From Fry to

600 Complete Quick and Easy Air Fryer Recipes for Beginner and Advanced Users

A.J. McTindal

ISBN: 9781737839866

ISBN: 9781737839866

Warning-Disclaimer

All the information presented in this book is aimed to be as accurate as possible. However, it is for informational purposes only and comes with no guarantees. The author and publisher shall have neither liability nor responsibility to anyone with respect to any loss or damage caused, or alleged to be caused, directly or indirectly by the information provided in this book.

QUICK AND EASY

1. Here's a simple recipe for French fries made in an air fryer:

Ingredients:

1 pound of potatoes, sliced into thin fries
1 tablespoon of olive oil
1 teaspoon of salt

Instructions:

Rinse the sliced potatoes and pat dry with a paper towel.
Place the potatoes in a bowl and toss with olive oil to coat.
Season with salt.
Place the potatoes in the air fryer basket in a single layer, making sure they are not crowded or overlapping.
Cook at 400°F for 20-25 minutes, flipping the fries halfway through, until golden brown and crispy.
Serve hot with your favorite dipping sauce. Enjoy!

2. Here's a simple recipe for spicy paprika curly fries made in an air fryer:

Ingredients:

1 package of frozen curly fries
1 tablespoon of olive oil
1 teaspoon of paprika
1/2 teaspoon of garlic powder
1/2 teaspoon of salt

Instructions:

Preheat the air fryer to 400°F.
In a bowl, mix the frozen curly fries with olive oil.
Add the paprika, garlic powder, and salt, and toss to evenly coat the fries.
Place the seasoned fries in a single layer in the air fryer basket.
Cook for 15-20 minutes, flipping halfway through, until crispy and golden brown.
Serve hot and enjoy!

3. Here's a simple recipe for baked potatoes in an air fryer:

Ingredients:

4 medium-sized potatoes, washed and dried
1 tablespoon of olive oil
Salt, to taste

Instructions:

Prick each potato a few times with a fork.
Rub each potato with olive oil and sprinkle with salt.
Place the potatoes in the air fryer basket in a single layer.
Cook at 400°F for 20-25 minutes, flipping the potatoes halfway through, until they are tender and the skin is crispy.
Serve hot and enjoy with your favorite toppings, such as butter, sour cream, cheese, or chives.
4. Here's a simple recipe for avocado egg rolls made in an air fryer:

Ingredients:

4 medium avocados, peeled, pitted, and mashed
1/2 cup of shredded Monterey Jack cheese
1/4 cup of diced red onion
1 jalapeño pepper, seeded and diced
1 tablespoon of chopped fresh cilantro
8 egg roll wrappers
Oil spray
Salt, to taste

Instructions:

In a bowl, mix the mashed avocados, cheese, onion, jalapeño, cilantro, and salt.
Place 2 tablespoons of the avocado mixture in the center of each egg roll wrapper.
Roll up the wrapper tightly, sealing the edges.
Spray the egg rolls with oil spray to help them crisp up.
Place the egg rolls in the air fryer basket in a single layer.
Cook at 400°F for 10-12 minutes, turning halfway through, until golden brown and crispy.
Serve with your favorite dipping sauce. Enjoy!

5. Here's a simple recipe for balsamic glazed Brussels sprouts made in an air fryer:

Ingredients:

1 pound of Brussels sprouts, trimmed and halved
1 tablespoon of olive oil
2 tablespoons of balsamic vinegar
1 teaspoon of brown sugar
Salt and pepper, to taste

Instructions:

In a bowl, mix the Brussels sprouts, olive oil, balsamic vinegar, brown sugar, salt, and pepper.
Place the Brussels sprouts in the air fryer basket in a single layer.
Cook at 400°F for 15-20 minutes, shaking the basket occasionally, until they are tender and caramelized.
Serve hot and enjoy!

6. Here's a simple recipe for Zucchini-Parmesan chips made in an air fryer:

Ingredients:

2 medium zucchinis, sliced into thin rounds
1/4 cup of grated Parmesan cheese
1 tablespoon of olive oil
Salt and pepper, to taste

Instructions:

In a bowl, mix the zucchini slices, Parmesan cheese, olive oil, salt, and pepper.
Place the zucchini slices in a single layer in the air fryer basket.
Cook at 400°F for 8-10 minutes, flipping halfway through, until they are crispy and golden brown.
Serve hot and enjoy!

7. Here's a simple recipe for crispy onion rings made in an air fryer:

Ingredients:

1 large onion, sliced into thick rounds
1 cup of all-purpose flour
2 teaspoons of paprika
1 teaspoon of garlic powder
Salt and pepper, to taste
1 cup of cold sparkling water
Oil spray

Instructions:

In a bowl, mix the flour, paprika, garlic powder, salt, and pepper.
Pour the sparkling water into the bowl and whisk until the mixture forms a smooth batter.
Dip each onion ring into the batter to coat.
Place the coated onion rings in the air fryer basket in a single layer.
Spray the onion rings with oil spray to help them crisp up.
Cook at 400°F for 10-12 minutes, flipping halfway through, until they are golden brown and crispy.
Serve with your favorite dipping sauce. Enjoy!

8. Here's a simple recipe for breaded mushrooms made in an air fryer:

Ingredients:

1 pound of button mushrooms, wiped clean
1 cup of all-purpose flour
2 teaspoons of dried basil
1 teaspoon of garlic powder
Salt and pepper, to taste
1 cup of cold sparkling water
Oil spray

Instructions:

In a bowl, mix the flour, basil, garlic powder, salt, and pepper.
Pour the sparkling water into the bowl and whisk until the mixture forms a smooth batter.
Dip each mushroom into the batter to coat.
Place the coated mushrooms in the air fryer basket in a single layer.
Spray the mushrooms with oil spray to help them crisp up.
Cook at 400°F for 10-12 minutes, flipping halfway through, until they are golden brown and crispy.
Serve as a snack or as a side dish. Enjoy!

9. Here's a simple recipe for herb and cheese stuffed mushrooms made in an air fryer:

Ingredients:
8 large mushrooms
1/4 cup grated Parmesan cheese
1/4 cup breadcrumbs
2 tablespoons chopped fresh parsley
2 cloves garlic, minced
2 tablespoons olive oil
Salt and pepper to taste

Instructions:

Clean the mushrooms and remove the stems. Reserve the stems for another use.

In a small bowl, mix the grated Parmesan cheese, breadcrumbs, chopped parsley, minced garlic, olive oil, salt, and pepper.
Spoon the mixture into the mushroom caps, filling each cap generously.
Place the mushrooms in the air fryer basket and set the temperature to 400°F.
Cook the mushrooms for 8-10 minutes or until they are tender and the filling is crispy and golden brown.
Serve the mushrooms warm, garnished with additional chopped parsley, if desired.

10. Here's a simple recipe for hot air-fried green tomatoes made in an air fryer:

Ingredients:

4 green tomatoes, sliced
1/2 cup all-purpose flour
1 teaspoon salt
1/2 teaspoon black pepper
2 eggs, beaten
1 cup breadcrumbs

Instructions:

Preheat the air fryer to 400°F.
In a shallow dish, mix the flour, salt, and pepper.
In another shallow dish, beat the eggs.
In a third shallow dish, place the breadcrumbs.
Dip each tomato slice first into the flour mixture, then into the beaten eggs, and finally into the breadcrumbs, making sure to coat well.
Place the coated tomato slices in the air fryer basket in a single layer, making sure they do not touch.
Cook the tomato slices in the air fryer for 8-10 minutes, or until they are golden brown and crispy.
Serve the hot air-fried green tomatoes as a side dish or as a snack. Enjoy!

11. Here's a simple recipe for classic zucchini fries in an air fryer:

Ingredients:

2 medium zucchinis, sliced into fries
1/4 cup all-purpose flour
1 teaspoon garlic powder
1 teaspoon paprika
Salt and pepper to taste
1 egg, beaten
1/2 cup breadcrumbs

Instructions:

Slice the zucchini into the fries.
In a bowl, mix the flour, garlic powder, paprika, salt, and pepper.
Dip the zucchini fries into the beaten egg, then coat them in the flour mixture.
Place the coated zucchini fries in the air fryer basket, making sure they are not overcrowded.
Air fry at 400°F for 10-12 minutes, flipping the fries halfway through, until they are golden brown and crispy.
Serve hot with your favorite dipping sauce.

12. Here's a simple recipe for corn on the cob in an air fryer:

Ingredients:

4 ears of corn, husked

1 tablespoon melted butter
Salt and pepper to taste

Instructions:

Place the husked corn in the air fryer basket.
Air fry at 400°F for 8-10 minutes, flipping the corn halfway through.
Brush the melted butter over the corn, and season with salt and pepper to taste.
Serve hot and enjoy!

13. Here's a simple recipe for perfectly cooked eggs in an air fryer:

Ingredients:

Eggs
Salt and pepper to taste (optional)

Instructions:

Crack an egg into a small bowl or ramekin.
Place the bowl or ramekin in the air fryer basket. Repeat for each egg you'd like to cook.
Air fry at 330°F for 4-6 minutes, or until the whites are set but the yolks are still runny. For firmer yolks, cook for an additional 1-2 minutes.
Season with salt and pepper to taste, if desired.
Serve and enjoy your perfectly cooked eggs!

14. Here's a simple recipe for mac & cheese in an air fryer:

Ingredients:

1 cup macaroni
1 cup water
1 cup milk
1/4 cup unsalted butter
2 tablespoons all-purpose flour
2 cups shredded cheddar cheese
Salt and pepper to taste
Optional toppings: breadcrumbs, paprika, chopped herbs

Instructions:

Cook the macaroni according to package instructions in a saucepan with the water, until al dente. Drain and set aside.
In the same saucepan, heat the milk, butter, and flour over medium heat, whisking constantly, until the mixture thickens, about 5 minutes.
Remove the saucepan from heat and stir in the cheddar cheese until melted and smooth.
Add the cooked macaroni to the cheese sauce and stir until well combined.
Transfer the mac & cheese to a small baking dish that fits in your air fryer basket.
If desired, sprinkle breadcrumbs, paprika, or chopped herbs on top.
Air fry at 400°F for 10-12 minutes, or until the top is golden brown and crispy.
Serve and enjoy your delicious air fryer mac & cheese!

15. Here's a simple recipe for a morning frittata in an air fryer:

Ingredients:

6 eggs

1/2 cup milk
Salt and pepper to taste
1/2 cup cooked diced potatoes
1/2 cup diced cooked ham or bacon
1/2 cup shredded cheddar cheese
1/4 cup diced onion
1/4 cup diced bell pepper

Instructions:

In a large bowl, whisk together the eggs, milk, salt, and pepper until well combined.
Stir in the cooked potatoes, ham or bacon, cheddar cheese, onion, and bell pepper until evenly distributed.
Pour the egg mixture into a 9-inch pie dish or frittata pan that fits in your air fryer basket.
Air fry at 400°F for 10-12 minutes, or until the edges are set and the top is golden brown.
Let the frittata cool for 5 minutes, then slice and serve.
Enjoy your delicious air fryer frittata for breakfast!

16. Here's a simple recipe for Mediterranean bruschetta in an air fryer:

Ingredients:

4 slices of baguette
2 tablespoons extra-virgin olive oil
2 cloves of garlic, minced
1 medium ripe tomato, diced
1/4 cup diced red onion
1/4 cup diced cucumber
2 tablespoons chopped fresh basil
Salt and pepper to taste
Feta cheese crumbles, for topping (optional)

Instructions:

Brush both sides of each baguette slice with olive oil, then sprinkle with minced garlic.
Place the baguette slices in the air fryer basket, making sure they are not overcrowded.
Air fry at 400°F for 3-5 minutes, or until the bread is crispy and lightly golden brown.
In a medium bowl, mix the diced tomato, red onion, cucumber, basil, salt, and pepper.
Top each bruschetta slice with the tomato mixture, and sprinkle with feta cheese crumbles, if desired.
Serve and enjoy your delicious air fryer Mediterranean bruschetta!

17. Here's a simple recipe for mozzarella cheese sticks in an air fryer:

Ingredients:

8 mozzarella cheese sticks
1 cup all-purpose flour
2 eggs, beaten
1 1/2 cups panko breadcrumbs
Salt and pepper to taste

Instructions:

Place the flour, beaten eggs, and Panko breadcrumbs in separate shallow bowls.
Season the flour with salt and pepper to taste.
Dip each cheese stick first in the flour, then in the beaten eggs, and finally in the Panko breadcrumbs, making sure each stick is well coated.

Place the breaded cheese sticks in the air fryer basket, making sure they are not overcrowded.
Air fry at 400°F for 5-7 minutes, or until the cheese is melted and the coating is crispy and golden brown.
Serve with your favorite dipping sauce and enjoy your delicious air fryer mozzarella cheese sticks!

18. Here's a simple recipe for a "Bikini" ham and cheese sandwich in an air fryer:

Ingredients:

2 slices of sandwich bread
2 slices of ham
2 slices of Swiss cheese
1 tablespoon unsalted butter, melted
Salt and pepper to taste

Instructions:

Lay out the 2 slices of sandwich bread on a cutting board.
Place a slice of ham and a slice of Swiss cheese on each slice of bread.
Close the sandwich by pressing the two slices of bread together.
Brush both sides of the sandwich with melted butter.
Sprinkle salt and pepper over the buttered surface of the sandwich, if desired.
Place the sandwich in the air fryer basket, making sure it is not overcrowded.
Air fry at 400°F for 5-7 minutes, or until the cheese is melted and the bread is golden brown and crispy.
Serve and enjoy your delicious air fryer "Bikini" ham and cheese sandwich!

19. Here's a simple recipe for homemade Arancini (rice balls) in an air fryer:

Ingredients:

2 cups cooked arborio rice
1/2 cup grated parmesan cheese
2 tablespoons chopped fresh parsley
Salt and pepper to taste
2 eggs, beaten
1 cup all-purpose flour
2 cups panko breadcrumbs
Vegetable oil spray

Instructions:

In a large bowl, mix the cooked arborio rice, parmesan cheese, parsley, salt, and pepper until well combined.
Scoop out 2 tablespoons of the rice mixture and form it into a ball.
Make a small well in the center of the ball, then place a small piece of mozzarella cheese in the well.
Roll the rice ball around the cheese filling until it is fully encased in the rice mixture.
Repeat the process with the remaining rice mixture and cheese until you have made several arancini.
Place the beaten eggs in a shallow bowl, the flour in another shallow bowl, and the Panko breadcrumbs in a third shallow bowl.
Coat each Arancini first in the flour, then in the beaten eggs, and finally in the Panko breadcrumbs.
Place the coated arancini in the air fryer basket, making sure they are not overcrowded.
Lightly spray the arancini with vegetable oil spray.
Air fry at 400°F for 8-10 minutes, or until the arancini are crispy and golden brown.
Serve with your favorite dipping sauce and enjoy your delicious air fryer homemade arancini!

20. Here's a simple recipe for cheddar hash browns in an air fryer:

Ingredients:

2 medium-sized russet potatoes, grated
1/4 cup finely chopped onion
1/4 cup shredded cheddar cheese
Salt and pepper to taste
2 tablespoons olive oil

Instructions:

In a large bowl, mix the grated potatoes, onion, cheddar cheese, salt, and pepper.
Shape the mixture into 4 patties about 1/2 inch thick.
Brush both sides of each patty with olive oil.
Place the hash brown patties in the air fryer basket, making sure they are not overcrowded.
Air fry at 400°F for 12-15 minutes, or until the hash browns are crispy and golden brown.
Serve and enjoy your delicious air fryer cheddar hash browns!

21. Here's a simple recipe for bacon-wrapped chicken breasts in an air fryer:

Ingredients:

4 boneless, skinless chicken breasts
8 slices of bacon
Salt and pepper to taste

Instructions:

Preheat the air fryer to 400°F.
Season the chicken breasts with salt and pepper on both sides.
Wrap each chicken breast with 2 slices of bacon, securing the ends with toothpicks.
Place the bacon-wrapped chicken breasts in the air fryer basket in a single layer.
Cook for 20-25 minutes, flipping the chicken halfway through, until the internal temperature reaches 165°F and the bacon is crispy.
Remove the chicken from the air fryer and let it rest for 5 minutes before serving.
Enjoy your delicious bacon-wrapped chicken!

22. Here's an easy recipe for air-fried chicken popcorn:

Ingredients:

1 pound boneless, skinless chicken breast, cut into 1-inch cubes
1 cup all-purpose flour
2 teaspoons paprika
1 teaspoon garlic powder
1 teaspoon onion powder
1 teaspoon salt
1/2 teaspoon black pepper
2 large eggs, beaten
1 cup Panko breadcrumbs

Instructions:

In a large bowl, whisk together the flour, paprika, garlic powder, onion powder, salt, and pepper.
In another bowl, beat the eggs.
Place the Panko breadcrumbs in a third bowl.
Dip each chicken cube in the flour mixture, then the beaten eggs, and finally the breadcrumbs, making sure each cube is well coated.
Preheat the air fryer to 400°F.
Place the coated chicken cubes in a single layer in the air fryer basket.
Cook for 12-15 minutes, shaking the basket every 5 minutes, until the chicken is golden brown and cooked through (165°F internal temperature).
Serve the chicken popcorn with your favorite dipping sauce.
Enjoy your delicious and crispy air-fried chicken popcorn!

23. Here's a simple recipe for sweet garlicky chicken wings in an air fryer:

Ingredients:

1 pound chicken wings
3 cloves garlic, minced
3 tablespoons honey
2 tablespoons soy sauce
1 tablespoon rice vinegar
1 teaspoon sesame oil
1/4 teaspoon red pepper flakes (optional)
Salt and pepper to taste
Sesame seeds and chopped green onions for garnish (optional)

Instructions:

In a large bowl, whisk together the minced garlic, honey, soy sauce, rice vinegar, sesame oil, red pepper flakes, salt, and pepper.
Add the chicken wings to the bowl and toss to coat well.
Cover the bowl and marinate the wings in the refrigerator for at least 30 minutes, or up to 2 hours.
Preheat the air fryer to 400°F.
Place the chicken wings in a single layer in the air fryer basket, leaving some space between each wing.
Cook for 20-25 minutes, flipping the wings halfway through, until they are crispy and the internal temperature reaches 165°F.
Serve the wings hot, garnished with sesame seeds and chopped green onions if desired.
Enjoy your sweet and garlicky air-fried chicken wings!

24. Here's a simple recipe for spicy buffalo chicken wings in an air fryer:

Ingredients:

1 pound chicken wings
1/2 cup hot sauce
2 tablespoons unsalted butter, melted
1 teaspoon garlic powder
1 teaspoon onion powder
Salt and pepper to taste
Blue cheese or ranch dressing for serving (optional)
Celery sticks for serving (optional)

Instructions:

In a large bowl, whisk together the hot sauce, melted butter, garlic powder, onion powder, salt, and pepper.
Add the chicken wings to the bowl and toss to coat well.

Preheat the air fryer to 400°F.
Place the chicken wings in a single layer in the air fryer basket, leaving some space between each wing.
Cook for 20-25 minutes, flipping the wings halfway through, until they are crispy and the internal temperature reaches 165°F.
Serve the wings hot with your favorite blue cheese or ranch dressing, and celery sticks if desired.
Enjoy your spicy and delicious buffalo chicken wings!

25. Here's a simple recipe for effortless chicken drumsticks in an air fryer:

Ingredients:

8 chicken drumsticks
2 tablespoons olive oil
Salt and pepper to taste
Your favorite spices or herbs (optional)

Instructions:

Preheat the air fryer to 400°F.
Place the chicken drumsticks in a large bowl and drizzle with olive oil.
Season the drumsticks with salt, pepper, and any other spices or herbs of your choice.
Toss the drumsticks to coat well with the seasoning.
Place the drumsticks in a single layer in the air fryer basket, leaving some space between each one.
Cook for 20-25 minutes, flipping the drumsticks halfway through, until they are golden brown and the internal temperature reaches 165°F.
Serve the drumsticks hot, with your favorite dipping sauce or side dishes.
Enjoy your juicy and flavorful air-fried chicken drumsticks!

26. Here's a simple recipe for hot and spicy chicken wingettes in an air fryer:

Ingredients:

1 pound chicken wingettes
2 tablespoons hot sauce
2 tablespoons unsalted butter, melted
1 teaspoon garlic powder
1 teaspoon onion powder
Salt and pepper to taste

Instructions:

In a large bowl, whisk together the hot sauce, melted butter, garlic powder, onion powder, salt, and pepper.
Add the chicken wingettes to the bowl and toss to coat well.
Preheat the air fryer to 400°F.
Place the chicken wingettes in a single layer in the air fryer basket, leaving some space between each one.
Cook for 20-25 minutes, flipping the wingettes halfway through, until they are crispy and the internal temperature reaches 165°F.
Serve the wingettes hot, with your favorite dipping sauce or side dishes.
Enjoy your hot and spicy air-fried chicken wingettes!

27. Here's a simple recipe for air-fried turkey scotch eggs:

Ingredients:

6 large eggs
1 pound ground turkey
1/4 cup breadcrumbs
1 teaspoon dried thyme
1 teaspoon dried basil
1 teaspoon dried oregano
1 teaspoon garlic powder
Salt and pepper to taste
Flour for coating
2 beaten eggs for coating
Panko breadcrumbs for coating

Instructions:

Hard-boil the eggs by placing them in a saucepan and covering them with water. Bring the water to a boil, then reduce the heat to low and let the eggs simmer for 10 minutes. Drain and let the eggs cool.
In a large bowl, mix the ground turkey, breadcrumbs, thyme, basil, oregano, garlic powder, salt, and pepper.
Divide the turkey mixture into 6 equal portions.
Peel the eggs and wrap each one with a portion of the turkey mixture, forming a ball and making sure there are no cracks.
Set up a coating station with three shallow bowls: one with flour, one with the beaten eggs, and one with the Panko breadcrumbs.
Coat each turkey-wrapped egg in the flour, then the beaten eggs, and finally the Panko breadcrumbs.
Preheat the air fryer to 400°F.
Place the scotch eggs in the air fryer basket, leaving some space between each one.
Cook for 10-12 minutes, until the turkey is fully cooked and the eggs are heated through.
Serve the scotch eggs hot, with your favorite dipping sauce or side dishes.
Enjoy your delicious and healthy air-fried turkey scotch eggs!

28. Here's a simple recipe for air-fried pork popcorn bites:

Ingredients:

1 pound boneless pork shoulder, cut into 1-inch cubes
2 tablespoons cornstarch
2 teaspoons paprika
1 teaspoon garlic powder
1 teaspoon onion powder
1 teaspoon salt
1/2 teaspoon black pepper
2 tablespoons vegetable oil

Instructions:

Mix the pork cubes, cornstarch, paprika, garlic powder, onion powder, salt, and pepper in a large bowl.
Add the vegetable oil to the bowl and toss to coat well.
Preheat the air fryer to 400°F.
Place the pork cubes in a single layer in the air fryer basket, leaving some space between each one.
Cook for 15-18 minutes, flipping the cubes halfway through, until they are crispy and the internal temperature reaches 145°F.
Serve the pork popcorn bites hot, with your favorite dipping sauce or side dishes.
Enjoy your juicy and flavorful air-fried pork popcorn bites!

29. Here's a simple recipe for sesame pork skewers in an air fryer:

Ingredients:

1 pound boneless pork shoulder, cut into 1-inch cubes
1/4 cup soy sauce
2 tablespoons honey
2 tablespoons rice vinegar
2 tablespoons sesame oil
1 tablespoon minced garlic
1 tablespoon minced ginger
1 tablespoon toasted sesame seeds
Salt and pepper to taste
Wooden skewers, soaked in water for 30 minutes

Instructions:

In a large bowl, whisk together the soy sauce, honey, rice vinegar, sesame oil, garlic, ginger, sesame seeds, salt, and pepper.
Add the pork cubes to the bowl and toss to coat well.
Marinate the pork cubes in the refrigerator for at least 30 minutes or up to 2 hours.
Preheat the air fryer to 400°F.
Skewer the marinated pork cubes, leaving some space between each one.
Place the pork skewers in a single layer in the air fryer basket, leaving some space between each one.
Cook for 15-18 minutes, flipping the skewers halfway through, until the pork is browned and the internal temperature reaches 145°F.
Serve the sesame pork skewers hot, with your favorite dipping sauce or side dishes.
Enjoy your savory and aromatic air-fried sesame pork skewers!

30. Here's a simple recipe for air-fried teriyaki pork ribs:

Ingredients:

1 rack of pork ribs, cut into individual ribs
1/2 cup teriyaki sauce
2 tablespoons brown sugar
1 tablespoon minced garlic
1 tablespoon minced ginger
Salt and pepper to taste

Instructions:

In a large bowl, whisk together the teriyaki sauce, brown sugar, garlic, ginger, salt, and pepper.
Add the pork ribs to the bowl and toss to coat well.
Marinate the pork ribs in the refrigerator for at least 30 minutes or up to 2 hours.
Preheat the air fryer to 400°F.
Place the marinated pork ribs in a single layer in the air fryer basket, leaving some space between each one.
Cook for 15-20 minutes, flipping the ribs halfway through, until the teriyaki sauce is caramelized and the internal temperature of the ribs reaches 145°F.
Serve the teriyaki pork ribs hot, with your favorite dipping sauce or side dishes.
Enjoy your juicy and flavorful air-fried teriyaki pork ribs!

31. Here's a quick and easy air fryer recipe for gorgonzola cheeseburgers:

Ingredients:

1 pound ground beef
1/4 cup crumbled gorgonzola cheese
1 teaspoon garlic powder
1/2 teaspoon salt
1/4 teaspoon black pepper
4 burger buns
Optional toppings: lettuce, tomato, onion, ketchup, mustard, mayo

Instructions:

Preheat your air fryer to 375°F (190°C).
In a mixing bowl, combine the ground beef, gorgonzola cheese, garlic powder, salt, and pepper. Mix well.
Form the beef mixture into 4 equal-sized patties.
Place the patties in the air fryer basket and cook for 10-12 minutes, flipping halfway through, until the internal temperature reaches 160°F (71°C).
Toast the burger buns in the air fryer for 1-2 minutes.
Assemble the burgers with your desired toppings.
Enjoy your delicious air fryer gorgonzola cheeseburgers!

32. Here's a quick and easy air fryer recipe for beef steak fingers:

Ingredients:

1 pound beef steak, sliced into 1-inch thick strips
1 cup all-purpose flour
1 teaspoon garlic powder
1/2 teaspoon salt
1/4 teaspoon black pepper
2 eggs
1 cup Panko breadcrumbs
Cooking spray

Instructions:

Preheat your air fryer to 400°F (200°C).
In a shallow dish, combine the flour, garlic powder, salt, and pepper.
In another shallow dish, beat the eggs.
In a third shallow dish, place the Panko breadcrumbs.
Coat each beef strip with the flour mixture, then dip into the beaten eggs, and finally coat with the Panko breadcrumbs, pressing the breadcrumbs onto the beef to adhere well.
Place the breaded beef strips in the air fryer basket in a single layer, making sure they are not touching each other.
Spray the tops of the breaded beef strips with cooking spray.
Cook for 8-10 minutes, flipping halfway through, until the beef is cooked through and the coating is golden and crispy.
Serve hot with your favorite dipping sauce.
Enjoy your crispy and delicious air fryer beef steak fingers!

33. Here's a quick and easy air fryer recipe for easy salmon fillets:

Ingredients:

2 salmon fillets, skin-on or skinless
1 tablespoon olive oil
1/2 teaspoon salt

1/4 teaspoon black pepper
1/2 teaspoon garlic powder
1 lemon, sliced
Fresh herbs (such as dill or parsley), for garnish (optional)

Instructions:

Preheat your air fryer to 375°F (190°C).
Brush the salmon fillets with olive oil on both sides.
Sprinkle the salt, black pepper, and garlic powder on both sides of the salmon fillets.
Place the salmon fillets in the air fryer basket, skin-side down if using skin-on fillets.
Place the lemon slices on top of the salmon fillets.
Cook for 8-10 minutes, depending on the thickness of the salmon, until the salmon is cooked through and flakes easily with a fork.
Remove the salmon fillets from the air fryer and garnish with fresh herbs, if desired.
Squeeze the roasted lemon over the salmon fillets before serving.
Enjoy your quick and easy air fryer salmon fillets!

34. Here's a quick and easy air fryer recipe for classic fish and chips:

Ingredients:

1 pound white fish fillets (such as cod or haddock)
1/2 cup all-purpose flour
1 teaspoon paprika
1/2 teaspoon garlic powder
1/2 teaspoon salt
1/4 teaspoon black pepper
1/2 cup Panko breadcrumbs
2 large potatoes, peeled and cut into wedges
Cooking spray
Lemon wedges, for serving
Tartar sauce, for serving

Instructions:

Preheat your air fryer to 400°F (200°C).
In a shallow dish, combine the flour, paprika, garlic powder, salt, and black pepper.
In another shallow dish, place the Panko breadcrumbs.
Coat each fish fillet with the flour mixture, shaking off any excess, then dip into the Panko breadcrumbs, pressing the breadcrumbs onto the fish to adhere well.
Place the breaded fish fillets in the air fryer basket, making sure they are not touching each other.
Spray the tops of the fish fillets with cooking spray.
In a separate bowl, toss the potato wedges with a drizzle of olive oil and any seasoning of your choice (such as salt and pepper).
Place the seasoned potato wedges in the air fryer basket in a single layer, making sure they are not touching each other.
Spray the tops of the potato wedges with cooking spray.
Cook for 8-10 minutes, flipping the fish and stirring the potato wedges halfway through, until the fish is cooked through and the coating is golden and crispy, and the potato wedges are tender and golden.
Serve hot with lemon wedges and tartar sauce on the side.
Enjoy your delicious air fryer classic fish and chips!

35. Here's a quick and easy air fryer recipe for chipotle-lime prawn bowls:

Ingredients:

1 pound large prawns, peeled and deveined
1 tablespoon olive oil
1 chipotle pepper in adobo sauce, minced
2 garlic cloves, minced
1 teaspoon honey
1/2 teaspoon cumin
1/2 teaspoon smoked paprika
1/4 teaspoon salt
1 lime, juiced
4 cups cooked rice
1 can black beans, drained and rinsed
1 cup corn kernels
1/4 cup chopped fresh cilantro

Instructions:

Preheat your air fryer to 400°F (200°C).
In a large bowl, whisk together the olive oil, chipotle pepper, garlic, honey, cumin, smoked paprika, salt, and lime juice.
Add the prawns to the bowl and toss to coat well.
Place the prawns in the air fryer basket in a single layer, making sure they are not touching each other.
Cook for 5-6 minutes, shaking the basket halfway through, until the prawns are pink and cooked through.
In a separate bowl, combine the cooked rice, black beans, and corn kernels.
Divide the rice mixture among 4 bowls and top with the cooked prawns.
Garnish with chopped cilantro.
Enjoy your flavorful and easy air fryer chipotle-lime prawn bowls!

36. Here's a quick and easy air fryer recipe for simple calamari rings:

Ingredients:

1-pound calamari rings
1/2 cup all-purpose flour
1/2 teaspoon garlic powder
1/2 teaspoon salt
1/4 teaspoon black pepper
2 large eggs, beaten
1 cup Panko breadcrumbs
Cooking spray
Lemon wedges, for serving
Marinara sauce or aioli, for serving

Instructions:

Preheat your air fryer to 400°F (200°C).
In a shallow dish, combine the flour, garlic powder, salt, and black pepper.
In another shallow dish, place the beaten eggs.
In a third shallow dish, place the Panko breadcrumbs.
Coat each calamari ring with the flour mixture, shaking off any excess, then dip into the beaten eggs, and finally, coat in the Panko breadcrumbs, pressing the breadcrumbs onto the calamari to adhere well.
Place the breaded calamari rings in the air fryer basket, making sure they are not touching each other.
Spray the tops of the calamari rings with cooking spray.
Cook for 6-8 minutes, shaking the basket halfway through, until the calamari rings are golden and crispy.
Serve hot with lemon wedges and marinara sauce or aioli on the side.
Enjoy your delicious and easy air fryer calamari rings!

37. Here's a quick and easy air fryer recipe for Gambas al Ajillo (garlic shrimp):

Ingredients:

1 pound large shrimp, peeled and deveined
3 garlic cloves, minced
1/4 teaspoon red pepper flakes
1/4 teaspoon smoked paprika
1/4 teaspoon salt
2 tablespoons olive oil
1 tablespoon chopped fresh parsley
Lemon wedges, for serving

Instructions:

Preheat your air fryer to 400°F (200°C).
In a large bowl, combine the minced garlic, red pepper flakes, smoked paprika, salt, and olive oil.
Add the shrimp to the bowl and toss to coat well.
Place the shrimp in the air fryer basket in a single layer, making sure they are not touching each other.
Cook for 6-8 minutes, shaking the basket halfway through, until the shrimp are pink and cooked through.
Remove the cooked shrimp from the air fryer basket and place it in a serving dish.
Garnish with chopped fresh parsley and serve hot with lemon wedges.
Enjoy your delicious and easy air fryer Gambas al Ajillo (garlic shrimp)!

38. Here's a quick and easy air fryer recipe for crispy fish finger sticks:

Ingredients:

1 pound firm white fish (such as cod or tilapia), cut into finger-sized strips
1/2 cup all-purpose flour
1/2 teaspoon garlic powder
1/2 teaspoon paprika
1/2 teaspoon salt
1/4 teaspoon black pepper
2 large eggs, beaten
1 cup Panko breadcrumbs
Cooking spray
Lemon wedges, for serving
Tartar sauce or ketchup, for serving

Instructions:

Preheat your air fryer to 400°F (200°C).
In a shallow dish, combine the flour, garlic powder, paprika, salt, and black pepper.
In another shallow dish, place the beaten eggs.
In a third shallow dish, place the Panko breadcrumbs.
Coat each fish finger with the flour mixture, shaking off any excess, then dip into the beaten eggs, and finally coat in the Panko breadcrumbs, pressing the breadcrumbs onto the fish to adhere well.

Place the breaded fish fingers in the air fryer basket, making sure they are not touching each other.
Spray the tops of the fish fingers with cooking spray.
Cook for 8-10 minutes, shaking the basket halfway through, until the fish fingers are golden and crispy.
Serve hot with lemon wedges and tartar sauce or ketchup on the side.
Enjoy your delicious and easy air fryer crispy fish finger sticks!

39. Here's a quick and easy air fryer recipe for raspberry and vanilla pancakes:

Ingredients:

1 cup all-purpose flour
2 tablespoons granulated sugar
2 teaspoons baking powder
1/4 teaspoon salt
1 cup milk
1 large egg
1/2 teaspoon vanilla extract
1/2 cup fresh raspberries
Cooking spray
Maple syrup, for serving

Instructions:

Preheat your air fryer to 350°F (180°C).
In a large bowl, whisk together the flour, sugar, baking powder, and salt.
Whisk together the milk, egg, and vanilla extract in a separate bowl.
Pour the wet ingredients into the dry ingredients and mix until just combined.
Gently fold in the raspberries.
Spray the air fryer basket with cooking spray.
Pour 1/4 cup of batter onto the air fryer basket for each pancake, leaving space between them.
Cook for 5-6 minutes, until the pancakes are golden brown and cooked through.
Repeat until all the batter is used up, spraying the basket with cooking spray in between batches as needed.
Serve hot with maple syrup.
Enjoy your delicious and easy air fryer raspberry and vanilla pancakes!

40. Here's a quick and easy air fryer recipe for cinnamon French toast sticks:

Ingredients:

6 slices of bread, cut into sticks
2 large eggs
1/4 cup milk
1/2 teaspoon vanilla extract
1/2 teaspoon ground cinnamon
1/4 teaspoon salt
Cooking spray
Powdered sugar, for serving
Maple syrup, for serving

Instructions:

Preheat your air fryer to 350°F (180°C).
In a shallow bowl, whisk together the eggs, milk, vanilla extract, cinnamon, and salt.
Dip each breadstick into the egg mixture, making sure to coat all sides.
Place the coated bread sticks in the air fryer basket in a single layer, making sure they are not touching each other.

Spray the tops of the breadsticks with cooking spray.
Cook for 4-5 minutes, shaking the basket halfway through, until the French toast sticks are golden brown and crispy.
Remove the cooked French toast sticks from the air fryer basket and place them on a plate.
Dust with powdered sugar and serve hot with maple syrup.
Enjoy your delicious and easy air fryer cinnamon French toast sticks!

41. Here's a quick and easy air fryer recipe for air-fried cinnamon apples:

Ingredients:

2 apples, cored and cut into 1/4-inch slices
1 tablespoon unsalted butter, melted
1 teaspoon ground cinnamon
1 tablespoon brown sugar
Cooking spray
Vanilla ice cream (optional), for serving

Instructions:

Preheat your air fryer to 375°F (190°C).
In a large bowl, toss the apple slices with the melted butter, cinnamon, and brown sugar until evenly coated.
Spray the air fryer basket with cooking spray.
Arrange the apple slices in a single layer in the air fryer basket, making sure they are not touching each other.
Cook for 8-10 minutes, shaking the basket halfway through, until the apples are tender and lightly browned.
Serve hot with a scoop of vanilla ice cream, if desired.
Enjoy your delicious and easy air fryer cinnamon apples!

BRUNCH

42. Here's a quick and easy air fryer recipe for breakfast potatoes:

Ingredients:

2-3 medium-sized potatoes, peeled and chopped into small pieces
1 tablespoon olive oil
1/2 teaspoon garlic powder
1/2 teaspoon onion powder
1/2 teaspoon smoked paprika
Salt and pepper to taste

Instructions:

Preheat your air fryer to 400°F (200°C).
In a mixing bowl, toss the chopped potatoes with olive oil, garlic powder, onion powder, smoked paprika, salt, and pepper.
Spray the air fryer basket with cooking spray.
Add the potatoes to the air fryer basket in a single layer.
Cook for 10-12 minutes, shaking the basket halfway through, until the potatoes are golden brown and crispy.
Remove the potatoes from the air fryer and serve hot.
These easy air fryer breakfast potatoes are perfect as a side dish for breakfast or brunch or as a delicious snack any time of day. Enjoy!

43. Here's an easy air fryer recipe for morning potato skins:

Ingredients:

4 medium-sized potatoes, washed and dried
1 tablespoon olive oil
1/2 teaspoon garlic powder
1/2 teaspoon onion powder
Salt and pepper to taste
4 slices of cooked bacon, chopped
1/2 cup shredded cheddar cheese
2 eggs
Chopped fresh chives, for garnish

Instructions:

Preheat your air fryer to 400°F (200°C).
Pierce each potato several times with a fork and place them in the air fryer basket.
Brush the potatoes with olive oil and sprinkle with garlic powder, onion powder, salt, and pepper.
Cook the potatoes for 25-30 minutes, or until they are tender and can be easily pierced with a fork.
Remove the potatoes from the air fryer and cut them in half lengthwise. Scoop out the flesh, leaving a thin layer of potato in the skins.
Crack an egg into each potato skin and sprinkle the bacon and cheddar cheese on top.
Return the potato skins to the air fryer basket and cook for an additional 5-6 minutes, or until the egg is set and the cheese is melted.
Garnish with chopped fresh chives and serve hot.
These morning potato skins are a delicious and hearty breakfast or brunch option. Enjoy!

44. Here's an easy air fryer recipe for chili potato latkes (hash browns):

Ingredients:

2 medium-sized potatoes, peeled and grated
1/2 onion, finely chopped
1 tablespoon all-purpose flour
1 teaspoon chili powder
1/2 teaspoon garlic powder
1/2 teaspoon salt
1/4 teaspoon black pepper
1 egg, beaten
Cooking spray

Instructions:

Preheat your air fryer to 400°F (200°C).
In a mixing bowl, combine the grated potatoes, chopped onion, flour, chili powder, garlic powder, salt, black pepper, and beaten egg. Mix well.
Spray the air fryer basket with cooking spray.
Spoon the potato mixture into the air fryer basket, making sure to flatten each latke with a fork or spatula.
Cook for 8-10 minutes, then flip the latkes and cook for an additional 5-7 minutes or until crispy and golden brown.
Remove the latkes from the air fryer and serve hot.
These chili potato latkes are a great addition to any breakfast or brunch menu. They are crispy, flavorful, and easy to make in the air fryer. Enjoy!

45. Here's an easy air fryer recipe for Kaiserschmarrn, a German torn pancake:

Ingredients:

4 eggs, separated
1/4 cup sugar
1 cup all-purpose flour
1/4 cup unsalted butter, melted
1/2 cup milk
1/4 teaspoon salt
1/2 cup raisins (optional)
Powdered sugar for dusting
Fresh berries for serving (optional)
Instructions:

Preheat your air fryer to 375°F (190°C).
In a mixing bowl, beat the egg whites until stiff peaks form. Set aside.
In another mixing bowl, beat the egg yolks and sugar together until light and fluffy.
Add the flour, melted butter, milk, and salt to the egg yolk mixture and mix until smooth.
Fold in the beaten egg whites and raisins, if using.
Pour the batter into a greased 9-inch baking pan or an air fryer-safe baking dish.
Place the baking pan or dish in the air fryer basket and cook for 12-15 minutes, or until the pancake is set and golden brown.
Using a spatula, tear the pancake into small pieces and flip them over.
Cook for an additional 5-7 minutes, or until the torn pancake is crispy on both sides.
Dust with powdered sugar and serve with fresh berries, if desired.
This air fryer recipe for Kaiserschmarrn is an easy and delicious breakfast or brunch dish that is sure to impress. Enjoy!

46. Here's an easy air fryer recipe for a three-meat cheesy omelet:

Ingredients:

4 large eggs
1/4 cup milk
1/4 teaspoon salt
1/8 teaspoon black pepper
1/4 cup cooked ham, diced
1/4 cup cooked bacon, crumbled
1/4 cup cooked sausage, crumbled
1/2 cup shredded cheddar cheese
Cooking spray

Instructions:

Preheat your air fryer to 375°F (190°C).
In a mixing bowl, whisk together the eggs, milk, salt, and black pepper.
Stir in the diced ham, crumbled bacon, crumbled sausage, and shredded cheddar cheese.
Spray a small baking dish or a ramekin with cooking spray.
Pour the egg mixture into the baking dish or ramekin.
Place the dish or ramekin in the air fryer basket and cook for 10-12 minutes, or until the omelet is set and golden brown on top.
Remove the omelet from the air fryer and let it cool for a few minutes before slicing and serving.
This three-meat cheesy omelet is a hearty and delicious breakfast dish that is easy to make in the air fryer. Feel free to add your favorite ingredients to customize it to your liking. Enjoy!

47. Here's an easy air fryer recipe for Masala Omelet, the Indian way:

Ingredients:

2 large eggs
1/4 cup finely chopped onion
1/4 cup finely chopped tomato
1/4 cup finely chopped cilantro
1/4 teaspoon cumin powder
1/4 teaspoon coriander powder
1/4 teaspoon red chili powder (optional)
Salt to taste
Cooking spray

Instructions:

Preheat your air fryer to 375°F (190°C).
In a mixing bowl, whisk together the eggs, cumin powder, coriander powder, red chili powder (if using), and salt.
Stir in the chopped onion, tomato, and cilantro.
Spray a small baking dish or a ramekin with cooking spray.
Pour the egg mixture into the baking dish or ramekin.
Place the dish or ramekin in the air fryer basket and cook for 8-10 minutes, or until the omelet is set and golden brown on top.
Remove the omelet from the air fryer and let it cool for a few minutes before slicing and serving.
This Masala Omelet is a flavorful and healthy breakfast or brunch dish that is easy to make in the air fryer. You can also serve it with some bread, chapati, or rice for a more filling meal. Enjoy!

48. Here's an easy air fryer recipe for a Japanese-style omelet:

Ingredients:

2 large eggs
1 tablespoon mirin (sweet rice wine)
1 tablespoon soy sauce
1 teaspoon sugar
1/4 teaspoon salt
Cooking spray

Instructions:

Preheat your air fryer to 375°F (190°C).
In a mixing bowl, whisk together the eggs, mirin, soy sauce, sugar, and salt.
Spray a small baking dish or a ramekin with cooking spray.
Pour the egg mixture into the baking dish or ramekin.
Place the dish or ramekin in the air fryer basket and cook for 8-10 minutes, or until the omelet is set and golden brown on top.
Remove the omelet from the air fryer and let it cool for a few minutes before slicing and serving.
This Japanese-style omelet, also known as Tamagoyaki, is a simple and delicious breakfast or snack that can be served on its own or with some rice and vegetables. You can also add some chopped scallions or sesame seeds for extra flavor and texture. Enjoy!

49. Here's an easy air fryer recipe for a baked kale omelet:

Ingredients:

2 large eggs
1/4 cup chopped kale

1/4 cup chopped red bell pepper
1/4 cup shredded cheddar cheese
Salt and black pepper to taste
Cooking spray

Instructions:

Preheat your air fryer to 375°F (190°C).
In a mixing bowl, whisk together the eggs and season with salt and black pepper.
Add in the chopped kale, red bell pepper, and shredded cheddar cheese.
Spray a small baking dish or a ramekin with cooking spray.
Pour the egg mixture into the baking dish or ramekin.
Place the dish or ramekin in the air fryer basket and cook for 8-10 minutes, or until the omelet is set and golden brown on top.
Remove the omelet from the air fryer and let it cool for a few minutes before slicing and serving.
This baked kale omelet is a healthy and tasty breakfast or brunch dish that is easy to make in the air fryer. You can also experiment with different types of vegetables or cheese to suit your taste. Enjoy!

50. Here's an easy air fryer recipe for a ham and cheddar omelet:

Ingredients:

2 large eggs
1/4 cup diced ham
1/4 cup shredded cheddar cheese
Salt and black pepper to taste
Cooking spray

Instructions:

Preheat your air fryer to 375°F (190°C).
In a mixing bowl, whisk together the eggs and season with salt and black pepper.
Add in the diced ham and shredded cheddar cheese.
Spray a small baking dish or a ramekin with cooking spray.
Pour the egg mixture into the baking dish or ramekin.
Place the dish or ramekin in the air fryer basket and cook for 8-10 minutes, or until the omelet is set and golden brown on top.
Remove the omelet from the air fryer and let it cool for a few minutes before slicing and serving.
This ham and cheddar omelet is a classic breakfast dish that is easy to make in the air fryer. You can also add some chopped vegetables like bell peppers or onions to add more flavor and nutrition to the dish. Enjoy!

51. Here's an easy air fryer recipe for omelet bread cups:

Ingredients:

4 slices of bread
4 large eggs
1/4 cup milk
1/4 cup shredded cheddar cheese
1/4 cup diced ham or cooked bacon
Salt and black pepper to taste
Cooking spray

Instructions:

Preheat your air fryer to 350°F (175°C).

Use a rolling pin to flatten each slice of bread and then press them into muffin tins to form cups.
In a mixing bowl, whisk together the eggs, milk, salt, and black pepper.
Stir in the shredded cheddar cheese and diced ham or cooked bacon.
Pour the egg mixture into each bread cup, filling about 2/3 of the way.
Spray the air fryer basket with cooking spray and place the muffin tin inside.
Cook for 12-15 minutes or until the egg is set and the bread cups are golden brown.
Remove the bread cups from the air fryer and let them cool for a few minutes before serving.
These omelet bread cups are a fun and easy way to serve omelets for breakfast or brunch. You can experiment with different fillings, such as sautéed mushrooms, diced bell peppers, or chopped spinach.
Enjoy!

52. Here's an easy air fryer recipe for a Greek-style frittata:

Ingredients:

6 large eggs
1/4 cup milk
1/2 cup crumbled feta cheese
1/2 cup diced cherry tomatoes
1/4 cup chopped fresh spinach
1/4 cup sliced black olives
1/4 cup chopped red onion
Salt and black pepper to taste
Cooking spray

Instructions:

Preheat your air fryer to 350°F (175°C).
In a mixing bowl, whisk together the eggs, milk, salt, and black pepper.
Stir in the crumbled feta cheese, diced cherry tomatoes, chopped spinach, sliced black olives, and chopped red onion.
Spray a small baking dish or a ramekin with cooking spray.
Pour the egg mixture into the baking dish or ramekin.
Place the dish or ramekin in the air fryer basket and cook for 12-15 minutes, or until the frittata is set and golden brown on top.
Remove the frittata from the air fryer and let it cool for a few minutes before slicing and serving.
This Greek-style frittata is a flavorful and healthy breakfast or brunch dish that is easy to make in the air fryer. You can also add in some chopped bell peppers or mushrooms for more flavor and nutrition.
Enjoy!

53. Here's an easy air fryer recipe for a Spanish chorizo frittata:

Ingredients:

6 large eggs
1/4 cup milk
1/2 cup diced Spanish chorizo
1/4 cup chopped red bell pepper
1/4 cup chopped green onions
1/4 cup grated Manchego cheese
Salt and black pepper to taste
Cooking spray

Instructions:

Preheat your air fryer to 350°F (175°C).
In a mixing bowl, whisk together the eggs, milk, salt, and black pepper.

Stir in the diced Spanish chorizo, chopped red bell pepper, and chopped green onions.
Spray a small baking dish or a ramekin with cooking spray.
Pour the egg mixture into the baking dish or ramekin.
Sprinkle the grated Manchego cheese on top.
Place the dish or ramekin in the air fryer basket and cook for 12-15 minutes, or until the frittata is set and golden brown on top.
Remove the frittata from the air fryer and let it cool for a few minutes before slicing and serving.
This Spanish chorizo frittata is a hearty and flavorful breakfast or brunch dish that is easy to make in the air fryer. You can also add in some chopped potatoes or mushrooms for more texture and flavor. Enjoy!

54. Here's an easy air fryer recipe for Vienna sausage & cherry tomato frittata:

Ingredients:

6 large eggs
1/4 cup milk
1 can Vienna sausages, chopped
1 cup cherry tomatoes, halved
1/4 cup chopped red onion
1/4 cup shredded cheddar cheese
Salt and black pepper to taste
Cooking spray

Instructions:

Preheat your air fryer to 350°F (175°C).
In a mixing bowl, whisk together the eggs, milk, salt, and black pepper.
Stir in the chopped Vienna sausages, halved cherry tomatoes, and chopped red onion.
Spray a small baking dish or a ramekin with cooking spray.
Pour the egg mixture into the baking dish or ramekin.
Sprinkle the shredded cheddar cheese on top.
Place the dish or ramekin in the air fryer basket and cook for 12-15 minutes, or until the frittata is set and golden brown on top.
Remove the frittata from the air fryer and let it cool for a few minutes before slicing and serving.
This Vienna sausage & cherry tomato frittata is a quick and easy breakfast or brunch dish that is perfect for busy mornings. The salty and savory Vienna sausages are balanced out by the sweet and juicy cherry tomatoes, and the melted cheddar cheese adds a creamy and comforting touch. Enjoy!

55. Here's an easy air fryer recipe for air-fried shirred eggs:

Ingredients:

2 large eggs
2 teaspoons heavy cream
Salt and pepper to taste
Cooking spray
Fresh herbs for garnish (optional)

Instructions:

Preheat your air fryer to 325°F (160°C).
Lightly spray two small oven-safe ramekins with cooking spray.
Crack one egg into each ramekin.
Add one teaspoon of heavy cream to each ramekin and sprinkle with salt and pepper.
Place the ramekins in the air fryer basket and cook for 8-10 minutes, or until the whites are set but the yolks are still slightly runny.
Carefully remove the ramekins from the air fryer using oven mitts or tongs, as they will be hot.

Garnish with fresh herbs if desired and serve immediately.
Shirred eggs are a simple and delicious breakfast dish that is usually baked in the oven, but this air fryer version is quicker and easier. The eggs cook to perfection in just a few minutes, and the creamy heavy cream adds richness and flavor. You can enjoy these shirred eggs as they are or serve them with toast, bacon, or other breakfast favorites.

56. Here's an easy air fryer recipe for prosciutto, mozzarella, and eggs in a cup:

Ingredients:

2 slices of prosciutto
2 large eggs
1/4 cup shredded mozzarella cheese
Salt and pepper to taste
Cooking spray

Instructions:

Preheat your air fryer to 325°F (160°C).
Lightly spray two small oven-safe ramekins with cooking spray.
Place one slice of prosciutto in the bottom of each ramekin, making sure it covers the bottom and sides.
Crack one egg into each ramekin.
Sprinkle 2 tablespoons of shredded mozzarella cheese over each egg and season with salt and pepper.
Place the ramekins in the air fryer basket and cook for 8-10 minutes, or until the whites are set but the yolks are still slightly runny.
Carefully remove the ramekins from the air fryer using oven mitts or tongs, as they will be hot.
Let the eggs cool for a few minutes, then use a spoon to carefully remove them from the ramekins.
Serve immediately, garnished with additional cheese and prosciutto if desired.
This recipe is a tasty and easy way to enjoy a protein-packed breakfast that's ready in minutes. The prosciutto adds a salty, savory flavor to the dish, while the mozzarella cheese provides richness and creaminess. You can also add other ingredients like diced tomatoes, fresh herbs, or sliced mushrooms to customize the recipe to your taste.

57. Here's an easy air fryer recipe for buttered eggs in a hole:

Ingredients:

2 slices of bread
2 large eggs
2 tablespoons of butter
Salt and pepper to taste

Instructions:

Preheat your air fryer to 360°F (182°C).
Using a round cookie cutter or the rim of a drinking glass, cut a hole in the center of each slice of bread.
Melt 1 tablespoon of butter in a microwave-safe dish or on the stovetop, then brush it on both sides of each bread slice.
Place the bread slices in the air fryer basket and cook for 2 minutes.
Flip the bread slices over and crack one egg into the center of each hole.
Sprinkle the eggs with salt and pepper to taste, then place a small pat of butter on top of each egg.
Cook for an additional 3-5 minutes, or until the whites are set but the yolks are still slightly runny.
Use a spatula to carefully remove the eggs in a hole from the air fryer and serve immediately.
This recipe is a delicious and simple way to enjoy a classic breakfast dish with a crispy, air-fried twist. The butter adds richness and flavor to the eggs and bread, while the air fryer gives them a crunchy texture. You can also experiment with different types of bread, such as whole wheat, sourdough, or brioche, to customize the recipe to your taste. Enjoy!

58. Here's an easy air fryer recipe for breakfast shrimp and egg muffins:

Ingredients:

6 large eggs
1/2 cup cooked shrimp, chopped
1/4 cup shredded cheddar cheese
1/4 cup milk
1/4 teaspoon garlic powder
1/4 teaspoon onion powder
Salt and pepper to taste
Cooking spray

Instructions:

Preheat your air fryer to 350°F (180°C).
In a medium bowl, whisk together the eggs, milk, garlic powder, onion powder, salt, and pepper.
Stir in the chopped shrimp and shredded cheddar cheese.
Grease a muffin tin with cooking spray and pour the egg mixture evenly into each cup, filling them about 2/3 full.
Place the muffin tin in the air fryer basket and cook for 8-10 minutes, or until the eggs are set and lightly golden on top.
Use a spatula to carefully remove the breakfast shrimp and egg muffins from the air fryer and serve hot.
These breakfast shrimp and egg muffins are a delicious and protein-packed breakfast option that is perfect for busy mornings. The air fryer cooks them quickly and evenly, giving them a crispy outer layer and a fluffy, tender center. You can also customize this recipe by adding different types of vegetables or seasonings to the egg mixture, such as bell peppers, spinach, or cayenne pepper, to suit your taste. Enjoy!

59. Here's an easy air fryer recipe for cheese and ham breakfast egg cups:

Ingredients:

6 large eggs
1/2 cup diced ham
1/2 cup shredded cheddar cheese
1/4 cup milk
1/4 teaspoon garlic powder
1/4 teaspoon onion powder
Salt and pepper to taste
Cooking spray

Instructions:

Preheat your air fryer to 350°F (180°C).
In a medium bowl, whisk together the eggs, milk, garlic powder, onion powder, salt, and pepper.
Stir in the diced ham and shredded cheddar cheese.
Grease a muffin tin with cooking spray and pour the egg mixture evenly into each cup, filling them about 2/3 full.
Place the muffin tin in the air fryer basket and cook for 8-10 minutes, or until the eggs are set and lightly golden on top.
Use a spatula to carefully remove the cheese and ham breakfast egg cups from the air fryer and serve hot.
These cheese and ham breakfast egg cups are a simple and delicious breakfast option that is perfect for busy mornings. The air fryer cooks them quickly and evenly, giving them a crispy outer layer and a fluffy,

tender center. You can also customize this recipe by adding different types of vegetables or seasonings to the egg mixture, such as diced bell peppers, onions, or cayenne pepper, to suit your taste. Enjoy!

60. Here's an easy air fryer recipe for a tasty turkey and mushroom sandwich:

Ingredients:

2 slices of bread
2-3 oz. turkey breast, sliced
1/2 cup sliced mushrooms
1/2 tbsp olive oil
Salt and pepper to taste
Optional toppings: lettuce, tomato, cheese, mustard, mayonnaise

Instructions:

Preheat your air fryer to 375°F.
In a small bowl, toss sliced mushrooms with olive oil, salt, and pepper.
Place the mushrooms in the air fryer basket and cook for 4-5 minutes until they are tender and slightly browned.
Remove the mushrooms from the air fryer basket and set aside.
Place the sliced turkey breast in the air fryer basket and cook for 2-3 minutes until it's heated through.
Toast the bread slices if desired.
Assemble the sandwich by placing the turkey and mushrooms on one slice of bread and adding any desired toppings.
Top with the other slice of bread and enjoy!
This recipe is simple, delicious, and takes only a few minutes to prepare. You can customize the sandwich with your favorite toppings and enjoy it for lunch or dinner.

61. Here's an easy air fryer recipe for delicious air-fried sourdough sandwiches:

Ingredients:

4 slices of sourdough bread
4-6 oz. deli meat (such as ham, turkey, or roast beef)
4 slices of cheese (such as cheddar, Swiss, or provolone)
2 tbsp mayonnaise
1 tbsp Dijon mustard
1-2 tbsp butter, softened

Instructions:

Preheat your air fryer to 375°F.
In a small bowl, mix the mayonnaise and Dijon mustard.
Spread the mayonnaise mixture on one side of each slice of bread.
Place the deli meat and cheese on top of two slices of bread, and top with the remaining two slices to make two sandwiches.
Spread a thin layer of softened butter on the outside of each sandwich.
Place the sandwiches in the air fryer basket and cook for 5-7 minutes until the bread is toasted and the cheese is melted.
Flip the sandwiches halfway through cooking to ensure even browning.
Serve hot and enjoy!
This recipe is quick, easy, and perfect for a quick lunch or dinner. You can customize the sandwich with your favorite deli meat and cheese, and experiment with different spreads and toppings to create your perfect sandwich.

62. Here's an easy air fryer recipe for loaded egg pepper rings:

Ingredients:

2 large bell peppers
4 eggs
1/4 cup shredded cheddar cheese
1/4 cup diced cooked bacon
Salt and pepper to taste

Instructions:

Preheat your air fryer to 350°F.
Cut the bell peppers into 1/2-inch rings, removing the seeds and stems.
Place the bell pepper rings in the air fryer basket and cook for 3-4 minutes until they are slightly softened.
Crack an egg into each bell pepper ring.
Sprinkle shredded cheese and diced bacon on top of each egg.
Season with salt and pepper to taste.
Place the bell pepper rings back in the air fryer basket and cook for 8-10 minutes until the egg whites are set and the yolks are cooked to your liking.
Serve hot and enjoy!
This recipe is a fun twist on traditional breakfast eggs and is a great way to incorporate more veggies into your morning routine. You can experiment with different types of cheese and toppings, such as diced ham or chopped scallions, to make the recipe your own.

63. Here's an easy air fryer recipe for sausage and egg casserole:

Ingredients:

1 lb breakfast sausage, crumbled and cooked
6 eggs
1/2 cup milk
1/2 tsp salt
1/4 tsp black pepper
1/2 cup shredded cheddar cheese
Optional toppings: chopped fresh herbs, sliced scallions

Instructions:

Preheat your air fryer to 350°F.
In a large mixing bowl, beat the eggs with the milk, salt, and black pepper until well combined.
Add the cooked sausage to the bowl and mix well.
Grease a small casserole dish or baking dish that will fit in your air fryer basket.
Pour the egg and sausage mixture into the dish and sprinkle with shredded cheese.
Place the dish in the air fryer basket and cook for 20-25 minutes until the eggs are set and the cheese is melted and lightly browned.
Remove the dish from the air fryer and let it cool for a few minutes before serving.
Top with chopped fresh herbs or sliced scallions if desired.
Serve hot and enjoy!
This recipe is a great way to make a delicious breakfast or brunch dish in your air fryer. You can also make it ahead of time and reheat it in the air fryer for a quick and easy breakfast during the week.

64. Here's an easy air fryer recipe for a delicious grilled tofu sandwich with cabbage:

Ingredients:

1 block of firm or extra-firm tofu

1 tbsp olive oil
1 tsp garlic powder
1/2 tsp smoked paprika
Salt and pepper to taste
4 slices of bread
1/4 head of cabbage, shredded
2 tbsp mayonnaise
1 tbsp Dijon mustard

Instructions:

Preheat your air fryer to 375°F.
Drain the tofu and slice it into 1/2-inch thick slices.
In a small bowl, mix the olive oil, garlic powder, smoked paprika, salt, and pepper.
Brush the tofu slices with the oil mixture.
Place the tofu slices in the air fryer basket and cook for 10-12 minutes, flipping halfway through, until they are crispy and golden brown.
Toast the bread slices if desired.
In a small bowl, mix the mayonnaise and Dijon mustard.
Assemble the sandwich by spreading the mayonnaise mixture on one slice of bread and placing the tofu slices and shredded cabbage on top.
Top with the other slice of bread.
Serve hot and enjoy!
This recipe is a delicious and healthy option for a vegetarian or vegan lunch or dinner. The air fryer adds a nice crispy texture to the tofu, and the combination of the spicy oil mixture and tangy cabbage makes for a flavorful and satisfying sandwich.

65. Here's an easy air fryer recipe for French toast with vanilla filling:

Ingredients:

6 slices of bread
2 eggs
1/4 cup milk
1 tsp vanilla extract
1/4 cup cream cheese, softened
2 tbsp powdered sugar
Optional toppings: fresh fruit, whipped cream, maple syrup

Instructions:

Preheat your air fryer to 360°F.
In a small mixing bowl, beat the eggs with the milk and vanilla extract until well combined.
In a separate bowl, mix the softened cream cheese and powdered sugar until smooth.
Spread the cream cheese mixture evenly onto three slices of bread and top with the remaining three slices of bread to make sandwiches.
Dip each sandwich into the egg mixture, making sure to coat both sides.
Place the sandwiches in the air fryer basket and cook for 6-8 minutes, flipping halfway through, until they are golden brown and crispy.
Remove the sandwiches from the air fryer and let them cool for a few minutes before slicing.
Top with fresh fruit, whipped cream, and/or maple syrup if desired.
Serve hot and enjoy!
This recipe is a fun twist on classic French toast, and the creamy vanilla filling adds a delicious richness to the dish. The air fryer makes the French toast crispy on the outside and soft on the inside, creating the perfect texture. This dish is great for breakfast or brunch and can be easily customized with your favorite toppings.

66. Here's an easy air fryer recipe for brioche toast with Nutella:

Ingredients:

4 slices of brioche bread
Nutella or other chocolate hazelnut spread
Optional toppings: sliced bananas, strawberries, chopped nuts

Instructions:

Preheat your air fryer to 360°F.
Spread a generous amount of Nutella on each slice of brioche bread.
Place the bread slices in the air fryer basket and cook for 3-4 minutes, until the Nutella is melted and the bread is toasted.
Remove the bread slices from the air fryer and let them cool for a minute or two.
Top with sliced bananas, strawberries, chopped nuts, or any other toppings you like.
Serve hot and enjoy!
This recipe is a quick and easy way to enjoy a delicious breakfast or dessert. The air fryer melts the Nutella perfectly and toasts the brioche bread to perfection, creating a warm and crispy treat. You can also experiment with different toppings to add some extra flavor and texture to the dish.

67. Here's an easy air fryer recipe for a delicious bacon and egg sandwich:

Ingredients:

2 slices of bread
2 slices of bacon
1 egg
1 tbsp milk
Salt and pepper to taste
Optional toppings: cheese, lettuce, tomato, avocado, mayonnaise

Instructions:

Preheat your air fryer to 370°F.
Place the bacon slices in the air fryer basket and cook for 6-8 minutes, until they are crispy. Remove from the basket and set aside.
In a small bowl, whisk the egg with the milk, salt, and pepper.
Pour the egg mixture into a greased ramekin or small oven-safe dish that fits inside the air fryer basket.
Place the ramekin in the air fryer and cook for 6-8 minutes, until the egg is cooked through.
While the bacon and egg are cooking, toast the bread slices if desired.
Assemble the sandwich by placing the cooked bacon and egg on one slice of bread, and adding any optional toppings that you like.
Top with the other slice of bread.
Serve hot and enjoy!
This recipe is a classic breakfast or brunch favorite that is made even easier with the help of an air fryer. The bacon and egg cook up quickly and evenly in the air fryer, and the toasted bread adds a delicious crunch. You can customize the sandwich with your favorite toppings, such as cheese, lettuce, tomato, avocado, or mayonnaise, to make it your own.

68. Here's an easy air fryer recipe for a delicious Mediterranean avocado toast:

Ingredients:

2 slices of bread (preferably whole grain or sourdough)
1 ripe avocado
1/4 cup crumbled feta cheese

1 tbsp chopped fresh herbs (such as parsley or basil)
1 small garlic clove, minced
1/4 cup diced cherry tomatoes
1/4 cup sliced Kalamata olives
Salt and pepper to taste
Optional toppings: lemon wedges, red pepper flakes

Instructions:

Preheat your air fryer to 360°F.
Cut the avocado in half, remove the pit, and scoop the flesh into a small mixing bowl.
Mash the avocado with a fork until it is smooth, but still a little chunky.
Add the crumbled feta cheese, chopped herbs, minced garlic, diced cherry tomatoes, and sliced Kalamata olives to the bowl. Mix well to combine.
Toast the bread slices in the air fryer for 2-3 minutes, until they are crispy.
Spread the avocado mixture evenly on each slice of toasted bread.
Sprinkle with a little salt and pepper to taste.
Add optional toppings if desired, such as a squeeze of lemon juice or a sprinkle of red pepper flakes.
Serve immediately and enjoy!
This recipe is a delicious twist on classic avocado toast, with the added flavors of Mediterranean ingredients like feta cheese, olives, and tomatoes. The air fryer toasts the bread slices perfectly and evenly, creating a crunchy base for the creamy avocado mixture. You can also experiment with different herbs and spices to add even more flavor to the dish.

69. Here's an easy air fryer recipe for very berry breakfast puffs:

Ingredients:

1 cup all-purpose flour
1 tsp baking powder
1/4 tsp salt
2 tbsp granulated sugar
1/2 cup milk
1 large egg
1/4 cup unsalted butter, melted
1/2 cup mixed berries (such as raspberries, blueberries, and blackberries)
Powdered sugar for dusting

Instructions:

Preheat your air fryer to 350°F.
Whisk together the flour, baking powder, salt, and granulated sugar in a large mixing bowl.
Whisk together the milk, egg, and melted butter in a separate bowl.
Pour the wet ingredients into the dry ingredients and mix until just combined.
Gently fold in the mixed berries.
Grease a muffin tin with cooking spray or butter.
Divide the batter evenly between the muffin cups, filling each about 2/3 full.
Place the muffin tin in the air fryer basket and cook for 8-10 minutes, until the puffs are golden brown and a toothpick inserted in the center comes out clean.
Remove the muffin tin from the air fryer and let the puffs cool for a few minutes.
Dust with powdered sugar before serving.
Serve warm and enjoy!
This recipe is a fun and easy way to enjoy a delicious breakfast treat. The air fryer puffs up the batter, creating light and fluffy muffins that are studded with juicy mixed berries. You can also experiment with different types of fruit or add a drizzle of honey or maple syrup on top for extra sweetness.

70. Here's an easy air fryer recipe for Romanian polenta fries:

Ingredients:

1 cup yellow cornmeal
3 cups water
1 tsp salt
1/2 cup grated Parmesan cheese
1/2 tsp garlic powder
1/2 tsp paprika
Cooking spray

Instructions:

In a medium saucepan, bring the water to a boil.
Slowly pour the cornmeal into the boiling water, stirring constantly with a whisk.
Reduce the heat to low and continue stirring for 10-15 minutes, until the mixture thickens and pulls away from the sides of the pan.
Remove from the heat and stir in the Parmesan cheese, garlic powder, and paprika.
Spread the mixture onto a baking sheet or flat surface and let it cool for at least 30 minutes.
Cut the polenta into thin fries or wedges, about 1/2 inch thick.
Preheat your air fryer to 400°F.
Spray the polenta fries with cooking spray and place them in the air fryer basket in a single layer.
Cook for 10-12 minutes, flipping the fries halfway through, until they are crispy and golden brown.
Serve immediately and enjoy!
These Romanian polenta fries are a delicious and unique twist on classic french fries. The air fryer gives them a crispy exterior while the inside stays soft and creamy. They are perfect as a snack or as a side dish to any meal. You can also experiment with different spices and dipping sauces to customize the flavor to your liking.

71. Here's an easy air fryer recipe for Soppressata pizza:

Ingredients:

1 prepared pizza crust (homemade or store-bought)
1/2 cup tomato sauce
1 cup shredded mozzarella cheese
1/4 cup grated Parmesan cheese
3 oz. sliced soppressata
1/4 cup sliced red onion
1 tbsp olive oil
Salt and pepper to taste

Instructions:

Preheat your air fryer to 375°F.
Brush the pizza crust with olive oil and season with salt and pepper.
Spread the tomato sauce evenly over the crust, leaving a small border around the edges.
Sprinkle the shredded mozzarella cheese and grated Parmesan cheese over the tomato sauce.
Top with the sliced Soppressata and red onion.
Place the pizza in the air fryer basket and cook for 10-12 minutes, or until the cheese is melted and the crust is crispy.
Remove the pizza from the air fryer and let it cool for a few minutes.

Slice and serve immediately.
This air fryer Soppressata pizza is a delicious and easy meal that can be made in minutes. The air fryer gives the crust a crispy texture while the toppings become melty and delicious. You can customize the toppings to your liking, adding more or less of your favorite ingredients. It's perfect for a quick lunch or dinner or as a fun appetizer for your next party.

72. Here's an easy air fryer recipe for air-fried Italian calzone:

Ingredients:

1 pound pizza dough
1/2 cup marinara sauce
1 cup shredded mozzarella cheese
1/2 cup ricotta cheese
1/4 cup grated Parmesan cheese
1/2 teaspoon garlic powder
1/2 teaspoon dried basil
1/4 teaspoon salt
1/4 teaspoon black pepper
Cooking spray
1 egg, beaten

Instructions:

Preheat your air fryer to 375°F.
Divide the pizza dough into 4 equal portions.
On a floured surface, roll out each portion into a circle.
In a small bowl, mix the marinara sauce, mozzarella cheese, ricotta cheese, Parmesan cheese, garlic powder, dried basil, salt, and black pepper.
Spread the marinara cheese mixture on one half of each dough circle, leaving a small border around the edge.
Fold the other half of the dough over the filling and use a fork to crimp the edges together.
Spray the calzones with cooking spray on both sides.
Place the calzones in the air fryer basket and brush with beaten egg.
Cook for 10-12 minutes or until golden brown and crispy.
Serve hot.
This air fryer Italian calzone recipe is a delicious and healthier version of a classic Italian dish. The air fryer gives the calzone a crispy crust while the filling remains hot and melty. You can experiment with different fillings and spices to create your unique calzone recipe. It's perfect for a quick and easy dinner or a fun appetizer for your next party.

73. Here's an easy air fryer recipe for breakfast banana bread:

Ingredients:

2 ripe bananas, mashed
1/4 cup vegetable oil
1/2 cup granulated sugar
1 large egg
1 tsp vanilla extract
1 cup all-purpose flour
1/2 tsp baking soda
1/2 tsp baking powder
1/2 tsp salt
Cooking spray

Instructions:

In a mixing bowl, combine the mashed bananas, vegetable oil, granulated sugar, egg, and vanilla extract.
In another mixing bowl, whisk together the flour, baking soda, baking powder, and salt.
Add the dry ingredients to the wet ingredients and mix until just combined.
Grease a 6-inch cake pan with cooking spray and pour in the banana bread batter.
Preheat your air fryer to 300°F.
Place the cake pan in the air fryer basket and cook for 20-25 minutes or until a toothpick inserted into the center comes out clean.
Remove the banana bread from the air fryer and let it cool for a few minutes before serving.
This air fryer banana bread recipe is a delicious and easy way to enjoy a classic breakfast treat. The air fryer gives the bread a crispy crust while keeping the inside moist and tender. You can enjoy it as is or with a dollop of whipped cream or a drizzle of honey. It's perfect for a quick breakfast or a sweet snack anytime.

74. Here's an easy air fryer recipe for prosciutto and mozzarella bruschetta:

Ingredients:

4 slices of crusty bread
2 tbsp olive oil
2 garlic cloves, minced
4 thin slices of prosciutto
4 slices of fresh mozzarella cheese
4-6 cherry tomatoes, halved
Fresh basil leaves, chopped
Salt and pepper, to taste

Instructions:

Preheat your air fryer to 400°F.
In a small bowl, combine the olive oil and minced garlic.
Brush the mixture onto each slice of bread.
Place the bread in the air fryer basket and cook for 3-5 minutes or until crispy and lightly golden.
Remove the bread from the air fryer and top each slice with a slice of prosciutto, a slice of mozzarella cheese, and a few cherry tomato halves.
Sprinkle salt and pepper to taste over the top of each slice.
Return the bread to the air fryer and cook for an additional 2-3 minutes, or until the cheese has melted.
Remove the bruschetta from the air fryer and sprinkle chopped fresh basil leaves over the top of each slice.
Serve hot and enjoy!
This air fryer prosciutto and mozzarella bruschetta recipe is a quick and easy way to enjoy a classic Italian appetizer. The air fryer makes the bread crispy and golden while keeping the toppings hot and melty. You can also experiment with different toppings and sauces to create your unique bruschetta recipe. It's perfect for a party or a quick snack anytime.

75. Here's an easy air fryer recipe for quick feta triangles:

Ingredients:

6-8 sheets of phyllo pastry
1/2 cup crumbled feta cheese
1/4 cup chopped fresh parsley
1/4 cup chopped scallions
1/4 tsp black pepper

3 tbsp melted butter

Instructions:

Preheat your air fryer to 375°F.
In a mixing bowl, combine the crumbled feta cheese, chopped fresh parsley, chopped scallions, and black pepper.
Lay out one sheet of phyllo pastry on a flat surface and brush it lightly with melted butter.
Cut the phyllo pastry sheet into three equal strips.
Place a small spoonful of the feta mixture at one end of each strip.
Fold the phyllo pastry over the feta mixture to form a triangle and continue to fold the pastry in a triangular shape until you reach the end of the strip.
Repeat the process with the remaining phyllo pastry sheets and feta mixture.
Brush the triangles with melted butter and place them in the air fryer basket.
Cook for 6-8 minutes or until the triangles are golden brown and crispy.
Serve hot and enjoy!
This air fryer feta triangles recipe is a quick and easy appetizer that is perfect for any occasion. The phyllo pastry is light and crispy, while the feta cheese filling is tangy and flavorful. You can also experiment with different herbs and spices to create your unique feta triangle recipe. It's a delicious and simple way to impress your guests or to enjoy a quick snack anytime.

76. Here's an easy air fryer recipe for toasted herb and garlic bagels:

Ingredients:

2 bagels, sliced in half
2 tbsp butter, melted
1 tsp garlic powder
1 tsp dried oregano
1 tsp dried thyme
Salt and black pepper to taste

Instructions:

Preheat your air fryer to 375°F.
In a small mixing bowl, combine the melted butter, garlic powder, dried oregano, dried thyme, salt, and black pepper.
Place the bagel halves in the air fryer basket, cut side up.
Brush the butter and herb mixture over each bagel half.
Place the basket in the air fryer and cook for 4-6 minutes or until the bagels are lightly toasted and golden brown.
Remove the bagels from the air fryer and let them cool for a few minutes before serving.
Serve with your favorite toppings or spreads and enjoy!
This air fryer toasted herb and garlic bagel recipe is a simple way to add extra flavor to your breakfast or snack. The air fryer ensures that the bagels are perfectly toasted and crispy, while the butter and herb mixture adds a delicious savory taste. You can also experiment with different herbs and spices to create your unique bagel recipe. It's perfect for a quick and easy breakfast or a tasty snack any time of day.

77. Here's an easy air fryer recipe for pumpkin and sultana bread:

Ingredients:

1 1/2 cups all-purpose flour
1/2 cup whole wheat flour
1 tsp baking soda
1 tsp baking powder
1/2 tsp salt

1 tsp ground cinnamon
1/2 tsp ground nutmeg
1/4 tsp ground ginger
1/4 tsp ground cloves
1 cup pumpkin puree
1/2 cup vegetable oil
1/2 cup brown sugar
2 eggs
1/2 cup sultanas
Cooking spray

Instructions:

Preheat your air fryer to 330°F.
In a large mixing bowl, combine the all-purpose flour, whole wheat flour, baking soda, baking powder, salt, cinnamon, nutmeg, ginger, and cloves.
In a separate mixing bowl, whisk together the pumpkin puree, vegetable oil, brown sugar, and eggs.
Gradually add the wet mixture to the dry mixture and mix until well combined.
Fold in the sultanas.
Grease a 7-inch cake pan with cooking spray and pour the batter into the pan.
Place the pan in the air fryer basket and cook for 25-30 minutes or until a toothpick inserted into the center of the bread comes out clean.
Remove the pan from the air fryer and let the bread cool for a few minutes before slicing and serving.
Enjoy the pumpkin and sultana bread warm or at room temperature with butter, jam, or your favorite spread.
This air fryer pumpkin and sultana bread recipe is a delicious and healthy way to enjoy the flavors of fall. The air fryer ensures that the bread is perfectly baked and moist, while the pumpkin and spices give it a wonderful aroma and taste. The sultanas add a natural sweetness and a touch of texture to the bread. It's perfect for breakfast or as a snack, and it's a great way to use up any leftover pumpkin puree.

78. Here's an easy air fryer recipe for a grilled apple and brie sandwich:

Ingredients:

4 slices of bread
1 medium apple, cored and sliced
4 oz brie cheese, thinly sliced
2 tbsp honey
1 tbsp Dijon mustard
1 tbsp butter, softened

Instructions:

Preheat your air fryer to 375°F.
In a small bowl, mix the honey and Dijon mustard.
Spread the butter on one side of each slice of bread.
Place the brie slices on two of the bread slices, on the unbuttered side.
Top the brie with the apple slices.
Drizzle the honey mustard mixture over the apple slices.
Place the remaining slices of bread, butter side up, on top of the apple slices.
Place the sandwiches in the air fryer basket and cook for 5 minutes.
Carefully flip the sandwiches over and cook for an additional 3-5 minutes or until the cheese is melted and the bread is golden brown.
Remove the sandwiches from the air fryer and let them cool for a few minutes before slicing and serving.
Enjoy the delicious and easy-to-make air-fried grilled apple and brie sandwich!
This air fryer grilled apple and brie sandwich is a perfect balance of savory and sweet flavors, with the creamy and nutty brie cheese complementing the juicy and slightly tart apple slices. The honey and

Dijon mustard mixture adds a tangy sweetness to the sandwich, while the air fryer ensures that the bread is crispy and golden brown on the outside and warm and soft on the inside. It's a quick and satisfying lunch or snack that's perfect for fall.

79. Here's an easy air fryer recipe for blueberry and maple toast:

Ingredients:

2 slices of bread
2 tbsp cream cheese, softened
1/4 cup fresh blueberries
1 tbsp maple syrup
1 tbsp butter, melted

Instructions:

Preheat your air fryer to 375°F.
In a small bowl, mix the softened cream cheese and maple syrup until well combined.
Spread the cream cheese mixture evenly on both slices of bread.
Sprinkle the fresh blueberries on top of the cream cheese mixture, dividing them evenly between the two slices of bread.
Brush the melted butter on top of the blueberries and bread.
Place the slices of bread in the air fryer basket and cook for 3-4 minutes, or until the bread is golden brown and crispy.
Remove the toast from the air fryer and let it cool for a few minutes before slicing and serving.
Enjoy the delicious and easy-to-make air-fried blueberry and maple toast!
This air fryer blueberry and maple toast is a perfect breakfast or snack that's quick to make and bursting with sweet and creamy flavors. The cream cheese and maple syrup mixture provides a sweet and tangy base for the fresh blueberries, which are baked to perfection in the air fryer, creating a juicy and flavorful topping for the crispy toast. The addition of melted butter on top of the blueberries and bread adds a rich and savory note to the dish, making it a satisfying and indulgent treat that's sure to be a hit with blueberry and toast lovers alike.

80. Here's an easy air fryer recipe for spicy egg and bacon tortilla wraps:

Ingredients:

2 large eggs
2 slices of bacon, chopped
1/4 onion, diced
1/4 red bell pepper, diced
1/4 tsp chili powder
1/4 tsp paprika
1/8 tsp cayenne pepper
Salt and pepper, to taste
2 medium tortillas

Instructions:

Preheat your air fryer to 375°F.
In a small bowl, whisk together the eggs, chili powder, paprika, cayenne pepper, salt, and pepper.
In a small frying pan over medium heat, cook the chopped bacon until crispy, then remove from the pan and set aside on a paper towel to drain.
In the same pan, sauté the onion and red bell pepper until soft, then add the egg mixture and stir occasionally until the eggs are fully cooked.
Warm the tortillas in the microwave for about 15 seconds or until soft and pliable.

Divide the egg mixture and chopped bacon evenly between the two tortillas, placing the filling in the center of each tortilla.
Roll up the tortillas, tucking in the sides to form a wrap.
Place the tortilla wraps in the air fryer basket and cook for 3-4 minutes, or until the tortillas are crispy and lightly browned.
Remove the wraps from the air fryer and let them cool for a few minutes before slicing and serving.
Enjoy the spicy and flavorful air-fried egg and bacon tortilla wraps!
This air fryer recipe for spicy egg and bacon tortilla wraps is a quick and easy breakfast or lunch option that's perfect for those who love a little heat in their meals. The combination of eggs, bacon, onion, and red bell pepper creates a hearty filling that's packed with protein and flavor, while the mix of chili powder, paprika, and cayenne pepper adds a spicy kick that's sure to wake up your taste buds. Air frying the tortilla wraps results in a crispy and golden exterior that complements the soft and savory filling, making for a satisfying and delicious meal that can be enjoyed any time of the day.

81. Here's an easy air fryer recipe for paprika rarebit:

Ingredients:

2 tbsp unsalted butter
2 tbsp all-purpose flour
1/2 tsp Dijon mustard
1/2 tsp Worcestershire sauce
1/4 tsp smoked paprika
1/4 tsp salt
1/4 tsp black pepper
1/2 cup milk
1 cup shredded sharp cheddar cheese
4 slices of bread
Instructions:

Preheat your air fryer to 375°F.
In a small saucepan over medium heat, melt the butter.
Add the flour and stir constantly for about 1-2 minutes until the mixture turns light brown.
Add the mustard, Worcestershire sauce, smoked paprika, salt, and black pepper and whisk until well combined.
Gradually pour in the milk while whisking continuously until the mixture is smooth.
Add the shredded cheddar cheese and whisk until the cheese is fully melted and the mixture is thick and smooth.
Toast the bread slices in the air fryer for 2-3 minutes.
Spread the cheese mixture generously over the toasted bread slices.
Place the cheese-covered bread slices in the air fryer and cook for 2-3 minutes or until the cheese is bubbly and slightly golden on top.
Serve hot and enjoy the deliciously cheesy and smoky air-fried paprika rarebit!
This air fryer recipe for paprika rarebit is a simple yet flavorful twist on the classic Welsh rarebit dish. The combination of melted sharp cheddar cheese, Dijon mustard, Worcestershire sauce, and smoked paprika creates a rich and savory cheese sauce that's perfect for smothering over toasted bread slices. Air frying the rarebit gives it a crispy and slightly charred exterior that complements the gooey and cheesy interior, making for a delicious and satisfying meal that can be enjoyed for breakfast, lunch, or dinner.

82. Here's an easy air fryer recipe for mango bread:

Ingredients:

1 1/2 cups all-purpose flour
1 tsp baking soda
1/2 tsp ground cinnamon

1/4 tsp ground ginger
1/4 tsp salt
2 large eggs
1/2 cup vegetable oil
1 cup mashed ripe mango (about 2 medium mangoes)
1/2 cup granulated sugar
1/4 cup brown sugar
1 tsp vanilla extract
1/2 cup chopped nuts (optional)

Instructions:

Preheat your air fryer to 320°F.
In a medium bowl, whisk together the flour, baking soda, cinnamon, ginger, and salt.
In another bowl, beat the eggs, oil, mashed mango, granulated sugar, brown sugar, and vanilla extract until well combined.
Add the dry ingredients to the wet ingredients and stir until just combined.
Fold in the chopped nuts (if using).
Grease a loaf pan that fits in your air fryer and pour in the batter.
Place the loaf pan in the air fryer and cook for 35-40 minutes or until a toothpick inserted in the center comes out clean.
Remove the pan from the air fryer and let the bread cool in the pan for 10 minutes.
Remove the bread from the pan and let it cool completely on a wire rack.
Slice and serve the deliciously moist and flavorful air-fried mango bread!
This air fryer recipe for mango bread is a great way to use up ripe mangoes and create a delicious and healthy breakfast or snack. The combination of spices like cinnamon and ginger adds warmth and depth to the bread, while the mashed mangoes provide natural sweetness and moisture. You can also add chopped nuts like walnuts or pecans for some extra crunch and texture. Air frying the bread results in a perfectly cooked loaf that's evenly browned and moist on the inside. Enjoy a slice of this delicious mango bread with your morning coffee or tea or as a snack any time of the day!

83. Here's an easy air fryer recipe for crustless Mediterranean feta quiche:

Ingredients:

4 large eggs
1/2 cup milk
1/2 cup crumbled feta cheese
1/2 cup chopped spinach
1/2 cup chopped cherry tomatoes
1/4 cup chopped kalamata olives
1/4 cup chopped red onion
1/4 tsp salt
1/4 tsp black pepper
Cooking spray

Instructions:

Preheat your air fryer to 320°F.
In a large mixing bowl, whisk together the eggs and milk.
Stir in the crumbled feta cheese, chopped spinach, cherry tomatoes, kalamata olives, and red onion.
Season with salt and black pepper.
Grease a baking dish that fits in your air fryer with cooking spray.
Pour the egg mixture into the baking dish.
Place the baking dish in the air fryer and cook for 15-20 minutes, or until the quiche is set in the center and the edges are lightly browned.
Remove the baking dish from the air fryer and let the quiche cool for a few minutes.

Slice and serve the delicious crustless Mediterranean feta quiche!
This air fryer recipe for crustless Mediterranean feta quiche is a delicious and healthy breakfast or brunch option that's full of flavor and nutrition. The combination of feta cheese, spinach, cherry tomatoes, kalamata olives, and red onion creates a classic Mediterranean flavor profile that's sure to satisfy your taste buds. The absence of crust in this quiche recipe also makes it a lighter and healthier option. Air frying the quiche results in a perfectly cooked dish that's evenly browned and fluffy on the inside. Enjoy this delicious and easy air fryer recipe for crustless Mediterranean feta quiche for breakfast, brunch, or any time of the day!

84. Here's an easy air fryer recipe for crustless broccoli & mushroom pie:

Ingredients:

1 medium head of broccoli, chopped into small florets
8 oz. mushrooms, sliced
1/2 cup chopped onion
3 cloves garlic, minced
4 large eggs
1/2 cup milk
1/2 cup shredded cheddar cheese
1/4 cup grated parmesan cheese
1/4 tsp salt
1/4 tsp black pepper
Cooking spray

Instructions:

Preheat your air fryer to 320°F.
In a large mixing bowl, whisk together the eggs and milk.
Stir in the shredded cheddar cheese, grated parmesan cheese, salt, and black pepper.
In a separate bowl, combine the chopped broccoli, sliced mushrooms, chopped onion, and minced garlic.
Spray a baking dish that fits in your air fryer with cooking spray.
Spread the broccoli and mushroom mixture at the bottom of the baking dish.
Pour the egg mixture over the top of the vegetables.
Place the baking dish in the air fryer and cook for 15-20 minutes, or until the pie is set in the center and the edges are lightly browned.
Remove the baking dish from the air fryer and let the pie cool for a few minutes.
Slice and serve the delicious crustless broccoli & mushroom pie!
This air fryer recipe for crustless broccoli & mushroom pie is a healthy and delicious option for a vegetarian breakfast or brunch. The combination of broccoli, mushrooms, onions, and garlic creates a savory and satisfying flavor profile that's complemented by the creamy and cheesy egg mixture. The absence of crust in this pie recipe also makes it a lighter and healthier option. Air frying the pie results in a perfectly cooked dish that's evenly browned and fluffy on the inside. Enjoy this delicious and easy air fryer recipe for crustless broccoli & mushroom pie for breakfast, brunch, or any time of the day!

85. Here's an easy air fryer recipe for flaxseed porridge:

Ingredients:

1/2 cup flaxseeds
1 cup water
1/2 cup milk
1/4 tsp cinnamon
1/4 tsp vanilla extract
1 tbsp honey or maple syrup (optional)
Toppings of your choice (e.g. sliced fruit, nuts, seeds, etc.)

Instructions:

Preheat your air fryer to 300°F.
In a blender or food processor, grind the flaxseeds into a fine powder.
In a mixing bowl, whisk together the ground flaxseeds, water, milk, cinnamon, and vanilla extract.
Pour the mixture into a heat-resistant container that fits in your air fryer.
Place the container in the air fryer and cook for 10-15 minutes, stirring occasionally, until the mixture thickens and becomes porridge-like in consistency.
Remove the container from the air fryer and stir in the honey or maple syrup, if desired.
Top the flaxseed porridge with your favorite toppings, such as sliced fruit, nuts, and seeds.
Serve the delicious and nutritious flaxseed porridge hot and enjoy!
This air fryer recipe for flaxseed porridge is a healthy and filling breakfast option that's high in fiber, omega-3 fatty acids, and other nutrients. The air frying process helps to cook the porridge evenly and gives it a slightly toasted flavor. You can customize this recipe by adding different spices, sweeteners, and toppings to suit your taste preferences. This recipe is also suitable for those following a vegan or gluten-free diet. Enjoy this delicious and easy air fryer recipe for flaxseed porridge to start your day on a healthy note!

86. Here's an easy air fryer recipe for zucchini muffins:

Ingredients:

1 1/2 cups all-purpose flour
1/2 cup whole wheat flour
1/2 cup brown sugar
2 tsp baking powder
1/2 tsp baking soda
1/2 tsp salt
1 tsp ground cinnamon
1/4 tsp ground nutmeg
1 egg
1/2 cup milk
1/2 cup plain Greek yogurt
1/4 cup vegetable oil
1 tsp vanilla extract
1 cup grated zucchini
1/2 cup chopped walnuts (optional)

Instructions:

Preheat your air fryer to 320°F.
In a mixing bowl, combine the all-purpose flour, whole wheat flour, brown sugar, baking powder, baking soda, salt, cinnamon, and nutmeg.
In another mixing bowl, whisk together the egg, milk, Greek yogurt, vegetable oil, and vanilla extract.
Pour the wet mixture into the dry mixture and stir until just combined.
Fold in the grated zucchini and chopped walnuts (if using).
Grease a muffin tin with cooking spray and spoon the batter evenly into the cups, filling each about 2/3 full.
Place the muffin tin in the air fryer and cook for 12-15 minutes, or until a toothpick inserted into the center of a muffin comes out clean.
Remove the muffin tin from the air fryer and let the muffins cool for a few minutes before removing them from the tin.
Serve the delicious and healthy zucchini muffins warm or at room temperature.
These zucchini muffins are a great way to incorporate more vegetables into your diet and make a tasty breakfast or snack. The air frying process helps to cook the muffins evenly and gives them a slightly crispy exterior. You can customize this recipe by adding different spices, nuts, or fruits to the batter. This

recipe is also suitable for those following a vegetarian diet. Enjoy this easy air fryer recipe for zucchini muffins as a healthy and delicious treat!

87. Here's an easy air fryer recipe for banana and hazelnut muffins:

Ingredients:

1 1/2 cups all-purpose flour
1/2 cup granulated sugar
2 teaspoons baking powder
1/4 teaspoon salt
1/3 cup vegetable oil
1 egg
1/3 cup milk
2 ripe bananas, mashed
1/2 cup chopped hazelnuts

Instructions:

Preheat your air fryer to 320°F (160°C) for 5 minutes.
In a mixing bowl, whisk together the flour, sugar, baking powder, and salt.
In another bowl, whisk together the oil, egg, milk, and mashed bananas.
Add the wet ingredients to the dry ingredients and mix until just combined.
Fold in the chopped hazelnuts.
Grease a muffin pan with cooking spray.
Fill the muffin cups 2/3 full with the batter.
Place the muffin pan in the air fryer basket and air fry at 320°F (160°C) for 15-18 minutes, or until a toothpick inserted in the center of a muffin comes out clean.
Remove the muffins from the air fryer and let them cool for a few minutes before serving.
Enjoy your delicious banana and hazelnut muffins!

88. Here's an easy air fryer recipe for Italian sausage patties:

Ingredients:

1 pound ground pork
1 teaspoon salt
1 teaspoon fennel seeds
1 teaspoon dried oregano
1/2 teaspoon garlic powder
1/2 teaspoon black pepper
1/4 teaspoon red pepper flakes
Cooking spray

Instructions:

In a large mixing bowl, combine the ground pork, salt, fennel seeds, oregano, garlic powder, black pepper, and red pepper flakes.
Mix the ingredients with your hands until well combined.
Divide the mixture into 8 equal portions and shape each portion into a patty.
Preheat your air fryer to 375°F (190°C) for 5 minutes.
Spray the air fryer basket with cooking spray.
Place the sausage patties in a single layer in the air fryer basket.
Air fry at 375°F (190°C) for 10-12 minutes, flipping the patties halfway through cooking, until they are browned and cooked through.
Use a meat thermometer to check that the internal temperature of the patties has reached 160°F (71°C).
Remove the sausage patties from the air fryer and let them rest for a few minutes before serving.

Serve these Italian sausage patties with your favorite sides for a delicious and easy meal!

89. Here's an easy air fryer recipe for Kiwi Muffins with Pecans:

Ingredients:

2 kiwis, peeled and mashed
1/2 cup vegetable oil
1/2 cup granulated sugar
2 eggs
1 teaspoon vanilla extract
1 cup all-purpose flour
1/2 cup pecans, chopped
1 teaspoon baking powder
1/2 teaspoon baking soda
1/2 teaspoon salt

Instructions:

Preheat your air fryer to 320°F (160°C) for 5 minutes.
In a large mixing bowl, whisk together the mashed kiwis, vegetable oil, granulated sugar, eggs, and vanilla extract.
Add the all-purpose flour, chopped pecans, baking powder, baking soda, and salt to the bowl. Mix everything until just combined.
Grease a muffin tin with cooking spray or line it with muffin liners.
Divide the batter equally among 6 muffin cups, filling each one about 3/4 full.
Place the muffin tin in the air fryer basket and air fry at 320°F (160°C) for 15-18 minutes, or until a toothpick inserted into the center of a muffin comes out clean.
Remove the muffin tin from the air fryer and let the muffins cool for a few minutes before removing them from the muffin cups.
Enjoy these delicious Kiwi Muffins with pecan as a sweet breakfast or snack option!

90. Here's an easy air fryer recipe for kiwi muffins with pecans that you can try:

Ingredients:

1 cup all-purpose flour
1/2 cup granulated sugar
1 tsp baking powder
1/2 tsp baking soda
1/4 tsp salt
1/2 cup chopped pecans
1 large egg
1/4 cup vegetable oil
1/4 cup plain Greek yogurt
1/4 cup milk
1 tsp vanilla extract
2 kiwis, peeled and chopped

Instructions:

Preheat your air fryer to 325°F (160°C).
In a mixing bowl, combine the flour, sugar, baking powder, baking soda, and salt. Mix well.
Add the chopped pecans and mix until combined.

In another mixing bowl, whisk the egg, vegetable oil, Greek yogurt, milk, and vanilla extract until smooth.
Add the chopped kiwis and mix until combined.
Add the dry ingredients to the wet ingredients and mix until just combined. Do not over mix.
Spoon the batter evenly into 6 muffin cups.
Place the muffin cups into the air fryer basket and cook for 12-15 minutes, or until a toothpick inserted into the center of a muffin comes out clean.
Remove the muffin cups from the air fryer and let them cool for a few minutes before serving.
Enjoy your delicious kiwi muffins with pecans!

91. Here is an easy air fryer recipe for orange creamy cupcakes:

Ingredients:

For the cupcakes:
1 1/2 cups all-purpose flour
1/2 cup granulated sugar
1 tsp baking powder
1/2 tsp baking soda
1/4 tsp salt
1/3 cup vegetable oil
1/2 cup fresh orange juice
1 tbsp orange zest
1 tsp vanilla extract
1 large egg
For the cream cheese frosting:
4 oz cream cheese, at room temperature
1/4 cup unsalted butter, at room temperature
1/2 tsp vanilla extract
1 1/2 cups powdered sugar

Instructions:

Preheat your air fryer to 320°F (160°C).
In a mixing bowl, combine the flour, sugar, baking powder, baking soda, and salt. Mix well.
In another mixing bowl, whisk together the vegetable oil, orange juice, orange zest, vanilla extract, and egg until well combined.
Add the dry ingredients to the wet ingredients and mix until just combined. Do not over mix.
Spoon the batter into 6 cupcake liners.
Place the cupcake liners in the air fryer basket and cook for 12-15 minutes, or until a toothpick inserted into the center of a cupcake comes out clean.
Remove the cupcakes from the air fryer and let them cool completely.
To make the cream cheese frosting, beat the cream cheese, unsalted butter, and vanilla extract until creamy.
Gradually add the powdered sugar, beating until well combined.
Spread the frosting on top of the cooled cupcakes.
Serve and enjoy your delicious orange-creamy cupcakes!
Note: This recipe can be easily doubled or tripled to make more cupcakes.

92. Here's an easy air fryer recipe for coconut and oat cookies:

Ingredients:

1 cup rolled oats
1/2 cup shredded sweetened coconut
1/2 cup all-purpose flour
1/2 cup granulated sugar
1/2 tsp baking powder
1/4 tsp salt
1/2 cup unsalted butter, softened
1 large egg
1 tsp vanilla extract

Instructions:

Preheat your air fryer to 325°F (160°C).
In a mixing bowl, combine the rolled oats, shredded sweetened coconut, all-purpose flour, granulated sugar, baking powder, and salt. Mix well.
In another mixing bowl, cream the unsalted butter until smooth.
Add the egg and vanilla extract to the creamed butter and mix until well combined.
Add the dry ingredients to the wet ingredients and mix until just combined. Do not over mix.
Roll the cookie dough into balls about the size of a golf ball.
Place the cookie dough balls on a parchment-lined air fryer basket, spacing them about 1 inch apart.
Flatten the cookie dough balls slightly with the palm of your hand.
Place the air fryer basket in the preheated air fryer and cook for 8-10 minutes, or until the cookies are golden brown.
Remove the cookies from the air fryer and let them cool on a wire rack.
Serve and enjoy your delicious coconut and oat cookies!
Note: This recipe makes about 12 cookies. You can easily double or triple the recipe to make more cookies.

93. Here's an easy air fryer recipe for cherry and almond scones:

Ingredients:

2 cups all-purpose flour
1/4 cup granulated sugar
2 tsp baking powder
1/2 tsp baking soda
1/2 tsp salt
1/2 cup unsalted butter, chilled and cubed
1/2 cup dried cherries, chopped
1/2 cup sliced almonds, toasted
1/2 cup buttermilk
1 large egg
1 tsp almond extract
1 tbsp turbinado sugar (optional)

Instructions:

Preheat your air fryer to 375°F (190°C).
In a mixing bowl, combine the all-purpose flour, granulated sugar, baking powder, baking soda, and salt. Mix well.
Add the chilled and cubed unsalted butter to the dry ingredients and use a pastry cutter or two knives to cut the butter into the flour mixture until it resembles coarse crumbs.
Add the chopped dried cherries and toasted sliced almonds to the mixture and mix well.
In another mixing bowl, whisk together the buttermilk, egg, and almond extract.
Add the wet ingredients to the dry ingredients and mix until just combined. Do not over mix.

Transfer the dough to a lightly floured surface and shape it into an 8-inch circle.
Cut the dough into 8 wedges.
Place the scones on a parchment-lined air fryer basket, spacing them about 1 inch apart.
Sprinkle Turbinado sugar over the tops of the scones, if desired.
Place the air fryer basket in the preheated air fryer and cook for 12-15 minutes, or until the scones are golden brown.
Remove the scones from the air fryer and let them cool on a wire rack.
Serve and enjoy your delicious cherry and almond scones!
Note: This recipe makes 8 scones. You can easily double or triple the recipe to make more scones.

94. Here's an easy air fryer recipe for blueberry oat bars:

Ingredients:

1 cup all-purpose flour
1/2 cup rolled oats
1/2 cup brown sugar
1/2 tsp baking powder
1/4 tsp salt
1/2 cup unsalted butter, melted
1/2 cup blueberry jam
1/4 cup sliced almonds

Instructions:

Preheat your air fryer to 325°F (160°C).
In a mixing bowl, combine the all-purpose flour, rolled oats, brown sugar, baking powder, and salt. Mix well.
Add the melted unsalted butter to the dry ingredients and mix until well combined.
Set aside 1/2 cup of the mixture for the topping.
Press the remaining mixture into the bottom of a 6-inch square baking dish.
Spread the blueberry jam evenly over the top of the mixture.
Sprinkle the reserved mixture and sliced the almonds over the top of the blueberry jam.
Place the baking dish in the air fryer basket and cook for 20-25 minutes, or until the top is golden brown and the jam is bubbling.
Remove the baking dish from the air fryer and let it cool on a wire rack.
Cut the blueberry oat bars into squares and serve.
Enjoy your delicious blueberry oat bars!
Note: This recipe makes about 9 bars. You can easily double or triple the recipe to make more bars.

95. Here is an easy air fryer recipe for sweet bread pudding with raisins:

Ingredients:

6 cups cubed day-old bread
1/2 cup raisins
3 eggs
1/2 cup granulated sugar
2 cups whole milk
1 tsp vanilla extract
1/2 tsp ground cinnamon
1/4 tsp ground nutmeg

Instructions:

Preheat your air fryer to 325°F (160°C).
In a large mixing bowl, combine the cubed day-old bread and raisins. Mix well.
In another mixing bowl, whisk together the eggs, granulated sugar, whole milk, vanilla extract, ground cinnamon, and ground nutmeg until well combined.
Pour the egg mixture over the bread and raisins. Mix until the bread is coated and the raisins are evenly distributed.
Let the bread mixture sit for 10-15 minutes, so the bread can absorb the egg mixture.
Transfer the bread mixture to a 6-inch baking dish that fits in your air fryer basket.
Place the baking dish in the air fryer basket and cook for 20-25 minutes, or until the bread pudding is set and the top is golden brown.
Remove the baking dish from the air fryer and let it cool on a wire rack for a few minutes.
Cut the sweet bread pudding into squares and serve warm.
Enjoy your delicious sweet bread pudding with raisins!
Note: This recipe makes about 6 servings. You can easily double or triple the recipe to make more servings.

96. Here is an easy air fryer recipe for simple crispy bacon:

Ingredients:

6-8 slices of bacon

Instructions:

Preheat your air fryer to 400°F (200°C).
Line the air fryer basket with parchment paper.
Place the bacon slices in a single layer in the air fryer basket. You may need to do this in batches, depending on the size of your air fryer.
Cook the bacon in the air fryer for 8-10 minutes, or until it reaches your desired level of crispiness.
Check on the bacon halfway through cooking and flip it over with tongs to ensure it cooks evenly.
Once the bacon is cooked to your liking, remove it from the air fryer and place it on a plate lined with paper towels to absorb any excess grease.
Serve the crispy bacon hot and enjoy!
Note: The cooking time may vary depending on the thickness of the bacon slices and the power of your air fryer. Keep an eye on the bacon and adjust the cooking time as needed.

97. Here is an easy air fryer recipe for crispy croutons:

Ingredients:

4 cups of cubed day-old bread
2 tablespoons of olive oil
1/2 teaspoon of garlic powder
1/2 teaspoon of dried basil
1/2 teaspoon of dried oregano
1/4 teaspoon of salt
1/4 teaspoon of black pepper

Instructions:

Preheat your air fryer to 375°F (190°C).

In a mixing bowl, combine the cubed day-old bread, olive oil, garlic powder, dried basil, dried oregano, salt, and black pepper. Mix well, ensuring the bread cubes are coated evenly.
Transfer the bread mixture to the air fryer basket in a single layer. You may need to do this in batches, depending on the size of your air fryer.
Cook the croutons in the air fryer for 5-7 minutes, or until they are golden brown and crispy. Check on the croutons halfway through cooking and shake the basket to ensure they cook evenly.
Once the croutons are cooked, remove them from the air fryer and let them cool on a wire rack.
Serve the crispy croutons as desired on top of salads, soups, or as a snack.
Note: The cooking time may vary depending on the size and thickness of your bread cubes and the power of your air fryer. Keep an eye on the croutons and adjust the cooking time as needed. Store any leftover croutons in an airtight container at room temperature for up to a week.

98. Here is an easy air fryer recipe for avocado tempura:

Ingredients:

1 large ripe avocado, pitted and sliced
1/2 cup all-purpose flour
1/2 cup cornstarch
1 teaspoon baking powder
1/2 teaspoon salt
1/2 cup cold water
1 egg, beaten
1 cup panko breadcrumbs
Cooking spray

Instructions:

Preheat your air fryer to 390°F (200°C).
In a mixing bowl, whisk together the all-purpose flour, cornstarch, baking powder, and salt. Gradually add the cold water and beaten egg, stirring until a smooth batter is formed.
Place the panko breadcrumbs in a shallow dish.
Dip the avocado slices into the batter, ensuring they are coated evenly.
Dredge the battered avocado slices in the panko breadcrumbs, pressing them gently to adhere.
Place the avocado slices in a single layer in the air fryer basket. You may need to do this in batches, depending on the size of your air fryer.
Lightly spray the avocado slices with cooking spray.
Cook the avocado tempura in the air fryer for 8-10 minutes, or until they are golden brown and crispy. Check on the avocado slices halfway through cooking and flip them over with tongs to ensure they cook evenly.
Once the avocado tempura is cooked, remove them from the air fryer and let them cool on a wire rack.
Serve the avocado tempura with your favorite dipping sauce and enjoy!
Note: You can also add additional seasonings to the panko breadcrumbs or the batter, such as garlic powder, cumin, or chili powder, to give the avocado tempura extra flavor. The cooking time may vary depending on the size and thickness of the avocado slices and the power of your air fryer. Keep an eye on the avocado tempura and adjust the cooking time as needed.

99. Here is an easy air fryer recipe for baked avocado with eggs and cilantro:

Ingredients:

2 ripe avocados, halved and pitted
4 eggs
2 tablespoons chopped fresh cilantro
Salt and pepper to taste

Instructions:

Preheat your air fryer to 350°F (175°C).
Place the avocado halves cut-side up in the air fryer basket.
Crack an egg into each avocado half, making sure not to overfill.
Season the eggs with salt and pepper to taste.
Place the air fryer basket in the air fryer and bake the avocado and eggs for 8-10 minutes, or until the egg whites are set and the yolks are cooked to your liking.
Remove the avocado halves from the air fryer and sprinkle the chopped cilantro on top.
Serve the baked avocado with eggs and cilantro hot and enjoy!
Note: You can also add additional toppings to the baked avocado, such as shredded cheese, diced tomatoes, or chopped bacon, to give it extra flavor and texture. The cooking time may vary depending on the size and power of your air fryer and the desired level of doneness for the eggs. Keep an eye on the baked avocado and eggs and adjust the cooking time as needed.

100. Here is an easy air fryer recipe for roasted asparagus with Serrano ham:

Ingredients:

1 pound asparagus, trimmed
4-6 thin slices of Serrano ham
2 tablespoons olive oil
Salt and pepper to taste

Instructions:

Preheat your air fryer to 400°F (200°C).
Toss the asparagus with olive oil, salt, and pepper in a bowl until coated evenly.
Cut the Serrano ham slices into thin strips.
Wrap each asparagus spear with a slice of Serrano ham, placing the ham near the top of the asparagus and wrapping it around the stem.
Place the asparagus spears in the air fryer basket in a single layer.
Roast the asparagus in the air fryer for 8-10 minutes, or until they are tender and lightly browned.
Remove the asparagus from the air fryer and let them cool for a minute before serving.
Serve the roasted asparagus with Serrano ham hot and enjoy!
Note: You can also add additional seasonings to the asparagus, such as garlic powder, paprika, or lemon juice, to give it extra flavor. The cooking time may vary depending on the size and thickness of the asparagus and the power of your air fryer. Keep an eye on the asparagus and adjust the cooking time as needed. If the Serrano ham starts to burn, you can remove it from the asparagus spears and crisp it separately in the air fryer for a few minutes.

101. Here is an easy air fryer recipe for the hearty banana pastry:

Ingredients:

1 sheet puff pastry, thawed
2 ripe bananas, sliced
1/4 cup chopped walnuts
1/4 cup brown sugar
1 teaspoon ground cinnamon
1 egg, beaten

Instructions:

Preheat your air fryer to 375°F (190°C).
Roll out the puff pastry sheet on a lightly floured surface and cut it into 4 equal pieces.
Place the sliced bananas on one half of each pastry piece.
Sprinkle the chopped walnuts, brown sugar, and cinnamon on top of the bananas.

Fold the other half of the pastry over the banana mixture and seal the edges with a fork.
Brush the top of each pastry with the beaten egg.
Place the pastries in the air fryer basket in a single layer.
Bake the pastries in the air fryer for 10-12 minutes, or until they are golden brown and puffed up.
Remove the pastries from the air fryer and let them cool for a minute before serving.
Serve the hearty banana pastries warm and enjoy!
Note: You can also add additional toppings to the banana pastries, such as chocolate chips or shredded coconut, to give them extra flavor and texture. The cooking time may vary depending on the size and power of your air fryer. Keep an eye on the pastries and adjust the cooking time as needed.

SNACKS & SIDE DISHES

102. Here is an easy air fryer recipe for air-fried hot wings:

Ingredients:

2 pounds of chicken wings, tips removed, and drumettes and flats separated
2 teaspoons baking powder
1/2 teaspoon salt
1/4 teaspoon black pepper
1/4 teaspoon garlic powder
1/4 teaspoon onion powder
1/4 teaspoon smoked paprika
1/4 cup hot sauce (such as Frank's RedHot)
2 tablespoons unsalted butter, melted

Instructions:

Preheat your air fryer to 400°F (200°C).
In a bowl, combine the baking powder, salt, black pepper, garlic powder, onion powder, and smoked paprika.
Add the chicken wings to the bowl and toss them in the seasoning mixture until they are coated evenly.
Place the chicken wings in the air fryer basket in a single layer, making sure they don't touch.
Air fry the wings for 24-28 minutes, flipping them halfway through the cooking time until they are crispy and golden brown.
In a separate bowl, mix the hot sauce and melted butter.
Toss the cooked wings in the hot sauce mixture until they are coated evenly.
Place the wings back in the air fryer basket and air fry for an additional 2-3 minutes to set the sauce.
Remove the wings from the air fryer and let them cool for a minute before serving.
Serve the air-fried hot wings with your favorite dipping sauce and enjoy!
Note: You can adjust the amount of hot sauce and butter to your liking, depending on how spicy you want the wings to be. You can also use different seasoning blends for the chicken wings. The cooking time may vary depending on the size and power of your air fryer. Keep an eye on the wings and adjust the cooking time as needed.

103. Here is an air fryer recipe for crispy Alfredo chicken wings:

Ingredients:

2 pounds of chicken wings, tips removed, and drumettes and flats separated
1/2 cup all-purpose flour
1/2 teaspoon salt
1/4 teaspoon black pepper
1/4 teaspoon garlic powder
1/4 teaspoon onion powder
1/4 cup unsalted butter, melted

1/2 cup Alfredo sauce
1/4 cup grated Parmesan cheese
Chopped fresh parsley, for garnish

Instructions:

Preheat your air fryer to 375°F (190°C).
In a bowl, mix the flour, salt, black pepper, garlic powder, and onion powder.
Toss the chicken wings in the flour mixture until they are coated evenly.
Place the chicken wings in the air fryer basket in a single layer, making sure they don't touch.
Air fry the wings for 20 minutes, flipping them halfway through the cooking time until they are crispy and golden brown.
In a separate bowl, mix the melted butter, Alfredo sauce, and grated Parmesan cheese.
Toss the cooked wings in the Alfredo sauce mixture until they are coated evenly.
Place the wings back in the air fryer basket and air fry for an additional 3-4 minutes to set the sauce.
Remove the wings from the air fryer and sprinkle with chopped fresh parsley for garnish.
Serve the crispy Alfredo chicken wings warm and enjoy!
Note: You can adjust the amount of Parmesan cheese and Alfredo sauce to your liking. You can also use different seasoning blends for the chicken wings. The cooking time may vary depending on the size and power of your air fryer. Keep an eye on the wings and adjust the cooking time as needed.

104. Here is an air fryer recipe for crunchy ranch chicken wings:

Ingredients:

2 pounds of chicken wings, tips removed, and drumettes and flats separated
1/2 cup all-purpose flour
1/2 teaspoon salt
1/4 teaspoon black pepper
1/4 teaspoon garlic powder
1/4 teaspoon onion powder
1/4 cup unsalted butter, melted
1/4 cup ranch dressing
1/2 cup panko breadcrumbs

Instructions:

Preheat your air fryer to 375°F (190°C).
In a bowl, mix the flour, salt, black pepper, garlic powder, and onion powder.
Toss the chicken wings in the flour mixture until they are coated evenly.
In a separate bowl, mix the melted butter and ranch dressing.
Dip each chicken wing into the ranch dressing mixture, then roll it in the panko breadcrumbs, pressing them onto the chicken to coat.
Place the chicken wings in the air fryer basket in a single layer, making sure they don't touch.
Air fry the wings for 20-22 minutes, flipping them halfway through the cooking time until they are crispy and golden brown.
Remove the wings from the air fryer and let them cool for a minute before serving.
Serve the crunchy ranch chicken wings with additional ranch dressing for dipping and enjoy!
Note: You can adjust the amount of ranch dressing to your liking, depending on how much flavor you want. You can also use different seasoning blends for the chicken wings. The cooking time may vary depending on the size and power of your air fryer. Keep an eye on the wings and adjust the cooking time as needed.

105. Here is an air fryer recipe for Korean chili chicken wings:

Ingredients:

2 pounds of chicken wings, tips removed, and drumettes and flats separated
1/4 cup soy sauce
1/4 cup Gochujang (Korean chili paste)
2 tablespoons honey
2 tablespoons rice vinegar
1 tablespoon sesame oil
1 tablespoon grated fresh ginger
1 tablespoon minced garlic
1/2 teaspoon salt
1/4 teaspoon black pepper
Sliced scallions and sesame seeds, for garnish

Instructions:

Preheat your air fryer to 375°F (190°C).
In a bowl, mix the soy sauce, gochujang, honey, rice vinegar, sesame oil, ginger, garlic, salt, and black pepper.
Toss the chicken wings in the marinade until they are coated evenly.
Place the chicken wings in the air fryer basket in a single layer, making sure they don't touch.
Air fry the wings for 20-22 minutes, flipping them halfway through the cooking time until they are crispy and golden brown.
Remove the wings from the air fryer and place them in a bowl.
Drizzle the remaining marinade over the wings and toss them to coat evenly.
Place the wings back in the air fryer basket and air fry for an additional 2-3 minutes to set the sauce.
Remove the wings from the air fryer and sprinkle with sliced scallions and sesame seeds for garnish.
Serve the Korean chili chicken wings hot and enjoy!
Note: You can adjust the amount of gochujang and honey to your liking, depending on how spicy and sweet you want the wings to be. You can also marinate the wings for a few hours or overnight for extra flavor. The cooking time may vary depending on the size and power of your air fryer. Keep an eye on the wings and adjust the cooking time as needed.

106. Here's an air fryer recipe for teriyaki chicken wings that you can try:

Ingredients:

2 pounds of chicken wings, tips removed, and drumettes and flats separated
1/4 cup teriyaki sauce
2 tablespoons honey
1 tablespoon rice vinegar
1 tablespoon sesame oil
1 tablespoon minced garlic
1/2 teaspoon salt
1/4 teaspoon black pepper
Sliced scallions and sesame seeds, for garnish

Instructions:

Preheat your air fryer to 375°F (190°C).
In a bowl, whisk together the teriyaki sauce, honey, rice vinegar, sesame oil, garlic, salt, and black pepper.
Toss the chicken wings in the marinade until they are coated evenly.
Place the chicken wings in the air fryer basket in a single layer, making sure they don't touch.
Air fry the wings for 20-22 minutes, flipping them halfway through the cooking time until they are crispy and golden brown.
Remove the wings from the air fryer and place them in a bowl.
Drizzle the remaining marinade over the wings and toss them to coat evenly.
Place the wings back in the air fryer basket and air fry for an additional 2-3 minutes to set the sauce.

Remove the wings from the air fryer and sprinkle with sliced scallions and sesame seeds for garnish.
Serve the teriyaki chicken wings hot and enjoy!
Note: You can adjust the amount of honey and teriyaki sauce to your liking, depending on how sweet and salty you want the wings to be. You can also marinate the wings for a few hours or overnight for extra flavor. The cooking time may vary depending on the size and power of your air fryer. Keep an eye on the wings and adjust the cooking time as needed.

107. Here's an air fryer recipe for chicken wings with gorgonzola dip that you can try:

Ingredients:

2 pounds of chicken wings, tips removed, and drumettes and flats separated
1 tablespoon olive oil
1/2 teaspoon salt
1/4 teaspoon black pepper
1/2 cup crumbled Gorgonzola cheese
1/2 cup mayonnaise
1/4 cup sour cream
1 tablespoon lemon juice
1/2 teaspoon garlic powder
1/4 teaspoon onion powder
2 tablespoons chopped fresh parsley, for garnish

Instructions:

Preheat your air fryer to 375°F (190°C).
In a bowl, toss the chicken wings with olive oil, salt, and black pepper until they are coated evenly.
Place the chicken wings in the air fryer basket in a single layer, making sure they don't touch.
Air fry the wings for 20-22 minutes, flipping them halfway through the cooking time until they are crispy and golden brown.
While the wings are cooking, prepare the gorgonzola dip by combining the Gorgonzola cheese, mayonnaise, sour cream, lemon juice, garlic powder, and onion powder in a bowl.
Mix the ingredients until they are well combined.
Once the wings are done cooking, remove them from the air fryer and let them cool for a few minutes.
Serve the wings hot with the gorgonzola dip on the side.
Garnish with chopped parsley and enjoy!
Note: You can adjust the amount of Gorgonzola cheese and other ingredients to your liking, depending on how strong or mild you want the dip to be. If you prefer a smoother dip, you can use a food processor or blender to blend the ingredients until they are smooth. The cooking time may vary depending on the size and power of your air fryer. Keep an eye on the wings and adjust the cooking time as needed.

108. Here's an air fryer recipe for Piri Piri chicken wings that you can try:

Ingredients:

2 pounds of chicken wings, tips removed, and drumettes and flats separated
1 tablespoon olive oil
1/2 teaspoon salt
1/4 teaspoon black pepper
2 tablespoons piri piri sauce
1 tablespoon honey
1 tablespoon lime juice
1 garlic clove, minced
1 tablespoon chopped fresh parsley, for garnish

Instructions:

Preheat your air fryer to 375°F (190°C).
In a bowl, toss the chicken wings with olive oil, salt, and black pepper until they are coated evenly.
Place the chicken wings in the air fryer basket in a single layer, making sure they don't touch.
Air fry the wings for 20-22 minutes, flipping them halfway through the cooking time until they are crispy and golden brown.
While the wings are cooking, prepare the piri piri sauce by combining the piri piri sauce, honey, lime juice, and minced garlic in a bowl.
Mix the ingredients until they are well combined.
Once the wings are done cooking, transfer them to a bowl and add the piri piri sauce.
Toss the wings with the sauce until they are coated evenly.
Serve the wings hot with chopped parsley on top.
Note: You can adjust the amount of piri piri sauce and other ingredients to your liking, depending on how spicy or mild you want the wings to be. You can also marinate the wings in the piri piri sauce for a few hours before cooking them to enhance the flavor. The cooking time may vary depending on the size and power of your air fryer. Keep an eye on the wings and adjust the cooking time as needed.

109. Here's a simple air fryer recipe for juicy and flavorful chicken thighs:

Ingredients:

4 bone-in, skin-on chicken thighs
1 teaspoon paprika
1 teaspoon garlic powder
1 teaspoon onion powder
1 teaspoon dried thyme
1 teaspoon salt
1/2 teaspoon black pepper
Cooking spray

Instructions:

Preheat your air fryer to 400°F (200°C).
In a small bowl, mix paprika, garlic powder, onion powder, thyme, salt, and black pepper to create a dry rub.
Pat the chicken thighs dry with paper towels, then rub the dry rub all over the chicken thighs, making sure to coat them evenly.
Spray the air fryer basket with cooking spray, then place the chicken thighs in the basket, skin side up.
Air fry the chicken thighs for 22-25 minutes, flipping them halfway through the cooking time until they are cooked through and the internal temperature reaches 165°F (74°C).
Let the chicken thighs rest for a few minutes before serving.
Note: You can adjust the cooking time depending on the size and thickness of your chicken thighs. You can also experiment with different seasonings and spices to create your unique flavor profile. If you want crispy skin, you can broil the chicken thighs in the oven for a few minutes after air frying.

110. Here's a tasty air fryer recipe for mustard-honey chicken thighs:

Ingredients:

4 bone-in, skin-on chicken thighs
1 tablespoon Dijon mustard
2 tablespoons honey
2 cloves garlic, minced
1/2 teaspoon paprika
1/2 teaspoon salt
1/4 teaspoon black pepper

Cooking spray

Instructions:

Preheat your air fryer to 400°F (200°C).
In a small bowl, mix Dijon mustard, honey, minced garlic, paprika, salt, and black pepper to create a marinade.
Pat the chicken thighs dry with paper towels, then brush the marinade all over the chicken thighs, making sure to coat them evenly.
Spray the air fryer basket with cooking spray, then place the chicken thighs in the basket, skin side up.
Air fry the chicken thighs for 20-25 minutes, flipping them halfway through the cooking time until they are cooked through and the internal temperature reaches 165°F (74°C).
Let the chicken thighs rest for a few minutes before serving.
Note: You can adjust the cooking time depending on the size and thickness of your chicken thighs. You can also add more honey or mustard to the marinade to suit your taste. If you want crispy skin, you can broil the chicken thighs in the oven for a few minutes after air frying.

111. Here's an easy and delicious air fryer recipe for crispy chicken nuggets:

Ingredients:

1 pound boneless, skinless chicken breasts
1 cup all-purpose flour
1 teaspoon garlic powder
1 teaspoon onion powder
1 teaspoon paprika
1 teaspoon salt
1/2 teaspoon black pepper
2 large eggs, beaten
2 cups panko breadcrumbs
Cooking spray

Instructions:

Cut the chicken breasts into bite-sized pieces and set aside.
In a shallow dish, mix the flour, garlic powder, onion powder, paprika, salt, and black pepper.
In another shallow dish, beat the eggs.
In a third shallow dish, place the panko breadcrumbs.
Dredge each piece of chicken in the flour mixture, shaking off any excess.
Dip the chicken into the beaten eggs, then coat in the panko breadcrumbs, pressing the breadcrumbs onto the chicken to ensure a good coating.
Spray the air fryer basket with cooking spray, then place the chicken nuggets in the basket, making sure they are not touching.
Air fry the chicken nuggets at 400°F (200°C) for 8-10 minutes, flipping them halfway through the cooking time, until they are golden brown and crispy.
Serve with your favorite dipping sauce.
Note: You can adjust the cooking time depending on the size and thickness of your chicken nuggets. You can also experiment with different seasonings and spices to create your unique flavor profile. If you want extra crispy chicken nuggets, you can spray them with a little more cooking spray before air frying.

112. Here's an easy and flavorful air fryer recipe for paprika chicken fingers:

Ingredients:

1 pound boneless, skinless chicken breasts, cut into strips
1 cup all-purpose flour
1 teaspoon paprika

1 teaspoon garlic powder
1 teaspoon onion powder
1 teaspoon salt
1/2 teaspoon black pepper
2 large eggs, beaten
1 1/2 cups panko breadcrumbs
Cooking spray

Instructions:

In a shallow dish, mix the flour, paprika, garlic powder, onion powder, salt, and black pepper.
In another shallow dish, beat the eggs.
In a third shallow dish, place the panko breadcrumbs.
Dredge each chicken strip in the flour mixture, shaking off any excess.
Dip the chicken into the beaten eggs, then coat in the panko breadcrumbs, pressing the breadcrumbs onto the chicken to ensure a good coating.
Spray the air fryer basket with cooking spray, then place the chicken fingers in the basket, making sure they are not touching.
Air fry the chicken fingers at 400°F (200°C) for 10-12 minutes, flipping them halfway through the cooking time, until they are golden brown and cooked through.
Serve with your favorite dipping sauce.
Note: You can adjust the seasoning to your taste by adding more or less paprika, garlic powder, or other spices. For extra crunch, you can use crushed cornflakes or crushed crackers instead of panko breadcrumbs. Enjoy!

113. Here's a tasty air fryer recipe for corn-crusted chicken tenders that are crispy on the outside and juicy on the inside:

Ingredients:

1 pound boneless, skinless chicken breasts, cut into strips
1/2 cup all-purpose flour
1 teaspoon garlic powder
1 teaspoon onion powder
1 teaspoon paprika
1 teaspoon salt
1/2 teaspoon black pepper
2 large eggs, beaten
1 cup cornmeal
Cooking spray

Instructions:

Preheat your air fryer to 400°F (200°C).
In a shallow dish, mix the flour, garlic powder, onion powder, paprika, salt, and black pepper.
In another shallow dish, beat the eggs.
In a third shallow dish, place the cornmeal.
Dredge each chicken strip in the flour mixture, shaking off any excess.
Dip the chicken into the beaten eggs, then coat in the cornmeal, pressing the cornmeal onto the chicken to ensure a good coating.
Spray the air fryer basket with cooking spray, then place the chicken tenders in the basket, making sure they are not touching.
Air fry the chicken tenders for 10-12 minutes, flipping them halfway through the cooking time until they are golden brown and cooked through.
Serve with your favorite dipping sauce.

Note: You can adjust the seasoning to your taste by adding more or less garlic powder, onion powder, or other spices. For extra flavor, you can mix some grated Parmesan cheese into the cornmeal coating. Enjoy!

114. Here's an air fryer recipe for delicious chicken and oat croquettes that are packed with flavor and perfect as a snack or appetizer:

Ingredients:

1 pound ground chicken
1 cup quick oats
1/2 cup breadcrumbs
1 egg
1/2 cup grated Parmesan cheese
2 tablespoons chopped fresh parsley
1 teaspoon garlic powder
1 teaspoon onion powder
1 teaspoon salt
1/2 teaspoon black pepper
Cooking spray

Instructions:

Preheat your air fryer to 400°F (200°C).
In a large bowl, mix the ground chicken, quick oats, breadcrumbs, egg, Parmesan cheese, parsley, garlic powder, onion powder, salt, and black pepper until well combined.
Using your hands, form the mixture into small croquettes about the size of a golf ball.
Spray the air fryer basket with cooking spray, then place the croquettes in the basket, making sure they are not touching.
Air fry the croquettes for 10-12 minutes, flipping them halfway through the cooking time until they are golden brown and cooked through.
Serve the croquettes hot with your favorite dipping sauce.
Note: You can also add other spices and seasonings to the mixture to suit your taste. These croquettes can be stored in the refrigerator for up to 3 days or in the freezer for up to 1 month. To reheat, simply air fry them for a few minutes until they are heated through and crispy again. Enjoy!

115. Here's an air fryer recipe for delicious and crunchy chicken egg rolls that are packed with flavor and perfect as an appetizer or snack:

Ingredients:

1 pound ground chicken
2 cups shredded cabbage
1 cup shredded carrots
1/2 cup chopped green onions
1 tablespoon grated ginger
2 cloves minced garlic
2 tablespoons soy sauce
1 tablespoon sesame oil
1 tablespoon cornstarch
Salt and pepper to taste
8 egg roll wrappers
Cooking spray

Instructions:

Preheat your air fryer to 375°F (190°C).
In a large bowl, mix the ground chicken, shredded cabbage, shredded carrots, green onions, ginger, garlic, soy sauce, sesame oil, cornstarch, salt, and pepper until well combined.
Lay out an egg roll wrapper on a clean surface, with one of the corners facing you.
Spoon about 2-3 tablespoons of the chicken mixture onto the center of the wrapper, leaving some space around the edges.
Fold the corner closest to you over the filling, then fold in the sides, and roll the wrapper tightly away from you.
Use a little bit of water to seal the remaining corner and press it down gently to seal the egg roll.
Repeat with the remaining wrappers and filling.
Spray the air fryer basket with cooking spray, then place the egg rolls in the basket, making sure they are not touching.
Air fry the egg rolls for 10-12 minutes, flipping them halfway through the cooking time until they are golden brown and crispy.
Serve the egg rolls hot with your favorite dipping sauce.
Note: You can also add other vegetables or seasonings to the mixture to suit your taste. These egg rolls can be stored in the refrigerator for up to 3 days or in the freezer for up to 1 month. To reheat, simply air fry them for a few minutes until they are heated through and crispy again. Enjoy!

116. Here's an air fryer recipe for tasty and crispy Asian veggie spring rolls that are perfect as an appetizer or light meal:

Ingredients:

8 spring roll wrappers
2 cups shredded cabbage
1 cup shredded carrots
1/2 cup chopped green onions
1/2 cup sliced mushrooms
1 tablespoon grated ginger
2 cloves minced garlic
2 tablespoons soy sauce
1 tablespoon sesame oil
Salt and pepper to taste
Cooking spray

Instructions:

Preheat your air fryer to 375°F (190°C).
In a large bowl, mix the shredded cabbage, shredded carrots, green onions, sliced mushrooms, ginger, garlic, soy sauce, sesame oil, salt, and pepper until well combined.
Lay out a spring roll wrapper on a clean surface, with one of the corners facing you.
Spoon about 2-3 tablespoons of the veggie mixture onto the center of the wrapper, leaving some space around the edges.
Fold the corner closest to you over the filling, then fold in the sides, and roll the wrapper tightly away from you.
Use a little bit of water to seal the remaining corner and press it down gently to seal the spring roll.
Repeat with the remaining wrappers and filling.
Spray the air fryer basket with cooking spray, then place the spring rolls in the basket, making sure they are not touching.
Air fry the spring rolls for 8-10 minutes, flipping them halfway through the cooking time until they are golden brown and crispy.
Serve the spring rolls hot with your favorite dipping sauce.

Note: You can also add other vegetables or seasonings to the mixture to suit your taste. These spring rolls can be stored in the refrigerator for up to 3 days or in the freezer for up to 1 month. To reheat, simply air fry them for a few minutes until they are heated through and crispy again. Enjoy!

117. Here's an air fryer recipe for delicious and flavorful herby meatballs that are perfect for serving as an appetizer or main course:

Ingredients:

1 pound ground beef (or a combination of beef and pork)
1/2 cup breadcrumbs
1/2 cup grated Parmesan cheese
2 cloves minced garlic
1/4 cup chopped fresh herbs (such as parsley, basil, and oregano)
1 egg, lightly beaten
Salt and pepper to taste
Cooking spray

Instructions:

Preheat your air fryer to 375°F (190°C).
In a large bowl, mix the ground beef, breadcrumbs, Parmesan cheese, minced garlic, chopped herbs, beaten egg, salt, and pepper until well combined.
Use your hands to shape the mixture into small meatballs, about 1-2 inches in diameter.
Spray the air fryer basket with cooking spray, then place the meatballs in the basket, making sure they are not touching.
Air fry the meatballs for 10-12 minutes, flipping them halfway through the cooking time until they are browned and cooked through.
Serve the herby meatballs hot with your favorite dipping sauce or tomato sauce, and garnish with additional herbs if desired.
Note: You can also make a larger batch of these meatballs and freeze them for later use. To freeze, place the uncooked meatballs on a baking sheet lined with parchment paper and freeze for 1 hour, then transfer them to a freezer-safe container and freeze for up to 3 months. To cook from frozen, simply air fry them for a few extra minutes until they are heated through and browned. Enjoy!

118. Here's an air fryer recipe for delicious and easy chili cheese balls that are perfect for serving as a snack or appetizer:

Ingredients:

8 ounces of cream cheese, softened
1/4 cup chopped green chilies
1/4 cup shredded cheddar cheese
1/4 teaspoon garlic powder
1/4 teaspoon onion powder
1/4 teaspoon chili powder
Salt and pepper to taste
1/2 cup breadcrumbs
1/4 cup all-purpose flour
1 egg, lightly beaten
Cooking spray

Instructions:

In a large bowl, mix the softened cream cheese, chopped green chilies, shredded cheddar cheese, garlic powder, onion powder, chili powder, salt, and pepper until well combined.
Use your hands to shape the mixture into small balls, about 1-2 inches in diameter.

In a shallow dish, mix the breadcrumbs and flour.
Dip each cheese ball in the beaten egg, then roll it in the breadcrumb mixture until it is fully coated.
Spray the air fryer basket with cooking spray, then place the coated cheese balls in the basket, making sure they are not touching.
Air fry the cheese balls for 8-10 minutes until they are crispy and golden brown on the outside and heated through on the inside.
Serve the chili cheese balls hot with your favorite dipping sauce, such as salsa, ranch, or sour cream.
Note: You can also freeze these chili cheese balls before cooking. Simply place the uncooked cheese balls on a baking sheet lined with parchment paper and freeze for 1 hour, then transfer them to a freezer-safe container and freeze for up to 3 months. To cook from frozen, air fry them for a few extra minutes until they are heated through and crispy. Enjoy!

119. Here's an air fryer recipe for cheesy sticks with a sweet Thai dipping sauce that is perfect for serving as a snack or appetizer:

Ingredients:

For the cheesy sticks:
1 cup panko breadcrumbs
1 cup grated parmesan cheese
2 eggs, lightly beaten
8 mozzarella cheese sticks
Cooking spray
For the sweet Thai sauce:
1/4 cup honey
1/4 cup soy sauce
1 tablespoon rice vinegar
1 tablespoon sesame oil
1 tablespoon Sriracha sauce
1 garlic clove, minced
1/2 teaspoon ground ginger

Instructions:

Preheat your air fryer to 375°F.
In a shallow dish, mix the panko breadcrumbs and grated parmesan cheese.
Dip each mozzarella cheese stick in the beaten eggs, then roll it in the breadcrumb mixture until it is fully coated.
Place the coated cheese sticks in the air fryer basket, making sure they are not touching.
Lightly spray the cheese sticks with cooking spray.
Air fry the cheese sticks for 5-6 minutes until they are crispy and golden brown on the outside and melted and gooey on the inside.
While the cheese sticks are cooking, make the sweet Thai sauce by whisking together the honey, soy sauce, rice vinegar, sesame oil, Sriracha sauce, minced garlic, and ground ginger in a small bowl.
Once the cheese sticks are done, remove them from the air fryer basket and serve them hot with the sweet Thai sauce on the side for dipping.
Note: If you prefer a spicier sauce, you can add more Sriracha sauce or red pepper flakes to taste.
Enjoy!

120. Here's an air fryer recipe for crispy potato chips with chives that is easy to make and delicious:

Ingredients:

2 medium-sized potatoes, thinly sliced
2 tablespoons olive oil
1/2 teaspoon salt
1/4 teaspoon black pepper

2 tablespoons chopped fresh chives

Instructions:

Preheat your air fryer to 375°F.
In a large bowl, toss the thinly sliced potatoes with the olive oil, salt, and black pepper until they are evenly coated.
Place the potato slices in a single layer in the air fryer basket, making sure they are not overlapping.
Air fry the potato slices for 8-10 minutes, flipping them halfway through until they are golden brown and crispy.
Once the potato chips are done, remove them from the air fryer basket and transfer them to a serving bowl.
Sprinkle the chopped fresh chives over the top of the potato chips and toss gently to combine.
Serve the potato chips immediately while they are still warm and crispy.
Note: You can experiment with different seasonings to flavor the potato chips, such as garlic powder, paprika, or rosemary. Enjoy!

121. Here's an air fryer recipe for quick and easy pickle chips that are crispy and flavorful:

Ingredients:

1 large cucumber, thinly sliced
1/2 cup white vinegar
1/2 cup water
2 tablespoons sugar
1 tablespoon salt
1/2 teaspoon black pepper
1/2 teaspoon garlic powder
1/2 teaspoon dried dill

Instructions:

Preheat your air fryer to 375°F.
In a small bowl, whisk together the white vinegar, water, sugar, salt, black pepper, garlic powder, and dried dill until the sugar and salt are fully dissolved.
Place the thinly sliced cucumber in a large bowl and pour the pickling liquid over the top, making sure that the cucumber slices are fully submerged.
Let the cucumber slices marinate in the pickling liquid for at least 10 minutes.
Remove the cucumber slices from the pickling liquid and pat them dry with a paper towel.
Place the cucumber slices in a single layer in the air fryer basket, making sure they are not overlapping.
Air fry the pickle chips for 5-7 minutes until they are golden brown and crispy.
Once the pickle chips are done, remove them from the air fryer basket and transfer them to a serving bowl.
Serve the pickle chips immediately while they are still warm and crispy.
Note: You can experiment with different spices and herbs to flavor the pickle chips, such as red pepper flakes, mustard seeds, or fresh parsley. Enjoy!

122. Air Fryer Garlicky Potato Chips with Herbs Recipe:

Ingredients:

2 large russet potatoes, thinly sliced
2 cloves of garlic, minced
1 tsp salt
1 tsp dried rosemary
1 tsp dried thyme
1/4 cup olive oil

Instructions:

Soak potato slices in cold water for about 30 minutes, then drain and pat dry with a paper towel.
In a mixing bowl, combine the potato slices with olive oil, minced garlic, salt, rosemary, and thyme. Toss until the potato slices are evenly coated.
Place the potato slices in a single layer in the air fryer basket.
Set the air fryer to 375°F and cook for 10-12 minutes or until the potato chips are crispy and golden brown.
Sprinkle more salt and herbs on top of the chips before serving.
Enjoy your delicious and flavorful air fryer garlicky potato chips with herbs!

123. Air Fryer Hot Carrot Crisps Recipe:

Ingredients:

2 large carrots, peeled and sliced into thin rounds
2 tbsp olive oil
1 tsp smoked paprika
1/2 tsp garlic powder
1/4 tsp cayenne pepper
Salt and pepper, to taste

Instructions:

In a mixing bowl, combine the sliced carrots with olive oil, smoked paprika, garlic powder, cayenne pepper, salt, and pepper. Toss until the carrots are evenly coated.
Place the carrot slices in a single layer in the air fryer basket.
Set the air fryer to 375°F and cook for 10-12 minutes or until the carrot crisps are crispy and slightly golden brown.
Serve hot and enjoy your spicy and crunchy air fryer carrot crisps!
Note: You can adjust the amount of cayenne pepper according to your spice tolerance level.

124. Air Fryer Root Vegetable Chips Recipe:

Ingredients:

1 sweet potato, peeled and sliced thinly
1 parsnip, peeled and sliced thinly
1 beetroot, peeled and sliced thinly
1 tbsp olive oil
Salt and pepper, to taste

Instructions:

In a mixing bowl, combine the sliced sweet potato, parsnip, and beetroot with olive oil, salt, and pepper. Toss until the vegetables are evenly coated.
Place the vegetable slices in a single layer in the air fryer basket.
Set the air fryer to 375°F and cook for 10-12 minutes or until the root vegetable chips are crispy and slightly golden brown.
Serve hot and enjoy your delicious and healthy air fryer root vegetable chips!
Note: You can use any root vegetables of your choice, such as carrots, turnips, or rutabagas. Make sure to slice them thinly and evenly to ensure even cooking. Also, keep an eye on them while cooking as the cooking time may vary depending on the thickness of the slices.

125. Air Fryer Mexican-Style Nachos Recipe:

Ingredients:

1 bag tortilla chips
1 cup cooked and shredded chicken
1 cup shredded cheese
1/2 cup diced tomatoes
1/4 cup diced red onions
1 jalapeño, seeded and diced
1/4 cup sliced black olives
1/4 cup chopped fresh cilantro
1 tbsp taco seasoning
Salsa and sour cream, for serving

Instructions:

Preheat the air fryer to 400°F.
Spread a layer of tortilla chips in the air fryer basket.
Top the chips with shredded chicken, shredded cheese, diced tomatoes, red onions, jalapeños, and black olives.
Sprinkle taco seasoning over the nachos.
Cook in the air fryer for 5-7 minutes or until the cheese is melted and bubbly.
Sprinkle with chopped cilantro and serve with salsa and sour cream.
Note: You can customize the toppings to your liking. You can also use ground beef, beans, or tofu as a protein source. This recipe is perfect for a quick and easy appetizer or snack. Enjoy your delicious and crispy air fryer Mexican-style nachos!

126. Here's an air fryer recipe for asparagus with Romesco sauce:

Ingredients:

1 bunch asparagus, trimmed
1/4 cup almonds
1 slice of bread
1 roasted red pepper, skin and seeds removed
1 clove garlic
1 tablespoon sherry vinegar
1/4 cup olive oil
Salt and pepper to taste

Instructions:

Preheat the air fryer to 400°F.
In a food processor, pulse the almonds and bread until finely ground.
Add the roasted red pepper, garlic, and sherry vinegar to the food processor and pulse until smooth.
With the food processor running, slowly pour in the olive oil until the sauce is emulsified. Season with salt and pepper to taste.
Arrange the asparagus in a single layer in the air fryer basket.
Air fry the asparagus for 8-10 minutes, or until tender and lightly browned.
Serve the asparagus hot with the romesco sauce on the side for dipping.
Enjoy your delicious and healthy air fryer asparagus with romesco sauce!

127. Sure! Here's a recipe for air fryer parmesan artichoke hearts:

Ingredients:

1 can of artichoke hearts, drained and rinsed
1/2 cup of breadcrumbs

1/2 cup of grated parmesan cheese
1/2 teaspoon of garlic powder
1/2 teaspoon of dried oregano
Salt and pepper to taste
Olive oil spray

Instructions:

Preheat the air fryer to 400°F.
In a small bowl, mix the breadcrumbs, parmesan cheese, garlic powder, dried oregano, salt, and pepper.
Dip each artichoke heart in the breadcrumb mixture, pressing down to ensure that it sticks.
Arrange the breaded artichoke hearts in the air fryer basket. Spray them with olive oil.
Cook for 8-10 minutes or until they are golden brown and crispy.
Serve the parmesan artichoke hearts as an appetizer or side dish.
Enjoy your crispy and delicious parmesan artichoke hearts!

128. Air Fried Cheesy Brussels Sprouts Recipe:

Ingredients:

1 pound of Brussels sprouts, trimmed and halved
2 tablespoons of olive oil
1/2 teaspoon of garlic powder
Salt and pepper to taste
1/4 cup of grated parmesan cheese
1/4 cup of shredded cheddar cheese

Instructions:

Preheat your air fryer to 375°F.
In a large bowl, toss the Brussels sprouts with olive oil, garlic powder, salt, and pepper until well-coated.
Place the Brussels sprouts in the air fryer basket in a single layer.
Air fry for 8-10 minutes, shaking the basket every 2-3 minutes, until the Brussels sprouts are golden brown and crispy.
Sprinkle the parmesan and cheddar cheese on top of the Brussels sprouts.
Air fry for an additional 1-2 minutes until the cheese is melted and bubbly.
Serve hot and enjoy!

129. Here's a recipe for crispy kale chips made in an air fryer:

Ingredients:

1 bunch kale
1 tablespoon olive oil
Salt and pepper, to taste

Instructions:

Preheat your air fryer to 375°F (190°C).
Rinse the kale and pat dry with a paper towel.
Remove the kale leaves from the stems and tear them into bite-sized pieces.
In a large bowl, toss the kale with olive oil and season with salt and pepper to taste.
Place the kale leaves in a single layer in the air fryer basket.
Cook for 5-7 minutes or until the kale is crispy and lightly browned. Check frequently to ensure the kale doesn't burn.
Remove from the air fryer and serve immediately.
Enjoy your crispy and healthy snack!

130. Here's an air fryer recipe for crispy cauliflower in buffalo sauce:

Ingredients:

1 head of cauliflower, chopped into bite-sized pieces
1/2 cup all-purpose flour
1 teaspoon garlic powder
1/2 teaspoon paprika
Salt and pepper, to taste
1/2 cup buffalo sauce
2 tablespoons melted butter or olive oil
Ranch or blue cheese dressing for serving

Instructions:

Preheat your air fryer to 375°F (190°C).
In a large mixing bowl, combine the flour, garlic powder, paprika, salt, and pepper.
Toss the cauliflower pieces in the flour mixture until evenly coated.
Arrange the cauliflower in a single layer in the air fryer basket, and cook for 10-12 minutes or until golden brown and crispy. Flip the pieces halfway through cooking.
In a separate mixing bowl, combine the buffalo sauce and melted butter or olive oil.
Remove the cauliflower from the air fryer and toss in the buffalo sauce mixture until evenly coated.
Return the cauliflower to the air fryer and cook for an additional 2-3 minutes until the sauce is sticky and caramelized.
Serve hot with ranch or blue cheese dressing for dipping.
Enjoy your crispy and spicy buffalo cauliflower!

131. Here's an air fryer recipe for crunchy cauliflower bites:

Ingredients:

1 head cauliflower, cut into bite-sized florets
1/2 cup all-purpose flour
1 teaspoon garlic powder
1 teaspoon onion powder
1/2 teaspoon paprika
1/2 teaspoon salt
1/4 teaspoon black pepper
2 eggs, beaten
1 cup panko breadcrumbs
Cooking spray

Instructions:

Preheat your air fryer to 375°F (190°C).
In a small bowl, mix the flour, garlic powder, onion powder, paprika, salt, and black pepper.
In another small bowl, beat the eggs.
Place the panko breadcrumbs in a third small bowl.
Working in batches, coat the cauliflower florets in the flour mixture, shaking off any excess, then dip them into the beaten eggs, and finally coat them in the panko breadcrumbs.
Place the coated cauliflower florets in a single layer in the air fryer basket. Lightly spray them with cooking spray.
Air fry for 10-12 minutes, flipping the florets halfway through, until they are golden brown and crispy.
Serve the cauliflower bites with your favorite dipping sauce.
Enjoy your crunchy and delicious air-fried cauliflower bites!

132. Here's an air fryer recipe for crispy yellow squash chips:

Ingredients:

2 medium yellow squash
1/2 cup all-purpose flour
1 tsp garlic powder
1 tsp paprika
1/2 tsp salt
1/4 tsp black pepper
2 eggs, beaten
1 1/2 cups panko breadcrumbs
Cooking spray

Instructions:

Preheat the air fryer to 375°F (190°C).
Cut the yellow squash into thin slices, about 1/8-inch thick.
In a shallow bowl, mix the flour, garlic powder, paprika, salt, and black pepper.
Dip each slice of yellow squash into the flour mixture, shaking off any excess.
Dip the flour-coated squash into the beaten eggs, then into the panko breadcrumbs, pressing the breadcrumbs onto the squash to help them adhere.
Place the breaded squash in a single layer in the air fryer basket. You may need to work in batches.
Spray the breaded squash with cooking spray.
Air fry for 8-10 minutes, or until the squash is golden brown and crispy.
Serve immediately as a snack or side dish.
Enjoy your crispy yellow squash chips!

133. here's an easy air fryer recipe for avocado wedges:

Ingredients:

1 ripe avocado
1/4 cup all-purpose flour
1/2 tsp garlic powder
1/2 tsp paprika
1/2 tsp salt
1/4 tsp black pepper
1 egg, beaten
1/2 cup breadcrumbs
Cooking spray

Instructions:

Preheat your air fryer to 375°F (190°C).
Cut the avocado in half lengthwise, then remove the pit and slice each half into four equal wedges.
In a shallow dish, combine the flour, garlic powder, paprika, salt, and black pepper.
In another shallow dish, beat the egg.
In a third shallow dish, add the breadcrumbs.
Dredge each avocado wedge in the flour mixture, shaking off any excess. Then dip it into the egg mixture, letting any excess drip off. Finally, coat it with breadcrumbs, pressing gently to adhere.
Place the avocado wedges in a single layer in the air fryer basket, making sure they're not touching.
Spray with cooking spray.
Air fry the avocado wedges for 5-6 minutes or until golden brown and crispy.
Serve with your favorite dipping sauce and enjoy!
Note: You can adjust the seasonings to your liking and use seasoned breadcrumbs for added flavor.

134. Here's a recipe for air fryer fried pimiento-stuffed green olives:

Ingredients:

1 cup pimiento-stuffed green olives
1/2 cup all-purpose flour
1/2 teaspoon garlic powder
1/2 teaspoon smoked paprika
1/4 teaspoon salt
1/4 teaspoon black pepper
1 egg
1 tablespoon water
1 cup panko bread crumbs
Cooking spray

Instructions:

Preheat your air fryer to 375°F (190°C).
In a small bowl, whisk together the flour, garlic powder, smoked paprika, salt, and black pepper.
In another small bowl, whisk together the egg and water.
Place the panko bread crumbs in a third small bowl.
Dip each olive into the flour mixture, then into the egg mixture, and finally into the panko bread crumbs, making sure to coat well.
Place the olives in a single layer in the air fryer basket. Spray them lightly with cooking spray.
Air fry the olives for 8 to 10 minutes or until they are crispy and golden brown, shaking the basket halfway through cooking.
Serve immediately as a snack or appetizer.
Enjoy your crispy, air fryer-fried pimiento-stuffed green olives!

135. Air Fryer Mini Spinach & Mushroom Empanadas Recipe:

Ingredients:

1 tablespoon olive oil
1/2 cup finely chopped onion
1 clove garlic, minced
2 cups baby spinach, roughly chopped
1 cup chopped mushrooms
Salt and pepper to taste
1 package of empanada dough (which can be found in the frozen section of most grocery stores)
1 egg, beaten

Instructions:

Preheat your air fryer to 350°F.
In a large skillet over medium heat, heat olive oil. Add chopped onion and garlic and cook until softened about 2-3 minutes.
Add chopped spinach and mushrooms to the skillet and cook until vegetables are tender and any excess moisture has cooked off about 5-7 minutes. Season with salt and pepper to taste.
Remove the skillet from the heat and allow the filling to cool for a few minutes.
Roll out the empanada dough on a lightly floured surface and cut it into circles using a cookie cutter or round pastry cutter.
Spoon a small amount of the spinach and mushroom filling onto each empanada circle. Fold the dough over and seal the edges with a fork.
Brush the empanadas with beaten eggs and place them in the air fryer basket.
Air fry the empanadas for 8-10 minutes, or until they are golden brown and crispy.
Serve hot and enjoy!

136. Here's an air fryer recipe for kielbasa and mushroom pierogi:

Ingredients:

1 package of frozen pierogi (about 12-16 pieces)
1/2 pound of sliced kielbasa
1 cup of sliced mushrooms
1 tablespoon of olive oil
Salt and pepper, to taste
Sour cream, for serving

Instructions:

Preheat your air fryer to 400°F.
In a medium bowl, toss the sliced mushrooms with olive oil and season with salt and pepper.
Add the sliced kielbasa to the bowl and toss to combine.
Place the pierogi in the air fryer basket in a single layer.
Spoon the kielbasa and mushroom mixture over the pierogi.
Place the air fryer basket into the air fryer and cook for 8-10 minutes, shaking the basket halfway through.
Serve with a dollop of sour cream on top.
Enjoy your delicious kielbasa and mushroom pierogi cooked to perfection in the air fryer!

137. Here is a recipe for low-carb air fryer radish chips:

Ingredients:

1 bunch of radishes
1 tablespoon olive oil
1/2 teaspoon salt
1/4 teaspoon garlic powder
1/4 teaspoon onion powder

Instructions:

Preheat your air fryer to 375°F.
Wash and slice the radishes into thin rounds.
In a bowl, mix the radish slices with olive oil, salt, garlic powder, and onion powder.
Place the radish slices in a single layer in the air fryer basket.
Cook for 8-10 minutes, shaking the basket every 3-4 minutes, until the radish chips are crispy and golden brown.
Serve immediately as a snack or side dish.
Enjoy your low-carb air fryer radish chips!

138. Here's an air fryer recipe for green bean crisps:

Ingredients:

1 pound fresh green beans, washed and trimmed
1 tablespoon olive oil
1/2 teaspoon garlic powder
1/2 teaspoon onion powder
1/2 teaspoon paprika
Salt and pepper, to taste

Instructions:

Preheat the air fryer to 375°F.
In a mixing bowl, toss green beans with olive oil, garlic powder, onion powder, paprika, salt, and pepper until well coated.
Place the seasoned green beans in the air fryer basket, spreading them out evenly.
Air fry the green beans for 8-10 minutes, shaking the basket halfway through the cooking time to ensure they cook evenly.
Check the green beans for crispness. If they need more time, return them to the air fryer and cook for an additional 2-3 minutes until they are crispy and golden brown.
Serve hot and enjoy!
Note: You can also try dipping them in a low-fat dip or sauce of your choice for added flavor.

139. Here's a recipe for air fryer smoked fish balls:

Ingredients:

8 oz smoked fish, flaked
1/2 cup breadcrumbs
1/4 cup chopped scallions
1/4 cup chopped parsley
1/4 cup mayonnaise
1 egg
1 tbsp Dijon mustard
1 tbsp lemon juice
1/4 tsp salt
1/4 tsp black pepper
cooking spray

Instructions:

Preheat your air fryer to 400°F (200°C).
In a large bowl, combine the smoked fish, breadcrumbs, scallions, parsley, mayonnaise, egg, Dijon mustard, lemon juice, salt, and black pepper.
Mix everything until well combined.
Using a cookie scoop or a spoon, form the mixture into balls.
Spray the air fryer basket with cooking spray and place the fish balls in a single layer.
Cook for 10-12 minutes or until golden brown and crispy on the outside.
Serve the smoked fish balls hot with your favorite dipping sauce.
Enjoy your delicious and crispy air fryer smoked fish balls!

140. Here's a recipe for air fryer salmon mini tarts:

Ingredients:

1 sheet of puff pastry, thawed
1/2 lb. cooked salmon, flaked
2 tbsp cream cheese, softened
2 tbsp mayonnaise
1 tbsp chopped chives
1 tbsp chopped dill
1 tbsp lemon juice
Salt and pepper to taste
1 egg, beaten

Instructions:

Preheat your air fryer to 375°F.

Cut the puff pastry sheet into 9 equal squares and place them in the air fryer basket, leaving some space in between each square.
In a mixing bowl, combine the cooked salmon, cream cheese, mayonnaise, chives, dill, lemon juice, salt, and pepper. Mix well.
Spoon the salmon mixture onto each pastry square, spreading it out evenly.
Brush the beaten egg over the edges of each pastry square.
Air fry for 10-12 minutes or until the pastry is golden brown and crispy.
Serve warm and enjoy!

141. here's a recipe for easy air fryer coconut shrimp:

Ingredients:

1 lb large shrimp, peeled and deveined
1/2 cup all-purpose flour
1 tsp garlic powder
1 tsp onion powder
1/2 tsp paprika
1/2 tsp salt
1/4 tsp black pepper
2 eggs, beaten
1 1/2 cups shredded sweetened coconut
Cooking spray

Directions:

In a shallow dish, mix the flour, garlic powder, onion powder, paprika, salt, and black pepper.
In another shallow dish, beat the eggs.
Place the shredded coconut in a third shallow dish.
Dip each shrimp into the flour mixture, shaking off any excess, then dip it into the beaten eggs, and finally coat it in the shredded coconut.
Place the coated shrimp onto a plate or tray.
Preheat the air fryer to 400°F (200°C) for 5 minutes.
Spray the air fryer basket with cooking spray.
Place the coated shrimp into the air fryer basket, in a single layer.
Spray the top of the shrimp with cooking spray.
Air fry for 6-8 minutes, or until golden brown and crispy, flipping halfway through cooking.
Serve with your favorite dipping sauce. Enjoy!

142. Here is an air fryer recipe for salmon croquettes:

Ingredients:

1 can (14.75 oz) salmon, drained and flaked
1/4 cup diced onion
1/4 cup diced celery
1/4 cup diced red bell pepper
1/2 teaspoon garlic powder
1/2 teaspoon salt
1/4 teaspoon black pepper
1/4 teaspoon cayenne pepper
1/4 cup almond flour
2 eggs, beaten
1/2 cup almond flour (for coating)
Cooking spray

Instructions:

In a large bowl, mix the salmon, onion, celery, red bell pepper, garlic powder, salt, black pepper, cayenne pepper, and 1/4 cup almond flour.
Add the beaten eggs to the mixture and stir until well combined.
Form the mixture into 8-10 small patties.
Place the remaining 1/2 cup almond flour in a shallow dish.
Coat each salmon patty in almond flour and shake off any excess.
Preheat the air fryer to 400°F (200°C).
Spray the air fryer basket with cooking spray.
Place the salmon patties in the air fryer basket, making sure to leave enough space between each patty.
Air fry the salmon patties for 8-10 minutes or until golden brown and crispy on the outside.
Serve the salmon croquettes warm with your favorite dipping sauce. Enjoy!

143. here's a recipe for air fryer cod fingers:

Ingredients:

1 pound cod fillets, cut into finger-sized pieces
1/2 cup all-purpose flour
2 large eggs, beaten
1 cup panko breadcrumbs
1/2 teaspoon garlic powder
1/2 teaspoon onion powder
Salt and pepper to taste
Cooking spray

Instructions:

Preheat your air fryer to 375°F (190°C).
Season the cod pieces with garlic powder, onion powder, salt, and pepper.
Set up a breading station with three bowls: one with flour, one with beaten eggs, and one with panko breadcrumbs.
Dredge each codpiece in the flour, shaking off any excess.
Dip the cod in the beaten eggs, making sure it's fully coated.
Roll the cod in the panko breadcrumbs, pressing the breadcrumbs to adhere to the fish.
Spray the air fryer basket with cooking spray.
Place the cod fingers in the air fryer basket, making sure they're not touching.
Air fry the cod fingers for 10-12 minutes, flipping them halfway through the cooking time, until golden brown and crispy.
Serve the cod fingers hot with your favorite dipping sauce.

144. Here's a recipe for parsley and lemon air-fried shrimp:

Ingredients:

1 lb large shrimp, peeled and deveined
1/2 cup all-purpose flour
1/2 teaspoon salt
1/4 teaspoon black pepper
1/2 teaspoon garlic powder
2 eggs, beaten
1 cup panko breadcrumbs
1/4 cup grated Parmesan cheese
2 tablespoons chopped fresh parsley
1 tablespoon lemon zest
1/4 teaspoon cayenne pepper
Cooking spray

Instructions:

Preheat your air fryer to 400°F.
In a shallow bowl, combine flour, salt, black pepper, and garlic powder.
In a second shallow bowl, beat the eggs.
In a third shallow bowl, combine panko breadcrumbs, Parmesan cheese, parsley, lemon zest, and cayenne pepper.
Dip each shrimp into the flour mixture, then into the beaten eggs, and finally coat it with the breadcrumb mixture.
Spray the air fryer basket with cooking spray, then arrange the shrimp in a single layer in the basket.
Air fry for 6-8 minutes or until the shrimp are golden brown and cooked through, flipping halfway through the cooking time.
Serve immediately with lemon wedges and tartar sauce or your favorite dipping sauce. Enjoy!

145. Here's a recipe for air fryer prawn and cabbage egg rolls:

Ingredients:

1/2 lb. large prawns, peeled and deveined
2 cups shredded cabbage
1 cup shredded carrots
2 cloves garlic, minced
2 green onions, sliced
1 tbsp soy sauce
1 tsp sesame oil
1/2 tsp ground ginger
1/4 tsp black pepper
8 egg roll wrappers
Cooking spray

Instructions:

Preheat your air fryer to 375°F.
In a large mixing bowl, combine the prawns, cabbage, carrots, garlic, green onions, soy sauce, sesame oil, ginger, and black pepper. Mix well.
Lay out an egg roll wrapper and place 2-3 tablespoons of the prawn mixture on the wrapper. Roll the wrapper tightly around the filling, folding in the sides as you go.
Repeat with the remaining egg roll wrappers and prawn mixture.
Spray the egg rolls lightly with cooking spray.
Place the egg rolls in the air fryer basket, making sure they are not touching.
Cook the egg rolls for 10-12 minutes, flipping them over halfway through cooking, until they are crispy and golden brown.
Serve the egg rolls hot with your favorite dipping sauce.

146. Here's a recipe for mouth-watering beef sticks in the air fryer:

Ingredients:

1 pound ground beef
1/4 cup breadcrumbs
1/4 cup milk
1 egg
1 teaspoon salt
1/2 teaspoon black pepper
1/2 teaspoon garlic powder
1/2 teaspoon onion powder

1/2 teaspoon paprika
Cooking spray

Instructions:

Preheat the air fryer to 375°F (190°C).
In a mixing bowl, combine ground beef, breadcrumbs, milk, egg, salt, black pepper, garlic powder, onion powder, and paprika.
Mix well until all ingredients are combined.
Divide the mixture into equal portions and shape each portion into a stick shape.
Lightly coat the beef sticks with cooking spray.
Place the beef sticks in the air fryer basket, leaving space between them.
Cook for 10-12 minutes, or until the beef sticks are cooked through and golden brown.
Flip the beef sticks halfway through the cooking time to ensure even cooking.
Serve hot with your favorite dipping sauce.
Enjoy your delicious and crispy beef sticks made in the air fryer!

147. here's an easy recipe for cheesy bacon fries in the air fryer:

Ingredients:

4-5 medium-sized potatoes
1 tsp paprika
1/2 tsp garlic powder
1/2 tsp onion powder
Salt and black pepper to taste
1/2 cup shredded cheddar cheese
4-5 strips of bacon, cooked and crumbled
2 tbsp chopped fresh parsley

Instructions:

Wash and peel the potatoes. Cut them into thin, even strips.
In a large mixing bowl, toss the potato strips with paprika, garlic powder, onion powder, salt, and black pepper.
Preheat your air fryer to 400°F.
Place the potato strips in the air fryer basket and cook for 15-18 minutes or until crispy, shaking the basket every 5 minutes to ensure even cooking.
Once the fries are cooked, remove them from the air fryer basket and transfer them to a large mixing bowl.
Add the shredded cheese and crumbled bacon to the bowl, and toss to combine.
Return the fries to the air fryer basket and cook for another 1-2 minutes, or until the cheese is melted and bubbly.
Sprinkle the chopped parsley over the top of the fries before serving.
Enjoy your delicious cheesy bacon fries straight out of the air fryer!

148. Here's a recipe for crispy bacon with butter bean dip made in the air fryer:

Ingredients:

8-10 slices of bacon
1 can of butter beans, drained and rinsed
1 tablespoon olive oil
1 tablespoon lemon juice

1 clove of garlic, minced
Salt and pepper, to taste

Instructions:

Preheat your air fryer to 400°F (200°C).
Lay out the bacon slices in the air fryer basket in a single layer, making sure they don't overlap.
Air fry the bacon for 8-10 minutes or until crispy, flipping halfway through. The cooking time may vary depending on the thickness of the bacon.
Remove the bacon from the air fryer and place it on a paper towel to drain off the excess grease.
In a food processor or blender, combine the butter beans, olive oil, lemon juice, garlic, salt, and pepper. Pulse until smooth.
Transfer the butter bean dip to a small serving bowl.
Serve the crispy bacon alongside the butter bean dip.
Enjoy your crispy bacon with a creamy and flavorful dip!

149. Here's a recipe for air fryer bacon-wrapped avocados:

Ingredients:

2 ripe avocados
6 slices of bacon
Salt and pepper to taste
Toothpicks

Instructions:

Preheat the air fryer to 375°F (190°C).
Cut the avocados in half and remove the pits.
Cut each avocado half into 3-4 wedges.
Wrap each avocado wedge with a slice of bacon, and secure it with a toothpick.
Season with salt and pepper to taste.
Place the bacon-wrapped avocado wedges in the air fryer basket, and cook for 10-12 minutes, or until the bacon is crispy and the avocados are tender.
Remove from the air fryer and let cool for a few minutes before serving.
Enjoy your delicious air fryer bacon-wrapped avocados!

150. Here's an air fryer recipe for bacon-wrapped chicken jalapeño bites:

Ingredients:

4 large jalapeño peppers, sliced in half lengthwise and seeded
4 boneless, skinless chicken thighs, cut into 8 strips
8 slices of bacon, cut in half
1/4 cup cream cheese, softened
1/4 cup shredded cheddar cheese
1/4 teaspoon garlic powder
1/4 teaspoon onion powder
Salt and pepper to taste
Toothpicks

Instructions:

Preheat the air fryer to 375°F.
In a small bowl, mix the cream cheese, cheddar cheese, garlic powder, onion powder, salt, and pepper.
Stuff each jalapeño half with a spoonful of the cheese mixture.
Wrap each chicken strip around a stuffed jalapeño half.

Wrap each bacon half around the chicken-wrapped jalapeño, securing it with a toothpick.
Place the bacon-wrapped jalapeño bites in a single layer in the air fryer basket.
Air fry for 10-12 minutes, flipping halfway through, or until the bacon is crispy and the chicken is cooked through.
Serve immediately and enjoy!

151. Here is a recipe for black bean and corn flatbreads made in an air fryer:

Ingredients:

1 can of black beans, drained and rinsed
1 cup of corn kernels
1/2 cup of chopped onion
1/2 cup of chopped red bell pepper
1 teaspoon of ground cumin
1 teaspoon of chili powder
Salt and black pepper, to taste
4 small whole wheat tortillas
1/2 cup of shredded cheddar cheese
2 tablespoons of chopped fresh cilantro

Instructions:

In a mixing bowl, combine the black beans, corn, onion, red bell pepper, cumin, chili powder, salt, and black pepper. Mix well.
Preheat the air fryer to 350°F (180°C).
Lay out the tortillas on a flat surface, and divide the black bean and corn mixture evenly among them.
Spread it out in the center of each tortilla.
Sprinkle shredded cheddar cheese over the top of each tortilla.
Fold the tortillas in half to enclose the filling.
Place the folded tortillas in the air fryer basket, making sure they don't touch each other.
Air fry the flatbreads for 5-7 minutes, or until the tortillas are crispy and the cheese is melted.
Remove the flatbreads from the air fryer basket and sprinkle chopped cilantro over the top.
Serve the black bean and corn flatbreads hot.
Enjoy your delicious and healthy air fryer black bean and corn flatbreads!

152. Here's an air fryer recipe for BBQ chicken naan pizza:

Ingredients:

2 pieces of Naan bread
1/2 cup BBQ sauce
1 1/2 cups shredded cooked chicken
1/2 cup shredded mozzarella cheese
1/4 cup thinly sliced red onion
1/4 cup chopped fresh cilantro

Instructions:

Preheat your air fryer to 370°F (190°C).
Place the Naan bread on a clean surface and spread 1/4 cup of BBQ sauce on each piece.

Top each Naan bread with 3/4 cup of shredded chicken, 1/4 cup of shredded mozzarella cheese, and a few slices of red onion.
Place the Naan pizzas in the air fryer basket and cook for 5-6 minutes, or until the cheese is melted and the Naan is crispy.
Remove the Naan pizzas from the air fryer and sprinkle with chopped cilantro.
Serve immediately and enjoy your delicious BBQ chicken Naan pizza!

153. Air Fryer Italian Pork Sausage Pizza Recipe:

Ingredients:

1 pre-made pizza dough
1/2 cup marinara sauce
2 Italian pork sausages, sliced
1/2 cup shredded mozzarella cheese
1/2 cup sliced bell peppers
1/2 cup sliced red onions
1/4 cup sliced black olives
1/4 cup sliced pepperoni
1/4 cup chopped fresh basil

Instructions:

Preheat your air fryer to 375°F.
Roll out the pizza dough to fit the size of your air fryer basket.
Spread the marinara sauce on top of the dough, leaving a small border around the edges.
Top the sauce with sliced Italian pork sausages, shredded mozzarella cheese, sliced bell peppers, sliced red onions, black olives, and pepperoni.
Place the pizza in the air fryer basket and cook for 8-10 minutes, or until the cheese is melted and the crust is crispy.
Remove the pizza from the air fryer and sprinkle with chopped fresh basil before serving.
Enjoy your delicious Italian pork sausage pizza made in the air fryer!

154. Here's an air fryer recipe for chorizo pita pizzas:

Ingredients:

4 small whole wheat pitas
1/2 cup pizza sauce
1/2 cup shredded mozzarella cheese
1/2 cup crumbled chorizo
1/4 cup chopped red onion
1/4 cup chopped fresh cilantro

Instructions:

Preheat your air fryer to 375°F (190°C).
Spread about 2 tablespoons of pizza sauce onto each pita.
Sprinkle about 2 tablespoons of shredded mozzarella cheese onto each pita.
Divide the crumbled chorizo and chopped red onion evenly among the pitas.
Place the pitas into the air fryer basket and cook for 5-7 minutes, or until the cheese is melted and the crust is crispy.
Remove from the air fryer and sprinkle with chopped cilantro before serving.
Enjoy your delicious chorizo pita pizzas!

155. Here's an air fryer recipe for crispy pepperoni pizza:

Ingredients:

1 pre-made pizza crust
1/2 cup of pizza sauce
1 cup of shredded mozzarella cheese
1/2 cup of sliced pepperoni
1 teaspoon of dried oregano

Instructions:

Preheat your air fryer to 375°F.
Place the pre-made pizza crust in the air fryer basket.
Spread the pizza sauce over the crust, leaving a small border around the edge.
Sprinkle the shredded mozzarella cheese over the sauce.
Arrange the pepperoni slices on top of the cheese.
Sprinkle the dried oregano over the top.
Place the pizza in the air fryer and cook for 8-10 minutes or until the cheese is melted and the crust is crispy.
Remove the pizza from the air fryer and let it cool for a few minutes.
Slice and serve hot. Enjoy!

156. Here's a recipe for air fryer bacon-wrapped dates:

Ingredients:

12 Medjool dates, pitted
6 strips of bacon, cut in half
Toothpicks

Instructions:

Preheat the air fryer to 390°F (200°C).
Take each date and stuff it with a small piece of blue cheese or goat cheese.
Wrap each stuffed date with a half-strip of bacon and secure it with a toothpick.
Place the bacon-wrapped dates in the air fryer basket, making sure they are not touching each other.
Air fry for 7-10 minutes or until the bacon is crispy and the dates are heated through.
Remove from the air fryer basket and let cool for a few minutes before serving.
Enjoy your delicious and easy air fryer bacon-wrapped dates!

157. Here's an air fryer recipe for delicious chicken tortillas:

Ingredients:

2 boneless, skinless chicken breasts, sliced into strips
1 tablespoon chili powder
1 teaspoon cumin
1 teaspoon garlic powder
1 teaspoon onion powder
1/2 teaspoon salt

1/4 teaspoon black pepper
1 tablespoon olive oil
8 small flour tortillas
1/2 cup shredded cheddar cheese
1/4 cup diced tomatoes
1/4 cup chopped fresh cilantro

Instructions:

Preheat your air fryer to 375°F.
In a small bowl, mix the chili powder, cumin, garlic powder, onion powder, salt, and black pepper.
In a separate bowl, toss the sliced chicken with the olive oil and the spice mixture until well-coated.
Place the chicken strips in the air fryer basket and cook for 8-10 minutes, flipping halfway through, until cooked through and crispy.
Remove the chicken from the air fryer and set aside.
Place the tortillas in the air fryer basket and cook for 1-2 minutes, until warm and slightly crispy.
Top each tortilla with some of the cooked chicken, shredded cheddar cheese, diced tomatoes, and chopped cilantro.
Place the tortillas back in the air fryer and cook for an additional 1-2 minutes, until the cheese is melted and bubbly.
Serve hot and enjoy!

158. Here's a recipe for air fryer chicken burgers with horseradish sauce:

Ingredients:

1 lb ground chicken
1/4 cup breadcrumbs
1 egg
1/2 teaspoon garlic powder
1/2 teaspoon onion powder
Salt and pepper, to taste
4 hamburger buns
1/4 cup mayonnaise
1 tablespoon prepared horseradish
1/2 teaspoon honey
Lettuce and tomato, for serving

Instructions:

In a large mixing bowl, combine ground chicken, breadcrumbs, egg, garlic powder, onion powder, salt, and pepper. Mix well until everything is evenly combined.
Shape the chicken mixture into four equal patties.
Preheat the air fryer to 400°F.
Spray the air fryer basket with cooking spray.
Place the chicken patties in the basket and air fry for 10-12 minutes, flipping halfway through, until fully cooked and crispy.
While the chicken patties are cooking, make the horseradish sauce. In a small bowl, whisk together the mayonnaise, horseradish, and honey.
Toast the hamburger buns if desired.
Assemble the burgers by spreading the horseradish sauce on the bottom bun, topping with a chicken patty, lettuce, and tomato. Add the top bun and enjoy!

159. here's an air fryer recipe for classic beef meatballs:

Ingredients:

1 pound ground beef
1/2 cup bread crumbs
1/4 cup grated Parmesan cheese
1 egg
1/4 cup milk
1/4 cup chopped fresh parsley
2 cloves garlic, minced
1 teaspoon dried oregano
1/2 teaspoon salt
1/4 teaspoon black pepper

Instructions:

Preheat your air fryer to 375°F (190°C).
In a large bowl, mix the ground beef, bread crumbs, Parmesan cheese, egg, milk, parsley, garlic, oregano, salt, and pepper until well combined.
Shape the mixture into 1-2 inch balls.
Place the meatballs in a single layer in the air fryer basket.
Cook for 10-12 minutes or until the meatballs are browned and cooked through.
Serve the meatballs hot with your favorite sauce or pasta.
Enjoy your delicious air-fried classic beef meatballs!

160. Here's an air fryer recipe for paprika beef fajitas:

Ingredients:

1 pound beef sirloin, sliced into thin strips
2 bell peppers, sliced
1 onion, sliced
2 teaspoons paprika
1 teaspoon garlic powder
1 teaspoon onion powder
1 teaspoon cumin
1/2 teaspoon salt
1/4 teaspoon black pepper
1 tablespoon olive oil
Flour or corn tortillas, for serving
Optional toppings: shredded cheese, diced tomatoes, sour cream, avocado, lime wedges

Instructions:

Preheat your air fryer to 400°F.
In a bowl, combine the paprika, garlic powder, onion powder, cumin, salt, and black pepper.
Add the sliced beef to the bowl and toss to coat evenly with the spice mixture.
In a separate bowl, toss the sliced peppers and onions with olive oil.
Place the beef strips in a single layer in the air fryer basket and cook for 6-8 minutes or until browned and cooked through.
Add the peppers and onions to the air fryer basket and cook for an additional 4-5 minutes or until tender.
Warm the tortillas in the air fryer for 1-2 minutes.
Assemble the fajitas by placing the beef, peppers, and onions onto a tortilla and adding any desired toppings. Serve immediately. Enjoy!

161. Here's an air fryer recipe for South Asian Pork Momos:

Ingredients:

1 lb ground pork
2 cups finely chopped cabbage
1/2 cup finely chopped onion
1/4 cup chopped fresh cilantro
1 tbsp freshly grated ginger
1 tbsp soy sauce
1 tbsp sesame oil
1 tsp ground cumin
1 tsp ground coriander
1/2 tsp ground turmeric
1/4 tsp ground cinnamon
1/4 tsp ground cloves
24-30 wonton wrappers

Instructions:

Preheat your air fryer to 375°F.
In a large mixing bowl, combine the ground pork, cabbage, onion, cilantro, ginger, soy sauce, sesame oil, cumin, coriander, turmeric, cinnamon, and cloves. Mix until well combined.
Place a wonton wrapper on a clean surface, and spoon a tablespoon of the pork mixture into the center.
Moisten the edges of the wonton wrapper with water and fold it in half to form a half-moon shape. Press the edges together to seal.
Repeat with the remaining wonton wrappers and pork mixture.
Place the momos in a single layer in the air fryer basket, and cook for 8-10 minutes or until the wonton wrappers are golden brown and the pork filling is cooked through.
Serve the momos hot with your favorite dipping sauce. Enjoy!

162. Here's a recipe for Spanish chorizo with Brussels sprouts in the air fryer:

Ingredients:

1 lb Brussels sprouts, trimmed and halved
8 oz Spanish chorizo, sliced into bite-sized pieces
1 tablespoon olive oil
1/2 teaspoon smoked paprika
Salt and black pepper to taste

Instructions:

Preheat your air fryer to 400°F (200°C).
In a large mixing bowl, toss the Brussels sprouts with olive oil, smoked paprika, salt, and black pepper.
Add the sliced chorizo to the bowl and mix well to combine.
Transfer the Brussels sprouts and chorizo mixture to the air fryer basket and spread it out evenly.
Air fry for 10-12 minutes, shaking the basket halfway through, until the Brussels sprouts are tender and the chorizo is crispy.
Serve hot as a side dish or appetizer.
Enjoy your Spanish chorizo with Brussels sprouts!

163. Air Fryer Cheesy Sausage Balls Recipe:

Ingredients:

1 pound ground breakfast sausage
2 cups shredded cheddar cheese
1 1/2 cups all-purpose flour
2 teaspoons baking powder
1/2 teaspoon salt

1/4 teaspoon cayenne pepper
1/4 cup milk
Cooking spray

Instructions:

Preheat your air fryer to 350°F (175°C).
In a large mixing bowl, combine the ground breakfast sausage, shredded cheddar cheese, all-purpose flour, baking powder, salt, cayenne pepper, and milk. Mix well until everything is well combined.
Roll the sausage mixture into small balls, about 1 inch in diameter.
Spray the air fryer basket with cooking spray, then place the sausage balls inside, making sure they don't touch.
Air fry the sausage balls for 12-15 minutes, or until they are golden brown and cooked through.
Serve the sausage balls hot with your favorite dipping sauce. Enjoy!

164. Here is an air fryer recipe for baked potatoes with bacon:

Ingredients:

4 medium-sized potatoes
4 strips of bacon
2 tablespoons olive oil
Salt and pepper to taste
Sour cream (optional)
Chopped chives (optional)

Instructions:

Preheat your air fryer to 400°F (200°C).
Wash and scrub the potatoes, and then pat them dry with a paper towel.
Rub the potatoes with olive oil and season with salt and pepper.
Place the potatoes in the air fryer basket and cook for 35-40 minutes, flipping them halfway through.
While the potatoes are cooking, cook the bacon in a skillet until crispy. Once done, chop the bacon into small pieces.
Once the potatoes are cooked, remove them from the air fryer and let them cool for a few minutes.
Cut the potatoes in half and top with the chopped bacon, sour cream, and chopped chives (optional).
Enjoy your delicious air fryer baked potatoes with bacon!

165. here's a recipe for air fryer chive roasted red potatoes:

Ingredients:

1 pound small red potatoes, washed and quartered
2 tablespoons olive oil
1 teaspoon garlic powder
1 teaspoon onion powder
1 teaspoon dried chives
Salt and pepper to taste

Instructions:

Preheat your air fryer to 400°F (200°C) for 5 minutes.
In a large mixing bowl, combine the quartered potatoes with olive oil, garlic powder, onion powder, dried chives, salt, and pepper. Mix until the potatoes are evenly coated.
Transfer the seasoned potatoes to the air fryer basket and cook for 15-20 minutes, shaking the basket every 5 minutes, until the potatoes are golden brown and crispy on the outside and tender on the inside.
Remove the basket from the air fryer and transfer the potatoes to a serving dish.

Sprinkle additional chives over the top of the potatoes for garnish, if desired. Serve hot and enjoy!

166. Air Fryer Recipe for Feta French Fries:

Ingredients:

2 large russet potatoes, cut into fries
1 tablespoon olive oil
1/4 teaspoon garlic powder
1/4 teaspoon onion powder
1/4 teaspoon paprika
Salt and pepper to taste
1/2 cup crumbled feta cheese
2 tablespoons chopped fresh parsley

Instructions:

Preheat your air fryer to 375°F (190°C).
In a large bowl, toss the potato fries with olive oil, garlic powder, onion powder, paprika, salt, and pepper.
Place the seasoned fries in the air fryer basket and cook for 15-20 minutes or until golden brown and crispy, shaking the basket halfway through the cooking time.
Once the fries are done, remove them from the air fryer and sprinkle with crumbled feta cheese and chopped parsley.
Serve immediately and enjoy your delicious feta French fries!

167. here's an air fryer recipe for crispy Hasselback potatoes:

Ingredients:

4 medium-sized potatoes
2 tbsp olive oil
Salt and pepper to taste
2 tbsp grated Parmesan cheese
1 tbsp chopped fresh parsley

Instructions:

Scrub the potatoes clean and pat them dry. Cut slits across the potatoes, leaving about 1/4 inch at the bottom uncut, making sure not to cut all the way through.
Preheat your air fryer to 375°F.
Rub olive oil all over the potatoes, making sure to get them in the slits. Season with salt and pepper.
Place the potatoes in the air fryer basket and cook for 25-30 minutes, or until the potatoes are tender and the skin is crispy.
Sprinkle grated Parmesan cheese over the potatoes and cook for an additional 2-3 minutes, until the cheese is melted and bubbly.
Sprinkle chopped fresh parsley over the potatoes and serve hot.
Enjoy your crispy and flavorful Hasselback potatoes straight out of the air fryer!

168. Here's an air fryer recipe for sweet potato boats:

Ingredients:

2 sweet potatoes
1/4 cup diced red onion
1/4 cup black beans
1/4 cup corn kernels
1/4 cup diced red bell pepper
1/4 cup shredded cheddar cheese
1/4 tsp cumin
1/4 tsp chili powder
1/4 tsp garlic powder
1 tbsp olive oil
Salt and pepper, to taste
Optional toppings: avocado, diced tomatoes, cilantro, sour cream

Instructions:

Preheat your air fryer to 400°F (200°C).
Wash the sweet potatoes and slice them in half lengthwise. Scoop out the flesh, leaving a 1/4-inch thick layer of sweet potato on the skin. Reserve the flesh for another use.
In a medium bowl, combine the diced red onion, black beans, corn kernels, red bell pepper, cheddar cheese, cumin, chili powder, garlic powder, olive oil, salt, and pepper. Mix well.
Divide the mixture evenly among the four sweet potato skins, pressing down gently to make sure it stays in place.
Place the sweet potato boats in the air fryer basket, skin side down. Cook for 12-15 minutes, or until the sweet potato skins are crispy and the filling is heated through.
Serve hot with your favorite toppings, such as diced avocado, tomatoes, cilantro, or sour cream. Enjoy!
169. Here's an air fryer recipe for thyme & garlic sweet potato wedges:

Ingredients:

2 large sweet potatoes, washed and cut into wedges
2 tbsp olive oil
2 garlic cloves, minced
1 tbsp fresh thyme leaves
Salt and pepper, to taste

Instructions:

Preheat your air fryer to 400°F (200°C).
In a mixing bowl, whisk together olive oil, minced garlic, and fresh thyme leaves.
Add the sweet potato wedges into the bowl and toss to coat with the oil mixture.
Arrange the sweet potato wedges in a single layer in the air fryer basket.
Season with salt and pepper to taste.
Air fry for 12-15 minutes or until crispy and golden brown, flipping the wedges halfway through.
Remove from the air fryer and serve immediately.
Enjoy your crispy and flavorful thyme & garlic sweet potato wedges!

170. Here's an air fryer recipe for prosciutto and cheese Stromboli:

Ingredients:

1 package of refrigerated pizza dough
8 thin slices of prosciutto
8 ounces of shredded mozzarella cheese
1/4 cup of grated Parmesan cheese
2 tablespoons of chopped fresh basil
2 tablespoons of chopped fresh parsley

1/2 teaspoon of garlic powder
1/2 teaspoon of onion powder
1 egg, beaten
Marinara sauce, for dipping

Instructions:

Preheat your air fryer to 375°F.
Roll out the pizza dough on a lightly floured surface into a rectangular shape.
Layer the prosciutto on top of the pizza dough, leaving a 1-inch border around the edges.
Sprinkle the mozzarella cheese, Parmesan cheese, basil, parsley, garlic powder, and onion powder over the prosciutto.
Starting from one of the long edges, roll the dough tightly into a log shape, sealing the edges.
Brush the beaten egg over the surface of the Stromboli.
Place the Stromboli in the air fryer basket and cook for 12-15 minutes, or until the crust is golden brown and the cheese is melted.
Remove the Stromboli from the air fryer and let it cool for a few minutes.
Slice the Stromboli into pieces and serve with marinara sauce for dipping.
Enjoy your delicious prosciutto and cheese Stromboli!

171. Here's a recipe for air fryer Fava bean falafel bites:

Ingredients:

1 can (15.5 oz) fava beans, drained and rinsed
1/2 cup chopped fresh parsley
1/2 cup chopped fresh cilantro
1/4 cup chopped red onion
2 cloves garlic, minced
1 tsp ground cumin
1 tsp ground coriander
1/2 tsp salt
1/4 tsp black pepper
2 tbsp all-purpose flour
1 tbsp olive oil
Cooking spray

Instructions:

In a food processor, pulse the fava beans, parsley, cilantro, red onion, garlic, cumin, coriander, salt, and black pepper until the mixture is finely ground.
Add the flour and pulse a few more times to combine.
Form the mixture into small balls (about 1 tablespoon each) and flatten slightly to form patties.
Brush the patties with olive oil and place them in the air fryer basket in a single layer.
Spray the patties with cooking spray.
Air fry at 375°F for 10-12 minutes, flipping halfway through, until the falafel bites are golden brown and crispy.
Serve the falafel bites with your favorite dipping sauce or in a pita with vegetables and tahini sauce.
Enjoy your delicious air fryer fava bean falafel bites!

172. Here is an air fryer recipe for plum and pancetta bombs:

Ingredients:

12 plums, pitted
12 thin slices of pancetta
1/4 cup balsamic vinegar
2 tablespoons honey
Salt and pepper to taste

Instructions:

Preheat your air fryer to 400°F (200°C).
Wrap each plum with a slice of pancetta and secure it with a toothpick.
Place the plum and pancetta bombs in the air fryer basket, making sure they are not touching each other.
Air fry the plum and pancetta bombs for 8 to 10 minutes, or until the pancetta is crispy and the plums are soft and juicy.
While the plum and pancetta bombs are cooking, make the glaze by whisking together the balsamic vinegar and honey in a small bowl. Season with salt and pepper to taste.
Remove the plum and pancetta bombs from the air fryer and brush them with the balsamic glaze.
Serve immediately and enjoy!
173. Here's an air fryer recipe for fried sausage ravioli:

Ingredients:

1 package frozen sausage ravioli (12 oz)
1 cup seasoned breadcrumbs
1/4 cup grated Parmesan cheese
2 large eggs, beaten
Marinara sauce, for serving

Instructions:

Preheat your air fryer to 375°F (190°C).
In a shallow dish, mix the breadcrumbs and Parmesan cheese.
Dip each ravioli in the beaten eggs, then coat it in the breadcrumb mixture.
Place the coated ravioli in a single layer in the air fryer basket. Repeat with remaining ravioli.
Air fry the ravioli for 6-8 minutes, or until golden and crispy, flipping them halfway through cooking.
Serve with a warm marinara sauce for dipping.
Enjoy your crispy and delicious fried sausage ravioli!

174. Here's an air fryer recipe for roasted hot chickpeas:

Ingredients:

1 can chickpeas (15 oz)
1 tablespoon olive oil
1 teaspoon smoked paprika
1/2 teaspoon cumin
1/2 teaspoon garlic powder
1/4 teaspoon cayenne pepper
Salt and black pepper to taste

Instructions:

Drain and rinse the chickpeas, then pat them dry with a paper towel.
In a small bowl, mix the olive oil, smoked paprika, cumin, garlic powder, cayenne pepper, salt, and black pepper.
Add the chickpeas to the spice mixture and toss until evenly coated.
Preheat the air fryer to 400°F.

Place the chickpeas in the air fryer basket in a single layer.
Air fry for 10-12 minutes, shaking the basket every 3-4 minutes to ensure even cooking.
Remove from the air fryer and let cool for a few minutes before serving.
Enjoy your hot and crispy roasted chickpeas as a healthy and tasty snack!

175. here's a recipe for paprika-baked parsnips in the air fryer:

Ingredients:

4 medium parsnips, peeled and cut into sticks
1 tablespoon olive oil
1 teaspoon smoked paprika
1/2 teaspoon garlic powder
Salt and pepper, to taste
Instructions:

Preheat the air fryer to 390°F (200°C).
In a bowl, mix the olive oil, smoked paprika, garlic powder, salt, and pepper.
Add the parsnip sticks to the bowl and toss to coat them with the spice mixture.
Arrange the parsnip sticks in a single layer in the air fryer basket.
Cook for 10 to 12 minutes, shaking the basket halfway through the cooking time, until the parsnips are tender and golden brown.
Serve hot as a side dish or snack.
Enjoy your paprika-baked parsnips!

176. here's a recipe for air-fried cheesy broccoli with garlic:

Ingredients:

1 head of broccoli, cut into florets
2 tablespoons olive oil
3 cloves garlic, minced
Salt and pepper, to taste
1/2 cup grated cheddar cheese

Instructions:

Preheat the air fryer to 375°F (190°C).
In a bowl, toss the broccoli florets with olive oil, minced garlic, salt, and pepper until well coated.
Arrange the broccoli in a single layer in the air fryer basket. You may need to cook in batches.
Cook the broccoli in the air fryer for 8-10 minutes or until tender and slightly crispy.
Sprinkle grated cheddar cheese over the broccoli and cook for an additional 2-3 minutes or until the cheese is melted and bubbly.
Remove from the air fryer and serve hot as a side dish or snack.
Enjoy your delicious and healthy air-fried cheesy broccoli with garlic!

177. here is a recipe for air fryer roasted coconut carrots:

Ingredients:

4-5 medium-sized carrots, peeled and sliced into sticks
2 tablespoons coconut oil, melted
1/4 cup unsweetened shredded coconut
Salt and pepper to taste

Instructions:

Preheat your air fryer to 375°F (190°C).
In a bowl, mix the sliced carrots and melted coconut oil until the carrots are coated evenly.
Add the shredded coconut, salt, and pepper to the bowl, and mix well.
Place the coated carrots in the air fryer basket, making sure they are not overlapping.
Air fry the carrots for 12-15 minutes, shaking the basket occasionally to ensure even cooking until they are tender and slightly crispy.
Serve hot as a side dish or snack. Enjoy!

178. here's a recipe for air fryer pumpkin wedges:

Ingredients:

1 small pumpkin
2 tbsp olive oil
1 tsp paprika
1/2 tsp garlic powder
1/2 tsp salt
1/4 tsp black pepper

Instructions:

Preheat your air fryer to 375°F (190°C).
Cut the pumpkin into wedges, removing the seeds and pulp.
In a bowl, mix the olive oil, paprika, garlic powder, salt, and black pepper.
Add the pumpkin wedges to the bowl and toss until they are evenly coated with the seasoning mixture.
Place the pumpkin wedges in the air fryer basket, making sure they are in a single layer.
Cook for 12-15 minutes, flipping the wedges halfway through the cooking time, until they are tender and golden brown.
Serve hot as a side dish or snack.
Enjoy your delicious air-fried pumpkin wedges!

179. Here's a recipe for baked butternut squash in the air fryer:

Ingredients:

1 medium-sized butternut squash
2 tablespoons olive oil
1 teaspoon dried thyme
1 teaspoon garlic powder
Salt and pepper, to taste

Instructions:

Preheat your air fryer to 375°F (190°C).
Cut the butternut squash in half lengthwise and remove the seeds and pulp.
Cut the squash into 1-inch thick slices.
In a bowl, mix the olive oil, thyme, garlic powder, salt, and pepper.
Dip each slice of squash into the mixture and coat evenly.
Place the coated squash slices into the air fryer basket in a single layer.
Cook for 12-15 minutes, or until the squash is tender and golden brown.
Serve hot and enjoy!

180. Here's an air fryer recipe for cheesy mushrooms:

Ingredients:

8 oz mushrooms
2 tbsp olive oil
1/4 tsp garlic powder
Salt and pepper to taste
1/2 cup shredded cheddar cheese
1 tbsp chopped fresh parsley

Instructions:

Clean the mushrooms and remove the stems. Cut the mushroom caps into bite-sized pieces.
In a bowl, mix the olive oil, garlic powder, salt, and pepper. Add the mushroom pieces and toss to coat evenly.
Preheat the air fryer to 375°F.
Place the seasoned mushroom pieces in the air fryer basket in a single layer.
Air fry for 8-10 minutes, shaking the basket halfway through the cooking time.
Sprinkle the shredded cheddar cheese over the mushrooms and air fry for another 1-2 minutes, until the cheese is melted and bubbly.
Serve the cheesy mushrooms hot, garnished with chopped fresh parsley if desired. Enjoy!

181. here's a recipe for walnut and cheese-filled mushrooms made in an air fryer:

Ingredients:

12 large mushrooms
1/2 cup chopped walnuts
1/2 cup ricotta cheese
1/2 cup shredded Parmesan cheese
1 tbsp chopped fresh thyme
1 tbsp chopped fresh parsley
Salt and pepper, to taste
Olive oil spray

Instructions:

Preheat the air fryer to 375°F (190°C).
Wash the mushrooms and remove the stems.
In a bowl, mix the walnuts, ricotta cheese, Parmesan cheese, thyme, parsley, salt, and pepper.
Stuff the mushroom caps with the walnut and cheese mixture.
Lightly spray the stuffed mushrooms with olive oil spray.
Place the stuffed mushrooms in the air fryer basket in a single layer.
Air fry for 8-10 minutes, until the mushrooms are cooked through and the filling is lightly browned.
Serve hot.
Enjoy your delicious air-fried walnut and cheese-stuffed mushrooms!

182. here's a recipe for paprika Serrano peppers in the air fryer:

Ingredients:

8-10 serrano peppers
1 tablespoon olive oil
1 teaspoon smoked paprika
Salt to taste

Instructions:

Wash and dry the Serrano peppers. Cut off the stem and slice them in half lengthwise. Remove the seeds and membranes from the inside.

In a bowl, mix the olive oil, smoked paprika, and salt.
Toss the sliced peppers in the mixture to coat them evenly.
Preheat the air fryer to 375°F (190°C).
Place the sliced peppers in the air fryer basket in a single layer.
Air fry for 5-7 minutes or until the peppers are tender and slightly charred, flipping them halfway through.
Serve hot as a side dish or appetizer. Enjoy!

183. Here's a recipe for air fryer chili edamame:

Ingredients:

1 pound frozen edamame in pods
1 tablespoon olive oil
2 teaspoons chili powder
1 teaspoon garlic powder
1 teaspoon cumin
1/2 teaspoon salt
1/4 teaspoon black pepper

Instructions:

Preheat your air fryer to 400°F (200°C).
In a bowl, mix the olive oil, chili powder, garlic powder, cumin, salt, and black pepper.
Add the frozen edamame to the bowl and toss until the edamame is well coated with the spice mixture.
Place the edamame in the air fryer basket in a single layer.
Air fry for 8-10 minutes or until the edamame is hot and crispy, shaking the basket halfway through cooking.
Serve the edamame immediately and enjoy it as a snack or side dish.
Note: You can adjust the amount of chili powder and other spices to your liking, depending on how spicy you prefer your edamame.

184. Air Fryer Brie Cheese Croutons with Herbs Recipe:

Ingredients:

8 oz brie cheese
1/2 cup all-purpose flour
1/2 tsp garlic powder
1/2 tsp onion powder
1/2 tsp dried thyme
1/2 tsp dried rosemary
1/4 tsp salt
1/4 tsp black pepper
1 egg, beaten
1 cup seasoned breadcrumbs
Cooking spray

Instructions:

Cut the brie cheese into small cubes, about 1 inch in size.
In a small bowl, whisk together the flour, garlic powder, onion powder, thyme, rosemary, salt, and black pepper.
In another small bowl, beat the egg.
Place the seasoned breadcrumbs in a third small bowl.
Dip each brie cheese cube into the flour mixture, then the beaten egg, and finally the breadcrumbs.
Press the breadcrumbs onto the cheese to make sure they adhere well.

Place the breaded brie cheese cubes in a single layer in the air fryer basket, making sure they are not touching each other.
Lightly spray the cheese cubes with cooking spray.
Air fry the cheese cubes at 375°F for 6-8 minutes or until golden brown and crispy.
Remove the brie cheese croutons from the air fryer and serve immediately as a snack or a topping for salads or soups. Enjoy!

185. Here is a recipe for air fryer super cabbage canapés:

Ingredients:

6 large cabbage leaves
1/2 cup cooked quinoa
1/2 cup cooked black beans
1/4 cup diced tomatoes
1/4 cup diced red onion
1 tablespoon chopped fresh cilantro
1 tablespoon fresh lime juice
1/2 teaspoon ground cumin
Salt and pepper to taste

Instructions:

Preheat your air fryer to 375°F.
Blanch cabbage leaves in boiling water for 1-2 minutes. Drain and set aside.
In a mixing bowl, combine quinoa, black beans, tomatoes, red onion, cilantro, lime juice, cumin, salt, and pepper. Mix well.
Place about 1-2 tablespoons of the quinoa mixture in the center of each cabbage leaf.
Roll up each cabbage leaf around the filling and secure with toothpicks.
Place the cabbage rolls in the air fryer basket and cook for 12-15 minutes, until the cabbage leaves are crispy.
Serve the super cabbage canapés hot and enjoy!

186. here's a recipe for air fryer broccoli cheese quiche:

Ingredients:

1 refrigerated pie crust
2 cups chopped broccoli florets
4 large eggs
1 cup whole milk
1/2 teaspoon salt
1/4 teaspoon black pepper
1/4 teaspoon garlic powder
1/4 teaspoon onion powder
1/2 cup shredded cheddar cheese

Instructions:

Preheat the air fryer to 375°F.
Roll out the pie crust and press it into a 9-inch pie pan, trimming the edges as needed.
In a large bowl, whisk together the eggs, milk, salt, pepper, garlic powder, and onion powder until well combined.
Stir in the chopped broccoli and shredded cheddar cheese.
Pour the mixture into the pie crust.
Place the quiche in the air fryer basket and cook for 20-25 minutes or until the center is set and the edges are golden brown.

Let the quiche cool for a few minutes before slicing and serving.
Enjoy your delicious air fryer broccoli cheese quiche!

187. Here is an air fryer recipe for an easy parmesan sandwich:

Ingredients:

2 slices of bread
1 tablespoon of mayonnaise
1/4 cup of grated parmesan cheese
1/4 teaspoon of garlic powder
Salt and pepper to taste

Instructions:

Preheat your air fryer to 370°F (188°C) for 5 minutes.
Spread the mayonnaise on one side of each slice of bread.
Mix the parmesan cheese, garlic powder, salt, and pepper together in a small bowl.
Sprinkle the parmesan mixture over the mayonnaise on one slice of bread.
Place the other slice of bread on top to make a sandwich.
Place the sandwich in the air fryer basket and air fry for 4-5 minutes, or until the bread is crispy and the cheese is melted.
Carefully remove the sandwich from the air fryer and let it cool for a minute or two before slicing and serving.
Enjoy your easy parmesan sandwich!

188. Here's an air fryer recipe for carrot cookies:

Ingredients:

1 cup all-purpose flour
1 tsp baking powder
1/2 tsp ground cinnamon
1/4 tsp ground nutmeg
1/4 tsp salt
1/2 cup unsalted butter, at room temperature
1/2 cup brown sugar
1 large egg
1 tsp vanilla extract
1 cup grated carrots

Instructions:

Preheat your air fryer to 350°F (180°C).
In a medium bowl, whisk together flour, baking powder, cinnamon, nutmeg, and salt.
In a separate bowl, cream together the butter and brown sugar until light and fluffy.
Beat in the egg and vanilla extract.
Gradually add the dry ingredients to the wet mixture and mix until just combined.
Fold in the grated carrots until evenly distributed.
Use a small cookie scoop or spoon to drop spoonfuls of dough onto the air fryer basket.
Gently press down on each cookie to flatten it slightly.
Air fry for 8-10 minutes, or until the cookies are golden brown on the bottom and cooked through.
Let cool for a few minutes before serving.
Enjoy your delicious and healthy carrot cookies!

189. here's a recipe for mini cheese scones in the air fryer:

Ingredients:

1 1/2 cups self-raising flour
1/4 tsp salt
1/4 tsp cayenne pepper
1/4 cup cold unsalted butter, cut into small pieces
1/2 cup grated cheddar cheese
1/2 cup milk
1 egg, beaten

Instructions:

In a large mixing bowl, combine the self-raising flour, salt, and cayenne pepper. Add the cold butter and use a pastry cutter or fork to cut the butter into the flour mixture until it resembles coarse crumbs.
Stir in the grated cheddar cheese.
Gradually add the milk and stir until a sticky dough forms.
Turn the dough out onto a lightly floured surface and knead lightly until it comes together. Do not over-knead.
Roll out the dough to about 1/2 inch thickness and use a small biscuit cutter or a glass to cut out mini scones.
Brush the beaten egg over the tops of the scones.
Preheat the air fryer to 375°F (190°C).
Place the scones in the air fryer basket in a single layer, leaving some space between them. You may need to air fry in batches.
Air fry for 8-10 minutes or until the scones are golden brown and cooked through.
Serve warm.
Enjoy your delicious mini cheese scones!

190. Here is a recipe for cheddar cheese biscuits made in an air fryer:

Ingredients:

1 cup all-purpose flour
1/2 teaspoon baking powder
1/4 teaspoon baking soda
1/2 teaspoon salt
2 tablespoons cold unsalted butter, cut into small pieces
1/2 cup shredded cheddar cheese
1/4 cup buttermilk
1 large egg
1 tablespoon chopped fresh parsley (optional)

Instructions:

In a mixing bowl, whisk together the flour, baking powder, baking soda, and salt until well combined.
Add the cold butter and use a pastry blender or your fingers to cut it into the dry ingredients until the mixture resembles coarse crumbs.
Add the shredded cheddar cheese and toss to coat evenly.
In a small bowl, whisk together the buttermilk and egg until smooth.
Pour the buttermilk mixture into the mixing bowl with the flour mixture, and use a fork or spatula to stir until a sticky dough forms.
Use a cookie scoop or spoon to portion the dough into 6 to 8 balls, and place them in the air fryer basket lined with parchment paper.
Set the air fryer to 350°F (175°C) and air fry the biscuits for 8 to 10 minutes until golden brown and cooked through.
Sprinkle the chopped parsley on top of the biscuits, if desired.
Serve warm and enjoy your delicious air-fried cheddar cheese biscuits!

191. Here's a recipe for air fryer cauliflower and tofu croquettes:

Ingredients:

1 head cauliflower, chopped into florets
1/2 block of firm tofu, pressed and crumbled
1/2 cup breadcrumbs
1/4 cup grated Parmesan cheese
1 egg
1 tablespoon chopped fresh parsley
1 tablespoon chopped fresh chives
1/2 teaspoon garlic powder
Salt and pepper, to taste
Olive oil cooking spray

Instructions:

Preheat the air fryer to 375°F (190°C).
In a large mixing bowl, combine the cauliflower florets and crumbled tofu.
Add in the breadcrumbs, Parmesan cheese, egg, parsley, chives, garlic powder, salt, and pepper.
Mix all the ingredients until well combined.
Using your hands, shape the mixture into small croquette shapes.
Place the croquettes in the air fryer basket in a single layer, making sure they are not touching each other.
Lightly spray the croquettes with olive oil cooking spray.
Cook the croquettes for 10-12 minutes, or until they are golden brown and crispy on the outside.
Remove the croquettes from the air fryer and serve hot.
Enjoy your delicious air fryer cauliflower and tofu croquettes!

192. Here's a recipe for Cheesy Mushroom and Cauliflower Balls made in the air fryer:

Ingredients:

1 small head of cauliflower, cut into florets
1 cup of chopped mushrooms
1/2 cup of grated cheddar cheese
1/4 cup of grated parmesan cheese
1/4 cup of breadcrumbs
1/4 cup of chopped parsley
2 cloves of garlic, minced
1 egg
Salt and pepper to taste
Olive oil cooking spray

Instructions:

Preheat your air fryer to 360°F (180°C).
Place the cauliflower florets in a microwave-safe bowl, cover with a lid or plastic wrap and microwave for 5-7 minutes until tender.
Mash the cooked cauliflower with a fork or potato masher until it forms a chunky paste.

In a pan, cook the mushrooms and garlic until softened.
In a mixing bowl, combine the mashed cauliflower, cooked mushrooms, cheddar cheese, parmesan cheese, breadcrumbs, parsley, egg, salt, and pepper.
Use your hands to form the mixture into small balls, about the size of a ping pong ball.
Place the balls in a single layer in the air fryer basket, making sure they are not touching.
Spray the balls with olive oil cooking spray.
Air fry for 10-12 minutes, or until the balls are crispy and golden brown.
Serve hot with your favorite dipping sauce.
Enjoy your Cheesy Mushroom and Cauliflower Balls made in the air fryer!

193. Here's a recipe for spicy cheese rings made in an air fryer:

Ingredients:

1 cup all-purpose flour
1 teaspoon paprika
1 teaspoon garlic powder
1 teaspoon onion powder
1/2 teaspoon salt
1/4 teaspoon cayenne pepper
1/2 cup milk
2 cups shredded cheddar cheese
1 egg, beaten
1 cup breadcrumbs
Instructions:
In a mixing bowl, whisk together the flour, paprika, garlic powder, onion powder, salt, and cayenne pepper.
Add the milk and whisk until a smooth batter forms.
Fold in the shredded cheddar cheese and mix until the cheese is evenly distributed.
Roll the mixture into small balls and place them onto a plate lined with parchment paper.
Chill the balls in the refrigerator for 10-15 minutes to help them set.
Preheat the air fryer to 400°F (200°C).
Dip each ball into the beaten egg and roll in the breadcrumbs to coat.
Place the balls into the air fryer basket, making sure they are not touching each other.
Air fry for 6-8 minutes or until the cheese rings are golden brown and crispy.
Serve the cheese rings hot with your favorite dipping sauce.

194. Here's an air fryer recipe for cocktail meatballs that's easy to make:

Ingredients:

1 pound ground beef
1/2 cup breadcrumbs
1/4 cup milk
1 egg
1 tablespoon Worcestershire sauce
1/2 teaspoon garlic powder
1/2 teaspoon onion powder
Salt and pepper, to taste
1/2 cup barbecue sauce
1/2 cup grape jelly

Instructions:

Preheat your air fryer to 375°F.
In a large bowl, combine ground beef, breadcrumbs, milk, egg, Worcestershire sauce, garlic powder, onion powder, salt, and pepper. Mix until well combined.

Roll the mixture into small meatballs, about 1 inch in diameter.
Place the meatballs in the air fryer basket, making sure they are not touching each other.
Cook the meatballs for 10 minutes, flipping them halfway through.
While the meatballs are cooking, mix together the barbecue sauce and grape jelly in a small saucepan.
Heat the sauce over low heat until the jelly is melted and the sauce is smooth.
Brush the meatballs with the sauce and cook for an additional 2-3 minutes.
Serve the meatballs hot with toothpicks for easy snacking. Enjoy!

195. Here's an air fryer recipe for French beans with toasted almonds:

Ingredients:

1 lb French beans, trimmed
2 tbsp olive oil
1/2 tsp salt
1/4 tsp black pepper
1/4 cup sliced almonds

Instructions:

Preheat your air fryer to 375°F (190°C) for 5 minutes.
Toss the trimmed French beans with olive oil, salt, and black pepper in a bowl until well coated.
Place the French beans in the air fryer basket and cook for 10-12 minutes, shaking the basket every 3-4 minutes, until they are tender and lightly browned.
While the beans are cooking, toast the sliced almonds in a dry skillet over medium heat until lightly browned and fragrant, about 3-4 minutes.
When the French beans are done, remove them from the air fryer and place them in a serving dish. Top with the toasted almonds and serve immediately.
Enjoy your crispy and flavorful French beans with toasted almonds!

196. Here's a recipe for cheddar black bean burritos made in an air fryer:

Ingredients:

4 large flour tortillas
1 can of black beans, drained and rinsed
1/2 cup of corn
1/4 cup of diced onions
1/4 cup of diced bell peppers
1/4 teaspoon of cumin
1/4 teaspoon of chili powder
1/4 teaspoon of garlic powder
Salt and pepper, to taste
1 cup of shredded cheddar cheese
Cooking spray

Instructions:

Preheat your air fryer to 370°F (188°C).
In a mixing bowl, combine black beans, corn, onions, bell peppers, cumin, chili powder, garlic powder, salt, and pepper.
Take one tortilla and spoon 1/4 of the black bean mixture onto the center. Sprinkle with 1/4 cup of shredded cheddar cheese.
Fold the bottom of the tortilla up over the filling, then fold in the sides and roll up tightly.
Repeat with the remaining tortillas and filling.
Spray the tops of the burritos with cooking spray and place them seam-side down in the air fryer basket.

Cook for 5 minutes, then flip the burritos over and cook for another 5 minutes.
Remove the burritos from the air fryer and let them cool for a few minutes before serving.
Enjoy your delicious and crispy cheddar black bean burritos!

197. Here's a recipe for smoky air-fryer hazelnuts:

Ingredients:

2 cups hazelnuts
2 tablespoons olive oil
1 tablespoon smoked paprika
1/2 teaspoon garlic powder
1/2 teaspoon sea salt

Instructions:

Preheat your air fryer to 360°F (182°C).
In a large bowl, mix together the olive oil, smoked paprika, garlic powder, and sea salt.
Add the hazelnuts to the bowl and toss until they are fully coated with the spice mixture.
Place the coated hazelnuts in the air fryer basket.
Air fry for 8-10 minutes, shaking the basket every 2-3 minutes to ensure even cooking.
Once the hazelnuts are fragrant and golden brown, remove them from the air fryer and let them cool for a few minutes.
Serve the hazelnuts as a snack or as a topping for salads, soups, or other dishes.
Enjoy your smoky and crunchy hazelnuts!

198. Here's an air fryer recipe for spiced almonds:

Ingredients:

2 cups raw almonds
1 tablespoon olive oil
1 teaspoon ground cumin
1 teaspoon smoked paprika
1/2 teaspoon garlic powder
1/2 teaspoon onion powder
1/4 teaspoon cayenne pepper
1/2 teaspoon salt

Instructions:

Preheat your air fryer to 350°F (180°C).
In a medium bowl, whisk together the olive oil, cumin, smoked paprika, garlic powder, onion powder, cayenne pepper, and salt.
Add the almonds to the bowl and stir until they are well coated with the spice mixture.
Place the almonds in the air fryer basket and spread them out in a single layer.
Cook the almonds for 8-10 minutes, shaking the basket occasionally, until they are lightly browned and fragrant.
Remove the almonds from the air fryer and let them cool for a few minutes before serving. Enjoy as a snack or use them as a topping for salads or roasted vegetables.

199. here's an air fryer recipe for roasted pumpkin seeds with cardamom:

Ingredients:

1 cup pumpkin seeds

1 tablespoon olive oil
1/2 teaspoon ground cardamom
1/2 teaspoon ground cinnamon
1/2 teaspoon salt
1/4 teaspoon cayenne pepper

Instructions:

Rinse pumpkin seeds in a colander and remove any remaining pumpkin flesh.
Spread the seeds in a single layer on a paper towel to dry for a few hours.
Preheat the air fryer to 325°F (160°C) for 3 minutes.
In a mixing bowl, toss the pumpkin seeds with olive oil, cardamom, cinnamon, salt, and cayenne pepper.
Transfer the seasoned pumpkin seeds to the air fryer basket in a single layer.
Air fry the seeds for 8 to 10 minutes or until they turn golden brown.
Toss the pumpkin seeds once in between cooking to ensure even roasting.
Remove from the air fryer and let them cool before serving.
Enjoy your crunchy and flavorful roasted pumpkin seeds with cardamom!

200. here's a recipe for air fryer masala cashew nuts:

Ingredients:

1 cup raw cashews
1/2 teaspoon salt
1 teaspoon garam masala
1/2 teaspoon turmeric
1/2 teaspoon cumin
1/2 teaspoon paprika
1/4 teaspoon garlic powder
1/4 teaspoon onion powder
1 tablespoon olive oil

Instructions:

Preheat your air fryer to 350°F (175°C).
In a bowl, mix together the salt, garam masala, turmeric, cumin, paprika, garlic powder, onion powder, and olive oil.
Add the cashews to the bowl and toss to coat them with the spice mixture.
Transfer the cashews to the air fryer basket and cook for 5-6 minutes, shaking the basket every couple of minutes, until the cashews are lightly browned and toasted.
Remove the cashews from the air fryer and let them cool before serving.
Enjoy your delicious and spicy air fryer masala cashew nuts!

201. Here's an air fryer recipe for sweet mixed nuts:

Ingredients:

1 cup mixed nuts (such as almonds, cashews, and pecans)
1/4 cup honey
1 tbsp melted butter
1/2 tsp ground cinnamon
1/4 tsp ground ginger
1/4 tsp salt

Instructions:

Preheat your air fryer to 350°F (180°C).
In a medium bowl, mix the honey, melted butter, cinnamon, ginger, and salt.
Add the mixed nuts to the bowl and stir to coat evenly.
Place the coated nuts in the air fryer basket and cook for 5-6 minutes, shaking the basket halfway through the cooking time.
Remove the basket from the air fryer and let the nuts cool for a few minutes.
Serve the sweet mixed nuts as a snack or sprinkle them over your favorite salad for extra crunch and sweetness. Enjoy!

PORK, BEEF & LAMB

202. Here is a recipe for honey and BBQ spare ribs made in an air fryer:

Ingredients:

2 lbs pork spare ribs, cut into individual pieces
1/4 cup honey
1/4 cup BBQ sauce
2 tbsp soy sauce
1 tbsp vegetable oil
1 tsp garlic powder
1 tsp onion powder
1/2 tsp paprika
1/2 tsp salt
1/4 tsp black pepper

Instructions:

In a small bowl, whisk together the honey, BBQ sauce, soy sauce, vegetable oil, garlic powder, onion powder, paprika, salt, and black pepper.
Brush the mixture onto the spare ribs, making sure they are coated evenly.
Place the spare ribs in the air fryer basket, making sure they are not overlapping.
Air fry at 375°F for 25-30 minutes, flipping the ribs halfway through cooking.
Brush the spare ribs with the remaining honey and BBQ sauce mixture and air fry for an additional 3-5 minutes until the sauce is caramelized and the spare ribs are fully cooked.
Remove the spare ribs from the air fryer and let them rest for a few minutes before serving.
Enjoy your honey and BBQ spare ribs made in the air fryer!

203. Here's a recipe for air fryer Char Siu pork ribs:

Ingredients:

1 lb pork spare ribs
2 cloves garlic, minced
2 tbsp char siu sauce

1 tbsp honey
1 tbsp soy sauce
1 tsp sesame oil
1/2 tsp five-spice powder
Salt and pepper, to taste
Optional garnish: chopped scallions and sesame seeds

Instructions:

Preheat your air fryer to 375°F (190°C).
Cut the pork spare ribs into individual pieces, then season with salt and pepper.
In a bowl, mix together the minced garlic, char siu sauce, honey, soy sauce, sesame oil, and five-spice powder until well combined.
Brush the mixture onto the pork spare ribs, coating them evenly on all sides.
Place the pork spare ribs in the air fryer basket, making sure to leave some space in between each piece.
Air fry for 10 minutes, then flip the ribs over and air fry for another 10 minutes.
Check the internal temperature of the pork ribs with a meat thermometer – it should read 145°F (63°C) or higher.
If the pork ribs are not fully cooked, continue air frying for another 5-10 minutes.
Once fully cooked, remove the pork ribs from the air fryer and let them rest for 5 minutes before serving.
Garnish with chopped scallions and sesame seeds, if desired. Serve hot and enjoy!

204. Here's a recipe for Memphis-style pork ribs in the air fryer:

Ingredients:

1 rack of pork ribs
1/4 cup brown sugar
2 tablespoons paprika
1 tablespoon garlic powder
1 tablespoon onion powder
1 tablespoon dried oregano
1 tablespoon dried thyme
1 teaspoon salt
1/2 teaspoon black pepper
1/4 teaspoon cayenne pepper

Instructions:

Mix together the brown sugar, paprika, garlic powder, onion powder, oregano, thyme, salt, black pepper, and cayenne pepper in a small bowl to make the rub.
Remove the membrane from the back of the pork ribs and season both sides with the rub, pressing the rub into the meat to adhere.
Preheat the air fryer to 350°F.
Place the pork ribs in the air fryer basket and cook for 25 minutes.
After 25 minutes, increase the temperature to 400°F and continue to cook for an additional 10-15 minutes until the ribs are tender and the outside is crispy.
Let the ribs rest for 5 minutes before slicing and serving. Enjoy your Memphis-style pork ribs!

205. Here's an air fryer recipe for roasted pork rack with macadamia nuts:

Ingredients:

1 (3-4 lb) pork rack
1/2 cup macadamia nuts, chopped
2 cloves garlic, minced

1 tablespoon olive oil
1 teaspoon paprika
1/2 teaspoon salt
1/4 teaspoon black pepper

Instructions:

Preheat your air fryer to 400°F (200°C).
In a small bowl, mix together the chopped macadamia nuts, minced garlic, olive oil, paprika, salt, and black pepper.
Score the fat on the pork rack with a sharp knife.
Rub the macadamia nut mixture all over the pork rack, making sure to get it into the scored fat.
Place the pork rack in the air fryer basket, bone-side down.
Air fry for 20-25 minutes or until the internal temperature of the pork reaches 145°F (63°C).
Let the pork rest for 10 minutes before slicing and serving.
Enjoy your delicious roasted pork rack with macadamia nuts!

206. Sure, here's a recipe for Chinese sticky ribs in the air fryer:

Ingredients:

2 lbs pork ribs
2 tablespoons hoisin sauce
2 tablespoons soy sauce
2 tablespoons honey
1 tablespoon rice vinegar
1 tablespoon vegetable oil
1 tablespoon Chinese five spice
1 teaspoon garlic powder
1 teaspoon ginger powder
Salt and pepper, to taste
Sesame seeds and green onions, for garnish

Instructions:

In a bowl, whisk together hoisin sauce, soy sauce, honey, rice vinegar, vegetable oil, Chinese five spice, garlic powder, ginger powder, salt, and pepper.
Place the pork ribs in a large bowl and pour the marinade over them. Make sure the ribs are evenly coated. Cover the bowl with plastic wrap and refrigerate for at least 2 hours, or overnight.
Preheat the air fryer to 375°F (190°C).
Remove the ribs from the marinade and place them in the air fryer basket. Discard the leftover marinade.
Air fry the ribs for 20 minutes, flipping them halfway through the cooking time. If the ribs are not yet crispy, cook them for an additional 5-10 minutes.
Once done, remove the ribs from the air fryer and let them rest for a few minutes.
Garnish with sesame seeds and chopped green onions, if desired. Serve hot and enjoy!

207. Here's an air fryer recipe for pork sausage with butter bean ratatouille:

Ingredients:

4 pork sausages
1 can butter beans, drained and rinsed
1 small onion, diced
1 small eggplant, diced
1 small zucchini, diced
1 red bell pepper, diced
2 cloves garlic, minced

1 tbsp olive oil
1 tsp dried basil
1 tsp dried thyme
Salt and pepper, to taste

Instructions:

Preheat the air fryer to 375°F (190°C).
In a large bowl, combine the onion, eggplant, zucchini, red bell pepper, garlic, olive oil, dried basil, dried thyme, salt, and pepper. Toss to combine.
Place the sausage links in the air fryer basket and arrange the butter beans and vegetable mixture around them.
Air fry for 15-20 minutes, or until the sausages are cooked through and the vegetables are tender, stirring the vegetables occasionally to ensure even cooking.
Serve hot, garnished with fresh herbs if desired.

208. Here's a recipe for maple mustard pork balls in the air fryer:

Ingredients:

1 lb ground pork
1/4 cup breadcrumbs
1/4 cup chopped onion
2 tablespoons Dijon mustard
1 tablespoon maple syrup
1/2 teaspoon garlic powder
1/2 teaspoon smoked paprika
Salt and pepper to taste
Cooking spray

Instructions:

In a bowl, combine ground pork, breadcrumbs, chopped onion, Dijon mustard, maple syrup, garlic powder, smoked paprika, salt, and pepper. Mix well.
Form mixture into 1-inch balls.
Spray the air fryer basket with cooking spray.
Place the pork balls in the air fryer basket and spray with cooking spray.
Air fry at 375°F for 10-12 minutes, shaking the basket halfway through cooking time.
Check that the internal temperature of the pork balls reaches 165°F.
Serve hot with your favorite dipping sauce.
Enjoy your maple mustard pork balls!

209. Here's a recipe for a pork meatball noodle bowl made in an air fryer:

Ingredients:

1 lb ground pork
1/2 cup breadcrumbs
2 cloves garlic, minced
1 tbsp soy sauce
1 tbsp hoisin sauce
1 egg, beaten
Salt and pepper to taste
4 cups chicken broth
8 oz rice noodles
2 cups chopped bok choy
1 red bell pepper, sliced

1 carrot, sliced into ribbons
1/4 cup chopped fresh cilantro
1/4 cup chopped green onions
2 tbsp sesame oil
2 tbsp soy sauce
2 tbsp rice vinegar
1 tbsp honey
Sriracha sauce (optional)

Instructions:

Preheat the air fryer to 375°F.
In a large mixing bowl, combine the ground pork, breadcrumbs, garlic, soy sauce, hoisin sauce, beaten egg, salt, and pepper. Mix well and form into small meatballs.
Place the meatballs in the air fryer basket and cook for 10-12 minutes, flipping halfway through, until they are browned and cooked through.
While the meatballs cook, prepare the noodle bowl. In a large pot, bring the chicken broth to a boil. Add the rice noodles and cook for 3-5 minutes, until tender. Drain and set aside.
In a small mixing bowl, whisk together the sesame oil, soy sauce, rice vinegar, and honey.
In a large mixing bowl, combine the cooked rice noodles, chopped Bok Choy, sliced red bell pepper, sliced carrot, cilantro, green onions, and the sesame oil mixture. Toss well to coat everything.
To serve, divide the noodle mixture among bowls and top with the cooked pork meatballs. Drizzle with Sriracha sauce if desired. Enjoy!

210. Here's an air fryer recipe for traditional Swedish meatballs:

Ingredients:

1 lb ground beef
1/2 lb ground pork
1/2 cup breadcrumbs
1/4 cup milk
1 egg
1/4 cup finely chopped onion
1/4 cup finely chopped fresh parsley
1 tsp salt
1/2 tsp black pepper
1/2 tsp ground allspice
1/4 tsp ground nutmeg
Cooking spray
For the gravy:
2 tbsp butter
2 tbsp all-purpose flour
2 cups beef broth
1/2 cup heavy cream
1 tbsp Worcestershire sauce
Salt and pepper to taste

Instructions:

Preheat your air fryer to 375°F (190°C).
In a large bowl, combine the ground beef, ground pork, breadcrumbs, milk, egg, onion, parsley, salt, pepper, allspice, and nutmeg. Mix well with your hands.
Using a cookie scoop or a spoon, form the mixture into 1-inch balls and place them in the air fryer basket in a single layer. You may need to cook them in batches.
Spray the meatballs with cooking spray and cook for 10-12 minutes, or until they are browned and cooked through.

While the meatballs are cooking, prepare the gravy. Melt the butter in a saucepan over medium heat. Add the flour and whisk until smooth. Cook for 1-2 minutes, or until the mixture turns golden brown. Gradually whisk in the beef broth and heavy cream, then add the Worcestershire sauce, salt, and pepper. Bring to a simmer and cook for 5-10 minutes, or until the gravy thickens.
Once the meatballs are cooked, transfer them to a serving platter and pour the gravy over them. Serve hot with mashed potatoes, lingonberry sauce, and/or pickled cucumbers, if desired. Enjoy!

211. Here's a recipe for air fryer pork burgers that are sure to be delicious!

Ingredients:

1 lb ground pork
1/2 cup breadcrumbs
1/4 cup finely chopped onion
1/4 cup finely chopped fresh parsley
1 egg
1 teaspoon garlic powder
1 teaspoon onion powder
1/2 teaspoon salt
1/4 teaspoon black pepper
Burger buns and toppings of your choice

Instructions:

In a large bowl, mix together the ground pork, breadcrumbs, onion, parsley, egg, garlic powder, onion powder, salt, and black pepper until well combined.
Form the mixture into four equal-sized patties.
Preheat your air fryer to 375°F (190°C).
Place the patties in the air fryer basket and cook for 8 to 10 minutes, flipping halfway through, until the internal temperature reaches 160°F (71°C).
Toast the burger buns in the air fryer for 1 to 2 minutes.
Assemble the burgers with your desired toppings and enjoy!

212. Air Fryer Pork and Pear Blue Cheese Patties Recipe:

Ingredients:

1 pound ground pork
1 medium pear, peeled and grated
1/4 cup crumbled blue cheese
2 tablespoons chopped fresh parsley
1 tablespoon Dijon mustard
1/2 teaspoon garlic powder
1/2 teaspoon salt
1/4 teaspoon black pepper

Instructions:

In a large mixing bowl, combine ground pork, grated pear, crumbled blue cheese, chopped parsley, Dijon mustard, garlic powder, salt, and black pepper. Mix well.
Divide the mixture into 4 equal parts and shape each part into a patty.
Preheat your air fryer to 375°F for 5 minutes.
Place the pork patties in the air fryer basket, leaving some space between them.
Air fry the patties for 8-10 minutes, flipping them halfway through cooking until they are cooked through and browned on both sides.
Serve the patties with your favorite burger toppings, such as lettuce, tomato, onion, and a bun. Enjoy!

213. Here is a recipe for Serbian pork skewers with a yogurt sauce that can be made in an air fryer:

Ingredients:

1 pound pork shoulder, cut into 1-inch cubes
1 red onion, cut into chunks
1 red bell pepper, cut into chunks
1 green bell pepper, cut into chunks
1 teaspoon paprika
1 teaspoon garlic powder
1 teaspoon onion powder
1/2 teaspoon salt
1/4 teaspoon black pepper
2 tablespoons olive oil
1/2 cup plain Greek yogurt
2 tablespoons chopped fresh dill
1 tablespoon lemon juice
Salt and black pepper, to taste

Instructions:

Preheat your air fryer to 400°F (200°C).
In a large bowl, combine the pork cubes, onion, red and green bell peppers, paprika, garlic powder, onion powder, salt, pepper, and olive oil. Toss to coat well.
Thread the pork and vegetables onto skewers, alternating between them.
Place the skewers in the air fryer basket and cook for 12-15 minutes, flipping once halfway through, until the pork is cooked through and the vegetables are tender and slightly charred.
In a small bowl, whisk together the Greek yogurt, dill, lemon juice, salt, and pepper.
Serve the pork skewers hot with the yogurt sauce on the side for dipping. Enjoy!

214. Here's an air fryer recipe for Italian fennel and pork balls:

Ingredients:

1 pound ground pork
1/2 cup breadcrumbs
1/4 cup grated Parmesan cheese
1 tablespoon chopped fresh parsley
1 tablespoon chopped fresh fennel fronds
1 teaspoon fennel seeds, crushed
1/2 teaspoon garlic powder
1/2 teaspoon onion powder
1/2 teaspoon salt
1/4 teaspoon black pepper

Instructions:

Preheat your air fryer to 400°F.
In a large mixing bowl, combine ground pork, breadcrumbs, Parmesan cheese, parsley, fennel fronds, fennel seeds, garlic powder, onion powder, salt, and black pepper. Mix until well combined.
Using your hands, form the mixture into small meatballs, about 1 inch in diameter.
Place the meatballs in the air fryer basket, leaving some space between them.
Air fry for 10-12 minutes, shaking the basket halfway through cooking, until the meatballs are browned and cooked through.
Serve the fennel and pork balls with your favorite dipping sauce, such as marinara sauce or garlic aioli. Enjoy!

215. Here's a recipe for Mediterranean Pork Kabobs made in an air fryer:

Ingredients:

1 lb. pork tenderloin, cut into 1-inch cubes
1 red bell pepper, cut into 1-inch pieces
1 yellow bell pepper, cut into 1-inch pieces
1 red onion, cut into 1-inch pieces
8-10 cherry tomatoes
1 tsp. dried oregano
1 tsp. dried basil
1 tsp. dried thyme
1/2 tsp. garlic powder
Salt and pepper, to taste
2 tbsp. olive oil

Instructions:

Preheat your air fryer to 400°F.
In a bowl, mix together the dried oregano, basil, thyme, garlic powder, salt, and pepper.
Add the pork cubes to the bowl and toss to coat with the seasoning mixture.
Thread the pork, bell peppers, onion, and cherry tomatoes onto skewers.
Brush the skewers with olive oil.
Place the skewers in the air fryer basket and cook for 10-12 minutes or until the pork is cooked through and the vegetables are tender, flipping the skewers halfway through.
Serve with a side salad or some rice.
Enjoy your Mediterranean Pork Kabobs made in an air fryer!

216. Here's an air fryer recipe for sausage sticks rolled in bacon:

Ingredients:

12 thin sausages
12 strips of bacon
1/4 cup BBQ sauce
1/4 cup honey
1 tablespoon Dijon mustard
1 teaspoon smoked paprika
Salt and black pepper to taste

Instructions:

Preheat your air fryer to 400°F (200°C).
In a small bowl, whisk together BBQ sauce, honey, Dijon mustard, smoked paprika, salt, and black pepper.
Wrap each sausage with a strip of bacon, securing the ends with toothpicks.
Brush the sauce generously over the bacon-wrapped sausages.
Place the sausages in the air fryer basket, leaving space between them.
Cook for 10-12 minutes, flipping halfway through and brushing with more sauce.
Once the sausages are browned and crispy, remove them from the air fryer and let them cool for a few minutes.
Remove the toothpicks and serve the sausage sticks warm with extra sauce on the side for dipping.
Enjoy!

217. Here's an air fryer recipe for veggies and pork Pinchos:

Ingredients:

1 lb pork loin, cut into cubes
1 red bell pepper, cut into bite-size pieces
1 green bell pepper, cut into bite-size pieces
1 zucchini, cut into bite-size pieces
1 yellow onion, cut into bite-size pieces
8 wooden skewers, soaked in water for 30 minutes
1 tsp smoked paprika
1 tsp garlic powder
Salt and black pepper, to taste
Olive oil

Instructions:

Preheat the air fryer to 400°F (200°C).
In a large bowl, mix the pork cubes with smoked paprika, garlic powder, salt, and black pepper.
Thread the pork cubes, bell peppers, zucchini, and onion onto the skewers.
Brush the skewers with olive oil.
Place the skewers in the air fryer basket and cook for 10-12 minutes, flipping the skewers halfway through, until the pork is cooked through and the vegetables are tender.
Serve hot and enjoy!

218. Great! Here's a recipe for spicy tricolor pork kebabs in the air fryer:

Ingredients:

1 pound pork tenderloin, cut into bite-sized pieces
1 red bell pepper, cut into bite-sized pieces
1 yellow bell pepper, cut into bite-sized pieces
1 green bell pepper, cut into bite-sized pieces
1 red onion, cut into bite-sized pieces
2 tablespoons olive oil
1 tablespoon smoked paprika
1 teaspoon garlic powder
1/2 teaspoon cumin
1/4 teaspoon cayenne pepper
Salt and pepper, to taste

Instructions:

Preheat the air fryer to 375°F.
In a bowl, combine the pork, peppers, onion, olive oil, smoked paprika, garlic powder, cumin, cayenne pepper, salt, and pepper. Toss to coat the pork and veggies evenly.
Thread the pork and veggies onto skewers, alternating between colors.
Place the kebabs in the air fryer basket and cook for 8-10 minutes, flipping halfway through, until the pork is cooked through and the veggies are tender.
Serve the kebabs immediately with your favorite dipping sauce.
Enjoy your delicious and spicy tricolor pork kebabs!

219. here's an air fryer recipe for sweet pork tenderloin:

Ingredients:

1 pound pork tenderloin
1/4 cup soy sauce
1/4 cup honey
2 tablespoons brown sugar

2 tablespoons ketchup
2 cloves garlic, minced
1 teaspoon grated fresh ginger
1/2 teaspoon black pepper
1/4 teaspoon red pepper flakes (optional)

Instructions:

Preheat your air fryer to 400°F (200°C).
In a bowl, whisk together the soy sauce, honey, brown sugar, ketchup, garlic, ginger, black pepper, and red pepper flakes (if using).
Cut the pork tenderloin into 1-inch thick medallions.
Add the pork medallions to the bowl with the marinade and toss to coat.
Let the pork marinate in the fridge for at least 30 minutes.
Spray the air fryer basket with cooking spray.
Place the pork medallions in the air fryer basket and cook for 12-15 minutes, flipping halfway through, until the internal temperature of the pork reaches 145°F (63°C).
Serve the sweet pork tenderloin with your favorite sides.
Enjoy your sweet and savory pork tenderloin!

220. Here's an air fryer recipe for stuffed pork tenderloin:

Ingredients:

1 pound pork tenderloin
2 tablespoons olive oil
2 cloves garlic, minced
1/4 cup chopped onion
1/4 cup chopped mushrooms
1/4 cup chopped spinach
1/4 cup crumbled feta cheese
Salt and pepper to taste

Instructions:

Preheat the air fryer to 375°F.
In a skillet, heat the olive oil over medium heat. Add the garlic, onion, mushrooms, and spinach. Cook for about 5 minutes or until the vegetables are tender.
Butterfly the pork tenderloin by slicing it lengthwise down the center, but not all the way through. Open the tenderloin up like a book and lay it flat on a cutting board.
Spoon the vegetable mixture over the tenderloin, leaving about 1/2 inch around the edges. Sprinkle the feta cheese on top.
Roll the tenderloin up tightly, tucking in the ends as you go.
Season the outside of the tenderloin with salt and pepper.
Place the tenderloin in the air fryer basket and cook for 25-30 minutes or until the internal temperature reaches 145°F.
Let the tenderloin rest for a few minutes before slicing and serving. Enjoy!

221. Here's an air fryer recipe for pork lettuce cups:

Ingredients:

1 lb ground pork
1 tablespoon olive oil
1/2 onion, chopped
2 cloves garlic, minced
1 tablespoon ginger, minced

1/4 cup hoisin sauce
1 tablespoon soy sauce
1 tablespoon rice vinegar
1 teaspoon sesame oil
1 head of lettuce, leaves separated
2 green onions, chopped
Salt and pepper, to taste

Instructions:

Preheat your air fryer to 375°F.
Heat olive oil in a large skillet over medium-high heat. Add onion, garlic, and ginger and cook until onion is softened.
Add the ground pork to the skillet and cook until browned, breaking it up into small pieces with a spoon.
In a small bowl, mix together hoisin sauce, soy sauce, rice vinegar, sesame oil, and salt and pepper.
Add the sauce mixture to the pork and cook for an additional 2-3 minutes until heated through.
Arrange lettuce leaves on a plate and spoon the pork mixture into each leaf.
Sprinkle chopped green onions over the top of the pork and serve.
Enjoy your delicious and healthy pork lettuce cups!

222. here's an air fryer recipe for sage-rubbed pork tenderloin:

Ingredients:

1 pork tenderloin
1 tablespoon olive oil
1 tablespoon finely chopped fresh sage leaves
1 teaspoon garlic powder
1/2 teaspoon salt
1/4 teaspoon black pepper

Instructions:

Preheat your air fryer to 375°F (190°C).
In a small bowl, mix together the olive oil, sage, garlic powder, salt, and black pepper to create a rub.
Rub the pork tenderloin with the spice mixture, making sure it is coated all over.
Place the tenderloin in the air fryer basket and cook for 15 to 20 minutes, or until the internal temperature reaches 145°F (63°C).
Remove the tenderloin from the air fryer and let it rest for 5 minutes before slicing and serving.
Enjoy your sage-rubbed pork tenderloin!

223. here's an air fryer recipe for zesty breaded pork chops:

Ingredients:

4 boneless pork chops
1/2 cup breadcrumbs
1/4 cup grated Parmesan cheese
1 tsp dried basil
1 tsp dried oregano
1 tsp garlic powder
1/2 tsp paprika
1/2 tsp salt
1/4 tsp black pepper
1 egg
1 tbsp olive oil

Instructions:

Preheat your air fryer to 375°F (190°C).
In a shallow dish, mix the breadcrumbs, Parmesan cheese, dried basil, dried oregano, garlic powder, paprika, salt, and black pepper.
In another shallow dish, beat the egg.
Dip each pork chop in the egg, then coat it in the breadcrumb mixture.
Brush the air fryer basket with olive oil.
Place the pork chops in the air fryer basket in a single layer.
Cook for 10 minutes, then flip the pork chops and cook for an additional 10 minutes or until the internal temperature reaches 145°F (63°C).
Serve immediately with your favorite sides. Enjoy!
Note: Cooking times may vary depending on the thickness of your pork chops. Be sure to use a meat thermometer to ensure the pork is cooked to the appropriate temperature.

224. Here's an air fryer recipe for Hungarian-style pork chops:

Ingredients:

4 boneless pork chops
1/2 cup all-purpose flour
1 teaspoon salt
1 teaspoon black pepper
1 teaspoon paprika
1 teaspoon garlic powder
1/2 teaspoon onion powder
1/2 teaspoon dried thyme
1/2 teaspoon dried oregano
2 eggs
1 tablespoon milk
1 cup seasoned breadcrumbs
Cooking spray

Instructions:

Preheat your air fryer to 375°F (190°C).
In a shallow dish, mix together the flour, salt, pepper, paprika, garlic powder, onion powder, dried thyme, and dried oregano.
In another shallow dish, whisk together the eggs and milk.
In a third shallow dish, place the seasoned breadcrumbs.
Coat each pork chop in the flour mixture, shaking off any excess.
Dip each pork chop in the egg mixture, then coat it in the seasoned breadcrumbs.
Lightly spray the pork chops with cooking spray.
Place the pork chops in the air fryer basket and cook for 10-12 minutes, flipping halfway through, until they are golden brown and cooked through.
Serve hot with your favorite sides.
Enjoy your Hungarian-style pork chops!

225. Here's an air fryer recipe for pork chops with mustard-apricot glaze:

Ingredients:

4 bone-in pork chops
Salt and pepper
1/2 cup apricot preserves
2 tbsp Dijon mustard
1 tbsp apple cider vinegar

1 tsp minced garlic
1/2 tsp ground ginger
1/4 tsp cayenne pepper

Instructions:

Preheat the air fryer to 375°F (190°C).
Season the pork chops with salt and pepper on both sides.
In a small bowl, whisk together the apricot preserves, Dijon mustard, apple cider vinegar, garlic, ginger, and cayenne pepper.
Brush the glaze generously over both sides of each pork chop.
Place the pork chops in the air fryer basket, making sure they don't overlap.
Cook for 12-15 minutes, flipping halfway through, until the internal temperature of the pork reaches 145°F (63°C).
Let the pork chops rest for 5 minutes before serving.
Enjoy your delicious pork chops with mustard-apricot glaze!

226. Here's an air fryer recipe for Southeast-Asian pork chops:

Ingredients:

4 bone-in pork chops
1/4 cup soy sauce
1/4 cup hoisin sauce
2 tablespoons honey
2 tablespoons rice vinegar
2 cloves garlic, minced
1 teaspoon ginger, minced
1 teaspoon sriracha sauce (or more to taste)
1/4 teaspoon black pepper
Sesame seeds, for garnish
Green onions, sliced, for garnish

Instructions:

Preheat your air fryer to 400°F (200°C).
In a small bowl, whisk together soy sauce, hoisin sauce, honey, rice vinegar, garlic, ginger, sriracha, and black pepper.
Place the pork chops in a large ziplock bag and pour the marinade over them. Seal the bag and gently massage to coat the pork chops in the marinade. Let them marinate for at least 30 minutes, or up to overnight.
Remove the pork chops from the marinade, shaking off any excess, and discard the remaining marinade.
Place the pork chops in the air fryer basket in a single layer, leaving some space in between them for air circulation.
Cook the pork chops for 12-15 minutes, flipping them halfway through, until the internal temperature reaches 145°F (63°C).
Remove the pork chops from the air fryer and let them rest for 5 minutes before serving.
Garnish with sesame seeds and sliced green onions, if desired.
Enjoy your flavorful and juicy Southeast-Asian pork chops!

227. Here's an air fryer recipe for Mexican pork chops with black beans:

Ingredients:

4 bone-in pork chops
1 tbsp chili powder

1 tsp cumin
1 tsp garlic powder
1 tsp onion powder
Salt and pepper, to taste
1 can black beans, drained and rinsed
1 can dice tomatoes with green chilies, drained
1/4 cup chopped cilantro
Juice of 1 lime
1 avocado, diced

Instructions:

Preheat the air fryer to 400°F (200°C).
In a small bowl, mix together the chili powder, cumin, garlic powder, onion powder, salt, and pepper.
Rub the seasoning mixture over both sides of the pork chops.
Place the pork chops in the air fryer basket and cook for 10-12 minutes, flipping halfway through, until cooked through and the internal temperature reaches 145°F (63°C).
While the pork chops are cooking, mix together the black beans, diced tomatoes, cilantro, lime juice, and diced avocado in a bowl.
Serve the pork chops with the black bean and avocado mixture on top. Enjoy!
228. here's a recipe for roasted pork chops with mushrooms in the air fryer:

Ingredients:

4 bone-in pork chops
1 cup sliced mushrooms
1 tablespoon olive oil
1 teaspoon garlic powder
1 teaspoon onion powder
1 teaspoon paprika
1/2 teaspoon salt
1/4 teaspoon black pepper

Instructions:

Preheat the air fryer to 400°F (200°C).
In a small bowl, mix together the garlic powder, onion powder, paprika, salt, and black pepper.
Rub the spice mixture all over the pork chops.
Place the pork chops in the air fryer basket.
Add the sliced mushrooms around the pork chops.
Drizzle the olive oil over the pork chops and mushrooms.
Cook for 10-12 minutes, flipping the pork chops halfway through, until the internal temperature of the pork reaches 145°F (63°C).
Remove from the air fryer and let rest for a few minutes before serving. Enjoy!

229. Here's an air fryer recipe for Italian-style apple pork chops:

Ingredients:

4 bone-in pork chops
1 large apple, sliced
1/4 cup Italian dressing
2 cloves garlic, minced
1 tsp dried rosemary
1 tsp dried thyme
Salt and pepper, to taste

Instructions:

Preheat the air fryer to 400°F (200°C).
Season the pork chops with salt and pepper.
In a small bowl, whisk together the Italian dressing, minced garlic, dried rosemary, and dried thyme.
Place the pork chops in the air fryer basket and brush with the Italian dressing mixture.
Add the sliced apple to the air fryer basket.
Air fry for 12-15 minutes, flipping the pork chops halfway through, until the internal temperature reaches 145°F (63°C).
Let the pork chops rest for a few minutes before serving with the cooked apple slices on top.
Enjoy your delicious Italian-style apple pork chops!

230. Here's an air fryer recipe for sweet French pork chops with blue cheese:

Ingredients:

4 bone-in pork chops
1/2 cup honey
2 tbsp Dijon mustard
2 tbsp apple cider vinegar
1/2 tsp dried thyme
1/2 tsp garlic powder
Salt and pepper, to taste
1/2 cup crumbled blue cheese

Instructions:

Preheat the air fryer to 400°F (200°C).
In a small bowl, whisk together the honey, Dijon mustard, apple cider vinegar, thyme, garlic powder, salt, and pepper.
Brush the pork chops with the honey mustard glaze.
Place the pork chops in the air fryer basket and cook for 10 minutes.
Flip the pork chops and brush with more of the glaze.
Sprinkle the crumbled blue cheese over the pork chops.
Cook for another 5-7 minutes, or until the pork chops are cooked through and the cheese is melted and bubbly.
Serve immediately with your favorite sides. Enjoy!

231. Here's an air fryer recipe for spicy-sweet pork chops:

Ingredients:

4 boneless pork chops
1/4 cup honey
1/4 cup soy sauce
1/4 cup sriracha sauce
2 tablespoons brown sugar
1 teaspoon garlic powder
1/2 teaspoon ground ginger
Salt and pepper, to taste

Instructions:

Preheat the air fryer to 400°F (200°C).
In a mixing bowl, whisk together the honey, soy sauce, sriracha sauce, brown sugar, garlic powder, and ground ginger.
Season the pork chops with salt and pepper on both sides.
Dip each pork chop into the sauce mixture, making sure it is well-coated.
Place the pork chops in the air fryer basket in a single layer.
Cook for 8-10 minutes on one side, then flip the pork chops over and cook for another 8-10 minutes on the other side, or until the internal temperature of the pork reaches 145°F (63°C).
Remove from the air fryer and let the pork chops rest for 3-5 minutes before serving.
Enjoy your spicy-sweet pork chops!

232. Here's an air fryer recipe for juicy double-cut pork chops:

Ingredients:

2 double-cut pork chops
1 tablespoon olive oil
1 teaspoon garlic powder
1 teaspoon paprika
1 teaspoon salt
1/2 teaspoon black pepper

Instructions:

Preheat your air fryer to 380°F (190°C).
Rub both sides of the pork chops with olive oil.
In a small bowl, mix the garlic powder, paprika, salt, and black pepper.
Rub the seasoning mixture all over the pork chops.
Place the pork chops in the air fryer basket and cook for 12-14 minutes, flipping once halfway through, or until the internal temperature of the pork reaches 145°F (63°C).
Let the pork chops rest for 5 minutes before slicing and serving.
Enjoy your juicy double-cut pork chops straight from the air fryer!

233. Here's an air fryer recipe for stuffed pork chops:

Ingredients:

4 bone-in pork chops, about 1-inch thick
4 ounces cream cheese, softened
1/4 cup grated Parmesan cheese
2 cloves garlic, minced
1/4 cup chopped fresh parsley
1/4 teaspoon salt
1/4 teaspoon black pepper
1/2 cup panko breadcrumbs
1 tablespoon olive oil

Instructions:

Preheat your air fryer to 380°F.
In a mixing bowl, combine cream cheese, Parmesan cheese, garlic, parsley, salt, and pepper.
Use a sharp knife to make a slit in the thickest part of each pork chop, creating a pocket.
Stuff each pork chop with 1/4 of the cheese mixture, using toothpicks to secure the opening.
In a shallow dish, combine panko breadcrumbs and olive oil.
Roll each stuffed pork chop in the breadcrumb mixture, pressing the crumbs onto the chops.

Place the stuffed pork chops in the air fryer basket, making sure they are not touching.
Air fry for 15 to 20 minutes, or until the internal temperature of the pork reaches 145°F.
Let the stuffed pork chops rest for a few minutes before serving. Enjoy!

234. Here's an air fryer recipe for pork escalopes with beet & cabbage salad:

Ingredients:

4 pork escalopes
1 cup bread crumbs
1/2 cup grated Parmesan cheese
1/2 teaspoon garlic powder
1/2 teaspoon onion powder
1/2 teaspoon paprika
1/2 teaspoon salt
1/4 teaspoon black pepper
2 tablespoons olive oil
2 beets, peeled and sliced into thin strips
1/2 head of cabbage, sliced into thin strips
1/4 cup apple cider vinegar
2 tablespoons honey
1 tablespoon Dijon mustard
Salt and pepper, to taste

Instructions:

Preheat the air fryer to 375°F (190°C).
In a shallow dish, mix together the bread crumbs, Parmesan cheese, garlic powder, onion powder, paprika, salt, and black pepper.
Brush each pork escalope with olive oil and dredge in the breadcrumb mixture, pressing the mixture onto the pork to ensure it sticks.
Place the breaded pork in the air fryer basket and cook for 12-15 minutes, flipping halfway through, or until the pork is cooked through and the coating is golden brown and crispy.
While the pork cooks, prepare the salad by mixing together the beets, cabbage, apple cider vinegar, honey, Dijon mustard, salt, and pepper in a bowl.
Serve the cooked pork escalopes hot with the beet and cabbage salad on the side. Enjoy!

235. Here's an Air Fryer recipe for Bavarian-style Crispy Pork Schnitzel:

Ingredients:

4 pork loin chops (boneless)
1 cup all-purpose flour
2 tsp. paprika
2 tsp. garlic powder
1 tsp. salt
1 tsp. black pepper
3 eggs
1 cup breadcrumbs
1/4 cup grated Parmesan cheese
Cooking spray

Instructions:

Preheat your air fryer to 375°F (190°C).
In a bowl, mix the flour, paprika, garlic powder, salt, and black pepper.
In another bowl, whisk the eggs.

In a third bowl, mix the breadcrumbs and Parmesan cheese.
Coat each pork chop in the flour mixture, shaking off any excess. Then dip it into the eggs, followed by the breadcrumb mixture, pressing it down to ensure it sticks.
Place the pork chops in the air fryer basket, leaving some space between them.
Spray the pork chops with cooking spray.
Cook in the air fryer for 10-12 minutes, flipping once halfway through, until golden brown and cooked through.
Serve hot with your favorite sides and toppings, such as mashed potatoes and gravy, sauerkraut, or lingonberry sauce. Enjoy!

236. Here's an air fryer recipe for Italian Pork Scallopini:

Ingredients:

4 boneless pork loin chops, pounded to 1/4 inch thickness
1/2 cup all-purpose flour
1 teaspoon salt
1/2 teaspoon black pepper
2 tablespoons olive oil
1 tablespoon butter
1/4 cup dry white wine
1/4 cup chicken broth
1/4 cup fresh lemon juice
2 tablespoons capers, drained
2 tablespoons chopped fresh parsley

Instructions:

Preheat your air fryer to 400°F (200°C).
In a shallow dish, mix the flour, salt, and pepper.
Dredge each pork chop in the flour mixture, shaking off any excess.
In a separate bowl, whisk together the white wine, chicken broth, lemon juice, and capers.
In a large skillet, heat the olive oil and butter over medium-high heat.
Cook the pork chops in the skillet for 2-3 minutes per side, until golden brown and crispy.
Transfer the pork chops to the air fryer basket and cook for an additional 5-6 minutes, until cooked through.
Remove the pork chops from the air fryer and place them on a serving plate.
Pour the wine mixture into the skillet and bring it to a boil.
Cook the sauce for 1-2 minutes, until it has thickened slightly.
Pour the sauce over the pork chops and sprinkle with fresh parsley before serving. Enjoy!

237. Here's an air fryer recipe for Provençal pork medallions:

Ingredients:

4 boneless pork loin medallions, about 1 inch thick
1 teaspoon dried thyme
1 teaspoon dried rosemary
1 teaspoon dried oregano
1 teaspoon garlic powder
1/2 teaspoon salt
1/4 teaspoon black pepper
2 tablespoons olive oil
1 tablespoon lemon juice
1 tablespoon Dijon mustard

Instructions:

Preheat your air fryer to 400°F (200°C).
In a small bowl, mix the thyme, rosemary, oregano, garlic powder, salt, and black pepper.
Rub the spice mixture all over the pork medallions.
In another small bowl, whisk together the olive oil, lemon juice, and Dijon mustard.
Brush the pork medallions with the olive oil mixture.
Place the pork medallions in the air fryer basket and cook for 8 to 10 minutes, flipping once halfway through cooking.
Once the pork medallions are cooked through and nicely browned, remove them from the air fryer and let them rest for a few minutes before serving.
For a complete Provençal meal, serve the pork medallions with a side of ratatouille and a glass of rosé wine. Enjoy!

238. Here's an air fryer recipe for thyme pork escalopes:

Ingredients:

4 pork escalopes
2 tablespoons olive oil
2 garlic cloves, minced
1 tablespoon fresh thyme leaves
Salt and pepper to taste

Instructions:

Preheat your air fryer to 400°F (200°C).
In a small bowl, mix the olive oil, minced garlic, fresh thyme leaves, salt, and pepper.
Brush both sides of the pork escalopes with the thyme mixture.
Place the pork escalopes in the air fryer basket and cook for 8-10 minutes, flipping halfway through, or until the internal temperature of the pork reaches 145°F (63°C).
Serve hot with your favorite sides.
Enjoy your delicious thyme pork escalopes made in the air fryer!

239. here's an air fryer recipe for Philippine-style pork belly:

Ingredients:

1 lb pork belly, sliced into 1-inch thick pieces
3 cloves garlic, minced
1/4 cup soy sauce
1/4 cup vinegar
2 tbsp brown sugar
1 tsp black pepper
1 tsp paprika
1 tsp chili flakes
1 bay leaf
1/4 cup water

Instructions:

In a mixing bowl, combine garlic, soy sauce, vinegar, brown sugar, black pepper, paprika, chili flakes, and bay leaf. Mix well.
Add pork belly pieces to the marinade and coat evenly. Let it marinate in the refrigerator for at least 1 hour, or overnight for best results.
Preheat your air fryer to 375°F.
Remove the pork belly from the marinade and shake off any excess marinade. Reserve the marinade.

Place the pork belly in the air fryer basket in a single layer, making sure they don't touch each other. Cook for 8-10 minutes.
After 8-10 minutes, take the basket out and flip the pork belly pieces. Brush the reserved marinade on top of the pork belly.
Return the basket to the air fryer and cook for an additional 5-6 minutes, or until the pork is cooked through and the skin is crispy.
Serve hot with rice and your favorite dipping sauce. Enjoy!

240. Here's an air fryer recipe for pork sandwiches with bacon and cheddar:

Ingredients:

4 boneless pork chops
Salt and pepper
1 cup flour
2 eggs, beaten
2 cups panko breadcrumbs
Cooking spray
8 slices bacon
4 brioche buns
4 slices cheddar cheese
Mayonnaise
Mustard
Lettuce and tomato (optional)

Instructions:

Preheat the air fryer to 400°F.
Season the pork chops with salt and pepper.
Place the flour in a shallow dish, the beaten eggs in a second shallow dish, and the panko breadcrumbs in a third shallow dish.
Dredge each pork chop in the flour, then dip in the beaten eggs, and finally coat in the panko breadcrumbs.
Place the pork chops in the air fryer basket and spray them with cooking spray.
Cook the pork chops for 12-15 minutes, flipping halfway through, until golden brown and cooked through.
While the pork chops are cooking, cook the bacon in a skillet until crispy.
To assemble the sandwiches, spread mayonnaise and mustard on the brioche buns.
Top each bun with a pork chop, a slice of cheddar cheese, and two slices of bacon.
Add lettuce and tomato if desired.
Serve hot and enjoy!

241. Here's an air fryer recipe for herbed pork belly:

Ingredients:

1 lb pork belly, sliced into 1-inch pieces
1 tsp dried rosemary
1 tsp dried thyme
1 tsp garlic powder
1/2 tsp salt
1/4 tsp black pepper
1 tbsp olive oil

Instructions:

In a small bowl, mix the rosemary, thyme, garlic powder, salt, and black pepper.

Rub the spice mixture all over the pork belly slices, making sure they are evenly coated.
Place the pork belly slices in the air fryer basket, making sure they are not touching each other.
Brush the pork belly slices with olive oil.
Air fry the pork belly at 400°F for 10-12 minutes, flipping halfway through, until crispy and golden brown.
Remove the pork belly slices from the air fryer and let them cool for a few minutes before serving.
Serve the herbed pork belly as an appetizer or main dish with your favorite sides. Enjoy!

242. Here's an air fryer recipe for beef steak strips with tomato sauce:

Ingredients:

1 lb beef steak strips
2 tablespoons olive oil
Salt and pepper to taste
1/2 cup tomato sauce
1/4 cup water
1 tablespoon Worcestershire sauce
1 tablespoon Dijon mustard
1 tablespoon honey
1 tablespoon soy sauce
1 teaspoon garlic powder
1 teaspoon onion powder

Instructions:

Preheat your air fryer to 400°F (200°C) for 5 minutes.
In a mixing bowl, combine the olive oil, salt, and pepper. Add the beef steak strips and toss to coat.
Place the steak strips in the air fryer basket and cook for 6-8 minutes, flipping halfway through.
While the steak strips are cooking, mix the tomato sauce, water, Worcestershire sauce, Dijon mustard, honey, soy sauce, garlic powder, and onion powder in a small bowl.
When the steak strips are done, transfer them to a serving dish and pour the tomato sauce mixture over them.
Serve hot and enjoy!

243. here's an air fryer recipe for effortless beef short ribs:

Ingredients:

2 lbs beef short ribs
Salt and black pepper, to taste
1 tbsp olive oil
1/2 cup beef broth
2 tbsp soy sauce
1 tbsp honey
2 cloves garlic, minced
1/2 tsp smoked paprika

Instructions:

Preheat your air fryer to 360°F.
Season the beef short ribs with salt and black pepper.
Brush the ribs with olive oil and place them in the air fryer basket in a single layer.
Air fry the ribs for 10 minutes.
In a small bowl, whisk together the beef broth, soy sauce, honey, garlic, and smoked paprika.
After 10 minutes, flip the ribs and brush them with the sauce.
Air fry for another 10-15 minutes or until the ribs are cooked to your desired level of doneness.
Serve hot with any additional sauce on top.

Enjoy your delicious and effortless beef short ribs!

244. Here's an air fryer recipe for ginger-garlic beef ribs with hot sauce:

Ingredients:

2 lbs beef ribs
2 tbsp grated ginger
2 tbsp minced garlic
1/4 cup soy sauce
1/4 cup honey
2 tbsp rice vinegar
1 tsp sesame oil
1/2 tsp black pepper
Hot sauce, for serving

Instructions:

Preheat your air fryer to 375°F.
In a mixing bowl, whisk together the ginger, garlic, soy sauce, honey, rice vinegar, sesame oil, and black pepper.
Coat the beef ribs in the mixture and let them marinate for at least 30 minutes, or up to overnight.
Place the beef ribs in the air fryer basket, making sure to leave some space between each rib.
Air fry for 25-30 minutes, flipping the ribs halfway through, until the ribs are crispy and browned on the outside and cooked through on the inside.
Serve the beef ribs with hot sauce on the side for dipping. Enjoy!

245. Here's an air fryer recipe for beef koftas in tomato sauce:

Ingredients:

1 lb ground beef
1 small onion, finely chopped
2 garlic cloves, minced
2 tablespoons chopped fresh parsley
1 tablespoon chopped fresh mint
1 teaspoon ground cumin
1/2 teaspoon ground cinnamon
Salt and pepper to taste
1 can (14 oz) crushed tomatoes
1/2 cup beef broth
1 tablespoon tomato paste
1 tablespoon olive oil

Instructions:

In a large mixing bowl, combine ground beef, chopped onion, minced garlic, chopped parsley, chopped mint, ground cumin, ground cinnamon, salt, and pepper. Mix well until all ingredients are well combined.
Shape the mixture into small meatballs or koftas and place them on a plate. Place the plate in the fridge for 15-20 minutes to chill.
Preheat your air fryer to 360°F.
Place the chilled koftas in the air fryer basket in a single layer. Cook for 8-10 minutes, flipping once, until browned and cooked through.
In a small bowl, whisk together crushed tomatoes, beef broth, tomato paste, and olive oil.
Pour the tomato sauce over the cooked koftas into the air fryer basket.
Return the air fryer basket to the air fryer and cook for an additional 5-7 minutes, until the tomato sauce is hot and bubbly.

Serve the beef koftas with tomato sauce, garnished with additional fresh herbs if desired.

246. Here's an air fryer recipe for beef meatballs with cranberry sauce:

Ingredients:

1 lb ground beef
1/2 cup breadcrumbs
1/4 cup chopped onion
1 egg
1 tsp salt
1/2 tsp black pepper
1/2 cup cranberry sauce
1/4 cup ketchup
1 tbsp Worcestershire sauce
1/4 cup water

Instructions:

Preheat the air fryer to 375°F.
In a mixing bowl, combine the ground beef, breadcrumbs, chopped onion, egg, salt, and black pepper. Mix well to combine.
Shape the mixture into 1-inch meatballs and place them in the air fryer basket.
Air fry the meatballs for 10-12 minutes, or until cooked through.
While the meatballs are cooking, make the cranberry sauce by mixing the cranberry sauce, ketchup, Worcestershire sauce, and water in a small saucepan.
Cook the cranberry sauce over medium heat for 5-7 minutes, or until it thickens slightly.
Serve the meatballs with the cranberry sauce on top.
Enjoy your delicious beef meatballs with cranberry sauce!

247. Here's an air fryer recipe for Greek-style beef meatballs:

Ingredients:

1 pound ground beef
1/2 cup breadcrumbs
1/4 cup crumbled feta cheese
1/4 cup chopped fresh parsley
1/4 cup chopped fresh mint
2 cloves garlic, minced
1 egg
1 teaspoon salt
1/2 teaspoon black pepper
Tzatziki sauce, for serving

Instructions:

Preheat your air fryer to 375°F.
In a large mixing bowl, combine the ground beef, breadcrumbs, feta cheese, parsley, mint, garlic, egg, salt, and black pepper. Mix well to combine.
Using your hands, form the mixture into 1 1/2-inch meatballs.
Place the meatballs in the air fryer basket in a single layer, leaving some space in between each meatball.
Air fry the meatballs for 10-12 minutes, flipping them over halfway through until they are browned and cooked through.
Serve the meatballs hot with tzatziki sauce for dipping.
Enjoy your Greek-style beef meatballs made in the air fryer!

248. Here's an air fryer recipe for Mexican beef cabbage wraps:

Ingredients:

1 lb ground beef
1 tbsp chili powder
1 tsp ground cumin
1 tsp smoked paprika
1/2 tsp garlic powder
1/2 tsp onion powder
1/4 tsp salt
1/4 tsp black pepper
1/2 head green cabbage, leaves separated and thick stem removed
1/2 cup shredded Mexican cheese blend
1/4 cup chopped fresh cilantro
1 avocado, diced
1 lime, cut into wedges

Instructions:

Preheat the air fryer to 400°F (200°C).
Mix the ground beef, chili powder, cumin, smoked paprika, garlic powder, onion powder, salt, and black pepper in a large bowl.
Form the beef mixture into small meatballs and place them in the air fryer basket.
Cook the meatballs in the air fryer for 10-12 minutes, or until they are browned and cooked through.
While the meatballs are cooking, place the cabbage leaves in a large pot of boiling water and cook for 1-2 minutes, or until they are slightly wilted.
Remove the cabbage leaves from the pot and let them cool slightly.
To assemble the wraps, place a spoonful of shredded cheese and cilantro in the center of each cabbage leaf.
Top the cheese and cilantro with a few meatballs and diced avocado.
Squeeze a lime wedge over each wrap and serve immediately.

249. Here's an air fryer recipe for California-style street beef taco rolls:

Ingredients:

1 lb. ground beef
1/2 onion, chopped
1 tsp. garlic powder
1 tsp. chili powder
1/2 tsp. ground cumin
1/2 tsp. paprika
Salt and pepper to taste
1/2 cup shredded cheddar cheese
8 egg roll wrappers
Cooking spray
Toppings: diced tomatoes, shredded lettuce, sour cream, guacamole, salsa

Instructions:

Preheat the air fryer to 375°F (190°C).
In a large skillet over medium-high heat, cook the ground beef and onions until the beef is browned and the onions are soft and translucent.

Add the garlic powder, chili powder, cumin, paprika, salt, and pepper to the skillet and stir to combine.
Remove the skillet from the heat and stir in the shredded cheddar cheese until melted.
Lay out an egg roll wrapper on a clean surface and spoon about 1/4 cup of the beef mixture onto one end of the wrapper.
Roll the wrapper tightly around the filling, tucking in the sides as you go.
Repeat with the remaining egg roll wrappers and beef mixture.
Lightly spray the air fryer basket with cooking spray.
Arrange the taco rolls in the basket in a single layer, leaving some space between them.
Spray the tops of the taco rolls with cooking spray.
Air fry the taco rolls at 375°F (190°C) for 8-10 minutes or until golden brown and crispy.
Serve the taco rolls hot with your favorite toppings.

250. Here's an air fryer recipe for smoked beef burgers with hoisin sauce:

Ingredients:

1 lb ground beef
2 tbsp liquid smoke
1 tsp garlic powder
1 tsp onion powder
1 tsp smoked paprika
Salt and pepper to taste
4 burger buns
1/4 cup hoisin sauce
1/4 cup mayonnaise
1 tbsp sriracha sauce
Lettuce leaves
Sliced red onions
Sliced pickles

Instructions:

In a large bowl, combine ground beef, liquid smoke, garlic powder, onion powder, smoked paprika, salt, and pepper. Mix well.
Divide the mixture into 4 equal portions and shape each portion into a patty.
Preheat the air fryer to 375°F.
Place the patties in the air fryer basket and cook for 10-12 minutes, flipping once halfway through.
While the burgers are cooking, prepare the sauce by mixing hoisin sauce, mayonnaise, and sriracha sauce in a small bowl.
Toast the burger buns in the air fryer for the last 1-2 minutes of cooking time.
Assemble the burgers by placing a lettuce leaf on the bottom bun, followed by a beef patty, sliced red onions, pickles, and a dollop of the hoisin sauce mixture. Serve immediately.

251. here's an air fryer recipe for South American arepas with cilantro sauce:

Ingredients:

2 cups pre-cooked yellow cornmeal (Masarepa)
2 cups hot water
1 teaspoon salt
2 tablespoons vegetable oil
1/2 pound ground beef
1/4 teaspoon cumin
1/4 teaspoon paprika
Salt and pepper to taste
1/4 cup chopped onion
1/4 cup chopped red pepper

1/4 cup chopped green pepper
1/4 cup chopped fresh cilantro
1/2 cup sour cream
1 tablespoon lime juice
Salt and pepper to taste

Instructions:

Preheat the air fryer to 400°F (200°C).
In a large mixing bowl, combine the pre-cooked yellow cornmeal, hot water, and salt. Mix well until a smooth dough forms.
Form the dough into small balls (about 2-3 inches in diameter) and flatten them slightly to form patties.
Brush the patties with vegetable oil and place them in the air fryer basket. Cook for 10-12 minutes, flipping them halfway through, until they are golden brown and crispy.
While the arepas are cooking, prepare the beef filling. In a skillet over medium-high heat, cook the ground beef until it's browned and fully cooked. Add the cumin, paprika, salt, and pepper, and stir to combine. Add the chopped onion, red pepper, and green pepper, and continue cooking for a few more minutes until the vegetables are softened.
In a small mixing bowl, whisk together the sour cream, lime juice, chopped cilantro, and salt and pepper to taste.
To assemble the arepas, cut them in half and fill each half with the beef mixture. Drizzle the cilantro sauce on top and serve immediately.
Enjoy your South American arepas with cilantro sauce!

252. Here's an air fryer recipe for healthy burgers:

Ingredients:

1 lb ground chicken or turkey
1/2 cup diced onion
1/2 cup grated zucchini
1/2 cup grated carrot
1/4 cup chopped fresh parsley
1/4 cup almond flour
1 egg
1 tsp garlic powder
1 tsp salt
1/2 tsp black pepper

Instructions:

In a large bowl, mix ground chicken or turkey, diced onion, grated zucchini, grated carrot, chopped fresh parsley, almond flour, egg, garlic powder, salt, and black pepper.
Mix well with your hands until all ingredients are well combined.
Form the mixture into 4-6 burger patties.
Preheat your air fryer to 375°F.
Place the burger patties in the air fryer basket and cook for 12-15 minutes, flipping halfway through.
Serve the burgers with your favorite toppings such as lettuce, tomato, avocado, and mustard.
Enjoy your healthy burgers!

253. here's an air fryer recipe for classic beef meatloaf:

Ingredients:

1 pound ground beef
1/2 cup bread crumbs
1/2 cup milk

1/2 onion, finely chopped
1 egg
1 tablespoon Worcestershire sauce
1 tablespoon ketchup
1/2 teaspoon salt
1/4 teaspoon black pepper

Instructions:

Preheat your air fryer to 350°F (175°C).
In a large bowl, combine ground beef, bread crumbs, milk, onion, egg, Worcestershire sauce, ketchup, salt, and pepper.
Mix well until all ingredients are evenly incorporated.
Form the mixture into a loaf shape and place it in the air fryer basket.
Air fry for 30-35 minutes or until the internal temperature reaches 160°F (71°C).
Let the meatloaf rest for a few minutes before slicing and serving.
Optional: You can top the meatloaf with ketchup or barbecue sauce before air frying for a delicious glaze. Enjoy!

254. here's an air fryer recipe for Stefánia beef meatloaf:

Ingredients:

1 pound ground beef
1/2 pound ground pork
1/2 cup breadcrumbs
1/2 cup milk
1 egg
1 onion, grated
1 clove garlic, minced
1 tsp paprika
1 tsp salt
1/2 tsp black pepper
4 slices of bacon

Instructions:

Preheat your air fryer to 350°F (175°C).
In a large bowl, mix the ground beef, ground pork, breadcrumbs, milk, egg, grated onion, minced garlic, paprika, salt, and black pepper until well combined.
Shape the mixture into a loaf shape and place it in the air fryer basket.
Wrap the bacon slices around the meatloaf, tucking the ends underneath.
Air fry the meatloaf for 25-30 minutes or until the internal temperature reaches 160°F (71°C).
Remove the meatloaf from the air fryer and let it rest for a few minutes before slicing and serving.
Enjoy your delicious Stefánia beef meatloaf!

255. Here's an air fryer recipe for homemade hot beef satay:

Ingredients:

1 lb beef sirloin, cut into thin strips
2 tbsp vegetable oil
1 tbsp sesame oil
1 tbsp soy sauce
1 tbsp fish sauce
2 tbsp red curry paste
2 tbsp brown sugar

1 tbsp lime juice
1/4 tsp ground cumin
1/4 tsp ground coriander
1/4 tsp ground turmeric
1 garlic clove, minced
1 small shallot, finely chopped
Skewers

Instructions:

In a mixing bowl, combine vegetable oil, sesame oil, soy sauce, fish sauce, red curry paste, brown sugar, lime juice, ground cumin, ground coriander, minced garlic, and finely chopped shallot. Mix well.
Add the beef strips into the bowl and coat them evenly with the marinade. Cover and refrigerate for at least 30 minutes, or up to 2 hours.
Preheat your air fryer to 400°F (200°C).
Thread the marinated beef strips onto skewers.
Place the skewers in the air fryer basket and cook for 8-10 minutes, flipping the skewers halfway through cooking.
Once done, remove the skewers from the air fryer basket and let them rest for 2-3 minutes before serving.
Enjoy your homemade hot beef satay!

256. here's an air fryer recipe for Argentinian beef empanadas:

Ingredients:

1 pound ground beef
1 onion, diced
1 red bell pepper, diced
1 green bell pepper, diced
2 cloves garlic, minced
1 teaspoon ground cumin
1/2 teaspoon smoked paprika
1/2 teaspoon dried oregano
1/4 teaspoon red pepper flakes
1 tablespoon tomato paste
1 tablespoon red wine vinegar
Salt and pepper to taste
1 package empanada dough (or homemade dough)
1 egg, beaten

Instructions:

Preheat the air fryer to 375°F (190°C).
In a large skillet, brown the ground beef over medium-high heat, breaking it up with a spatula, until no longer pink.
Add the onion, red and green bell peppers, and garlic to the skillet and cook until the vegetables are softened.
Add the cumin, smoked paprika, oregano, red pepper flakes, tomato paste, and red wine vinegar to the skillet and stir until well combined. Season with salt and pepper to taste.
On a lightly floured surface, roll out the empanada dough into 4-inch circles.
Place a spoonful of the beef filling in the center of each empanada circle.
Brush the edges of the empanada circles with beaten egg and fold them over to create a half-moon shape. Use a fork to crimp the edges and seal the empanadas closed.
Place the empanadas in the air fryer basket, making sure they are not touching. You may need to cook them in batches.
Air fry the empanadas for 10-12 minutes or until golden brown and crispy.

Serve hot with your favorite dipping sauce.

257. Here's an air fryer recipe for Mexican Chorizo and Beef Empanadas:

Ingredients:

1/2 pound ground beef
1/2 pound Mexican chorizo
1/2 cup diced onion
1/2 cup diced green bell pepper
1/2 cup diced red bell pepper
1/2 cup diced tomatoes
2 cloves garlic, minced
1/2 teaspoon ground cumin
1/2 teaspoon paprika
1/4 teaspoon chili powder
Salt and black pepper, to taste
1 package (2 sheets) prepared pie crust
1 egg, beaten
Queso fresco, crumbled (optional)
Fresh cilantro leaves, chopped (optional)

Instructions:

Preheat the air fryer to 375°F (190°C).
In a large skillet over medium-high heat, cook the ground beef and chorizo until browned and crumbled, about 8-10 minutes. Drain any excess fat.
Add the onions, bell peppers, tomatoes, garlic, cumin, paprika, chili powder, salt, and black pepper to the skillet. Cook until the vegetables are tender and the mixture is heated through about 5-7 minutes. Remove from heat and set aside.
Unroll the pie crusts and cut out circles using a cookie cutter or the rim of a glass. Re-roll the scraps and cut out additional circles until all the dough is used up.
Spoon 1-2 tablespoons of the meat mixture onto each circle. Fold the dough over to create a half-moon shape and crimp the edges with a fork to seal.
Brush the empanadas with the beaten egg.
Place the empanadas in the air fryer basket, making sure they don't touch each other. Cook for 8-10 minutes or until golden brown and crispy.
Remove the empanadas from the air fryer and let them cool for a few minutes. Serve with crumbled Queso fresco and chopped cilantro, if desired. Enjoy!

258. Here's an air fryer recipe for cheesy Italian beef meatloaf:

Ingredients:

1 lb ground beef
1/2 cup Italian-seasoned breadcrumbs
1/4 cup milk
1/4 cup grated Parmesan cheese
1/2 cup shredded mozzarella cheese
1/4 cup chopped fresh parsley
2 cloves garlic, minced
1 tsp dried oregano
1/2 tsp salt
1/4 tsp black pepper
1 egg
Marinara sauce, for serving

Instructions:

Preheat your air fryer to 375°F.
In a large bowl, combine the ground beef, breadcrumbs, milk, Parmesan cheese, mozzarella cheese, parsley, garlic, oregano, salt, pepper, and egg. Mix well to combine.
Shape the mixture into a loaf and place it in the air fryer basket.
Cook the meatloaf in the air fryer for 20-25 minutes, until it reaches an internal temperature of 160°F.
Let the meatloaf cool for a few minutes before slicing and serving with marinara sauce.
Enjoy your cheesy Italian beef meatloaf cooked to perfection in your air fryer!

259. Here's an air fryer recipe for mini beef sausage rolls:

Ingredients:

1 lb ground beef
1/2 cup breadcrumbs
1 egg, beaten
1/4 cup milk
1/2 onion, finely chopped
1 clove garlic, minced
1 tsp dried thyme
1 tsp dried rosemary
1/2 tsp salt
1/4 tsp black pepper
1 sheet frozen puff pastry, thawed
1 egg yolk, beaten with 1 tsp water

Instructions:

Preheat your air fryer to 400°F (200°C).
In a large bowl, mix ground beef, breadcrumbs, egg, milk, onion, garlic, thyme, rosemary, salt, and black pepper until well combined.
Roll out the puff pastry on a lightly floured surface and cut it into 6 rectangles.
Place a heaping tablespoon of the beef mixture on one end of each rectangle and roll up tightly, tucking in the ends.
Brush each sausage roll with the egg yolk mixture.
Place the sausage rolls in the air fryer basket, leaving space between them.
Air fry for 10-12 minutes, or until golden brown and cooked through.
Serve hot with your favorite dipping sauce. Enjoy!

260. Here's an air fryer recipe for garlic steak with Mexican salsa:

Ingredients:

1 pound flank steak
1 teaspoon salt
1 teaspoon black pepper
1 teaspoon garlic powder
1 teaspoon onion powder
1 teaspoon cumin
1 teaspoon chili powder
2 tablespoons olive oil
1/2 red onion, diced
1 jalapeño, diced
1 lime, juiced
1/4 cup chopped fresh cilantro

Instructions:

Preheat your air fryer to 400°F.
In a small bowl, mix the salt, black pepper, garlic powder, onion powder, cumin, and chili powder.
Rub the spice mixture onto both sides of the flank steak.
Drizzle the olive oil over the steak and use your hands to rub it into the meat.
Place the steak in the air fryer basket and cook for 10-12 minutes for medium-rare, or until your desired doneness is reached.
While the steak is cooking, prepare the salsa. In a medium bowl, mix the diced red onion, diced jalapeño, lime juice, and chopped cilantro.
Once the steak is done cooking, let it rest for 5 minutes before slicing it against the grain.
Serve the steak with the salsa on top or the side.
Enjoy your garlic steak with Mexican salsa!

261. Air Fryer Beef Steak with Mustard Sauce Recipe:

Ingredients:

2 beef steaks
Salt and pepper
2 tbsp olive oil
2 tbsp Dijon mustard
1 tbsp honey
1 tbsp red wine vinegar
1 garlic clove, minced
1/2 tsp dried thyme

Instructions:

Preheat your air fryer to 400°F (200°C).
Season both sides of the beef steaks with salt and pepper.
Place the steaks in the air fryer basket and drizzle with olive oil.
Air fry the steaks for 10-12 minutes for medium-rare or 12-15 minutes for medium-well, flipping them halfway through cooking.
While the steaks are cooking, prepare the mustard sauce by mixing the Dijon mustard, honey, red wine vinegar, minced garlic, and dried thyme in a small bowl.
Once the steaks are cooked to your desired doneness, remove them from the air fryer and let them rest for a few minutes.
Serve the steaks with the mustard sauce on the side. Enjoy!

262. Here's an air fryer recipe for chipotle rib-eye steak with avocado salsa:

Ingredients:

2 rib-eye steaks
1 tablespoon olive oil
1 teaspoon chipotle powder
1 teaspoon garlic powder
1 teaspoon smoked paprika
Salt and pepper to taste
For the avocado salsa:
2 ripe avocados, diced
1/2 cup cherry tomatoes, halved
1/4 cup chopped red onion
1/4 cup chopped cilantro
1 tablespoon lime juice

Salt and pepper to taste

Instructions:

Preheat your air fryer to 400°F (200°C).
In a small bowl, mix olive oil, chipotle powder, garlic powder, smoked paprika, salt, and pepper.
Rub the spice mixture over both sides of the rib-eye steaks.
Place the steaks in the air fryer basket and cook for 10-12 minutes, flipping halfway through.
While the steaks are cooking, make the avocado salsa. In a medium bowl, mix diced avocados, cherry tomatoes, red onion, cilantro, lime juice, salt, and pepper.
Once the steaks are done, let them rest for a few minutes before slicing.
Serve the sliced steak topped with avocado salsa.
Enjoy your chipotle rib-eye steak with avocado salsa!

263. Here's an air fryer recipe for gorgonzola rib eye steak:

Ingredients:

2 (8 oz) rib-eye steaks
Salt and pepper to taste
2 oz gorgonzola cheese, crumbled
1/4 cup heavy cream
1 tablespoon butter
1 tablespoon olive oil
1 garlic clove, minced
Fresh parsley, chopped (optional)

Instructions:

Preheat your air fryer to 400°F.
Season the rib-eye steaks with salt and pepper on both sides.
In a small saucepan, melt the butter over low heat. Add the minced garlic and cook for 1-2 minutes until fragrant.
Add the heavy cream and crumbled gorgonzola cheese to the saucepan. Cook, stirring occasionally, until the cheese has melted and the sauce has thickened.
Brush the steaks with olive oil on both sides and place them in the air fryer basket.
Cook the steaks for 7-10 minutes, depending on the desired level of doneness. Flip the steaks halfway through cooking.
Remove the steaks from the air fryer and let them rest for a few minutes.
Drizzle the gorgonzola sauce over the steaks and garnish with chopped parsley, if desired. Serve immediately.

264. Here's an air fryer recipe for Chimichurri New York steak:

Ingredients:

2 New York strip steaks
Salt and pepper
1/2 cup fresh parsley leaves, chopped
1/4 cup fresh oregano leaves, chopped
3 garlic cloves, minced
1/2 teaspoon red pepper flakes
1/2 cup olive oil
2 tablespoons red wine vinegar
Juice of 1/2 lime

Instructions:

Preheat your air fryer to 400°F (200°C).
Season the New York strip steaks with salt and pepper to taste.
Place the steaks in the air fryer basket and cook for 10-12 minutes for medium-rare or until they reach your desired level of doneness.
While the steaks are cooking, prepare the chimichurri sauce. In a bowl, mix the parsley, oregano, garlic, red pepper flakes, olive oil, red wine vinegar, and lime juice. Season with salt and pepper to taste.
When the steaks are done, remove them from the air fryer and let them rest for a few minutes.
Slice the steaks and serve with the chimichurri sauce on top. Enjoy!

265. Here's an air fryer recipe for tender rib eye steak:

Ingredients:

2 rib-eye steaks (1 inch thick)
1 tablespoon olive oil
1 tablespoon Montreal steak seasoning
Salt and pepper to taste

Instructions:

Preheat your air fryer to 400°F (200°C) for 5 minutes.
Rub the rib-eye steaks with olive oil on both sides.
Season the steaks with Montreal steak seasoning, salt, and pepper on both sides.
Place the seasoned steaks in the air fryer basket.
Cook the steaks for 10-12 minutes, flipping them halfway through the cooking time.
Once the steaks are cooked to your desired doneness, remove them from the air fryer and let them rest for a few minutes.
Slice the steaks against the grain and serve hot.
Note: Cooking times may vary depending on the thickness of your steaks and your air fryer model. Always check the internal temperature of your steak using a meat thermometer to ensure it reaches at least 145°F (63°C) for medium-rare, 160°F (71°C) for medium, and 170°F (77°C) for well-done.

266. Here's an air fryer recipe for parsley-crumbed beef strips:

Ingredients:

1 lb beef strips
1 cup panko breadcrumbs
1/4 cup chopped fresh parsley
1/2 tsp garlic powder
1/2 tsp paprika
1/2 tsp salt
1/4 tsp black pepper
2 eggs, beaten

Instructions:

Preheat the air fryer to 400°F (200°C).
In a shallow bowl, combine the panko breadcrumbs, parsley, garlic powder, paprika, salt, and black pepper.
Dip each beef strip in the beaten eggs, then coat with the breadcrumb mixture.
Place the coated beef strips in the air fryer basket in a single layer.
Cook for 8-10 minutes, or until the beef strips are cooked through and crispy on the outside.
Serve hot with your favorite dipping sauce.
Enjoy your delicious parsley-crumbed beef strips made in the air fryer!

267. Here's an air fryer recipe for pesto beef steaks:

Ingredients:

2 beef steaks (sirloin or ribeye)
2 tablespoons pesto sauce
Salt and pepper, to taste
Olive oil cooking spray

Instructions:

Preheat your air fryer to 400°F (200°C).
Season both sides of the beef steaks with salt and pepper.
Spread the pesto sauce evenly over the top of each steak.
Lightly spray the steaks with olive oil cooking spray.
Place the steaks in the air fryer basket and cook for 8-10 minutes, flipping halfway through.
Check the internal temperature of the steak using a meat thermometer, and cook for an additional 1-2 minutes if necessary to reach your desired level of doneness.
Let the steaks rest for a few minutes before slicing and serving.
Enjoy your delicious pesto beef steaks straight out of the air fryer!

268. Here's an air fryer recipe for beef with rice and broccoli:

Ingredients:

1 pound beef sirloin, sliced into thin strips
1 cup uncooked rice
2 cups water
2 cups broccoli florets
1 tablespoon olive oil
2 cloves garlic, minced
Salt and pepper, to taste
Soy sauce, for serving

Instructions:

Preheat the air fryer to 400°F.
In a pot, combine the rice and water. Bring to a boil, then reduce heat to low and cover. Cook for 18-20 minutes or until the rice is tender and the water has been absorbed.
While the rice is cooking, toss the beef strips with olive oil, minced garlic, salt, and pepper in a mixing bowl.
Arrange the seasoned beef strips in a single layer in the air fryer basket.
Air fry for 5-7 minutes or until the beef is cooked to your desired doneness, flipping the strips once halfway through.
Remove the beef from the air fryer and set aside.
Add the broccoli florets to the air fryer basket and air fry for 4-6 minutes or until tender-crisp.
To serve, divide the cooked rice, beef strips, and broccoli florets among four plates. Drizzle soy sauce over the beef, if desired. Enjoy!

269. Air Fryer French Style Entrecôte with Bordelaise Sauce Recipe:

Ingredients:

2 Entrecote steaks (about 1 inch thick)
2 tablespoons of olive oil
Salt and pepper to taste
1/2 cup red wine

1/2 cup beef stock
1/4 cup chopped shallots
2 garlic cloves, minced
1 tablespoon tomato paste
1 tablespoon butter

Instructions:

Preheat your air fryer to 400°F (200°C).
Rub both sides of the steaks with olive oil and season with salt and pepper.
Place the steaks in the air fryer basket and cook for 10-12 minutes for medium-rare, flipping halfway through.
While the steaks are cooking, prepare the Bordelaise sauce. In a saucepan, heat a tablespoon of olive oil over medium heat. Add the shallots and garlic, and cook until softened about 2-3 minutes.
Add the red wine and beef stock, and bring to a boil. Reduce the heat to low and let simmer until the liquid has reduced by half, about 8-10 minutes.
Add the tomato paste and stir until combined. Cook for another 2-3 minutes, then remove from heat and whisk in the butter until fully melted and incorporated.
Once the steaks are done, remove them from the air fryer and let them rest for a few minutes before slicing. Serve with the Bordelaise sauce drizzled over the top. Enjoy!

270. Here's an air fryer recipe for spicy sweet beef with veggie topping:

Ingredients:

1 lb beef sirloin, cut into thin strips
1/4 cup soy sauce
2 tablespoons honey
1 tablespoon sriracha sauce
1 teaspoon garlic powder
1 teaspoon onion powder
1 red bell pepper, sliced
1 green bell pepper, sliced
1 small red onion, sliced
Salt and black pepper
1 tablespoon olive oil

Instructions:

In a bowl, mix soy sauce, honey, sriracha sauce, garlic powder, and onion powder.
Add the beef strips to the bowl and toss to coat.
Preheat the air fryer to 400°F.
In a separate bowl, toss the sliced peppers and onions with olive oil, salt, and black pepper.
Add the marinated beef strips to the air fryer basket in a single layer.
Cook for 5-6 minutes, flipping halfway through.
Add the seasoned veggies to the air fryer basket and cook for an additional 4-5 minutes, stirring occasionally.
Once everything is cooked, remove it from the air fryer and serve hot.
Enjoy your spicy sweet beef with veggie topping!

271. Here's an air fryer recipe for sausage-stuffed beef rolls:

Ingredients:

4 thin beef steaks
4 sausages, casings removed
1/2 cup breadcrumbs

1/4 cup chopped parsley
1/4 cup grated Parmesan cheese
1 egg
Salt and pepper, to taste
Olive oil cooking spray

Instructions:

Preheat the air fryer to 375°F (190°C).
In a mixing bowl, combine the sausage meat, breadcrumbs, parsley, Parmesan cheese, egg, salt, and pepper.
Lay the beef steaks on a clean work surface and divide the sausage mixture evenly between them. Spread it in a thin layer, leaving a border around the edges.
Roll up each steak tightly, tucking in the sides as you go. Secure the rolls with toothpicks.
Spray the rolls with olive oil cooking spray on all sides.
Place the rolls in the air fryer basket, making sure they don't touch each other.
Cook for 10-12 minutes, flipping halfway through, until the beef is cooked through and the sausage filling is golden brown and crispy.
Remove the rolls from the air fryer basket and let them rest for 5 minutes.
Slice the rolls into 1-inch pieces and serve hot. Enjoy!

272. Here's an air fryer recipe for Thai roasted beef:

Ingredients:

1 lb beef roast, trimmed
2 tablespoons soy sauce
1 tablespoon fish sauce
1 tablespoon honey
2 tablespoons lime juice
1 tablespoon grated fresh ginger
2 cloves garlic, minced
1 tablespoon sesame oil
1 tablespoon red curry paste
Salt and pepper, to taste
Chopped fresh cilantro and sliced lime, for serving

Instructions:

Preheat your air fryer to 400°F.
In a small bowl, whisk together the soy sauce, fish sauce, honey, lime juice, ginger, garlic, sesame oil, red curry paste, salt, and pepper.
Brush the beef roast with the mixture, making sure to coat it thoroughly.
Place the beef roast in the air fryer basket and cook for 15-20 minutes, flipping halfway through, until the beef is cooked to your desired level of doneness.
Let the beef rest for a few minutes before slicing it thinly.
Serve the sliced beef with chopped cilantro and lime slices on the side.
Enjoy your flavorful and tender Thai roasted beef!

273. Here's an air fryer recipe for bloody Mary beef steak with avocado:

Ingredients:

2 beef steaks
1/4 cup vodka
1/4 cup tomato juice
1 tbsp Worcestershire sauce

1 tbsp hot sauce
1 tsp celery salt
1 tsp garlic powder
1 tsp smoked paprika
Salt and pepper to taste
1 avocado, diced

Instructions:

In a small bowl, whisk together the vodka, tomato juice, Worcestershire sauce, hot sauce, celery salt, garlic powder, smoked paprika, salt, and pepper.
Marinate the beef steaks in the bloody Mary mixture for at least 30 minutes.
Preheat the air fryer to 400°F (200°C).
Remove the steaks from the marinade and pat them dry with paper towels.
Place the steaks in the air fryer basket and cook for 8-10 minutes, flipping halfway through, or until they reach your desired doneness.
Let the steaks rest for 5 minutes before slicing them thinly.
Serve the sliced steak topped with diced avocado. Enjoy!

274. Here's an air fryer recipe for Mexican beef quesadillas:

Ingredients:

1 lb ground beef
1/2 tsp chili powder
1/2 tsp cumin
1/2 tsp paprika
1/2 tsp garlic powder
Salt and pepper to taste
4 large flour tortillas
1 cup shredded cheddar cheese
1/2 cup diced tomatoes
1/4 cup diced red onion
1/4 cup chopped fresh cilantro
1 avocado, diced

Instructions:

Preheat the air fryer to 375°F.
In a large skillet, brown the ground beef over medium heat. Add the chili powder, cumin, paprika, garlic powder, salt, and pepper, and stir to combine.
Place a tortilla on a flat surface and sprinkle 1/4 cup of cheese on one-half of the tortilla. Top with 1/4 of the beef mixture, 1/4 of the tomatoes, 1/4 of the red onion, and 1/4 of the cilantro.
Fold the tortilla in half and lightly press down on the edges to seal.
Repeat with the remaining tortillas and filling ingredients.
Place the quesadillas in the air fryer basket and cook for 5-6 minutes, until the cheese is melted and the tortillas are golden brown and crispy.
Remove from the air fryer and let cool for a few minutes before slicing into wedges.
Top with diced avocado and serve hot.
Enjoy your delicious and easy air fryer Mexican beef quesadillas!

275. here's a recipe for Korean beef bulgogi in the air fryer:

Ingredients:

1 pound beef sirloin, thinly sliced
1/4 cup soy sauce

2 tablespoons brown sugar
1 tablespoon sesame oil
1 tablespoon minced garlic
1 tablespoon minced ginger
1/2 teaspoon black pepper
2 green onions, chopped
1 tablespoon toasted sesame seeds
Vegetable oil for brushing

Instructions:

In a bowl, mix soy sauce, brown sugar, sesame oil, garlic, ginger, and black pepper.
Add the sliced beef to the bowl and stir to coat with the marinade. Cover and refrigerate for at least 30 minutes or up to overnight.
Preheat the air fryer to 400°F.
Remove the beef from the marinade and place on a plate.
Brush the air fryer basket with vegetable oil and place the beef slices in the basket, making sure they are not touching.
Air fry the beef for 6-8 minutes, shaking the basket halfway through.
Remove the beef from the air fryer and sprinkle with chopped green onions and sesame seeds.
Serve the beef bulgogi with rice and your favorite side dishes. Enjoy!

276. Here's an air fryer recipe for beef and veggie mix with hoisin sauce:

Ingredients:

1 pound beef sirloin, thinly sliced
1 red bell pepper, thinly sliced
1 green bell pepper, thinly sliced
1 onion, thinly sliced
2 garlic cloves, minced
1 tablespoon vegetable oil
1 tablespoon cornstarch
2 tablespoons hoisin sauce
1 tablespoon soy sauce
1 tablespoon honey
1 tablespoon rice vinegar
1 teaspoon sesame oil
Salt and pepper, to taste

Instructions:

Preheat the air fryer to 400°F (200°C).
In a large bowl, whisk together the cornstarch, hoisin sauce, soy sauce, honey, rice vinegar, sesame oil, salt, and pepper until well combined.
Add the beef slices to the bowl and toss until evenly coated with the marinade. Set aside.
In a separate bowl, toss the sliced red and green bell peppers and onion with the vegetable oil and minced garlic until evenly coated.
Arrange the beef slices and vegetable mixture in a single layer in the air fryer basket.
Cook in the air fryer for 8-10 minutes, flipping once halfway through, until the beef is cooked through and the vegetables are tender and slightly charred.
Serve hot and enjoy!

278. Here's an air fryer recipe for a beef roast with red potatoes:

Ingredients:

2 lbs beef roast
1 lb baby red potatoes, halved
1 onion, chopped
3 cloves garlic, minced
1 tsp dried thyme
1 tsp dried rosemary
1 tsp smoked paprika
1/2 tsp salt
1/4 tsp black pepper
2 tbsp olive oil

Instructions:

Preheat the air fryer to 400°F.
In a small bowl, mix the thyme, rosemary, smoked paprika, salt, and black pepper.
Rub the beef roast with 1 tablespoon of olive oil, then rub the spice mixture all over the roast.
Place the roast in the air fryer basket and cook for 20 minutes.
In a medium bowl, toss the halved red potatoes and chopped onion with the remaining 1 tablespoon of olive oil and minced garlic.
After the beef roast has cooked for 20 minutes, add the seasoned red potatoes and onions to the air fryer basket, spreading them out around the roast.
Cook for an additional 15-20 minutes or until the beef roast is cooked to your desired level of doneness and the potatoes are tender and browned.
Remove the beef roast and potatoes from the air fryer and let the roast rest for 5-10 minutes before slicing and serving.
Enjoy your delicious air fryer beef roast with red potatoes!

279. Here's a recipe for beef steak au Poivre in the air fryer:

Ingredients:

2 beef steaks (about 1 inch thick)
2 tbsp black peppercorns
1 tbsp olive oil
1 tbsp butter
1/2 cup beef broth
1/2 cup heavy cream
Salt, to taste

Instructions:

Preheat your air fryer to 400°F (200°C).
Crush the peppercorns with a mortar and pestle or in a plastic bag with a rolling pin.
Season the steaks with salt and coat both sides with the crushed peppercorns, pressing them onto the meat.
Brush both sides of the steaks with olive oil.
Place the steaks in the air fryer basket and cook for 8-10 minutes medium-rare or longer if you prefer your steak well done.
Remove the steaks from the air fryer and let them rest for a few minutes.
While the steaks are resting, melt the butter in a saucepan over medium heat.
Add the beef broth to the saucepan and let it simmer until it reduces by half.
Add the heavy cream to the saucepan and let it simmer until it thickens.
Serve the steaks with the creamy peppercorn sauce on top.
Enjoy your delicious beef steak au poivre!

280. Here's an air fryer recipe for fusion flank steak with Mexican dressing:

Ingredients:

1 pound flank steak
1 tablespoon olive oil
1 teaspoon ground cumin
1 teaspoon chili powder
1/2 teaspoon garlic powder
Salt and pepper, to taste
1/4 cup cilantro, chopped
1/4 cup lime juice
1/4 cup sour cream
1/4 cup mayonnaise
1/4 cup salsa
1 jalapeño pepper, seeded and finely chopped

Instructions:

Preheat your air fryer to 400°F (200°C).
In a small bowl, mix the cumin, chili powder, garlic powder, salt, and pepper.
Rub the spice mixture all over the flank steak.
Brush the steak with olive oil.
Place the steak in the air fryer basket and cook for 10-12 minutes for medium-rare doneness or longer for your desired level of doneness.
While the steak is cooking, prepare the Mexican dressing by whisking together the cilantro, lime juice, sour cream, mayonnaise, salsa, and jalapeño pepper in a bowl.
When the steak is done, remove it from the air fryer and let it rest for a few minutes before slicing it against the grain.
Serve the sliced steak with the Mexican dressing on top. Enjoy!

281. Here's an air fryer recipe for pesto beef rolls with spinach:

Ingredients:

4 thin beef steaks
4 tablespoons of pesto sauce
4 cups of fresh spinach leaves
Salt and pepper, to taste
Toothpicks

Instructions:

Preheat your air fryer to 375°F (190°C).
Place a beef steak between two pieces of parchment paper and use a meat mallet to pound the steak until it's thin and even in thickness.
Repeat with the other three steaks.
Season the steaks with salt and pepper to taste.
Spread 1 tablespoon of pesto sauce on each steak, leaving about 1/2 inch of space around the edges.
Place a handful of fresh spinach leaves on top of the pesto sauce.
Starting at one end, roll up the steak tightly and secure it with a toothpick.
Repeat with the remaining steaks.
Place the beef rolls in the air fryer basket and cook for 12-15 minutes, or until the beef is cooked through and the outside is crispy.
Serve hot and enjoy!

282. Here's an air fryer recipe for beef with veggies and oyster sauce:

Ingredients:

1 pound beef, sliced into thin strips
1 red bell pepper, sliced into thin strips
1 green bell pepper, sliced into thin strips
1 onion, sliced into thin strips
3 cloves garlic, minced
2 tablespoons oyster sauce
1 tablespoon soy sauce
1 teaspoon sugar
1 teaspoon cornstarch
2 tablespoons vegetable oil
Salt and pepper, to taste

Instructions:

Preheat your air fryer to 400°F (200°C) for 5 minutes.
In a mixing bowl, combine the oyster sauce, soy sauce, sugar, and cornstarch. Mix until well combined.
Add the beef strips to the bowl and mix well, making sure each piece is coated in the sauce mixture.
In another mixing bowl, toss the red and green bell peppers and onion with the vegetable oil and minced garlic.
Season the beef and veggies with salt and pepper, to taste.
Place the beef strips in the air fryer basket and cook for 5-7 minutes, flipping halfway through.
After 5-7 minutes, add the veggies to the air fryer basket and cook for an additional 5-7 minutes or until the beef is cooked through and the veggies are tender.
Serve hot with steamed rice or noodles.

283. Here's an air fryer recipe for beer-dredged corned beef:

Ingredients:

1 (3-4 pound) corned beef brisket
1 cup of beer (lager or stout)
1 tbsp whole-grain mustard
2 tbsp honey
2 cloves garlic, minced
1 tsp dried thyme
Salt and black pepper, to taste

Instructions:

Preheat the air fryer to 350°F (175°C).
Rinse the corned beef brisket under cold water to remove any excess salt.
Pat dry the brisket with paper towels.
In a small bowl, whisk together the beer, whole-grain mustard, honey, minced garlic, dried thyme, salt, and black pepper.
Place the corned beef brisket in the air fryer basket and pour the beer mixture over it.
Cover the air fryer basket with aluminum foil and place it in the air fryer.
Cook the corned beef brisket for 45 minutes.
After 45 minutes, remove the aluminum foil from the air fryer basket and continue cooking the corned beef brisket for another 15 minutes or until the internal temperature reaches 145°F (63°C).
Remove the corned beef brisket from the air fryer basket and let it rest for 10 minutes before slicing it thinly against the grain.
Serve with your favorite sides and enjoy!

284. here's an air fryer recipe for yummy London broil with parsley butter:

Ingredients:

1 pound London broil
Salt and pepper, to taste
2 tablespoons olive oil
1/4 cup butter, softened
2 tablespoons chopped fresh parsley

Instructions:

Preheat your air fryer to 400°F (200°C).
Season the London broil with salt and pepper on both sides.
Rub olive oil all over the London broil and place it in the air fryer basket.
Cook for 8-10 minutes for medium-rare or until the desired doneness, flipping once halfway through cooking.
Meanwhile, in a small bowl, mix softened butter and chopped parsley.
Once the London broil is done, remove it from the air fryer basket and let it rest for a few minutes.
Slice the London broil against the grain and serve with a dollop of parsley butter on top.
Enjoy your yummy London broil with parsley butter!

285. Here's an air fryer recipe for lamb meatballs with roasted veggie bake:

Ingredients:

1 pound ground lamb
1/2 cup breadcrumbs
1 egg
2 cloves garlic, minced
1 tablespoon chopped fresh rosemary
1 teaspoon ground cumin
1/2 teaspoon salt
1/4 teaspoon black pepper
1 zucchini, chopped
1 red bell pepper, chopped
1 yellow bell pepper, chopped
1 onion, chopped
2 tablespoons olive oil
Salt and pepper, to taste

Instructions:

Preheat your air fryer to 350°F.
In a large mixing bowl, combine the ground lamb, breadcrumbs, egg, garlic, rosemary, cumin, salt, and pepper. Mix well.
Roll the mixture into small meatballs, about 1-2 tablespoons each.
Arrange the meatballs in the air fryer basket, leaving space between them for even cooking.
Air fry the meatballs for 10-12 minutes, until they are browned and cooked through.
While the meatballs cook, toss the chopped vegetables with olive oil, salt, and pepper in a separate bowl.
Spread the vegetables on a baking sheet and place them in the air fryer basket with the meatballs. Cook for an additional 10-15 minutes, until the vegetables are roasted and tender.
Serve the meatballs and vegetables together for a tasty and healthy meal.

286. here's an air fryer recipe for simple roasted beef with herbs:

Ingredients:

1 lb beef roast (such as sirloin, tenderloin, or rib eye)
1 tbsp olive oil
1 tsp dried rosemary
1 tsp dried thyme
1 tsp garlic powder
1 tsp salt
1/2 tsp black pepper

Instructions:

Preheat the air fryer to 400°F (200°C).
Rub the beef roast with olive oil and sprinkle with rosemary, thyme, garlic powder, salt, and black pepper.
Place the beef roast in the air fryer basket and cook for 12-15 minutes for medium-rare, or until the internal temperature reaches 130°F (54°C) using a meat thermometer.
Remove the beef roast from the air fryer and let it rest for 5-10 minutes before slicing and serving.
Enjoy your simple and flavorful roasted beef with herbs!

287. Here's an air fryer recipe for crunchy beef escalopes:

Ingredients:

4 beef escalopes
1 cup breadcrumbs
1/2 cup grated parmesan cheese
1 tbsp dried oregano
1 tbsp dried basil
1/2 tsp garlic powder
Salt and pepper, to taste
2 eggs, beaten

Instructions:

Preheat the air fryer to 375°F (190°C).
In a shallow dish, mix the breadcrumbs, parmesan cheese, oregano, basil, garlic powder, salt, and pepper.
Dip each beef escalope into the beaten eggs, then coat with the breadcrumb mixture.
Place the coated escalopes in the air fryer basket in a single layer.
Air fry for 10-12 minutes, or until the escalopes are crispy and cooked through.
Serve hot with your favorite dipping sauce or sides.
Enjoy your crunchy beef escalopes cooked in the air fryer!

288. Here's an air fryer recipe for traditional lamb kabobs:

Ingredients:

1 lb. lamb, cut into 1-inch pieces
1/4 cup olive oil
2 tbsp. lemon juice
2 tbsp. minced garlic
1 tbsp. ground cumin
1 tbsp. ground coriander
1 tsp. smoked paprika
1/2 tsp. salt
1/4 tsp. black pepper
1 red onion, cut into 1-inch pieces
1 red bell pepper, cut into 1-inch pieces

1 green bell pepper, cut into 1-inch pieces
8-10 wooden skewers, soaked in water for 30 minutes

Instructions:

In a bowl, whisk together the olive oil, lemon juice, garlic, cumin, coriander, paprika, salt, and black pepper.
Add the lamb pieces to the bowl and toss to coat.
Thread the marinated lamb, red onion, and bell peppers onto the soaked wooden skewers.
Preheat your air fryer to 375°F (190°C).
Place the skewers in the air fryer basket in a single layer.
Air fry for 8-10 minutes or until the lamb is cooked to your desired level of doneness, flipping the skewers halfway through cooking.
Serve hot with your favorite dipping sauce. Enjoy!

289. Here's an air fryer recipe for wiener beef schnitzel:

Ingredients:

4 thin-sliced beef cutlets
1/2 cup all-purpose flour
1/2 tsp salt
1/2 tsp black pepper
2 large eggs, beaten
1 cup panko breadcrumbs
Cooking spray
Lemon wedges, for serving
Instructions:
Preheat the air fryer to 400°F (200°C).
In a shallow dish, mix the flour, salt, and pepper.
In another shallow dish, beat the eggs.
In a third shallow dish, add the panko breadcrumbs.
Dip each beef cutlet in the flour mixture, then in the beaten eggs, and finally in the panko breadcrumbs, making sure to coat each cutlet evenly.
Spray the air fryer basket with cooking spray, and place the breaded cutlets in the basket.
Cook for 10-12 minutes, flipping the cutlets halfway through, until golden brown and cooked through.
Serve with lemon wedges and your favorite side dishes.
Enjoy your crispy and delicious wiener beef schnitzel!

290. Here's an air fryer recipe for beef liver with onions:

Ingredients:

4 slices of beef liver
1 large onion, sliced
1/4 cup all-purpose flour
1/2 teaspoon salt
1/4 teaspoon black pepper
1/4 teaspoon paprika
2 tablespoons olive oil

Instructions:

Preheat your air fryer to 375°F (190°C).
In a small bowl, mix the flour, salt, black pepper, and paprika.
Dredge each liver slice in the flour mixture until well coated.
Place the liver slices in the air fryer basket, making sure they are not touching.

Drizzle the olive oil over the liver slices and top with the sliced onions.
Air fry for 10-12 minutes, flipping halfway through the cooking time, until the liver is cooked through and the onions are caramelized.
Serve hot and enjoy!

291. here's an air fryer recipe for African minty lamb kofta:

Ingredients:

1 lb ground lamb
1/2 onion, finely chopped
2 cloves garlic, minced
1/4 cup breadcrumbs
1 egg
1 tsp cumin
1 tsp paprika
1 tsp coriander
1/2 tsp salt
1/4 tsp black pepper
1/4 cup fresh mint leaves, chopped
Olive oil spray

Instructions:

Preheat the air fryer to 375°F.
In a mixing bowl, combine ground lamb, chopped onion, minced garlic, breadcrumbs, egg, cumin, paprika, coriander, salt, black pepper, and fresh mint leaves. Mix well.
Divide the lamb mixture into 8 equal portions and form them into oblong patties.
Lightly spray the air fryer basket with olive oil spray.
Place the lamb kofta patties in the air fryer basket in a single layer, leaving a little space in between each patty.
Air fry the lamb kofta for 10-12 minutes, or until the internal temperature reaches 160°F.
Serve hot with your favorite dipping sauce or side dish. Enjoy!

292. here's an air fryer recipe for lamb chops with lemony couscous:

Ingredients:

4 lamb chops
1 tsp olive oil
1 tsp dried oregano
Salt and pepper to taste
1/2 cup couscous
3/4 cup boiling water
1 tbsp lemon juice
1 tsp lemon zest
1 tbsp chopped fresh parsley

Instructions:

Preheat your air fryer to 375°F (190°C).
Season the lamb chops with olive oil, dried oregano, salt, and pepper.
Place the lamb chops in the air fryer basket and cook for 8-10 minutes or until they reach your desired level of doneness.

While the lamb chops are cooking, prepare the couscous. In a heatproof bowl, pour the boiling water over the couscous and cover with a lid or plastic wrap. Let it sit for 5 minutes until the couscous is cooked through.
Fluff the couscous with a fork and add lemon juice, lemon zest, chopped parsley, and salt to taste.
Serve the lamb chops with the lemony couscous on the side.
Enjoy your delicious lamb chops with lemony couscous cooked in the air fryer!

293. Here's an air fryer recipe for easy lamb chop bites:

Ingredients:

8 lamb chops
2 tablespoons olive oil
1 teaspoon garlic powder
1 teaspoon paprika
1 teaspoon dried oregano
Salt and black pepper, to taste

Instructions:

Preheat the air fryer to 400°F.
Season the lamb chops with olive oil, garlic powder, paprika, oregano, salt, and pepper. Rub the seasoning all over the lamb chops.
Arrange the lamb chops in a single layer in the air fryer basket.
Air fry the lamb chops for 8-10 minutes, flipping them halfway through the cooking time, until they are cooked to your desired doneness.
Remove the lamb chops from the air fryer and let them rest for 2-3 minutes before serving.
Serve the lamb chop bites with a side salad or roasted vegetables for a delicious and easy meal. Enjoy!

294. here's an air fryer recipe for sweet and sour lamb strips:

Ingredients:

1 pound lamb leg, cut into thin strips
2 tablespoons cornstarch
Salt and pepper to taste
1/2 cup pineapple juice
2 tablespoons soy sauce
2 tablespoons rice vinegar
1 tablespoon honey
1 tablespoon ketchup
1 tablespoon cornstarch
1 tablespoon water
2 garlic cloves, minced
1 red bell pepper, sliced
1 green bell pepper, sliced
1/2 onion, sliced
1 tablespoon vegetable oil
Sesame seeds, for garnish

Instructions:

Preheat the air fryer to 400°F.
Season the lamb strips with salt and pepper and coat with cornstarch.
In a small bowl, whisk together the pineapple juice, soy sauce, rice vinegar, honey, ketchup, cornstarch, and water until smooth.

In a large bowl, combine the seasoned lamb strips, garlic, sliced red and green bell peppers, and sliced onion.
Pour the sweet and sour sauce over the lamb and vegetables and toss to coat.
Brush the air fryer basket with vegetable oil.
Place the lamb and vegetables in the air fryer basket and cook for 8-10 minutes, shaking the basket occasionally.
Remove from the air fryer and serve with cooked rice or noodles.
Garnish with sesame seeds and enjoy!

295. Here's an air fryer recipe for thyme lamb chops with asparagus:

Ingredients:

4 lamb chops
1 tablespoon olive oil
1 tablespoon chopped fresh thyme
Salt and pepper, to taste
1 bunch asparagus, trimmed
1 tablespoon balsamic vinegar

Instructions:

Preheat the air fryer to 400°F (200°C).
Season the lamb chops with salt, pepper, and chopped thyme.
Brush the lamb chops with olive oil.
Place the lamb chops in the air fryer basket and cook for 8-10 minutes, flipping halfway through.
While the lamb chops are cooking, toss the asparagus in balsamic vinegar and season with salt and pepper.
After the lamb chops have cooked for 8-10 minutes, remove them from the air fryer and set them aside to rest.
Add the asparagus to the air fryer basket and cook for 5 minutes, shaking the basket halfway through.
Serve the lamb chops with the roasted asparagus on the side. Enjoy!

296. Here's an air fryer recipe for lamb taquitos:

Ingredients:

1 lb ground lamb
1/2 onion, chopped
2 cloves garlic, minced
1 tsp cumin
1 tsp chili powder
1/2 tsp paprika
1/4 tsp cayenne pepper
Salt and pepper to taste
10-12 corn tortillas
1/2 cup crumbled feta cheese
1/2 cup chopped fresh cilantro
Cooking spray

Instructions:

Preheat your air fryer to 400°F.
In a large skillet, cook the ground lamb, onion, and garlic over medium heat until the lamb is browned and cooked through.
Add the cumin, chili powder, paprika, cayenne pepper, salt, and pepper to the skillet and stir to combine.

Place the corn tortillas on a clean work surface and spoon a few tablespoons of the lamb mixture onto the center of each tortilla. Add some crumbled feta cheese and chopped cilantro on top.
Roll the tortillas tightly around the filling to form taquitos.
Lightly spray the air fryer basket with cooking spray. Arrange the taquitos in a single layer in the basket, seam side down.
Spray the tops of the taquitos with cooking spray.
Cook in the air fryer for 8-10 minutes, or until the taquitos are crispy and golden brown.
Serve hot with your favorite dipping sauce. Enjoy!

POULTRY

297. Here's an air fryer recipe for spice-rubbed jerk chicken wings:

Ingredients:

2 lbs chicken wings
2 tbsp jerk seasoning
1 tsp paprika
1/2 tsp garlic powder
1/2 tsp onion powder
1/2 tsp salt
1/4 tsp black pepper
Cooking spray

Instructions:

Preheat the air fryer to 375°F (190°C).
In a small bowl, mix together the jerk seasoning, paprika, garlic powder, onion powder, salt, and black pepper.
Place the chicken wings in a large bowl and sprinkle the seasoning mixture over them, tossing to coat evenly.
Spray the air fryer basket with cooking spray.
Place the chicken wings in the basket in a single layer, making sure they are not touching.
Air fry the wings for 15-20 minutes, flipping them halfway through cooking until they are crispy and cooked through with an internal temperature of 165°F (74°C).
Serve hot with your favorite dipping sauce.
Enjoy your delicious and flavorful spice-rubbed jerk chicken wings!

298. Here's a recipe for sticky chicken wings with coleslaw in the air fryer:

Ingredients for the chicken wings:

2 lbs chicken wings
1 tbsp olive oil
1 tsp garlic powder
1 tsp paprika
1 tsp salt
1/2 tsp black pepper
1/4 cup honey
1/4 cup soy sauce
2 tbsp ketchup
1 tbsp sriracha sauce
1 tbsp rice vinegar
1 tbsp cornstarch
2 tbsp water

Ingredients for the coleslaw:

3 cups shredded cabbage
1/4 cup shredded carrots
1/4 cup chopped fresh cilantro
1/4 cup mayonnaise
1 tbsp apple cider vinegar
1 tsp sugar
Salt and pepper to taste

Directions:

Preheat the air fryer to 380°F.
Pat the chicken wings dry with paper towels.
In a small bowl, mix together the olive oil, garlic powder, paprika, salt, and black pepper. Rub the seasoning mixture all over the chicken wings.
Place the chicken wings in the air fryer basket in a single layer, and cook for 12 minutes.
While the chicken wings are cooking, prepare the sticky sauce. In a small saucepan, combine the honey, soy sauce, ketchup, sriracha sauce, and rice vinegar. Cook over medium heat until the sauce thickens, about 5 minutes.
In a small bowl, mix together the cornstarch and water. Add the cornstarch mixture to the sauce and cook for an additional 1-2 minutes until the sauce is thick and glossy.
Remove the chicken wings from the air fryer and brush them generously with the sticky sauce.
Return the chicken wings to the air fryer and cook for an additional 5-6 minutes, until the sauce is caramelized and the chicken wings are crispy.
In a large bowl, mix together the shredded cabbage, shredded carrots, chopped cilantro, mayonnaise, apple cider vinegar, sugar, salt, and pepper.
Serve the sticky chicken wings with the coleslaw on the side. Enjoy!

299. Here's an air fryer recipe for sweet chili and ginger chicken wings:

Ingredients:

2 lbs chicken wings, separated into wingettes and drumettes
1/2 cup sweet chili sauce
1/4 cup soy sauce
1 tbsp grated fresh ginger
1 tbsp minced garlic
1 tbsp rice vinegar
1 tbsp honey
1 tsp sesame oil
1/2 tsp red pepper flakes
Salt and pepper, to taste
Green onions, thinly sliced, for garnish

Instructions:

Preheat your air fryer to 400°F.
In a large bowl, whisk together the sweet chili sauce, soy sauce, grated ginger, garlic, rice vinegar, honey, sesame oil, red pepper flakes, salt, and pepper until well combined.
Add the chicken wings to the bowl and toss to coat evenly.
Place the chicken wings in the air fryer basket in a single layer.
Cook for 10 minutes, then flip the wings and cook for an additional 5-7 minutes until cooked through and crispy.
Garnish with thinly sliced green onions and serve immediately.
Enjoy your sweet and spicy chicken wings with a side of coleslaw or rice for a delicious meal!

300. Here's an air fryer recipe for crispy chicken wings with buffalo sauce:

Ingredients:

2 lbs chicken wings, separated into drumettes and flats
2 tbsp olive oil
1 tsp garlic powder
1 tsp onion powder
1 tsp paprika
1/2 tsp salt
1/2 tsp black pepper
1/2 cup buffalo sauce
2 tbsp butter
Ranch dressing and celery sticks, for serving

Instructions:

Preheat your air fryer to 400°F (200°C).
In a large bowl, toss the chicken wings with olive oil, garlic powder, onion powder, paprika, salt, and black pepper.
Place the chicken wings in the air fryer basket, making sure they are not touching. You may need to cook the wings in batches, depending on the size of your air fryer.
Cook the chicken wings for 12-15 minutes, flipping halfway through, or until they are golden brown and crispy.
While the chicken wings are cooking, melt the butter in a small saucepan over low heat. Add the buffalo sauce and stir to combine.
When the chicken wings are done, transfer them to a large bowl and toss with the buffalo sauce mixture until evenly coated.
Serve the chicken wings hot with ranch dressing and celery sticks on the side.
Enjoy your delicious and crispy chicken wings with buffalo sauce!

301. Here's a recipe for Italian Parmesan chicken wings with herbs in the air fryer:

Ingredients:

2 pounds of chicken wings, separated into flats and drumettes
1/2 cup all-purpose flour
1/2 cup grated Parmesan cheese
1 tablespoon dried oregano
1 tablespoon dried basil
1 tablespoon garlic powder
1/2 teaspoon salt
1/4 teaspoon black pepper
2 eggs, beaten
Cooking spray

Instructions:

Preheat the air fryer to 375°F.
In a large bowl, mix together the flour, Parmesan cheese, oregano, basil, garlic powder, salt, and black pepper.
Dip each chicken wing first into the beaten eggs, and then coat in the flour mixture.
Place the chicken wings in the air fryer basket, making sure they are not touching each other. You may need to cook them in batches.
Spray the chicken wings with cooking spray.
Air fry the chicken wings at 375°F for 12-15 minutes, flipping them halfway through, until they are golden brown and crispy.

Serve hot with your favorite dipping sauce. Enjoy!

302. Here's an air fryer recipe for Greek-style chicken wings:

Ingredients:

2 lbs chicken wings
2 tbsp olive oil
1 tbsp dried oregano
1 tbsp dried thyme
1 tbsp garlic powder
1 tsp salt
1/2 tsp black pepper
1/2 lemon, juiced

Instructions:

Preheat the air fryer to 400°F (200°C).
Pat the chicken wings dry with paper towels and place them in a large bowl.
Drizzle the olive oil over the wings and toss until coated.
In a small bowl, mix the oregano, thyme, garlic powder, salt, and black pepper.
Sprinkle the herb mixture over the wings and toss until evenly coated.
Place the wings in the air fryer basket in a single layer. Cook for 12-15 minutes, flipping halfway through, or until the wings are golden brown and cooked through.
Squeeze the lemon juice over the wings and serve hot.
Optional: Serve with tzatziki sauce or your favorite dipping sauce. Enjoy!

303. Here's an air fryer recipe for hot chili chicken wings:

Ingredients:

2 lbs chicken wings
2 tbsp chili powder
1 tsp cumin
1 tsp garlic powder
1 tsp onion powder
1/2 tsp smoked paprika
1/2 tsp salt
1/4 tsp black pepper
2 tbsp olive oil
1/4 cup hot sauce
2 tbsp unsalted butter, melted
Ranch or blue cheese dressing for dipping

Instructions:

Preheat the air fryer to 375°F.
In a small bowl, mix together chili powder, cumin, garlic powder, onion powder, smoked paprika, salt, and black pepper.
Pat chicken wings dry with paper towels and place in a large bowl.
Drizzle olive oil over the chicken wings and toss to coat evenly.
Sprinkle the spice mixture over the chicken wings and toss until evenly coated.
Place the chicken wings in the air fryer basket and cook for 12 minutes.
Flip the chicken wings and cook for an additional 12 minutes.
In a separate bowl, whisk together hot sauce and melted butter.
Once the chicken wings are done, toss them in the hot sauce mixture until evenly coated.
Serve hot with ranch or blue cheese dressing for dipping. Enjoy!

304. Air Fryer One Tray Parmesan Chicken Wings Recipe:

Ingredients:

2 lbs chicken wings, cut into flats and drumettes
1/2 cup grated parmesan cheese
1 tsp garlic powder
1 tsp onion powder
1 tsp paprika
1/2 tsp dried basil
1/2 tsp dried oregano
1/2 tsp dried thyme
1/2 tsp salt
1/4 tsp black pepper
1/4 cup olive oil

Instructions:

Preheat your air fryer to 400°F (200°C) for 5 minutes.
In a small bowl, mix together the parmesan cheese, garlic powder, onion powder, paprika, basil, oregano, thyme, salt, and black pepper.
Add the chicken wings to a large bowl and drizzle with olive oil. Toss to coat.
Sprinkle the parmesan cheese mixture over the chicken wings and toss to coat evenly.
Place the chicken wings in a single layer in the air fryer basket.
Cook for 10 minutes, then flip the chicken wings over and cook for an additional 10-12 minutes or until the chicken wings are golden brown and crispy.
Serve immediately and enjoy!

305. Here's a recipe for Korean-style chicken wings in the air fryer:

Ingredients:

2 lbs chicken wings, separated into flats and drumettes
1/2 cup cornstarch
1 tsp salt
1 tsp garlic powder
1/2 tsp black pepper
1/4 cup gochujang (Korean chili paste)
2 tbsp honey
2 tbsp soy sauce
1 tbsp rice vinegar
1 tbsp sesame oil
2 cloves garlic, minced
1-inch ginger, grated
1 tbsp sesame seeds
1 green onion, thinly sliced

Instructions:

In a large bowl, combine the cornstarch, salt, garlic powder, and black pepper. Add the chicken wings and toss until they are coated in the mixture.
Preheat the air fryer to 400°F (200°C). Spray the air fryer basket with cooking spray.
Arrange the chicken wings in a single layer in the air fryer basket. You may need to do this in batches, depending on the size of your air fryer.
Air fry the wings for 20 minutes, flipping them over halfway through.

While the wings are cooking, prepare the sauce. In a small bowl, whisk together the gochujang, honey, soy sauce, rice vinegar, sesame oil, garlic, and ginger.
Once the wings are done cooking, transfer them to a large bowl. Pour the sauce over the wings and toss until they are coated.
Return the wings to the air fryer basket and air fry for an additional 5 minutes, until the sauce is sticky and caramelized.
Remove the wings from the air fryer and sprinkle with sesame seeds and green onions. Serve hot.
Enjoy your delicious Korean-style chicken wings made in the air fryer!

306. Here's a recipe for Air Fryer Thai Tom Yum Wings:

Ingredients:

1 lb chicken wings
1 tbsp fish sauce
2 tbsp soy sauce
2 tbsp lime juice
2 tbsp brown sugar
2 tbsp chopped lemongrass
1 tbsp grated ginger
1 tbsp chopped garlic
1 tsp red chili flakes
1/4 cup chopped cilantro

Instructions:

Preheat the air fryer to 400°F (200°C).
In a mixing bowl, whisk together the fish sauce, soy sauce, lime juice, brown sugar, lemongrass, ginger, garlic, and red chili flakes.
Add the chicken wings to the bowl and toss until well coated with the marinade.
Place the chicken wings in the air fryer basket in a single layer, making sure they don't touch.
Cook for 15-20 minutes, flipping the wings halfway through cooking, until the wings are golden brown and crispy.
Once cooked, remove the wings from the air fryer and transfer to a plate.
Garnish the wings with chopped cilantro and serve hot.
Enjoy your delicious Air Fryer Thai Tom Yum Wings!

307. Here's an air fryer recipe for homemade chicken patties:

Ingredients:

1 pound ground chicken
1/4 cup breadcrumbs
1/4 cup grated Parmesan cheese
1 egg
1/2 teaspoon garlic powder
1/2 teaspoon onion powder
1/2 teaspoon salt
1/4 teaspoon black pepper

Instructions:

Preheat the air fryer to 400°F (200°C).
In a large bowl, combine the ground chicken, breadcrumbs, Parmesan cheese, egg, garlic powder, onion powder, salt, and black pepper. Mix until well combined.
Divide the mixture into 8 equal portions and shape each into a patty.
Spray the air fryer basket with cooking spray and place the patties in a single layer in the basket.

Cook the chicken patties for 10-12 minutes, flipping halfway through, or until they are golden brown and cooked through.
Serve hot with your favorite toppings or use them to make chicken burgers.
Enjoy your homemade chicken patties!

308. Here's an air fryer recipe for Mongolian chicken wings:

Ingredients:

2 lbs chicken wings
1/4 cup cornstarch
2 tbsp vegetable oil
1/4 cup soy sauce
1/4 cup brown sugar
2 tbsp honey
2 cloves garlic, minced
1 tsp ginger, minced
1/4 tsp red pepper flakes
2 green onions, sliced

Instructions:

Preheat your air fryer to 375°F (190°C).
In a large bowl, toss the chicken wings with cornstarch until they are fully coated.
Place the wings in the air fryer basket and cook for 20 minutes, flipping halfway through.
While the wings are cooking, prepare the sauce. In a small saucepan, combine the soy sauce, brown sugar, honey, garlic, ginger, and red pepper flakes. Cook over medium heat until the sugar has dissolved and the sauce has thickened, about 5 minutes.
Once the wings are done cooking, remove them from the air fryer basket and place them in a large bowl.
Pour the sauce over the wings and toss until they are fully coated.
Return the wings to the air fryer basket and cook for an additional 5 minutes, or until the sauce has caramelized and the wings are crispy.
Remove the wings from the air fryer and garnish with sliced green onions before serving. Enjoy!

309. Here is an air fryer recipe for chicken fingers with red mayo dip:

Ingredients:

1 lb boneless, skinless chicken breasts, cut into strips
1 cup all-purpose flour
1 tsp garlic powder
1 tsp paprika
1 tsp salt
1/2 tsp black pepper
2 eggs
1 tbsp water
2 cups panko breadcrumbs
Cooking spray
1/2 cup mayonnaise
1 tbsp ketchup
1 tsp hot sauce
1/4 tsp smoked paprika
1/4 tsp garlic powder
Salt and pepper, to taste

Instructions:

Preheat the air fryer to 400°F (200°C).
In a shallow bowl, whisk together the flour, garlic powder, paprika, salt, and black pepper.
In another shallow bowl, whisk together the eggs and water.
Place the panko breadcrumbs in a third shallow bowl.
Coat each chicken strip in the flour mixture, shaking off any excess.
Dip the chicken strip in the egg mixture, then coat it in the panko breadcrumbs.
Place the chicken strips in the air fryer basket, making sure they are not touching each other.
Spray the chicken strips with cooking spray.
Air fry for 8-10 minutes, flipping the chicken strips halfway through, until they are golden brown and cooked through.
While the chicken is cooking, make the red mayo dip by whisking together the mayonnaise, ketchup, hot sauce, smoked paprika, garlic powder, salt, and pepper in a small bowl.
Serve the chicken fingers with the red mayo dip on the side.
Enjoy your crispy and delicious chicken fingers with a flavorful dipping sauce!

310. Here's an air fryer recipe for chicken kebabs with a spicy sriracha dipping sauce:

Ingredients:

1 pound boneless, skinless chicken breasts, cut into bite-sized pieces
1 red bell pepper, cut into bite-sized pieces
1 yellow onion, cut into bite-sized pieces
1 tablespoon olive oil
1 teaspoon garlic powder
1 teaspoon smoked paprika
1/2 teaspoon salt
1/4 teaspoon black pepper
Bamboo skewers, soaked in water for 30 minutes

For the dipping sauce:

1/4 cup mayonnaise
2 tablespoons sriracha sauce
1 tablespoon honey
1 tablespoon lime juice
Pinch of salt

Instructions:

Preheat the air fryer to 400°F.
In a large bowl, combine the chicken pieces, bell pepper, onion, olive oil, garlic powder, smoked paprika, salt, and black pepper. Toss to coat evenly.
Thread the chicken, bell pepper, and onion onto the soaked bamboo skewers, alternating as desired.
Place the skewers in the air fryer basket in a single layer, and air fry for 10-12 minutes or until the chicken is cooked through and the vegetables are tender, flipping halfway through cooking.
While the chicken is cooking, prepare the dipping sauce by whisking together the mayonnaise, sriracha sauce, honey, lime juice, and salt in a small bowl.
Serve the chicken kebabs hot with the spicy sriracha dipping sauce on the side. Enjoy!

311. Here's an air fryer recipe for chicken meatballs with Farfalle pasta:

Ingredients:

1 lb ground chicken
1/4 cup breadcrumbs
1/4 cup grated Parmesan cheese
1 egg

1 tsp garlic powder
1 tsp onion powder
1/2 tsp dried oregano
1/2 tsp dried basil
Salt and pepper to taste
8 oz farfalle pasta
2 tbsp olive oil
2 cups tomato sauce
1/4 cup chopped fresh basil
Shredded Parmesan cheese (optional)

Instructions:

Preheat the air fryer to 400°F (200°C).
In a bowl, mix together ground chicken, breadcrumbs, Parmesan cheese, egg, garlic powder, onion powder, oregano, basil, salt, and pepper until well combined.
Form the mixture into small meatballs, about 1-2 inches in diameter.
Place the meatballs in the air fryer basket and cook for 10-12 minutes, flipping halfway through, until golden brown and cooked through.
While the meatballs are cooking, cook the farfalle pasta according to package instructions. Drain and toss with olive oil.
In a saucepan, heat tomato sauce over medium heat. Add chopped fresh basil and stir to combine.
Serve the meatballs over the pasta, topped with tomato sauce and shredded Parmesan cheese (if desired).
Enjoy your delicious and easy air fryer chicken meatballs with farfalle pasta!

312. Here's an air fryer recipe for Mexican jalapeño quesadillas:

Ingredients:

4 large flour tortillas
1 cup shredded Mexican blend cheese
1/2 cup cooked and crumbled chorizo
1 jalapeño pepper, seeded and chopped
1/4 cup chopped fresh cilantro
1 tablespoon olive oil

Instructions:

Preheat your air fryer to 375°F (190°C).
In a bowl, mix together the shredded cheese, cooked chorizo, chopped jalapeño, and cilantro.
Place a flour tortilla on a flat surface and spread 1/4 of the cheese mixture over one half of the tortilla.
Fold the tortilla in half to cover the cheese mixture and press the edges together to seal.
Repeat with the remaining tortillas and cheese mixture.
Brush the outside of each quesadilla with olive oil.
Place the quesadillas in the air fryer basket and cook for 5-7 minutes or until they are golden brown and the cheese is melted.
Serve hot with your favorite toppings, such as guacamole, salsa, or sour cream.
Enjoy your Mexican jalapeño quesadillas!

313. Here's an air fryer recipe for crispy breaded chicken bites:

Ingredients:

1 pound boneless, skinless chicken breasts, cut into bite-sized pieces
1 cup panko bread crumbs
1/2 cup all-purpose flour

1 teaspoon garlic powder
1 teaspoon paprika
1/2 teaspoon salt
1/4 teaspoon black pepper
2 large eggs, beaten
Cooking spray

Instructions:

Preheat the air fryer to 400°F (200°C).
In a shallow bowl, mix together the panko bread crumbs, all-purpose flour, garlic powder, paprika, salt, and black pepper.
In another shallow bowl, beat the eggs.
Dip each chicken piece into the beaten eggs, then coat in the breadcrumb mixture, pressing the crumbs onto the chicken to help them adhere.
Place the breaded chicken bites in a single layer in the air fryer basket, leaving space between each piece.
Spray the chicken with cooking spray.
Cook the chicken bites in the air fryer for 8-10 minutes, flipping halfway through, until golden brown and cooked through.
Serve hot with your favorite dipping sauce. Enjoy!

314. Here's an air fryer recipe for spiced chicken tacos:

Ingredients:

1 lb boneless, skinless chicken breast, cut into bite-sized pieces
2 tbsp olive oil
2 tsp chili powder
1 tsp cumin
1 tsp smoked paprika
1/2 tsp garlic powder
Salt and pepper, to taste
8 small corn tortillas
Toppings (such as shredded lettuce, diced tomato, sliced avocado, chopped cilantro, and lime wedges)

Instructions:

Preheat the air fryer to 400°F.
In a large bowl, combine the chicken, olive oil, chili powder, cumin, smoked paprika, garlic powder, salt, and pepper. Mix well to coat the chicken.
Place the chicken in a single layer in the air fryer basket. Cook for 10-12 minutes, flipping the chicken halfway through, until it is golden brown and cooked through.
While the chicken is cooking, warm the tortillas in the microwave or on a skillet.
Assemble the tacos with the chicken and your desired toppings. Serve immediately.
Enjoy your spiced chicken tacos!

315. Here is an air fryer recipe for Spanish-style crusted chicken fingers:

Ingredients:

1 pound boneless, skinless chicken breasts, cut into strips
1 cup panko breadcrumbs
1/4 cup grated Parmesan cheese
1 tablespoon smoked paprika
1/2 teaspoon garlic powder
1/2 teaspoon onion powder

1/2 teaspoon salt
1/4 teaspoon black pepper
2 eggs, beaten
Cooking spray

Instructions:

In a shallow bowl, mix together the panko breadcrumbs, Parmesan cheese, smoked paprika, garlic powder, onion powder, salt, and black pepper.
In another shallow bowl, beat the eggs.
Dip each chicken strip into the beaten eggs, then coat it in the panko mixture, pressing the breadcrumbs onto the chicken to help them stick.
Place the chicken strips in the air fryer basket, making sure they are not touching each other. You may need to cook them in batches depending on the size of your air fryer.
Spray the chicken strips with cooking spray.
Air fry at 375°F for 8-10 minutes, or until the chicken is cooked through and the coating is crispy and golden brown.
Serve with your favorite dipping sauce, such as a spicy tomato sauce or garlic aioli. Enjoy!

316. Here's a recipe for quinoa chicken nuggets in the air fryer:

Ingredients:

1 pound ground chicken
1 cup cooked quinoa
1/4 cup finely chopped onion
2 cloves garlic, minced
1/2 teaspoon salt
1/4 teaspoon black pepper
1/4 teaspoon paprika
1/4 teaspoon cumin
1/4 teaspoon dried oregano
1/4 teaspoon chili powder
1/4 cup all-purpose flour
2 eggs, beaten
1 cup panko breadcrumbs

Instructions:

In a large bowl, mix together the ground chicken, cooked quinoa, chopped onion, minced garlic, salt, black pepper, paprika, cumin, dried oregano, and chili powder until well combined.
Shape the mixture into small nuggets.
Place the flour, beaten eggs, and panko breadcrumbs into separate shallow bowls.
Dip each nugget first into the flour, then the beaten eggs, and finally the panko breadcrumbs, pressing the breadcrumbs onto the nuggets to adhere.
Preheat the air fryer to 375°F (190°C).
Place the breaded nuggets into the air fryer basket in a single layer, making sure they are not touching each other.
Cook for 8-10 minutes or until the nuggets are golden brown and crispy.
Serve immediately with your favorite dipping sauce.
Enjoy your crispy and healthy quinoa chicken nuggets!

317. here's a recipe for air fryer Rice Krispies chicken Goujons:

Ingredients:

2 boneless, skinless chicken breasts

1/2 cup all-purpose flour
2 eggs, beaten
1 1/2 cups Rice Krispies cereal, crushed
1/2 tsp paprika
1/2 tsp garlic powder
Salt and pepper, to taste
Cooking spray
Instructions:

Preheat your air fryer to 400°F (200°C).
Cut the chicken breasts into strips or nuggets.
In a bowl, mix the flour, paprika, garlic powder, salt, and pepper.
In another bowl, beat the eggs.
In a third bowl, crush the Rice Krispies cereal.
Dip each chicken strip into the flour mixture, then into the beaten eggs, and finally coat with the crushed Rice Krispies.
Place the chicken strips into the air fryer basket, making sure they are not touching each other.
Spray the chicken strips with cooking spray.
Cook for 8-10 minutes or until golden brown and crispy, flipping halfway through the cooking time.
Serve with your favorite dipping sauce.
Enjoy your crispy and flavorful air fryer rice Krispies chicken goujons!

318. Here's an air fryer recipe for San Antonio Taco Chicken Strips:

Ingredients:

1 pound boneless, skinless chicken breasts, cut into strips
1/4 cup all-purpose flour
1 teaspoon chili powder
1 teaspoon garlic powder
1/2 teaspoon cumin
1/2 teaspoon smoked paprika
1/4 teaspoon salt
1/4 teaspoon black pepper
1/4 cup buttermilk
1 cup crushed tortilla chips
Cooking spray

Instructions:

Preheat the air fryer to 375°F (190°C).
In a small bowl, mix together the flour, chili powder, garlic powder, cumin, smoked paprika, salt, and black pepper.
In a separate bowl, pour in the buttermilk.
Dip each chicken strip into the flour mixture, coating it well on all sides. Then dip the chicken strip into the buttermilk, and then into the crushed tortilla chips, pressing the chips onto the chicken to create a coating.
Spray the chicken strips with cooking spray on both sides.
Place the chicken strips in the air fryer basket, making sure not to overcrowd them. Cook for 10-12 minutes or until the chicken is cooked through and the coating is golden brown and crispy.
Serve with your favorite dipping sauce and enjoy!

319. Here's an air fryer recipe for harissa chicken sticks:

Ingredients:

1 pound chicken breast, cut into strips

2 tablespoons Harissa paste
1 tablespoon olive oil
1/2 teaspoon garlic powder
1/2 teaspoon smoked paprika
Salt and pepper, to taste
Wooden skewers, soaked in water for 30 minutes

Instructions:

In a bowl, mix together the harissa paste, olive oil, garlic powder, smoked paprika, salt, and pepper.
Add the chicken strips to the bowl and toss until they are evenly coated with the harissa mixture.
Thread the chicken strips onto the wooden skewers.
Preheat the air fryer to 375°F (190°C).
Place the chicken skewers in the air fryer basket and cook for 10-12 minutes, flipping once halfway through, until the chicken is cooked through and the outside is crispy.
Serve the harissa chicken sticks with your favorite dipping sauce and enjoy!

320. Here is a recipe for South Asian-inspired air fryer chicken strips:

Ingredients:

1 pound boneless, skinless chicken breasts, cut into strips
1/2 cup plain Greek yogurt
2 tablespoons lemon juice
1 tablespoon minced garlic
1 tablespoon grated ginger
1 teaspoon ground cumin
1 teaspoon ground coriander
1/2 teaspoon turmeric
1/4 teaspoon cayenne pepper
Salt and pepper, to taste
Cooking spray

Instructions:

In a large bowl, whisk together the Greek yogurt, lemon juice, garlic, ginger, cumin, coriander, turmeric, cayenne pepper, salt, and pepper.
Add the chicken strips to the bowl and toss to coat well with the marinade.
Cover the bowl and refrigerate for at least 1 hour (or up to 24 hours) to marinate.
Preheat the air fryer to 400°F.
Lightly spray the air fryer basket with cooking spray.
Remove the chicken strips from the marinade and shake off any excess.
Place the chicken strips in the air fryer basket in a single layer.
Cook for 8-10 minutes, flipping halfway through, until the chicken is cooked through and crispy on the outside.
Serve hot with your favorite dipping sauce, such as raita or mango chutney.

321. Here is a recipe for crunchy coconut chicken dippers in the air fryer:

Ingredients:

1 lb chicken tenders
1/2 cup all-purpose flour
1/2 tsp garlic powder
1/2 tsp paprika
1/2 tsp salt
1/4 tsp black pepper

2 eggs
1 1/2 cups unsweetened shredded coconut
Cooking spray

Instructions:

Preheat your air fryer to 400°F (200°C).
In a shallow dish, whisk together the flour, garlic powder, paprika, salt, and black pepper.
In another shallow dish, beat the eggs.
In a third shallow dish, place the shredded coconut.
Dip each chicken tender into the flour mixture, shaking off any excess.
Dip the chicken tender into the beaten egg, then into the shredded coconut, pressing the coconut onto the chicken to ensure it sticks.
Spray the chicken tenders with cooking spray.
Place the chicken tenders into the air fryer basket in a single layer, making sure they do not touch.
Cook the chicken tenders for 10-12 minutes, flipping them halfway through cooking, until they are golden brown and crispy.
Serve with your favorite dipping sauce.
Enjoy your delicious crunchy coconut chicken dippers!

322. Here's an air fryer recipe for popcorn chicken tenders:

Ingredients:

1 lb chicken tenders, cut into bite-sized pieces
1 cup all-purpose flour
1 tsp garlic powder
1 tsp onion powder
1 tsp paprika
1 tsp salt
1/2 tsp black pepper
2 eggs, beaten
2 cups plain breadcrumbs
Cooking spray

Instructions:

Preheat your air fryer to 375°F (190°C).
In a large bowl, mix together flour, garlic powder, onion powder, paprika, salt, and black pepper.
In a separate bowl, beat the eggs.
In another bowl, add the breadcrumbs.
Dip each chicken tender into the flour mixture, then into the beaten eggs, and finally into the breadcrumbs, making sure to coat each piece well.
Spray the basket of your air fryer with cooking spray.
Place the chicken tenders in the basket in a single layer. You may need to work in batches, depending on the size of your air fryer.
Spray the top of the chicken tenders with cooking spray.
Cook the chicken tenders for 8-10 minutes or until golden brown and cooked through, flipping halfway through.
Serve hot with your favorite dipping sauce.
Enjoy your crispy and delicious popcorn chicken tenders!

323. Here is an air fryer recipe for chicken skewers with yogurt dip:

Ingredients:

1 lb chicken breast, cut into bite-sized pieces

1/2 cup plain Greek yogurt
1 tbsp olive oil
1 tbsp lemon juice
1 garlic clove, minced
1/2 tsp paprika
1/2 tsp cumin
1/2 tsp salt
Bamboo skewers

For the yogurt dip:

1/2 cup plain Greek yogurt
1 tbsp lemon juice
1 garlic clove, minced
Salt and pepper, to taste

Instructions:

Preheat your air fryer to 375°F.
In a mixing bowl, combine the chicken pieces, Greek yogurt, olive oil, lemon juice, garlic, paprika, cumin, and salt. Mix well until the chicken is evenly coated with the yogurt mixture.
Thread the chicken pieces onto bamboo skewers, leaving a little space between each piece.
Place the chicken skewers in the air fryer basket, making sure they are not touching each other.
Air fry the chicken skewers for 10-12 minutes or until golden brown and cooked through.
While the chicken is cooking, prepare the yogurt dip by mixing together the Greek yogurt, lemon juice, garlic, salt, and pepper in a small bowl.
Serve the chicken skewers hot with the yogurt dip on the side. Enjoy!

324. here's an air fryer recipe for chicken pinches with salsa verde:

Ingredients:

1 lb boneless, skinless chicken breasts, cut into cubes
1 tbsp olive oil
1 tsp smoked paprika
1/2 tsp garlic powder
1/2 tsp onion powder
Salt and pepper to taste
Wooden skewers, soaked in water for 30 minutes
For the salsa verde:
1 cup fresh cilantro, chopped
1/4 cup fresh parsley, chopped
1 garlic clove, minced
1 tbsp capers, drained and chopped
2 tbsp fresh lime juice
1/4 cup olive oil
Salt and pepper to taste

Instructions:

Preheat the air fryer to 400°F.
In a bowl, mix the chicken cubes with olive oil, smoked paprika, garlic powder, onion powder, salt, and pepper.
Thread the chicken onto the skewers.
Place the skewers in the air fryer basket and cook for 8-10 minutes, flipping once halfway through.
While the chicken is cooking, prepare the salsa verde by combining all ingredients in a bowl and mixing well.

Serve the chicken pinchos with the salsa verde on the side for dipping. Enjoy!

325. here's a recipe for ranch cheesy chicken tenders made in the air fryer:

Ingredients:

1 pound chicken tenders
1 cup panko breadcrumbs
1/2 cup grated parmesan cheese
1/2 teaspoon garlic powder
1/2 teaspoon onion powder
1/2 teaspoon dried parsley
1/2 teaspoon dried dill
1/4 teaspoon salt
1/4 teaspoon black pepper
1/4 cup all-purpose flour
1 large egg
1 tablespoon milk
1/2 cup ranch dressing, divided

Instructions:

Preheat your air fryer to 400°F (200°C).
In a bowl, mix together the panko breadcrumbs, parmesan cheese, garlic powder, onion powder, parsley, dill, salt, and black pepper.
In a separate bowl, whisk together the egg, milk, and 1/4 cup of the ranch dressing.
Place the flour in another bowl.
Coat each chicken tender in the flour, then dip it into the egg mixture, and finally coat it in the breadcrumb mixture.
Place the chicken tenders in the air fryer basket, making sure they are not touching each other.
Cook for 10-12 minutes, flipping halfway through, until the chicken is cooked through and the coating is golden brown and crispy.
Serve the chicken tenders with the remaining ranch dressing for dipping.
Enjoy your delicious air fryer ranch cheesy chicken tenders!

326. Here's a recipe for crispy chicken tenders with hot aioli:

Ingredients:

1 lb. chicken tenders
1 cup all-purpose flour
1 tsp. paprika
1 tsp. garlic powder
1 tsp. onion powder
1 tsp. salt
1/2 tsp. black pepper
2 eggs, beaten
1 1/2 cups panko breadcrumbs
Cooking spray

For the hot aioli:

1/2 cup mayonnaise
1 tbsp. hot sauce
1 tbsp. honey
1/2 tsp. garlic powder
1/2 tsp. smoked paprika

Salt and pepper, to taste

Instructions:

Preheat the air fryer to 400°F.
In a shallow dish, mix the flour, paprika, garlic powder, onion powder, salt, and black pepper.
In another shallow dish, beat the eggs.
In a third shallow dish, place the panko breadcrumbs.
Dredge each chicken tender in the flour mixture, then dip it in the beaten eggs, and coat it in the panko breadcrumbs, pressing the breadcrumbs onto the chicken to adhere.
Spray the air fryer basket with cooking spray.
Place the chicken tenders in the air fryer basket in a single layer, leaving space between them.
Spray the chicken tenders with cooking spray.
Cook the chicken tenders in the air fryer for 8-10 minutes, flipping them halfway through, until they are golden brown and cooked through.
While the chicken tenders are cooking, prepare the hot aioli by mixing together all of the aioli ingredients in a small bowl.
Serve the hot chicken tenders with the hot aioli dipping sauce.

327. Here's a recipe for juicy chicken fillets with peppers in the air fryer:

Ingredients:

2 chicken fillets
1 red bell pepper
1 yellow bell pepper
1 green bell pepper
1 tsp garlic powder
1 tsp smoked paprika
1/2 tsp salt
1/4 tsp black pepper
2 tbsp olive oil

Instructions:

Preheat the air fryer to 375°F (190°C).
Cut the chicken fillets into thin strips and place them in a bowl.
Add the garlic powder, smoked paprika, salt, black pepper, and olive oil to the bowl and mix well to coat the chicken.
Cut the bell peppers into thin strips and add them to the bowl with the chicken. Mix well.
Place the chicken and peppers in the air fryer basket in a single layer.
Cook for 8-10 minutes or until the chicken is cooked through and the peppers are slightly charred, stirring once halfway through.
Serve hot and enjoy!
Note: You can adjust the seasoning according to your taste preferences. You can also add other vegetables such as onions or mushrooms if you like.

328. Here's an air fryer recipe for effortless chicken scallopini:

Ingredients:

4 boneless, skinless chicken breasts
Salt and pepper, to taste
1/2 cup all-purpose flour
1/2 tsp garlic powder
1/2 tsp dried oregano
1/4 cup grated parmesan cheese

1/4 cup breadcrumbs
1 egg, beaten
2 tbsp olive oil
1 lemon, sliced
2 tbsp chopped fresh parsley

Instructions:

Preheat your air fryer to 400°F.
Season the chicken breasts with salt and pepper.
In a shallow bowl, combine the flour, garlic powder, oregano, parmesan cheese, and breadcrumbs.
In another shallow bowl, beat the egg.
Dip each chicken breast in the beaten egg, then coat it in the flour mixture.
Place the chicken breasts in the air fryer basket and drizzle them with olive oil.
Air fry the chicken for 10-12 minutes, flipping once halfway through, until golden brown and cooked through.
Remove the chicken from the air fryer and let it rest for a few minutes.
Serve the chicken with lemon slices and chopped parsley.
Enjoy your effortless chicken scallopini!

329. Here is an air fryer recipe for balsamic chicken with green beans:

Ingredients:

4 boneless, skinless chicken breasts
1/4 cup balsamic vinegar
2 tbsp olive oil
1 tbsp honey
1 tsp Dijon mustard
1 tsp dried thyme
1/2 tsp salt
1/4 tsp black pepper
2 cups fresh green beans, trimmed
2 cloves garlic, minced

Instructions:

Preheat your air fryer to 375°F.
In a small bowl, whisk together balsamic vinegar, olive oil, honey, Dijon mustard, thyme, salt, and black pepper.
In a large bowl, toss the chicken breasts with half of the balsamic mixture. Add the green beans and garlic to the same bowl and toss to coat.
Arrange the chicken and green beans in the air fryer basket in a single layer.
Cook for 12-15 minutes, or until the chicken is cooked through and the green beans are tender and slightly crispy.
Remove the basket from the air fryer and drizzle the remaining balsamic mixture over the chicken and green beans.
Serve immediately and enjoy!

330. here's a recipe for Cajun chicken tenders made in the air fryer:

Ingredients:

1 lb chicken tenderloins
1 tbsp olive oil
1 tbsp paprika
1 tbsp garlic powder

1 tbsp onion powder
1 tbsp dried oregano
1 tbsp dried thyme
1 tsp cayenne pepper
Salt and pepper to taste

Instructions:

Preheat your air fryer to 400°F.
In a small bowl, mix together the olive oil, paprika, garlic powder, onion powder, oregano, thyme, cayenne pepper, salt, and pepper.
Coat each chicken tenderloin with the spice mixture.
Place the chicken tenderloins in the air fryer basket in a single layer.
Cook for 8-10 minutes, flipping halfway through, or until the chicken is cooked through and golden brown on the outside.
Serve with your favorite dipping sauce.
Enjoy your crispy and flavorful Cajun chicken tenders!

331. Here's an air fryer recipe for crispy chicken tenderloins:

Ingredients:

1 lb chicken tenderloins
1 cup all-purpose flour
1 tsp paprika
1 tsp garlic powder
1 tsp onion powder
1 tsp salt
1/2 tsp black pepper
2 eggs, beaten
1 cup panko breadcrumbs
Cooking spray

Instructions:

Preheat the air fryer to 400°F.
In a shallow bowl, mix together the flour, paprika, garlic powder, onion powder, salt, and black pepper.
Place the beaten eggs in another shallow bowl.
In a third shallow bowl, add the panko breadcrumbs.
Dip each chicken tenderloin first in the flour mixture, then in the beaten eggs, and finally in the panko breadcrumbs.
Place the breaded chicken tenderloins in the air fryer basket in a single layer, making sure they are not touching.
Spray the chicken tenderloins with cooking spray.
Cook for 8-10 minutes, flipping halfway through, until the chicken is cooked through and the coating is crispy.
Serve hot with your favorite dipping sauce.
Enjoy your crispy and delicious chicken tenderloins!

332. here's an air fryer recipe for almond-fried crispy chicken:

Ingredients:

1 lb boneless, skinless chicken breasts, cut into strips
1/2 cup almond flour
1/2 cup finely ground almond meal
1 tsp smoked paprika

1 tsp garlic powder
1/2 tsp salt
1/4 tsp black pepper
2 eggs
1 tbsp water
Cooking spray

Instructions:

In a shallow bowl, whisk together almond flour, almond meal, smoked paprika, garlic powder, salt, and black pepper.
In another shallow bowl, whisk together eggs and water.
Dip each chicken strip into the egg mixture, then into the almond flour mixture, pressing the coating onto the chicken to ensure it sticks.
Place the chicken strips in a single layer in the air fryer basket. Spray the chicken with cooking spray.
Air fry the chicken at 375°F for 10-12 minutes, flipping halfway through, or until golden brown and crispy.
Serve hot with your favorite dipping sauce. Enjoy!
Note: You can also use regular flour instead of almond flour and bread crumbs instead of almond meal.

333. Here's a recipe for Jerusalem Matzah & Chicken Schnitzels in the air fryer:

Ingredients:

4 sheets of Jerusalem matzah
4 boneless, skinless chicken breasts
2 eggs
1/2 cup of all-purpose flour
1/2 cup of breadcrumbs
1/2 tsp of paprika
1/2 tsp of garlic powder
1/2 tsp of onion powder
1/4 tsp of salt
1/4 tsp of black pepper
Cooking spray

Instructions:

Preheat the air fryer to 400°F (200°C).
Cut each chicken breast into 2-3 pieces of equal size.
Place the Jerusalem matzah in a food processor or blender and pulse until it turns into fine crumbs.
In a shallow bowl, whisk the eggs until beaten.
In another shallow bowl, mix the flour, paprika, garlic powder, onion powder, salt, and black pepper.
In a third shallow bowl, add the matzah crumbs.
Dip each piece of chicken in the flour mixture, shaking off any excess. Then, dip it into the beaten egg mixture and finally coat it with the matzah crumbs, pressing the crumbs onto the chicken to make sure it sticks.
Place the chicken pieces in the air fryer basket, making sure they are not touching each other. Lightly spray the chicken with cooking spray.
Air fry for 8-10 minutes, then flip the chicken and spray with more cooking spray. Continue to air fry for another 6-8 minutes or until the chicken is golden brown and cooked through.
Serve with your favorite dipping sauce and enjoy!

Note: You can also prepare the chicken in advance and store it in the refrigerator until you're ready to air fry.

334. Here is an air fryer recipe for chicken fillets with sweet chili adobo:

Ingredients:

4 chicken fillets
1/4 cup sweet chili sauce
1 tablespoon adobo sauce
1 teaspoon garlic powder
1/2 teaspoon onion powder
1/2 teaspoon salt
1/4 teaspoon black pepper
1 tablespoon olive oil

Instructions:

Preheat your air fryer to 375°F.
In a bowl, mix together the sweet chili sauce, adobo sauce, garlic powder, onion powder, salt, pepper, and olive oil until well combined.
Add the chicken fillets to the bowl and coat them with the sauce mixture.
Place the chicken fillets in the air fryer basket and cook for 10-12 minutes, flipping halfway through the cooking time.
Check that the internal temperature of the chicken has reached 165°F before removing from the air fryer.
Serve hot with your favorite sides.
Enjoy your delicious chicken fillets with sweet chili adobo made in the air fryer!

335. Here is a recipe for air fryer chicken schnitzel with gypsy sauce:

Ingredients:

4 boneless, skinless chicken breasts
1 cup all-purpose flour
2 eggs, beaten
1 cup seasoned breadcrumbs
Salt and pepper, to taste
Cooking spray
1/2 cup mayonnaise
1/4 cup ketchup
1/4 cup diced pickles
1/4 cup diced onion
1 tablespoon Dijon mustard
1 tablespoon paprika
1 tablespoon apple cider vinegar
1 teaspoon sugar
1/2 teaspoon garlic powder
1/2 teaspoon cayenne pepper

Instructions:

Preheat the air fryer to 400°F (200°C).
Cut each chicken breast into 2 or 3 even pieces.
Place the flour in a shallow dish and season with salt and pepper.
Place the beaten eggs in another shallow dish.
Place the breadcrumbs in a third shallow dish.
Coat each piece of chicken in the flour, shaking off any excess.

Dip each piece of chicken in the egg mixture, letting any excess drip off.
Press each piece of chicken into the breadcrumbs, coating well.
Spray the air fryer basket with cooking spray.
Place the chicken pieces in the air fryer basket in a single layer, making sure they do not touch.
Spray the chicken with cooking spray.
Cook the chicken for 8-10 minutes, or until golden brown and crispy.
While the chicken is cooking, make the gypsy sauce.
In a small bowl, mix together the mayonnaise, ketchup, pickles, onion, Dijon mustard, paprika, apple cider vinegar, sugar, garlic powder, and cayenne pepper.
Serve the chicken with the gypsy sauce for dipping.
Enjoy your air fryer chicken schnitzel with gypsy sauce!

336. Here's an air fryer recipe for gluten-free crunchy chicken:

Ingredients:

4 boneless, skinless chicken breasts
1 cup gluten-free panko breadcrumbs
1/4 cup almond flour
1/4 cup grated parmesan cheese
1 teaspoon paprika
1/2 teaspoon garlic powder
1/2 teaspoon onion powder
1/2 teaspoon dried thyme
1/2 teaspoon salt
1/4 teaspoon black pepper
2 eggs, beaten
Cooking spray

Instructions:

Preheat your air fryer to 400°F.
Cut the chicken breasts into strips or nuggets.
In a shallow dish, mix together the panko breadcrumbs, almond flour, parmesan cheese, paprika, garlic powder, onion powder, dried thyme, salt, and black pepper.
Dip each piece of chicken into the beaten eggs, then coat with the breadcrumb mixture.
Spray the air fryer basket with cooking spray and arrange the chicken in a single layer.
Cook for 10-12 minutes, flipping the chicken halfway through, until the chicken is cooked through and the coating is crispy and golden brown.
Serve hot with your favorite dipping sauce.
Enjoy your gluten-free crunchy chicken!

337. Here's an air fryer recipe for sweet curried chicken cutlets:

Ingredients:

4 boneless, skinless chicken cutlets
1/2 cup gluten-free panko breadcrumbs
1/4 cup unsweetened shredded coconut
1 tbsp curry powder
1/2 tsp garlic powder
1/2 tsp paprika
1/4 tsp salt
1/4 tsp black pepper

1/4 cup honey
1 tbsp coconut aminos or soy sauce
1 tbsp apple cider vinegar
1 tsp minced fresh ginger
Cooking spray

Instructions:

Preheat the air fryer to 375°F.
In a shallow dish, mix together the panko breadcrumbs, shredded coconut, curry powder, garlic powder, paprika, salt, and black pepper.
In another shallow dish, whisk together the honey, coconut aminos or soy sauce, apple cider vinegar, and minced fresh ginger.
Dip each chicken cutlet into the honey mixture, then coat with the breadcrumb mixture, pressing the breadcrumbs onto the chicken to adhere.
Place the chicken cutlets in the air fryer basket in a single layer. Spray the tops with cooking spray.
Air fry for 10-12 minutes, flipping halfway through, until the chicken is cooked through and the coating is crispy and golden brown.
Serve with your favorite side dishes and enjoy!

338. Here is an air fryer recipe for Jamaican chicken fajitas:

Ingredients:

1 lb chicken breast, sliced into thin strips
1 green bell pepper, sliced into thin strips
1 red bell pepper, sliced into thin strips
1 yellow onion, sliced into thin strips
1 tablespoon Jamaican jerk seasoning
1 teaspoon ground cumin
1 teaspoon smoked paprika
1/2 teaspoon garlic powder
1/2 teaspoon onion powder
Salt and black pepper, to taste
1 tablespoon olive oil
Juice of 1 lime
Tortillas, for serving

Instructions:

Preheat your air fryer to 400°F (200°C).
In a large bowl, combine the chicken, bell peppers, onion, Jamaican jerk seasoning, cumin, smoked paprika, garlic powder, onion powder, salt, black pepper, and olive oil. Toss until the chicken and vegetables are evenly coated.
Arrange the chicken and vegetables in a single layer in the air fryer basket.
Cook for 10-12 minutes, shaking the basket halfway through, until the chicken is cooked through and the vegetables are tender.
Drizzle the lime juice over the cooked chicken and vegetables, and toss to coat.
Serve the Jamaican chicken fajitas in tortillas, with your favorite toppings such as shredded cheese, sour cream, and guacamole. Enjoy!

339. here's a recipe for Greek Chicken Gyros in the air fryer:
Ingredients:
1 lb boneless, skinless chicken breasts, sliced into thin strips
1 tbsp olive oil
2 cloves garlic, minced
1 tsp dried oregano

1/2 tsp dried thyme
1/2 tsp salt
1/4 tsp black pepper
4-6 pita pieces of bread
Tzatziki sauce
Sliced red onion
Sliced tomato
Crumbled feta cheese

Instructions:

Preheat your air fryer to 400°F.
In a mixing bowl, combine the olive oil, garlic, oregano, thyme, salt, and pepper.
Add the chicken to the bowl and toss until it is coated in the mixture.
Place the chicken in the air fryer basket in a single layer and cook for 8-10 minutes, flipping halfway through.
Warm the pita breads in the air fryer for 1-2 minutes until they are slightly crispy.
Assemble the gyros with chicken, tzatziki sauce, sliced red onion, sliced tomato, and crumbled feta cheese.
Serve hot and enjoy!

340. Here's an air fryer recipe for Swiss-style breaded chicken:

Ingredients:

4 chicken breasts
1/2 cup all-purpose flour
1/2 teaspoon garlic powder
1/2 teaspoon onion powder
1/2 teaspoon dried thyme
1/2 teaspoon dried oregano
Salt and pepper, to taste
2 eggs
2 tablespoons milk
1 1/2 cups breadcrumbs
1/2 cup grated Parmesan cheese
Cooking spray

Instructions:

Preheat your air fryer to 400°F.
Cut the chicken breasts into 1-inch strips.
In a shallow bowl, mix together the flour, garlic powder, onion powder, dried thyme, dried oregano, salt, and pepper.
In another shallow bowl, whisk together the eggs and milk.
In a third shallow bowl, mix together the breadcrumbs and Parmesan cheese.
Dredge each chicken strip in the flour mixture, then dip it in the egg mixture, and finally coat it in the breadcrumb mixture, pressing the crumbs onto the chicken to ensure they stick.
Spray the air fryer basket with cooking spray and place the breaded chicken strips in a single layer in the basket.
Spray the chicken with cooking spray.
Air fry for 8-10 minutes, flipping the chicken strips halfway through the cooking time, until they are golden brown and cooked through.
Serve hot with your favorite dipping sauce. Enjoy!

341. Here is a recipe for air fryer chicken teriyaki:

Ingredients:

4 boneless, skinless chicken thighs, cut into 1-inch pieces
1/4 cup soy sauce
1/4 cup mirin
2 tablespoons honey
2 tablespoons brown sugar
1 tablespoon rice vinegar
1 teaspoon grated fresh ginger
1 clove garlic, minced
1 tablespoon cornstarch
1 tablespoon water
Sesame seeds and chopped green onions, for garnish

Instructions:

In a small saucepan, whisk together the soy sauce, mirin, honey, brown sugar, rice vinegar, ginger, and garlic. Bring to a simmer over medium heat.
In a small bowl, whisk together the cornstarch and water. Slowly whisk the cornstarch mixture into the soy sauce mixture. Simmer until thickened, about 2-3 minutes.
Preheat the air fryer to 400°F (200°C).
Place the chicken pieces in a single layer in the air fryer basket. Cook for 8 minutes.
Brush the chicken pieces with the teriyaki sauce and cook for an additional 2-3 minutes, until the chicken is cooked through and the sauce is sticky and caramelized.
Garnish with sesame seeds and chopped green onions, if desired, and serve immediately.
Enjoy your air fryer chicken teriyaki!

342. Here's a recipe for air fryer chicken breasts with avocado mango salsa:

Ingredients:

2 boneless, skinless chicken breasts
Salt and pepper
1/2 teaspoon garlic powder
1/2 teaspoon paprika
1 tablespoon olive oil
1 avocado, diced
1 mango, diced
1/4 red onion, diced
1/2 jalapeño, seeded and diced
Juice of 1 lime
1 tablespoon chopped fresh cilantro

Instructions:

Preheat the air fryer to 375°F.
Season the chicken breasts with salt, pepper, garlic powder, and paprika.
Drizzle olive oil over the chicken breasts and rub to coat evenly.
Place the chicken breasts in the air fryer basket and cook for 12-15 minutes, flipping halfway through.
While the chicken is cooking, make the avocado mango salsa. In a bowl, combine the diced avocado, mango, red onion, jalapeño, lime juice, and cilantro. Mix well.
Once the chicken is done, let it rest for a few minutes before slicing.
Serve the chicken with the avocado mango salsa on top.
Enjoy your delicious and healthy air fryer chicken breasts with avocado mango salsa!

343. Here's an air fryer recipe for lemony chicken breast:

Ingredients:

2 boneless, skinless chicken breasts
2 tablespoons olive oil
2 tablespoons lemon juice
1 teaspoon garlic powder
1 teaspoon onion powder
1 teaspoon dried oregano
1 teaspoon dried thyme
Salt and black pepper, to taste
Lemon wedges, for serving

Instructions:

Preheat your air fryer to 375°F.
Pound the chicken breasts to an even thickness of about ½ inch.
In a small bowl, mix together the olive oil, lemon juice, garlic powder, onion powder, oregano, thyme, salt, and black pepper.
Coat the chicken breasts with the seasoning mixture on both sides.
Place the chicken breasts in the air fryer basket in a single layer.
Cook for 10-12 minutes, flipping halfway through, until the chicken is cooked through and the internal temperature reaches 165°F.
Serve the lemony chicken breast with lemon wedges on the side.
Enjoy your delicious and healthy lemony chicken breast!

344. here's a recipe for air fryer prosciutto-wrapped chicken breasts:

Ingredients:

4 boneless, skinless chicken breasts
4 thin slices of prosciutto
1 tablespoon olive oil
1 teaspoon garlic powder
Salt and pepper to taste

Instructions:

Preheat the air fryer to 400°F (200°C).
Season chicken breasts with garlic powder, salt, and pepper.
Wrap each chicken breast with a slice of prosciutto, making sure to cover the entire breast.
Drizzle olive oil over the wrapped chicken breasts.
Place the chicken breasts in the air fryer basket and cook for 15-20 minutes, or until the internal temperature of the chicken reaches 165°F (74°C).
Remove from the air fryer and let rest for 5 minutes.
Serve and enjoy!

345. Here's an air fryer recipe for French-style sweet chicken breasts:

Ingredients:

2 boneless chicken breasts
1 tablespoon olive oil
1 tablespoon honey
1 tablespoon Dijon mustard
1 tablespoon apple cider vinegar

1/2 teaspoon dried thyme
Salt and pepper to taste

Instructions:

Preheat your air fryer to 375°F (190°C).
In a small bowl, whisk together the olive oil, honey, Dijon mustard, apple cider vinegar, thyme, salt, and pepper.
Place the chicken breasts in a shallow dish and pour the marinade over them, making sure the chicken is coated evenly. Let it marinate for 10-15 minutes.
Place the chicken breasts in the air fryer basket, making sure they are not touching each other. Cook for 10-12 minutes or until the internal temperature reaches 165°F (74°C).
Let the chicken rest for a few minutes before slicing and serving. You can garnish with fresh herbs like thyme or parsley.
Enjoy your sweet and tangy French-style chicken breasts!

346. Here's an air fryer recipe for Creamy Asiago Chicken:

Ingredients:

4 boneless, skinless chicken breasts
1/2 cup all-purpose flour
1 teaspoon garlic powder
1 teaspoon paprika
Salt and pepper, to taste
1 egg
1/4 cup milk
1 cup seasoned breadcrumbs
1/4 cup grated Asiago cheese
Cooking spray
1 tablespoon butter
1 tablespoon olive oil
1/2 cup heavy cream
1/4 cup grated Asiago cheese
1/2 teaspoon dried basil
Salt and pepper, to taste

Instructions:

Preheat the air fryer to 380°F.
In a shallow bowl, mix together flour, garlic powder, paprika, salt, and pepper.
In another shallow bowl, beat egg and milk together.
In a third shallow bowl, mix together breadcrumbs and Asiago cheese.
Coat each chicken breast in the flour mixture, then dip in the egg mixture, and finally coat in the breadcrumb mixture.
Place chicken in the air fryer basket and spray with cooking spray.
Cook chicken for 20-25 minutes or until golden brown and cooked through.
In a small saucepan, melt butter and olive oil together over medium heat.
Add heavy cream, Asiago cheese, dried basil, salt, and pepper. Whisk until well combined and cheese is melted.
Serve chicken with the Asiago cream sauce poured over the top. Enjoy!
347. Air Fryer Chicken Parmigiana with Fresh Rosemary Recipe:

Ingredients:

4 boneless, skinless chicken breasts
1 cup Italian-seasoned breadcrumbs

1/2 cup grated Parmesan cheese
1/2 teaspoon garlic powder
1/2 teaspoon dried basil
1/2 teaspoon dried oregano
1/2 teaspoon salt
1/4 teaspoon black pepper
1 egg
1/2 cup all-purpose flour
Cooking spray
1 cup marinara sauce
1 cup shredded mozzarella cheese
Fresh rosemary, chopped

Instructions:

Preheat the air fryer to 375°F (190°C).
In a shallow bowl, mix together the breadcrumbs, Parmesan cheese, garlic powder, basil, oregano, salt, and black pepper.
In another shallow bowl, beat the egg.
Place the flour in a third shallow bowl.
Dredge each chicken breast in the flour, then dip in the beaten egg, and finally coat in the breadcrumb mixture.
Place the chicken breasts in the air fryer basket, making sure they don't touch each other. Spray them lightly with cooking spray.
Air fry for 12 to 15 minutes, or until the chicken is golden brown and cooked through, flipping once halfway through cooking.
Remove the chicken from the air fryer and spoon marinara sauce over each breast. Sprinkle shredded mozzarella cheese and chopped fresh rosemary on top.
Return the chicken to the air fryer and air fry for another 2-3 minutes, or until the cheese is melted and bubbly.
Serve the chicken parmesan hot with your favorite side dish. Enjoy!

348. Here's a recipe for chicken tikka masala cooked in an air fryer:

Ingredients:

1 lb boneless, skinless chicken breasts, cut into bite-sized pieces
1/2 cup plain Greek yogurt
1 tbsp lemon juice
1 tbsp garam masala
1 tbsp paprika
1 tsp cumin
1/2 tsp turmeric
1/2 tsp salt
1/4 tsp cayenne pepper
1/4 cup tomato paste
1/4 cup heavy cream
2 tbsp butter
2 cloves garlic, minced
1 small onion, diced
1/4 cup chicken broth
Fresh cilantro, chopped (optional)

Instructions:

Preheat your air fryer to 400°F (200°C).

In a medium bowl, whisk together the Greek yogurt, lemon juice, garam masala, paprika, cumin, turmeric, salt, and cayenne pepper.
Add the chicken pieces to the bowl and toss to coat.
Place the chicken in a single layer in the air fryer basket and cook for 8 to 10 minutes, or until browned and cooked through. Flip the chicken pieces halfway through cooking.
While the chicken is cooking, melt the butter in a medium saucepan over medium heat. Add the garlic and onion and cook for 2 to 3 minutes, or until softened.
Add the tomato paste and chicken broth to the saucepan and whisk until smooth. Simmer for 5 to 7 minutes, or until the sauce has thickened.
Add the heavy cream to the sauce and stir to combine.
Once the chicken is cooked, transfer it to the saucepan with the sauce and toss to coat.
Serve the chicken tikka masala over rice, topped with fresh cilantro, if desired. Enjoy!

349. Here's a recipe for easy chicken enchiladas made in the air fryer:

Ingredients:

1 pound boneless, skinless chicken breast, cooked and shredded
1 cup enchilada sauce
1/2 cup sour cream
1/2 cup shredded cheddar cheese
1/2 cup shredded Monterey Jack cheese
1/4 cup chopped fresh cilantro
8 small corn tortillas

Instructions:

Preheat the air fryer to 400°F (200°C).
In a medium mixing bowl, combine the cooked and shredded chicken, 1/2 cup of the enchilada sauce, and the sour cream. Mix well.
In another mixing bowl, combine the cheddar cheese, Monterey Jack cheese, and cilantro. Mix well.
Place one tortilla in the air fryer basket and cook for 1-2 minutes, or until it's soft and pliable.
Spoon 1/4 cup of the chicken mixture onto the center of the tortilla, then roll it up and place it seam-side down in the air fryer basket.
Repeat with the remaining tortillas and chicken mixture, making sure to leave a little bit of space between each enchilada in the air fryer basket.
Brush the remaining 1/2 cup of enchilada sauce over the tops of the enchiladas, then sprinkle the cheese and cilantro mixture over the top.
Cook the enchiladas in the air fryer for 6-8 minutes, or until the cheese is melted and bubbly.
Serve hot, garnished with extra chopped cilantro and a dollop of sour cream, if desired. Enjoy!

350. here's a recipe for air fryer Caprese chicken with balsamic sauce:

Ingredients:

2 boneless, skinless chicken breasts
Salt and pepper, to taste
1/2 teaspoon garlic powder
1/2 teaspoon onion powder
1/2 teaspoon dried basil
1/2 teaspoon dried oregano
1/2 cup cherry tomatoes, halved
1/2 cup fresh mozzarella cheese, sliced

1/4 cup fresh basil leaves, torn
1/4 cup balsamic vinegar
1 tablespoon honey
1 tablespoon olive oil

Instructions:

Preheat your air fryer to 375°F.
Season the chicken breasts with salt, pepper, garlic powder, onion powder, basil, and oregano.
Place the chicken breasts in the air fryer basket and cook for 12-15 minutes or until they reach an internal temperature of 165°F.
While the chicken is cooking, make the balsamic sauce. In a small saucepan, combine the balsamic vinegar and honey. Bring the mixture to a simmer and cook for 5-6 minutes or until the mixture has thickened.
Once the chicken is cooked, remove it from the air fryer and let it rest for a few minutes.
Top the chicken breasts with cherry tomatoes, mozzarella cheese, and torn basil leaves.
Drizzle the balsamic sauce over the chicken and serve immediately.
Enjoy your delicious air fryer caprese chicken with balsamic sauce!

351. here's a recipe for Texas BBQ Chicken Thighs in the air fryer:

Ingredients:

6 bone-in chicken thighs
1/2 cup BBQ sauce
2 tbsp olive oil
1 tbsp smoked paprika
1 tbsp garlic powder
1 tbsp onion powder
1 tbsp brown sugar
1 tsp chili powder
Salt and pepper, to taste

Instructions:

Preheat your air fryer to 400°F (200°C).
In a small bowl, mix together the olive oil, smoked paprika, garlic powder, onion powder, brown sugar, chili powder, salt, and pepper.
Pat the chicken thighs dry with paper towels and brush them with the spice mixture on both sides.
Place the chicken thighs in the air fryer basket, skin-side up, and cook for 10 minutes.
Flip the chicken thighs and brush them with BBQ sauce.
Cook for an additional 10-12 minutes, until the internal temperature of the chicken reaches 165°F (74°C).
Serve hot with additional BBQ sauce, if desired.
Enjoy your Texas-style BBQ chicken thighs!

352. Here's a recipe for spinach-loaded chicken breasts cooked in an air fryer:

Ingredients:

4 chicken breasts
2 cups fresh spinach
1/2 cup feta cheese
2 tablespoons olive oil
2 cloves garlic, minced
1 teaspoon dried oregano
Salt and pepper, to taste

Instructions:

Preheat the air fryer to 400°F (200°C).
In a mixing bowl, combine the spinach, feta cheese, olive oil, garlic, oregano, salt, and pepper. Mix well.
Cut a pocket into each chicken breast by slicing horizontally into the thickest part of the breast, being careful not to cut all the way through.
Stuff each chicken breast with the spinach mixture.
Rub the chicken breasts with a little bit of olive oil and season with salt and pepper.
Place the chicken breasts into the air fryer basket, making sure there is enough space between each one.
Cook for 12-15 minutes, or until the chicken is cooked through and the internal temperature reaches 165°F (74°C).
Let the chicken rest for a few minutes before serving.
Optional: You can also add a sprinkle of parmesan cheese on top of the chicken breasts before serving.
Enjoy!

353. Here's an air fryer recipe for Hawaiian Style Chicken:

Ingredients:

4 boneless, skinless chicken breasts
1/2 cup pineapple juice
1/4 cup low-sodium soy sauce
1/4 cup brown sugar
1/4 cup ketchup
1/4 cup chicken broth
2 teaspoons minced garlic
1 teaspoon ground ginger
1/2 teaspoon red pepper flakes
Salt and pepper, to taste
1 can (8 oz) pineapple chunks, drained
Sliced green onions and sesame seeds, for garnish

Instructions:

In a small bowl, whisk together pineapple juice, soy sauce, brown sugar, ketchup, chicken broth, minced garlic, ground ginger, red pepper flakes, salt and pepper until well combined.
Place chicken breasts in a ziplock bag and pour the marinade over the chicken. Seal the bag and massage the marinade into the chicken. Refrigerate for at least 1 hour, or up to 24 hours.
Preheat your air fryer to 380°F.
Remove the chicken from the marinade and discard the remaining marinade.
Place the chicken in the air fryer basket and cook for 10-12 minutes per side, or until the internal temperature reaches 165°F.
During the last 2 minutes of cooking, add the pineapple chunks to the air fryer basket and cook until heated through.
Serve the chicken and pineapple over rice or with a side salad. Garnish with sliced green onions and sesame seeds, if desired. Enjoy!

354. Here's a recipe for chicken breasts en papillote in the air fryer:

Ingredients:

2 boneless, skinless chicken breasts
1/2 red onion, sliced
1 bell pepper, sliced
1 zucchini, sliced
4 cloves garlic, minced

Salt and pepper, to taste
2 tbsp olive oil
2 tbsp butter
4 sprigs of fresh thyme
4 slices lemon
Parchment paper

Instructions:

Preheat your air fryer to 375°F (190°C).
Cut two large pieces of parchment paper and fold them in half.
Place half of the red onion, bell pepper, and zucchini on each folded parchment paper.
Season the vegetables with salt, pepper, and minced garlic.
Drizzle 1 tablespoon of olive oil over the vegetables on each parchment paper.
Place a chicken breast on top of each pile of vegetables and season with salt and pepper.
Place a sprig of thyme and a slice of lemon on top of each chicken breast.
Add a tablespoon of butter to each chicken breast.
Fold the parchment paper over the chicken and vegetables and tuck the edges under to create a sealed packet.
Place the packets in the air fryer basket and cook for 18-20 minutes, until the chicken is cooked through.
Carefully remove the packets from the air fryer basket and place them on plates.
Open the packets and serve the chicken and vegetables with the juices from the packets.
Enjoy your delicious chicken breasts en papillote cooked in the air fryer!

355. Here's an air fryer recipe for French-style chicken thighs:

Ingredients:

6 bone-in, skin-on chicken thighs
2 tablespoons olive oil
1 teaspoon dried thyme
1 teaspoon dried rosemary
1 teaspoon dried oregano
1 teaspoon garlic powder
1 teaspoon onion powder
1 teaspoon paprika
Salt and pepper, to taste

Instructions:

Preheat the air fryer to 400°F (200°C).
In a small bowl, mix together the olive oil, thyme, rosemary, oregano, garlic powder, onion powder, paprika, salt, and pepper.
Rub the chicken thighs with the seasoning mixture, making sure to coat them evenly.
Place the chicken thighs in the air fryer basket, skin side up.
Cook for 20-25 minutes or until the chicken thighs reach an internal temperature of 165°F (74°C) and the skin is crispy and golden brown.
Serve hot with your favorite side dishes.
Enjoy your French-style chicken thighs cooked to perfection in your air fryer!

356. Here's a recipe for an air-fried chicken bowl with black beans:

Ingredients:

1 lb boneless, skinless chicken breasts, cut into bite-sized pieces
1 tbsp olive oil

1 tsp chili powder
1 tsp cumin
1/2 tsp garlic powder
Salt and pepper, to taste
1 can black beans, drained and rinsed
1 cup cooked rice
1 cup salsa
1 avocado, sliced
Cilantro, for garnish

Instructions:

Preheat the air fryer to 400°F.
In a bowl, mix together the olive oil, chili powder, cumin, garlic powder, salt, and pepper.
Add the chicken pieces and toss to coat.
Arrange the chicken pieces in a single layer in the air fryer basket.
Cook for 10-12 minutes, flipping halfway through, until the chicken is cooked through and golden brown.
While the chicken is cooking, heat the black beans in a small saucepan on the stovetop.
Assemble the bowls by dividing the cooked rice, black beans, and chicken among four bowls.
Top each bowl with salsa, avocado slices, and cilantro.
Serve and enjoy!

357. Here's a recipe for ham and cheese stuffed chicken breasts cooked in an air fryer:

Ingredients:

4 boneless, skinless chicken breasts
4 slices of ham
4 slices of Swiss cheese
1/2 cup all-purpose flour
1 teaspoon paprika
1 teaspoon garlic powder
1 teaspoon onion powder
Salt and pepper to taste
2 eggs, beaten
1 cup panko bread crumbs

Instructions:

Preheat your air fryer to 400°F (200°C).
Use a meat tenderizer to pound the chicken breasts until they're an even thickness.
Place one slice of ham and one slice of Swiss cheese on each chicken breast, and roll up the chicken tightly around the filling. Secure each roll with toothpicks.
In a shallow bowl, combine the flour, paprika, garlic powder, onion powder, salt, and pepper. In a separate bowl, beat the eggs.
Dip each chicken roll in the flour mixture, shaking off any excess, then dip it in the beaten eggs, and finally coat it in the panko bread crumbs.
Place the chicken rolls in the air fryer basket, making sure they're not touching each other. Spray them with cooking spray.
Cook for 15 to 18 minutes, or until the chicken is cooked through and the bread crumbs are golden brown and crispy.
Remove the toothpicks before serving.
Enjoy your delicious and easy ham and cheese stuffed chicken breasts made in the air fryer!

358. Here's an air fryer recipe for chicken cheesy divan casserole:

Ingredients:

4 chicken breasts, cooked and shredded
2 cups broccoli florets, blanched
1 can cream of chicken soup
1/2 cup mayonnaise
1/2 cup sour cream
1 cup shredded cheddar cheese
1/2 teaspoon garlic powder
1/2 teaspoon onion powder
Salt and pepper, to taste
1 cup bread crumbs

Instructions:

Preheat the air fryer to 375°F.
In a bowl, mix together the cream of chicken soup, mayonnaise, sour cream, garlic powder, onion powder, salt, and pepper.
Add the shredded chicken and blanched broccoli to the bowl and mix well to combine.
Place the mixture in a baking dish and sprinkle the shredded cheddar cheese on top.
In a separate bowl, mix the bread crumbs with a tablespoon of olive oil.
Sprinkle the bread crumb mixture over the top of the casserole.
Place the baking dish in the air fryer and cook for 15-20 minutes or until the cheese is melted and the bread crumbs are golden brown.
Serve the chicken cheesy divan casserole hot and enjoy!

359. Here's an air fryer recipe for creamy onion chicken:

Ingredients:

4 boneless, skinless chicken breasts
Salt and pepper
1 tablespoon olive oil
1 tablespoon butter
1 large onion, sliced
1 tablespoon minced garlic
1/2 cup chicken broth
1/2 cup heavy cream
1/2 cup grated Parmesan cheese
2 tablespoons chopped fresh parsley

Instructions:

Preheat the air fryer to 375°F.
Season the chicken breasts with salt and pepper on both sides.
Place the chicken breasts in the air fryer basket and spray with cooking spray.
Air fry the chicken for 10-12 minutes, or until it reaches an internal temperature of 165°F.
While the chicken is cooking, melt the butter and olive oil in a large skillet over medium heat.
Add the sliced onion and minced garlic and cook until the onion is softened about 5-7 minutes.
Add the chicken broth to the skillet and bring to a simmer.
Stir in the heavy cream and Parmesan cheese until the cheese is melted and the sauce is smooth.
Reduce the heat to low and simmer the sauce for 5-7 minutes, stirring occasionally, until it thickens slightly.
Serve the cooked chicken with the creamy onion sauce on top, garnished with chopped parsley.
Enjoy your creamy onion chicken!

360. Here's an air fryer recipe for restaurant-style chicken with yogurt sauce:

Ingredients:

4 boneless, skinless chicken breasts
1 tsp paprika
1 tsp garlic powder
1 tsp onion powder
1 tsp dried thyme
Salt and pepper to taste
1/4 cup olive oil
1/4 cup Greek yogurt
2 tbsp lemon juice
2 tbsp chopped fresh parsley
2 tbsp chopped fresh dill
2 tbsp chopped fresh mint

Instructions:

Preheat your air fryer to 375°F.
In a small bowl, mix together the paprika, garlic powder, onion powder, thyme, salt, and pepper.
Rub the spice mixture all over the chicken breasts, making sure to coat both sides.
Place the chicken breasts in the air fryer basket and brush with olive oil.
Air fry for 10-12 minutes or until the chicken is cooked through and no longer pink in the middle.
While the chicken is cooking, make the yogurt sauce by whisking together the Greek yogurt, lemon juice, parsley, dill, and mint.
Serve the chicken hot with the yogurt sauce on top. Enjoy!

361. Here's an air fryer recipe for sweet wasabi chicken:

Ingredients:

4 boneless, skinless chicken thighs
2 tablespoons soy sauce
2 tablespoons honey
2 tablespoons rice vinegar
1 tablespoon sesame oil
1 tablespoon wasabi paste
1 teaspoon garlic powder
Salt and pepper, to taste
Sesame seeds and chopped green onions, for garnish

Instructions:

In a small bowl, whisk together the soy sauce, honey, rice vinegar, sesame oil, wasabi paste, garlic powder, salt, and pepper.
Add the chicken thighs to a large bowl and pour the marinade over them. Toss to coat the chicken evenly.
Cover the bowl with plastic wrap and let it marinate in the refrigerator for at least 30 minutes.
Preheat the air fryer to 375°F.
Remove the chicken from the marinade and place them in the air fryer basket.
Cook the chicken for 12-15 minutes, flipping halfway through, until they are crispy and golden brown.
Serve the chicken hot, garnished with sesame seeds and chopped green onions.
Enjoy your sweet and spicy air fryer chicken with a wasabi kick!

362. Here's an air fryer recipe for tasty Kyiv-style chicken:

Ingredients:

4 boneless, skinless chicken breasts
1/2 cup unsalted butter, softened
2 cloves garlic, minced
2 tbsp fresh parsley, finely chopped
2 tbsp fresh chives, finely chopped
1 tsp lemon zest
1/2 tsp salt
1/4 tsp black pepper
1 cup all-purpose flour
2 large eggs, beaten
2 cups panko breadcrumbs
Cooking spray
Instructions:

In a small bowl, mix together the softened butter, garlic, parsley, chives, lemon zest, salt, and pepper until well combined. Chill in the refrigerator until firm, about 20 minutes.
Cut a pocket in each chicken breast by making a slit in the thickest part of the breast, being careful not to cut through the other side. Divide the chilled butter mixture into four portions and stuff each chicken breast with one portion. Secure the opening with toothpicks.
Place the flour, beaten eggs, and panko breadcrumbs in three separate shallow bowls. Dip each chicken breast first into the flour, then the beaten eggs, and finally the panko breadcrumbs, pressing the breadcrumbs onto the chicken to help them adhere.
Preheat the air fryer to 375°F (190°C). Lightly spray the air fryer basket with cooking spray. Place the chicken breasts in the basket, making sure they do not touch each other.
Air fry for 18-20 minutes or until the internal temperature of the chicken reaches 165°F (74°C), flipping the chicken breasts over halfway through the cooking time for even browning. Let the chicken rest for a few minutes before removing the toothpicks and serving. Enjoy!

363. here's a recipe for tropical coconut chicken thighs in the air fryer:

Ingredients:

4 bone-in chicken thighs
1/2 cup coconut milk
1/2 cup unsweetened shredded coconut
1/4 cup all-purpose flour
1 tsp salt
1 tsp garlic powder
1/2 tsp ground ginger
1/4 tsp black pepper
1/4 cup pineapple juice
1 tbsp honey
1 tbsp lime juice
1/4 tsp red pepper flakes (optional)

Instructions:

Preheat the air fryer to 375°F.
In a shallow bowl, mix together the coconut milk, pineapple juice, honey, lime juice, and red pepper flakes (if using).
In another shallow bowl, mix together the shredded coconut, flour, salt, garlic powder, ginger, and black pepper.
Dip each chicken thigh in the coconut milk mixture, then dredge in the coconut flour mixture, pressing the mixture onto the chicken to adhere.
Place the chicken thighs in the air fryer basket in a single layer, skin-side down.

Air fry for 12 minutes, then flip the chicken thighs over and air fry for another 10-12 minutes, or until the internal temperature reaches 165°F.
Let the chicken rest for a few minutes before serving. Enjoy!

364. Here's an air fryer recipe for rosemary and oyster chicken breasts:

Ingredients:

2 boneless, skinless chicken breasts
1 tablespoon olive oil
1 tablespoon chopped fresh rosemary
1/2 teaspoon garlic powder
Salt and pepper to taste
2 oysters, shucked and chopped
2 tablespoons butter, melted

Instructions:

Preheat the air fryer to 375°F (190°C).
Season the chicken breasts with olive oil, chopped rosemary, garlic powder, salt, and pepper.
Place the chicken breasts in the air fryer basket and cook for 10 minutes.
Meanwhile, mix the chopped oysters and melted butter in a small bowl.
After 10 minutes, remove the chicken from the air fryer and spoon the oyster mixture over the top of each chicken breast.
Return the chicken to the air fryer and cook for an additional 5-7 minutes, until the chicken is cooked through and the oyster mixture is golden brown.
Serve immediately and enjoy!
Note: Make sure the oysters you use are fresh and have been properly shucked before chopping them up. If you're not a fan of oysters, you can omit them and just use the rosemary and garlic seasoning on the chicken for a delicious and simple meal.

365. Here's an air fryer recipe for cheesy marinara chicken:

Ingredients:

4 boneless, skinless chicken breasts
1 cup marinara sauce
1 cup shredded mozzarella cheese
1/4 cup grated parmesan cheese
1/4 cup chopped fresh basil
2 tablespoons olive oil
Salt and pepper to taste

Instructions:

Preheat your air fryer to 375°F (190°C).
Season the chicken breasts with salt and pepper.
Brush both sides of the chicken breasts with olive oil.
Place the chicken breasts in the air fryer basket and cook for 10 minutes.
After 10 minutes, spoon the marinara sauce over the chicken breasts.
Sprinkle the shredded mozzarella cheese and grated parmesan cheese over the chicken.
Place the chicken back in the air fryer and cook for another 5-7 minutes, or until the cheese is melted and bubbly.
Garnish with chopped fresh basil and serve hot.
Enjoy your delicious cheesy marinara chicken from the air fryer!

366. Here's an air fryer recipe for garlicky chicken cubes on a green bed:

Ingredients:

1 lb boneless, skinless chicken breast, cut into cubes
2 tablespoons olive oil
4 cloves garlic, minced
Salt and pepper, to taste
4 cups mixed greens
1/4 cup cherry tomatoes, halved
1/4 cup cucumber, sliced
1/4 cup red onion, sliced
Lemon wedges, for serving

Instructions:

Preheat your air fryer to 400°F.
In a bowl, mix together the chicken cubes, olive oil, minced garlic, salt, and pepper.
Place the chicken cubes in the air fryer basket and cook for 10-12 minutes, flipping the chicken halfway through, until the chicken is cooked through and crispy.
While the chicken is cooking, prepare your green salad by mixing together the mixed greens, cherry tomatoes, cucumber, and red onion in a large bowl.
Once the chicken is done, transfer it to a plate and serve it over the green salad. Squeeze lemon juice over the top of the chicken and salad, if desired.
Enjoy your garlicky chicken cubes on a bed of greens!

367. Here's an air fryer recipe for chicken thighs with herby tomatoes:

Ingredients:

4 bone-in chicken thighs
2 cups cherry tomatoes, halved
1 tbsp olive oil
1 tbsp chopped fresh rosemary
1 tbsp chopped fresh thyme
1 tsp garlic powder
1 tsp salt
1/2 tsp black pepper

Instructions:

Preheat your air fryer to 375°F (190°C).
In a mixing bowl, combine the olive oil, chopped rosemary, chopped thyme, garlic powder, salt, and black pepper.
Add the halved cherry tomatoes to the bowl and toss to coat.
Place the chicken thighs in the air fryer basket and brush them with the herby tomato mixture.
Add the coated cherry tomatoes to the basket around the chicken thighs.
Air fry for 18-20 minutes or until the chicken is cooked through and the tomatoes are slightly softened and blistered.
Let the chicken rest for a few minutes before serving with the roasted tomatoes on the side.
Enjoy your flavorful and juicy chicken thighs with herby tomatoes!

368. Here's an air fryer recipe for chicken thighs with parmesan crust:

Ingredients:

4 boneless, skinless chicken thighs
1/2 cup grated parmesan cheese

1/2 cup panko breadcrumbs
1 tsp garlic powder
1 tsp dried oregano
1/2 tsp salt
1/4 tsp black pepper
2 tbsp olive oil

Instructions:

Preheat the air fryer to 400°F (200°C).
In a shallow bowl, mix together the parmesan cheese, panko breadcrumbs, garlic powder, dried oregano, salt, and black pepper.
Brush the chicken thighs with olive oil, then coat them in the parmesan mixture, pressing the mixture onto the chicken to make sure it adheres.
Place the chicken thighs in the air fryer basket, making sure they don't touch.
Cook for 12-15 minutes, flipping the chicken halfway through, until the internal temperature of the chicken reaches 165°F (75°C) and the crust is golden brown and crispy.
Serve immediately, garnished with fresh parsley or chopped tomatoes, if desired.

369. Here's an air fryer recipe for classic buttermilk chicken thighs:

Ingredients:

6 bone-in, skin-on chicken thighs
1 cup buttermilk
1 tbsp hot sauce
1 tsp paprika
1 tsp garlic powder
1 tsp onion powder
1 tsp salt
1/2 tsp black pepper
1 1/2 cups panko breadcrumbs
1/2 cup all-purpose flour
2 large eggs, beaten
Cooking spray

Instructions:

In a large bowl, whisk together the buttermilk, hot sauce, paprika, garlic powder, onion powder, salt, and black pepper. Add the chicken thighs and toss to coat. Cover and refrigerate for at least 2 hours, or overnight.
Preheat the air fryer to 400°F (200°C).
In a shallow dish, combine the panko breadcrumbs and flour.
Dip each chicken thigh in the beaten eggs, then coat in the breadcrumb mixture, pressing to adhere.
Place the chicken thighs in a single layer in the air fryer basket. Spray the tops lightly with cooking spray.
Cook for 20-25 minutes, flipping halfway through, or until the chicken is golden brown and cooked through (internal temperature of 165°F/74°C).
Serve hot with your favorite dipping sauce.

370. Here's an air fryer recipe for traditional chicken mole:

Ingredients:

4 boneless, skinless chicken thighs
1 tablespoon vegetable oil
1/2 onion, diced

2 garlic cloves, minced
1 cup chicken broth
1/2 cup unsweetened cocoa powder
1/4 cup almond butter
2 tablespoons honey
2 teaspoons ground cumin
1 teaspoon ground cinnamon
1/2 teaspoon chili powder
1/2 teaspoon salt

Instructions:

Preheat your air fryer to 375°F (190°C).
Season the chicken thighs with salt and pepper.
Add the vegetable oil to the air fryer basket and place the chicken thighs in the basket.
Air fry the chicken for 10-12 minutes, flipping halfway through, or until they are cooked through.
While the chicken is cooking, heat a saucepan over medium heat and add the onion and garlic. Cook until softened, about 3-4 minutes.
Add the chicken broth, cocoa powder, almond butter, honey, cumin, cinnamon, chili powder, and salt to the saucepan. Whisk until smooth.
Bring the sauce to a simmer and let it cook for 10-15 minutes or until it has thickened slightly.
Once the chicken is done, serve it with the mole sauce on top.

371. Here's an air fryer recipe for chicken drumsticks with garlic butter sauce:

Ingredients:

6-8 chicken drumsticks
1/2 cup all-purpose flour
1 tsp paprika
1 tsp garlic powder
1 tsp onion powder
Salt and pepper to taste
1/4 cup unsalted butter, melted
3 garlic cloves, minced
1 tbsp chopped parsley

Instructions:

Preheat the air fryer to 375°F.
In a bowl, mix together flour, paprika, garlic powder, onion powder, salt and pepper.
Coat each chicken drumstick in the flour mixture and shake off any excess.
Place the chicken drumsticks in the air fryer basket and cook for 20-25 minutes, or until the chicken is golden brown and cooked through.
In a separate bowl, mix together melted butter, minced garlic and chopped parsley.
Brush the garlic butter sauce over the chicken drumsticks and continue cooking for another 2-3 minutes to allow the sauce to stick to the chicken.
Serve hot and enjoy!

372. here's an air fryer recipe for enchilada chicken thighs:

Ingredients:

6 chicken thighs, bone-in, skin-on
1/2 cup enchilada sauce
1/2 cup shredded cheddar cheese
1/4 cup diced green onions

Salt and pepper, to taste

Instructions:

Preheat your air fryer to 400°F.
Season the chicken thighs with salt and pepper on both sides.
Place the chicken thighs in the air fryer basket skin-side down and cook for 10 minutes.
Flip the chicken over and brush with enchilada sauce. Cook for another 10 minutes.
Brush with more enchilada sauce and sprinkle with cheddar cheese. Cook for an additional 2-3 minutes until the cheese is melted.
Top with diced green onions and serve.
Enjoy your delicious enchilada chicken thighs!

373. Here's a recipe for air fryer cauliflower oatmeal-crusted drumsticks:

Ingredients:

6 chicken drumsticks
1 cup cauliflower rice
1/2 cup rolled oats
1/4 cup grated parmesan cheese
1 tsp garlic powder
1 tsp onion powder
1 tsp smoked paprika
1/2 tsp salt
1/4 tsp black pepper
2 tbsp olive oil

Instructions:

Preheat your air fryer to 400°F.
In a food processor, pulse the cauliflower rice until it becomes finely chopped.
In a large bowl, combine the chopped cauliflower rice, rolled oats, parmesan cheese, garlic powder, onion powder, smoked paprika, salt, and black pepper.
Drizzle the olive oil over the mixture and toss until well combined.
Pat the chicken drumsticks dry with paper towels, then coat each drumstick in the cauliflower oatmeal mixture, pressing it onto the chicken to help it stick.
Place the coated drumsticks in the air fryer basket in a single layer.
Cook the drumsticks for 20-25 minutes, or until the internal temperature reaches 165°F and the coating is golden brown and crispy.
Serve hot and enjoy!

374. Here's an air fryer recipe for Indonesian Sambal chicken drumsticks:

Ingredients:

8 chicken drumsticks
2 tablespoons Sambal Oelek (Indonesian chili paste)
2 tablespoons honey
1 tablespoon soy sauce
1 tablespoon rice vinegar
1 tablespoon sesame oil
2 cloves garlic, minced
1 teaspoon ground ginger
Salt and pepper to taste
Chopped green onions and sesame seeds for garnish

Instructions:

In a mixing bowl, combine sambal Oelek, honey, soy sauce, rice vinegar, sesame oil, garlic, ginger, salt and pepper. Mix well.
Add chicken drumsticks into the mixture, and toss to coat evenly. Marinate for at least 30 minutes.
Preheat the air fryer to 375°F (190°C) for 5 minutes.
Arrange the chicken drumsticks in a single layer in the air fryer basket.
Cook for 15-18 minutes, flipping halfway through, until the internal temperature reaches 165°F (74°C) and the chicken is crispy and golden brown.
Serve hot, garnished with chopped green onions and sesame seeds.
Enjoy your spicy and flavorful Indonesian sambal chicken drumsticks!

375. Here's an air fryer recipe for chicken and baby potato Traybake:

Ingredients:

4-6 chicken thighs, bone-in, and skin-on
1 pound baby potatoes, halved
1 red onion, chopped
1 red bell pepper, chopped
2 cloves garlic, minced
2 tablespoons olive oil
1 teaspoon dried thyme
1 teaspoon dried rosemary
1/2 teaspoon salt
1/4 teaspoon black pepper
Fresh parsley, chopped (for garnish)

Instructions:

Preheat the air fryer to 375°F (190°C).
In a large bowl, toss the baby potatoes, red onion, red bell pepper, and minced garlic with olive oil, dried thyme, dried rosemary, salt, and black pepper until evenly coated.
Place the chicken thighs on top of the potato mixture in the air fryer basket.
Air fry for 25-30 minutes, flipping the chicken and stirring the potatoes halfway through, until the chicken is cooked through (reaches an internal temperature of 165°F/74°C) and the potatoes are tender and crispy.
Garnish with chopped fresh parsley before serving.
Enjoy your delicious and easy chicken and baby potato traybake!

376. Here's an air fryer recipe for southern-style fried chicken drumsticks:

Ingredients:

6 chicken drumsticks
1 cup buttermilk
1 cup all-purpose flour
2 tsp salt
1 tsp paprika
1 tsp garlic powder
1 tsp onion powder
1/2 tsp black pepper
Cooking spray

Instructions:

Soak the chicken drumsticks in buttermilk for at least 1 hour or overnight in the fridge.

In a large bowl, mix together flour, salt, paprika, garlic powder, onion powder, and black pepper.
Remove the chicken drumsticks from the buttermilk and let any excess buttermilk drip off.
Dredge the chicken drumsticks in the flour mixture, making sure they are well coated.
Preheat the air fryer to 375°F (190°C).
Spray the air fryer basket with cooking spray.
Place the chicken drumsticks in the air fryer basket in a single layer. Do not overcrowd.
Spray the chicken drumsticks with cooking spray.
Cook for 20-25 minutes, flipping halfway through, until the chicken is golden brown and crispy and the internal temperature reaches 165°F (75°C).
Serve immediately.
Enjoy your crispy and delicious southern-style fried chicken drumsticks!

377. Here's an air fryer recipe for crispy drumsticks with blue cheese sauce:

Ingredients:

8 chicken drumsticks
1/2 cup all-purpose flour
1 tsp smoked paprika
1 tsp garlic powder
1 tsp onion powder
1 tsp dried thyme
Salt and pepper
Cooking spray
1/4 cup blue cheese crumbles
1/4 cup sour cream
2 tbsp mayonnaise
1 tbsp lemon juice
1 clove garlic, minced
2 tbsp chopped fresh parsley

Instructions:

Preheat your air fryer to 400°F (200°C).
In a large bowl, whisk together the flour, smoked paprika, garlic powder, onion powder, dried thyme, salt, and pepper.
Coat the drumsticks in the flour mixture, shaking off any excess.
Spray the air fryer basket with cooking spray and place the drumsticks in the basket.
Spray the drumsticks with more cooking spray.
Cook the drumsticks for 25-30 minutes, flipping them over halfway through, or until they are golden brown and cooked through.
While the drumsticks are cooking, make the blue cheese sauce. In a small bowl, whisk together the blue cheese crumbles, sour cream, mayonnaise, lemon juice, garlic, and parsley.
Serve the drumsticks hot with the blue cheese sauce on the side for dipping.
Enjoy your crispy drumsticks with delicious blue cheese sauce!

378. Here's an air fryer recipe for peri-peri chicken legs:

Ingredients:

4 chicken legs
2 tablespoons peri-peri sauce
1 tablespoon olive oil
1 teaspoon paprika
1/2 teaspoon salt
1/4 teaspoon black pepper

Instructions:

Preheat the air fryer to 375°F (190°C).
In a small bowl, whisk together the peri peri sauce, olive oil, paprika, salt, and black pepper.
Rub the chicken legs all over with the marinade.
Place the chicken legs in the air fryer basket and cook for 20-25 minutes, flipping them halfway through.
Check that the internal temperature of the chicken has reached 165°F (74°C) using a meat thermometer.
Serve the chicken legs hot with your favorite sides.
Enjoy your peri peri chicken legs made in the air fryer!

379. here's an air fryer recipe for thyme-fried chicken legs:

Ingredients:

4 chicken legs
1/2 cup all-purpose flour
1 teaspoon salt
1 teaspoon black pepper
1 teaspoon dried thyme
1/2 teaspoon garlic powder
2 eggs
1/4 cup milk
1 cup panko bread crumbs
Cooking spray

Instructions:

Preheat your air fryer to 375°F (190°C).
In a shallow dish, whisk together the flour, salt, black pepper, dried thyme, and garlic powder.
In another shallow dish, whisk together the eggs and milk.
In a third shallow dish, add the panko bread crumbs.
Dredge each chicken leg in the flour mixture, shaking off any excess.
Dip each chicken leg into the egg mixture, then coat with the panko bread crumbs.
Lightly spray the chicken legs with cooking spray.
Place the chicken legs in the air fryer basket, being careful not to overcrowd.
Cook for 20-25 minutes, flipping the chicken legs halfway through the cooking time, until they are crispy and fully cooked with an internal temperature of 165°F (74°C).
Serve hot with your favorite dipping sauce. Enjoy!

380. Here's an air fryer recipe for Thai chicken satay:

Ingredients:

1 pound boneless, skinless chicken breasts, cut into strips
1/4 cup coconut milk
2 tablespoons soy sauce
2 tablespoons fish sauce
1 tablespoon honey
1 tablespoon lime juice
1 tablespoon red curry paste
1 teaspoon ground coriander
1/2 teaspoon ground cumin
1/4 teaspoon turmeric
1/4 teaspoon paprika
1/4 teaspoon garlic powder
Skewers

Instructions:

In a bowl, whisk together coconut milk, soy sauce, fish sauce, honey, lime juice, red curry paste, coriander, cumin, turmeric, paprika, and garlic powder.
Add chicken strips to the bowl and toss until evenly coated.
Marinate chicken in the refrigerator for at least 30 minutes (or up to overnight).
Preheat the air fryer to 375°F.
Thread the chicken strips onto skewers.
Place skewers in the air fryer basket and cook for 8-10 minutes, flipping halfway through, until the chicken is cooked through and lightly browned.
Serve with peanut sauce or sweet chili sauce, if desired.
Enjoy your delicious and healthy Thai chicken satay!

381. Here's an air fryer recipe for Asian-style chicken lollipops:

Ingredients:

12 chicken drumettes, skin removed from the bottom and pushed to the top to create a lollipop shape
1 tablespoon vegetable oil
2 teaspoons soy sauce
1 teaspoon sesame oil
1 teaspoon rice vinegar
1 teaspoon honey
1 teaspoon grated ginger
1 teaspoon grated garlic
Salt and pepper, to taste
Sesame seeds, for garnish
Green onions, thinly sliced, for garnish

Instructions:

Preheat the air fryer to 375°F (190°C).
In a large bowl, whisk together the vegetable oil, soy sauce, sesame oil, rice vinegar, honey, ginger, garlic, salt, and pepper.
Add the chicken lollipops to the bowl and toss until they are evenly coated in the marinade.
Place the chicken lollipops in the air fryer basket in a single layer, making sure they are not touching.
Air fry for 10-12 minutes, flipping halfway through, until the chicken is cooked through and crispy on the outside.
Sprinkle sesame seeds and green onions over the top of the chicken lollipops and serve with your favorite dipping sauce. Enjoy!

382. here's an air fryer recipe for chicken quarters with broccoli and carrots:

Ingredients:

4 chicken quarters
1 head of broccoli, chopped into florets
2 large carrots, sliced into thin rounds
2 tablespoons olive oil
1 teaspoon garlic powder
1 teaspoon paprika
1 teaspoon dried thyme
Salt and pepper, to taste

Instructions:

Preheat the air fryer to 375°F (190°C).

In a small bowl, mix together the garlic powder, paprika, dried thyme, salt, and pepper.
Place the chicken quarters in a large bowl and drizzle with olive oil. Add the spice mixture and toss until the chicken is evenly coated.
Place the chicken quarters in the air fryer basket, skin side up. Cook for 15 minutes.
After 15 minutes, add the broccoli and carrots to the air fryer basket around the chicken. Cook for an additional 10-12 minutes or until the chicken is cooked through and the vegetables are tender.
Serve the chicken quarters with the broccoli and carrots on the side. Enjoy!

383. Here's a recipe for Asian sticky chicken wingettes in the air fryer:

Ingredients:

1 lb chicken wingettes
2 tbsp soy sauce
2 tbsp honey
2 tbsp brown sugar
1 tbsp rice vinegar
1 tbsp sesame oil
1 tsp grated ginger
1 tsp minced garlic
1 tsp red pepper flakes
Salt and pepper, to taste
Sesame seeds and sliced green onions, for garnish

Instructions:

Preheat your air fryer to 380°F (190°C).
In a small bowl, whisk together the soy sauce, honey, brown sugar, rice vinegar, sesame oil, ginger, garlic, red pepper flakes, salt, and pepper.
Place the chicken wingettes in a large bowl and pour the sauce over them. Toss until the chicken is well coated.
Place the chicken in the air fryer basket in a single layer.
Cook for 10 minutes, then flip the chicken and cook for another 10 minutes.
Brush the chicken with any remaining sauce and cook for an additional 2-3 minutes to caramelize the sauce.
Garnish with sesame seeds and sliced green onions before serving.
Enjoy your deliciously sticky Asian chicken wingettes straight out of the air fryer!

384. Here's an air fryer recipe for roasted chicken with pancetta and thyme:

Ingredients:

1 whole chicken (3-4 lbs), rinsed and patted dry
4 oz pancetta, chopped
4 sprigs of fresh thyme
2 tbsp olive oil
1 tsp salt
1/2 tsp black pepper

Instructions:

Preheat the air fryer to 360°F.
In a small bowl, combine the olive oil, salt, and black pepper.
Rub the chicken with the olive oil mixture, making sure to coat all sides.
Place the chicken in the air fryer basket breast side up.
Scatter the chopped pancetta and fresh thyme sprigs over the chicken.
Cook for 30 minutes at 360°F.

After 30 minutes, flip the chicken and cook for another 20-25 minutes, or until the internal temperature of the thickest part of the chicken reads 165°F on a meat thermometer.
Let the chicken rest for 5-10 minutes before carving and serving.
Enjoy your delicious roasted chicken with pancetta and thyme!

385. here's an air fryer recipe for BBQ whole chicken:

Ingredients:

1 whole chicken, approximately 4 pounds
2 tbsp olive oil
1 tbsp smoked paprika
1 tbsp garlic powder
1 tbsp onion powder
1 tsp salt
1/2 tsp black pepper
1/2 cup BBQ sauce

Instructions:

Preheat your air fryer to 380°F.
Pat dry the chicken and remove the giblets.
In a small bowl, mix together the olive oil, smoked paprika, garlic powder, onion powder, salt, and black pepper.
Rub the spice mixture all over the chicken, making sure to get in all the nooks and crannies.
Place the chicken in the air fryer basket, breast side down.
Cook for 30 minutes at 380°F.
Flip the chicken over and brush it with the BBQ sauce.
Cook for another 25-30 minutes, or until the internal temperature of the chicken reaches 165°F.
Let the chicken rest for 5-10 minutes before carving and serving.
Enjoy your delicious and juicy BBQ whole chicken!

386. Here's an air fryer recipe for whole chicken with sage and garlic:

Ingredients:

1 whole chicken (about 4-5 pounds)
4 cloves garlic, minced
3 tbsp fresh sage, chopped
1 tsp salt
1/2 tsp black pepper
2 tbsp olive oil

Instructions:

Preheat your air fryer to 375°F.
Remove the giblets from the chicken and pat it dry with paper towels.
In a small bowl, mix the minced garlic, chopped sage, salt, and black pepper.
Rub the olive oil all over the chicken, then sprinkle the herb mixture evenly over the chicken, inside and out.
Place the chicken in the air fryer basket, breast side down.
Cook the chicken for 30 minutes, then flip it over and cook for another 30 minutes.
Check the internal temperature of the chicken using a meat thermometer. It should reach 165°F in the thickest part of the chicken.
If the chicken isn't fully cooked, continue cooking in 10-minute increments until it reaches the correct temperature.

Once the chicken is fully cooked, remove it from the air fryer and let it rest for 10 minutes before carving and serving.

387. Here's an air fryer recipe for Spanish-roasted whole chicken:

Ingredients:

1 whole chicken (3-4 pounds)
1 lemon, sliced
1 onion, chopped
4 garlic cloves, minced
2 tablespoons olive oil
2 teaspoons smoked paprika
1 teaspoon dried oregano
1/2 teaspoon ground cumin
Salt and pepper
Fresh parsley, chopped (optional)

Instructions:

Rinse the chicken and pat it dry with paper towels. Season the chicken with salt and pepper, both inside and outside.
In a small bowl, mix together the olive oil, smoked paprika, dried oregano, ground cumin, and minced garlic.
Brush the chicken with the spice mixture, making sure to coat it thoroughly.
Stuff the cavity of the chicken with the lemon slices and chopped onions.
Preheat the air fryer to 350°F.
Place the chicken in the air fryer basket, breast side down.
Cook for 30 minutes, then flip the chicken over and cook for an additional 30 minutes, until the internal temperature of the chicken reaches 165°F.
Let the chicken rest for 10-15 minutes before carving.
Garnish with fresh parsley and serve.
Enjoy your Spanish-roasted whole chicken!

388. here's a recipe for honey and lemon glazed stuffed chicken in the air fryer:

Ingredients:

4 boneless, skinless chicken breasts
1/2 cup breadcrumbs
1/2 cup grated Parmesan cheese
1 tsp garlic powder
1 tsp dried thyme
1/2 tsp salt
1/4 tsp black pepper
4 oz cream cheese, softened
2 tbsp honey
1 tbsp fresh lemon juice
1 tbsp olive oil

Instructions:

Preheat your air fryer to 375°F (190°C).
In a medium bowl, mix together the breadcrumbs, Parmesan cheese, garlic powder, thyme, salt, and pepper.
In another bowl, mix the cream cheese, honey, and lemon juice.

Use a sharp knife to cut a pocket into the side of each chicken breast. Stuff each chicken breast with 1/4 of the cream cheese mixture.
Rub the outside of each chicken breast with olive oil.
Coat each chicken breast with the breadcrumb mixture, pressing the crumbs onto the chicken to make sure they stick.
Place the chicken breasts in the air fryer basket, making sure they don't touch each other.
Air fry for 18-20 minutes, until the chicken is cooked through and the coating is golden brown and crispy.
Serve the chicken hot, garnished with extra lemon slices and fresh herbs if desired.
Enjoy your honey and lemon glazed stuffed chicken!

389. Here's a recipe for Greek-style whole chicken in the air fryer:

Ingredients:

1 whole chicken (3-4 pounds)
1/4 cup olive oil
3 cloves garlic, minced
2 tablespoons lemon juice
2 teaspoons dried oregano
1 teaspoon salt
1/2 teaspoon black pepper
Lemon wedges, for serving

Instructions:

Preheat your air fryer to 375°F.
Rinse the chicken and pat it dry with paper towels.
In a small bowl, whisk together the olive oil, garlic, lemon juice, oregano, salt, and black pepper.
Rub the seasoning mixture all over the chicken, making sure to get some under the skin and inside the cavity.
Place the chicken in the air fryer basket breast-side down and cook for 30 minutes.
Flip the chicken over and cook for an additional 20-30 minutes, or until the internal temperature of the thickest part of the chicken reaches 165°F.
Let the chicken rest for 10 minutes before carving.
Serve with lemon wedges on the side.
Enjoy your Greek-style whole chicken made in the air fryer!

390. Here's a recipe for Mediterranean-style whole chicken in the air fryer:

Ingredients:

1 whole chicken, about 4-5 lbs
2 tbsp olive oil
2 tbsp dried oregano
2 tbsp dried basil
1 tbsp dried thyme
1 tsp garlic powder
1 tsp onion powder
1 tsp salt
1/2 tsp black pepper
1 lemon, sliced
1/2 onion, sliced

Instructions:

Preheat the air fryer to 375°F (190°C).

In a small bowl, mix together the olive oil, oregano, basil, thyme, garlic powder, onion powder, salt, and black pepper.
Rub the spice mixture all over the chicken, making sure to coat it evenly.
Stuff the chicken cavity with the sliced lemon and onion.
Place the chicken in the air fryer basket, breast side down.
Cook for 30 minutes, then flip the chicken over and cook for another 30 minutes, or until the internal temperature of the thickest part of the chicken reaches 165°F (74°C).
Let the chicken rest for 10 minutes before carving and serving.
Enjoy your flavorful Mediterranean-style whole chicken!

391. Here's an air fryer recipe for whole chicken with Fresno chili sauce:

Ingredients:

1 whole chicken, about 4 lbs
2 tbsp olive oil
1 tbsp paprika
1 tbsp garlic powder
1 tsp salt
1 tsp black pepper
1 Fresno chili, seeded and minced
1 tbsp honey
1 tbsp apple cider vinegar
1 tbsp water
1 tbsp chopped fresh cilantro

Instructions:

Preheat the air fryer to 375°F (190°C).
Rinse the chicken and pat dry with paper towels. In a small bowl, combine the olive oil, paprika, garlic powder, salt, and black pepper.
Rub the spice mixture all over the chicken, making sure to coat the entire surface.
Place the chicken in the air fryer basket, breast side down. Cook for 30 minutes.
Meanwhile, make the Fresno chili sauce. In a small saucepan over medium heat, combine the Fresno chili, honey, apple cider vinegar, water, and cilantro. Cook for 5 minutes, stirring frequently, until the sauce has thickened.
After 30 minutes, flip the chicken over so it is breast side up. Continue to cook for an additional 30 minutes, or until the internal temperature of the chicken reaches 165°F (74°C) when tested with a meat thermometer.
Remove the chicken from the air fryer basket and let it rest for 5-10 minutes before carving.
Serve the chicken with the Fresno chili sauce on the side.

392. here is a recipe for Moroccan turkey meatballs made in an air fryer:

Ingredients:

1 lb ground turkey
1/2 onion, finely chopped
1/4 cup bread crumbs
1/4 cup chopped fresh parsley
1/4 cup chopped fresh cilantro
2 garlic cloves, minced
1 teaspoon ground cumin
1 teaspoon paprika
1/2 teaspoon ground cinnamon
1/4 teaspoon ground ginger
1/4 teaspoon ground allspice

Salt and pepper to taste
Olive oil cooking spray

Instructions:

Preheat your air fryer to 375°F.
In a large mixing bowl, combine ground turkey, onion, bread crumbs, parsley, cilantro, garlic, cumin, paprika, cinnamon, ginger, allspice, salt, and pepper.
Mix all the ingredients until well combined.
Form the mixture into 1 1/2-inch meatballs.
Spray the air fryer basket with cooking spray.
Arrange the meatballs in a single layer in the basket.
Air fry the meatballs for 10-12 minutes, turning them halfway through the cooking process.
Check the internal temperature of the meatballs, it should be at least 165°F.
Serve hot with a side of your choice.
Enjoy your Moroccan turkey meatballs!

393. Here's an air fryer recipe for honey-glazed turkey:

Ingredients:

1 pound boneless turkey breast
2 tablespoons honey
2 tablespoons soy sauce
1 tablespoon olive oil
1 teaspoon Dijon mustard
1/2 teaspoon garlic powder
Salt and pepper to taste

Instructions:

Preheat your air fryer to 400°F.
Season the turkey breast with salt and pepper.
In a small bowl, whisk together the honey, soy sauce, olive oil, Dijon mustard, and garlic powder.
Brush the glaze all over the turkey breast, making sure it's coated evenly.
Place the turkey breast in the air fryer basket and cook for 10 minutes.
After 10 minutes, flip the turkey breast over and brush with the remaining glaze.
Cook for an additional 10 minutes or until the internal temperature of the turkey reaches 165°F.
Remove the turkey breast from the air fryer and let it rest for a few minutes before slicing and serving.
Enjoy your delicious and easy honey-glazed turkey!

394. Here's a recipe for air fryer turkey burgers with cabbage slaw:

Ingredients:

1 lb ground turkey
1/2 teaspoon garlic powder
1/2 teaspoon onion powder
1/2 teaspoon paprika
Salt and pepper, to taste
4 hamburger buns
1 cup shredded cabbage
1/4 cup mayonnaise
1 tablespoon apple cider vinegar
1 teaspoon honey
1/4 teaspoon celery seed

Instructions:

Preheat the air fryer to 375°F.
In a mixing bowl, combine the ground turkey, garlic powder, onion powder, paprika, salt, and pepper. Mix well.
Form the mixture into four patties.
Place the patties in the air fryer basket and cook for 10 minutes, flipping halfway through.
While the burgers are cooking, make the slaw. In a mixing bowl, combine the shredded cabbage, mayonnaise, apple cider vinegar, honey, and celery seed. Mix well.
Toast the hamburger buns in the air fryer for 1-2 minutes.
Assemble the burgers by placing the cooked patty on the toasted bun and topping it with a scoop of slaw.
Serve and enjoy!

395. Here's a recipe for parmesan turkey meatballs cooked in an air fryer:

Ingredients:

1 pound ground turkey
1/2 cup seasoned breadcrumbs
1/4 cup grated parmesan cheese
1/4 cup chopped fresh parsley
1 teaspoon garlic powder
1 teaspoon onion powder
1/2 teaspoon salt
1/4 teaspoon black pepper
Cooking spray

Instructions:

Preheat your air fryer to 375°F.
In a mixing bowl, combine ground turkey, breadcrumbs, parmesan cheese, parsley, garlic powder, onion powder, salt, and black pepper. Mix well.
Roll the mixture into small meatballs, about 1 to 1.5 inches in diameter.
Place the meatballs in the air fryer basket, making sure they are not touching each other.
Spray the meatballs with cooking spray.
Air fry for 10-12 minutes or until the internal temperature of the meatballs reaches 165°F.
Serve hot with your favorite dipping sauce.
Enjoy your delicious parmesan turkey meatballs!

396. Here's an air fryer recipe for thyme turkey nuggets:

Ingredients:

1 pound ground turkey
1/4 cup breadcrumbs
1/4 cup grated parmesan cheese
1 tablespoon chopped fresh thyme leaves
1 teaspoon garlic powder
1/2 teaspoon onion powder
1/2 teaspoon salt
1/4 teaspoon black pepper
1 egg
Cooking spray

Instructions:

Preheat the air fryer to 375°F (190°C).
In a large bowl, combine the ground turkey, breadcrumbs, parmesan cheese, thyme leaves, garlic powder, onion powder, salt, black pepper, and egg. Mix well until all ingredients are combined.
Roll the turkey mixture into small balls, about 1-2 tablespoons each.
Spray the air fryer basket with cooking spray, and place the turkey nuggets inside in a single layer, without overcrowding.
Cook the turkey nuggets in the air fryer for 8-10 minutes, flipping halfway through, until they are golden brown and cooked through.
Serve hot with your favorite dipping sauce.
Enjoy your delicious and healthy thyme turkey nuggets!

397. here's an air fryer recipe for turkey and veggie skewers:

Ingredients:

1 pound turkey breast, cut into 1-inch cubes
1 red bell pepper, seeded and cut into 1-inch pieces
1 yellow bell pepper, seeded and cut into 1-inch pieces
1 zucchini, sliced into 1/2-inch rounds
1/2 red onion, cut into 1-inch pieces
2 tablespoons olive oil
1 tablespoon dried thyme
1 teaspoon garlic powder
1/2 teaspoon salt
1/4 teaspoon black pepper
Wooden skewers, soaked in water for 30 minutes

Instructions:

Preheat the air fryer to 375°F (190°C).
In a large bowl, combine the turkey, bell peppers, zucchini, and onion. Drizzle with olive oil and toss to coat.
In a small bowl, mix the thyme, garlic powder, salt, and black pepper.
Thread the turkey and vegetables onto the skewers, alternating between the different ingredients.
Sprinkle the seasoning mixture evenly over the skewers.
Place the skewers in the air fryer basket and cook for 8-10 minutes, or until the turkey is cooked through and the vegetables are tender.
Serve hot with your favorite dipping sauce. Enjoy!

398. Here's a recipe for air fryer turkey strips with cranberry glaze:

Ingredients:

1 pound turkey breast strips
1/2 cup cranberry sauce
2 tablespoons honey
1 tablespoon soy sauce
1 tablespoon olive oil
Salt and pepper, to taste
Optional: chopped fresh herbs for garnish

Instructions:

Preheat your air fryer to 380°F (190°C).
In a small bowl, whisk together the cranberry sauce, honey, soy sauce, and olive oil until well combined.
Season the turkey strips with salt and pepper.
Brush the turkey strips with the cranberry glaze, making sure they are evenly coated.

Place the turkey strips in the air fryer basket in a single layer, making sure they are not touching.
Air fry for 8-10 minutes or until the turkey strips are cooked through and golden brown, flipping halfway through and brushing with more cranberry glaze.
Serve hot, garnished with chopped fresh herbs if desired.
Enjoy your delicious and easy air fryer turkey strips with cranberry glaze!

399. Here's a recipe for Mediterranean-rubbed turkey tenderloins cooked in an air fryer:

Ingredients:

1 lb turkey tenderloins
1 tbsp olive oil
1 tsp dried oregano
1 tsp dried thyme
1 tsp dried basil
1/2 tsp garlic powder
1/2 tsp onion powder
Salt and pepper, to taste

Instructions:

Preheat your air fryer to 375°F (190°C).
In a small bowl, mix together the olive oil, oregano, thyme, basil, garlic powder, onion powder, salt, and pepper.
Rub the spice mixture all over the turkey tenderloins.
Place the turkey tenderloins in the air fryer basket.
Cook for 15-20 minutes, flipping the tenderloins halfway through cooking, until the internal temperature of the turkey reaches 165°F (74°C).
Let the turkey rest for 5 minutes before slicing and serving.
Enjoy your delicious Mediterranean rubbed turkey tenderloins!

400. Here is an air fryer recipe for roasted turkey with Brussels sprouts:

Ingredients:

1 lb. boneless turkey breast
1 lb. Brussels sprouts, trimmed and halved
2 tbsp. olive oil
1 tsp. garlic powder
1 tsp. dried thyme
1 tsp. dried rosemary
1 tsp. paprika
Salt and pepper, to taste

Instructions:

Preheat your air fryer to 400°F (200°C).
In a small bowl, mix together the garlic powder, thyme, rosemary, paprika, salt, and pepper.
Rub the spice mixture all over the turkey breast.
Toss the Brussels sprouts with 1 tablespoon of olive oil and salt and pepper to taste.
Place the turkey breast and Brussels sprouts in the air fryer basket.
Drizzle the remaining 1 tablespoon of olive oil over the Brussels sprouts.
Air fry for 20-25 minutes or until the turkey is cooked through and the Brussels sprouts are crispy and tender.
Serve hot.
Enjoy your roasted turkey with crispy and flavorful Brussels sprouts!

401. Here's an air fryer recipe for turkey tenderloins with fattoush salad:

Ingredients:

2 turkey tenderloins
1 tablespoon olive oil
1 teaspoon ground cumin
1 teaspoon ground coriander
1/2 teaspoon garlic powder
1/2 teaspoon paprika
Salt and black pepper

For the salad:

1/2 head romaine lettuce, chopped
1/2 cup cherry tomatoes, halved
1 small cucumber, sliced
1/2 small red onion, sliced
1/2 cup fresh parsley, chopped
1/2 cup fresh mint, chopped
Juice of 1 lemon
2 tablespoons olive oil
Salt and black pepper
Pita bread, for serving

Instructions:

Preheat your air fryer to 400°F (200°C).
In a small bowl, mix together the olive oil, cumin, coriander, garlic powder, paprika, salt, and black pepper.
Rub the turkey tenderloins with the spice mixture and place them in the air fryer basket.
Cook the turkey for 20-25 minutes, or until the internal temperature reaches 165°F (74°C).
While the turkey is cooking, make the salad. In a large bowl, combine the romaine lettuce, cherry tomatoes, cucumber, red onion, parsley, mint, lemon juice, olive oil, salt, and black pepper. Toss well.
Serve the turkey tenderloins with the fattoush salad and warm pita bread. Enjoy!

402. Here's a recipe for air fryer chipotle buttered turkey:

Ingredients:

1 pound turkey breast tenderloins
2 tbsp unsalted butter, melted
1 tbsp chipotle seasoning
1 tsp garlic powder
Salt and black pepper, to taste
Fresh cilantro, chopped (optional)

Instructions:

Preheat the air fryer to 400°F.
In a small bowl, mix together the melted butter, chipotle seasoning, garlic powder, salt, and black pepper.
Pat the turkey tenderloins dry with paper towels, then brush them with the chipotle butter mixture, making sure to coat them well.
Place the turkey tenderloins in the air fryer basket and cook for 12-15 minutes, flipping halfway through, until the internal temperature reaches 165°F.
Once cooked, remove the turkey tenderloins from the air fryer and let them rest for a few minutes.

Serve the chipotle buttered turkey hot, garnished with chopped cilantro if desired. Enjoy!

403. Here's a recipe for mini turkey meatloaves with hot sauce cooked in an air fryer:

Ingredients:

1 lb ground turkey
1/2 cup breadcrumbs
1/4 cup diced onion
1/4 cup diced green bell pepper
1/4 cup diced celery
1/4 cup hot sauce
1 egg, beaten
1 tsp garlic powder
1 tsp salt
1/2 tsp black pepper
Cooking spray

Instructions:

Preheat your air fryer to 375°F.
In a mixing bowl, combine the ground turkey, breadcrumbs, onion, bell pepper, celery, hot sauce, egg, garlic powder, salt, and black pepper. Mix until everything is evenly combined.
Divide the mixture into 6 equal portions and shape each into a mini meatloaf.
Lightly coat the basket of your air fryer with cooking spray, then place the meatloaves in the basket. You may need to cook them in batches depending on the size of your air fryer.
Cook the meatloaves for 15-20 minutes, or until they reach an internal temperature of 165°F.
Serve the meatloaves with additional hot sauce, if desired.

404. Here's an air fryer recipe for turkey-stuffed bell peppers:

Ingredients:

4 bell peppers, halved and seeded
1 pound ground turkey
1 cup cooked brown rice
1/2 cup diced onion
1/2 cup diced celery
1/2 cup diced carrot
1 clove garlic, minced
1 teaspoon salt
1/2 teaspoon black pepper
1 teaspoon paprika
1 teaspoon cumin
1/2 teaspoon chili powder
1/4 teaspoon cayenne pepper
1/2 cup shredded cheddar cheese

Instructions:

Preheat your air fryer to 360°F (180°C).
In a mixing bowl, combine the ground turkey, cooked brown rice, diced onion, diced celery, diced carrot, minced garlic, salt, black pepper, paprika, cumin, chili powder, and cayenne pepper. Mix well.
Stuff each bell pepper half with the turkey mixture.
Place the stuffed bell peppers in the air fryer basket, making sure they don't touch each other.
Air fry the bell peppers for 15-20 minutes, or until the turkey is fully cooked and the peppers are tender.

Remove the basket from the air fryer and sprinkle shredded cheddar cheese on top of the stuffed bell peppers.
Return the basket to the air fryer and air fry for another 1-2 minutes, or until the cheese is melted and bubbly.
Serve the turkey stuffed bell peppers hot and enjoy!

FISH & SEAFOOD

405. Here is an air fryer recipe for herbed crab croquettes:

Ingredients:

1 lb crab meat
1/4 cup bread crumbs
2 tablespoons chopped fresh parsley
2 tablespoons chopped fresh chives
1/4 teaspoon paprika
1/4 teaspoon garlic powder
1/4 teaspoon onion powder
1/4 teaspoon salt
1/8 teaspoon black pepper
1 egg, beaten
1 tablespoon mayonnaise
1 tablespoon Dijon mustard
Cooking spray

Instructions:

Preheat the air fryer to 375°F (190°C).
In a bowl, combine the crab meat, bread crumbs, parsley, chives, paprika, garlic powder, onion powder, salt, and black pepper.
In a separate bowl, whisk together the egg, mayonnaise, and Dijon mustard.
Add the egg mixture to the crab mixture and stir until well combined.
Form the mixture into small croquettes, about 2 tablespoons each.
Spray the air fryer basket with cooking spray.
Place the croquettes in the basket, making sure they are not touching.
Spray the tops of the croquettes with cooking spray.
Air fry for 8-10 minutes until the croquettes are golden brown and crispy.
Serve hot with your favorite dipping sauce.
Enjoy your herbed crab croquettes made in the air fryer!

406. Here's an air fryer recipe for crab fritters with sweet chili sauce:

Ingredients:

1 pound crab meat
1/2 cup breadcrumbs
1/4 cup finely chopped onion
2 cloves garlic, minced
1/4 cup chopped fresh cilantro
1/4 cup chopped scallions
1/4 cup mayonnaise
1 egg, beaten
1 tablespoon Dijon mustard
1 tablespoon Worcestershire sauce
1/2 teaspoon salt

1/4 teaspoon black pepper
Cooking spray
Sweet chili sauce for dipping

Instructions:

In a large bowl, combine the crab meat, breadcrumbs, onion, garlic, cilantro, scallions, mayonnaise, egg, Dijon mustard, Worcestershire sauce, salt, and pepper. Mix well.
Use your hands to form the mixture into small patties or fritters, about 2 inches in diameter.
Preheat the air fryer to 375°F.
Spray the air fryer basket with cooking spray.
Place the fritters in the basket in a single layer, making sure they don't touch each other.
Spray the tops of the fritters with cooking spray.
Air fry for 8-10 minutes, or until golden brown and crispy on the outside and cooked through on the inside.
Serve hot with sweet chili sauce for dipping.
Enjoy your delicious air fried crab fritters with sweet chili sauce!

407. Here's a recipe for Old Bay Sticks with Garlic Mayo in the air fryer:

Ingredients:

1 pound shrimp, peeled and deveined
1/2 cup all-purpose flour
1 tablespoon Old Bay seasoning
2 eggs, beaten
1 cup panko breadcrumbs
Cooking spray
1/4 cup mayonnaise
2 cloves garlic, minced
Salt and pepper to taste

Instructions:

Preheat the air fryer to 400°F (200°C).
In a small bowl, mix together the mayonnaise and minced garlic to make the garlic mayo. Set aside.
In a separate bowl, mix together the flour and Old Bay seasoning.
Dip each shrimp in the flour mixture, then in the beaten eggs, and finally in the panko breadcrumbs to coat well.
Spray the air fryer basket with cooking spray.
Arrange the breaded shrimp in a single layer in the air fryer basket.
Spray the shrimp with a light coating of cooking spray.
Air fry the shrimp for 6 to 8 minutes, or until golden brown and crispy, turning halfway through cooking.
Season with salt and pepper to taste.
Serve the Old Bay sticks hot with the garlic mayo on the side for dipping.
Enjoy your Old Bay Sticks with Garlic Mayo made in the air fryer!

408. Here's a recipe for crabmeat and veggie patties with basil dip in the air fryer:

Ingredients:

1 pound lump crabmeat, drained
1/2 cup bread crumbs
1/4 cup diced red bell pepper
1/4 cup diced onion
1/4 cup diced celery
1/4 cup diced carrots

2 tablespoons mayonnaise
1 egg, beaten
1 tablespoon Dijon mustard
1 tablespoon lemon juice
1 tablespoon Worcestershire sauce
1 teaspoon Old Bay seasoning
Salt and pepper, to taste
Cooking spray

For the basil dip:

1/2 cup mayonnaise
1/4 cup sour cream
1/4 cup chopped fresh basil
2 tablespoons lemon juice
Salt and pepper, to taste

Instructions:

Preheat your air fryer to 375°F.
In a large mixing bowl, combine the crabmeat, bread crumbs, red bell pepper, onion, celery, carrots, mayonnaise, egg, Dijon mustard, lemon juice, Worcestershire sauce, Old Bay seasoning, salt, and pepper. Mix well.
Shape the mixture into patties, about 1/4 cup each.
Spray the air fryer basket with cooking spray. Place the patties in the basket, making sure they don't touch.
Air fry the patties for 8-10 minutes, until golden brown and cooked through.
While the patties are cooking, make the basil dip by whisking together the mayonnaise, sour cream, basil, lemon juice, salt, and pepper in a small bowl.
Serve the crabmeat and veggie patties with the basil dip on the side.
Enjoy your delicious and healthy crabmeat and veggie patties with basil dip!

409. Here's an air fryer recipe for fiery prawns:

Ingredients:

1 pound large prawns, peeled and deveined
2 teaspoons smoked paprika
1 teaspoon cumin
1 teaspoon chili powder
1/2 teaspoon garlic powder
1/2 teaspoon salt
1/4 teaspoon cayenne pepper
2 tablespoons olive oil
1 lemon, cut into wedges

Instructions:

Preheat the air fryer to 400°F (200°C).
In a small bowl, mix together the smoked paprika, cumin, chili powder, garlic powder, salt, and cayenne pepper.
Place the prawns in a large bowl and toss with the spice mixture until evenly coated.
Drizzle the olive oil over the prawns and toss to coat.
Place the prawns in the air fryer basket and cook for 6-8 minutes, shaking the basket halfway through, until the prawns are pink and cooked through.
Serve hot with lemon wedges on the side.
Enjoy your fiery prawns!

410. Here's a recipe for crispy prawns in bacon wraps made in an air fryer:

Ingredients:

12 large prawns, peeled and deveined
6 slices of bacon, cut in half
1 teaspoon garlic powder
1/2 teaspoon paprika
1/4 teaspoon salt
1/4 teaspoon black pepper
Cooking spray

Instructions:

Preheat the air fryer to 400°F (200°C).
In a small bowl, mix garlic powder, paprika, salt, and black pepper.
Season each prawn with the spice mixture.
Wrap each seasoned prawn with a half slice of bacon and secure with a toothpick.
Spray the air fryer basket with cooking spray.
Place the prawns in the air fryer basket in a single layer.
Cook for 6-8 minutes, flipping halfway through, until the bacon is crispy and the prawns are cooked through.
Remove the prawns from the air fryer and let cool for a minute before serving.
Serve the crispy prawns in bacon wraps hot with your favorite dipping sauce. Enjoy!

411. Here's a recipe for air fryer Chinese garlic prawns:

Ingredients:

1 pound large raw prawns, peeled and deveined
2 tablespoons soy sauce
1 tablespoon honey
1 tablespoon rice vinegar
1 tablespoon minced garlic
1 teaspoon grated fresh ginger
1/2 teaspoon Chinese five-spice powder
1/4 teaspoon red pepper flakes (optional)
1 tablespoon vegetable oil
Chopped scallions, for garnish

Instructions:

In a bowl, whisk together the soy sauce, honey, rice vinegar, garlic, ginger, Chinese five-spice powder, and red pepper flakes (if using) until well combined.
Add the prawns to the bowl and toss to coat well.
Preheat the air fryer to 375°F.
Once the air fryer is preheated, brush the basket with the vegetable oil to prevent sticking.
Add the prawns to the air fryer basket in a single layer and cook for 4-5 minutes or until they are cooked through and pink.
Remove the prawns from the air fryer and transfer them to a serving dish.
Garnish with chopped scallions and serve hot.
Enjoy your delicious air fryer Chinese garlic prawns!

412. Here's a recipe for sesame prawns with firecracker sauce in the air fryer:

Ingredients:

1 lb large prawns, peeled and deveined
2 tbsp cornstarch
1 tsp salt
1/2 tsp black pepper
2 tbsp sesame seeds
1 egg
1 tbsp water
1/2 cup panko breadcrumbs
Cooking spray
1/4 cup sweet chili sauce
1 tbsp sriracha sauce
1 tbsp soy sauce
1 tsp garlic powder
1 tsp onion powder

Instructions:

Preheat your air fryer to 400°F (200°C).
In a small bowl, mix together the sweet chili sauce, sriracha sauce, soy sauce, garlic powder, and onion powder to make the firecracker sauce. Set aside.
In a separate bowl, mix together the cornstarch, salt, and black pepper.
In a third bowl, beat the egg with 1 tbsp of water.
Coat the prawns in the cornstarch mixture, then dip them in the beaten egg, and then coat them in the panko breadcrumbs mixed with the sesame seeds.
Place the prawns in a single layer in the air fryer basket, making sure they are not touching each other.
Lightly spray the prawns with cooking spray.
Air fry the prawns for 6-8 minutes, flipping them halfway through the cooking time, until they are crispy and golden brown.
Serve the prawns with the firecracker sauce on the side for dipping. Enjoy!

413. Here is a recipe for air fryer ale-battered scampi with tartare sauce:

Ingredients:

1 lb scampi tails, peeled and deveined
1 cup all-purpose flour
1 tsp baking powder
1/2 tsp salt
1/2 tsp garlic powder
1/2 tsp paprika
1/2 tsp onion powder
1/2 tsp dried oregano
1/4 tsp cayenne pepper
1/2 cup beer
1 egg
1/4 cup mayonnaise
2 tbsp sweet pickle relish
1 tbsp lemon juice
1 tbsp chopped fresh parsley
Salt and pepper to taste
Cooking spray

Instructions:

Preheat your air fryer to 400°F (200°C).

In a mixing bowl, whisk together the flour, baking powder, salt, garlic powder, paprika, onion powder, oregano, and cayenne pepper.
In another bowl, beat the egg and then stir in the beer.
Add the scampi tails to the flour mixture and toss to coat. Then dip the scampi into the beer mixture, making sure they are fully coated.
Place the scampi in a single layer in the air fryer basket, and spray them lightly with cooking spray.
Air fry the scampi for 8-10 minutes or until golden and crispy, shaking the basket halfway through cooking.
While the scampi are cooking, prepare the tartare sauce by mixing together the mayonnaise, sweet pickle relish, lemon juice, parsley, salt, and pepper.
Serve the scampi hot with the tartare sauce on the side for dipping. Enjoy!

414. here's a recipe for air fryer cayenne shrimp:

Ingredients:

1 lb large shrimp, peeled and deveined
1/4 cup all-purpose flour
1 tsp garlic powder
1 tsp paprika
1 tsp cayenne pepper
1/2 tsp salt
1/4 tsp black pepper
1 egg, beaten
1 cup panko breadcrumbs

Instructions:

Preheat your air fryer to 375°F (190°C).
In a shallow bowl, mix together the flour, garlic powder, paprika, cayenne pepper, salt, and black pepper.
In another shallow bowl, beat the egg.
Place the panko breadcrumbs in a third shallow bowl.
Dip each shrimp into the flour mixture, shaking off any excess. Next, dip the shrimp into the egg mixture, then coat with the panko breadcrumbs.
Place the breaded shrimp in the air fryer basket in a single layer.
Cook the shrimp in the air fryer for 5-7 minutes, or until they are golden brown and cooked through.
Serve the cayenne shrimp immediately with your favorite dipping sauce. Enjoy!

415. Here's a recipe for Louisiana-style shrimp in the air fryer:

Ingredients:

1 lb raw shrimp, peeled and deveined
1 tbsp olive oil
2 tbsp Cajun seasoning
1/2 tsp garlic powder
1/2 tsp onion powder
1/4 tsp cayenne pepper
Salt and pepper, to taste
Lemon wedges, for serving

Instructions:

Preheat your air fryer to 400°F (200°C).
In a large bowl, toss the shrimp with olive oil, Cajun seasoning, garlic powder, onion powder, cayenne pepper, salt, and pepper until evenly coated.

Place the shrimp in the air fryer basket in a single layer. Cook for 5-7 minutes, flipping the shrimp halfway through cooking, until they are pink and cooked through.
Serve hot with lemon wedges on the side.
Enjoy your delicious Louisiana-style shrimp made in the air fryer!

416. Here's a recipe for spicy shrimp with coconut avocado dip that you can make in an air fryer:

Ingredients for spicy shrimp:
1 pound large shrimp, peeled and deveined
1 tablespoon olive oil
1 teaspoon paprika
1/2 teaspoon cumin
1/4 teaspoon cayenne pepper
1/4 teaspoon garlic powder
1/4 teaspoon salt
1/8 teaspoon black pepper
Ingredients for coconut avocado dip:
1 ripe avocado, peeled and pitted
1/4 cup coconut milk
1 tablespoon lime juice
1 clove garlic, minced
1/4 teaspoon salt
1/4 teaspoon black pepper

Instructions:

Preheat the air fryer to 400°F (200°C).
In a bowl, toss the shrimp with the olive oil, paprika, cumin, cayenne pepper, garlic powder, salt, and black pepper until well coated.
Place the shrimp in the air fryer basket in a single layer.
Air fry the shrimp for 5-6 minutes, shaking the basket halfway through cooking time, until they are cooked through and crispy on the outside.
While the shrimp is cooking, prepare the coconut avocado dip by combining the avocado, coconut milk, lime juice, garlic, salt, and black pepper in a blender or food processor. Blend until smooth.
Serve the spicy shrimp with the coconut avocado dip on the side. Enjoy!

417. Here's a recipe for an Asian shrimp medley in the air fryer:

Ingredients:

1 lb. medium-sized shrimp, peeled and deveined
1 red bell pepper, sliced
1 yellow bell pepper, sliced
1 small onion, sliced
1 tbsp. olive oil
1 tsp. garlic powder
1 tsp. onion powder
1 tsp. paprika
Salt and pepper, to taste
1 tbsp. sesame oil
1 tbsp. soy sauce
1 tsp. honey
1 tsp. grated ginger
1 tbsp. chopped green onions
1 tbsp. sesame seeds

Instructions:

Preheat your air fryer to 400°F (200°C).
In a bowl, combine the shrimp, bell peppers, onion, olive oil, garlic powder, onion powder, paprika, salt, and pepper. Toss to coat everything evenly.
Arrange the shrimp and vegetables in the air fryer basket in a single layer.
Air fry for 8-10 minutes, shaking the basket halfway through.
While the shrimp and vegetables cook, make the sauce. In a small bowl, whisk together the sesame oil, soy sauce, honey, and grated ginger.
Once the shrimp and vegetables are cooked, transfer them to a serving dish and drizzle with the sauce.
Sprinkle with chopped green onions and sesame seeds, and serve immediately.
Enjoy your delicious Asian shrimp medley made in the air fryer!
418. Here's an air fryer recipe for mango shrimp skewers with hot sauce:

Ingredients:

1 lb large shrimp, peeled and deveined
1 ripe mango, peeled and cubed
1 red onion, cut into chunks
1 red bell pepper, cut into chunks
1/4 cup olive oil
2 tbsp lime juice
1 tbsp honey
1/2 tsp chili powder
1/4 tsp cumin
1/4 tsp salt
1/4 tsp black pepper
1/4 cup hot sauce

Instructions:

Preheat the air fryer to 400°F (200°C).
In a small bowl, whisk together olive oil, lime juice, honey, chili powder, cumin, salt, and black pepper.
Thread the shrimp, mango, red onion, and red bell pepper onto skewers, alternating ingredients.
Brush the skewers with the marinade.
Place the skewers in the air fryer basket and cook for 8-10 minutes, flipping halfway through, until the shrimp are pink and cooked through.
In a small saucepan, heat the hot sauce over low heat.
Serve the shrimp skewers with the hot sauce on the side for dipping. Enjoy!

419. here is a recipe for rosemary cashew shrimp cooked in an air fryer:

Ingredients:

1 lb. large shrimp, peeled and deveined
1 cup cashews, roughly chopped
2 tbsp. olive oil
2 tbsp. honey
2 tbsp. soy sauce
1 tbsp. minced fresh rosemary
1 tsp. garlic powder
Salt and pepper to taste

Instructions:

Preheat your air fryer to 400°F (200°C).
In a bowl, whisk together the olive oil, honey, soy sauce, minced rosemary, garlic powder, salt, and pepper.

Add the shrimp to the bowl and toss to coat well.
Add the chopped cashews to the bowl and mix well.
Place the shrimp and cashews in the air fryer basket in a single layer.
Cook for 6-8 minutes or until the shrimp are pink and cooked through, shaking the basket halfway through cooking to ensure even cooking.
Serve hot and enjoy!
Note: You can also add some sliced vegetables such as bell peppers or zucchini to the air fryer basket with the shrimp for a delicious and nutritious side dish.

420. Here's a recipe for Cajun-rubbed jumbo shrimp cooked in an air fryer:

Ingredients:

1 lb jumbo shrimp, peeled and deveined
1 tbsp olive oil
1 tsp Cajun seasoning
1/2 tsp garlic powder
1/2 tsp onion powder
Salt and pepper, to taste

Instructions:

Preheat the air fryer to 400°F.
In a small bowl, mix together the olive oil, Cajun seasoning, garlic powder, onion powder, salt, and pepper.
Add the shrimp to the seasoning mixture and toss to coat evenly.
Arrange the shrimp in a single layer in the air fryer basket.
Cook for 5-7 minutes or until the shrimp are pink and cooked through, flipping halfway through.
Serve hot with your favorite dipping sauce.
Enjoy your delicious Cajun rubbed jumbo shrimp cooked to perfection in your air fryer!

421. Here's a recipe for Greek-style air fryer fried mussels:

Ingredients:

1 pound of fresh mussels, cleaned and debearded
1/2 cup of all-purpose flour
1/2 teaspoon of garlic powder
1/2 teaspoon of dried oregano
1/4 teaspoon of salt
1/4 teaspoon of black pepper
2 eggs, beaten
1/2 cup of plain breadcrumbs
Cooking spray
Lemon wedges, for serving

Instructions:

Preheat your air fryer to 400°F.
In a shallow dish, mix together the flour, garlic powder, oregano, salt, and black pepper.
In another shallow dish, beat the eggs.
In a third shallow dish, place the breadcrumbs.
Dip each mussel first in the flour mixture, then in the beaten eggs, and finally in the breadcrumbs, making sure to coat it well.
Spray the air fryer basket with cooking spray and place the breaded mussels in a single layer in the basket.
Air fry for 6-8 minutes, until the mussels are crispy and golden brown.

Serve the fried mussels with lemon wedges on the side.
Enjoy your Greek-style air fryer fried mussels!

422. Here's an air fryer recipe for herbed garlic lobster:

Ingredients:

2 lobster tails
4 cloves garlic, minced
2 tbsp olive oil
1 tsp dried basil
1 tsp dried oregano
1/2 tsp salt
1/4 tsp black pepper
Lemon wedges, for serving

Instructions:

Preheat the air fryer to 375°F.
Use a sharp knife to split the lobster tails in half lengthwise, then remove the meat from the shell.
In a small bowl, mix together the minced garlic, olive oil, dried basil, dried oregano, salt, and black pepper.
Brush the garlic and herb mixture onto both sides of the lobster meat.
Place the lobster meat in the air fryer basket, shell-side down.
Cook for 8-10 minutes or until the lobster meat is fully cooked and opaque.
Serve the lobster tails with lemon wedges and enjoy!

423. Here's an air fryer recipe for breaded scallops:

Ingredients:

1 lb sea scallops, rinsed and patted dry
1/2 cup all-purpose flour
2 eggs, beaten
1 cup panko breadcrumbs
1/2 tsp garlic powder
1/2 tsp onion powder
Salt and pepper, to taste
Cooking spray

Instructions:

Preheat your air fryer to 400°F (200°C).
Set up a breading station by putting the flour in a shallow dish, the beaten eggs in another shallow dish, and mixing the panko breadcrumbs with garlic powder, onion powder, salt, and pepper in a third shallow dish.
Coat each scallop in flour, shaking off any excess.
Dip the floured scallop in the beaten eggs, then coat it in the seasoned panko breadcrumbs, pressing gently to adhere.
Place the breaded scallops in a single layer in the air fryer basket. Spray lightly with cooking spray.
Cook the scallops for 6-8 minutes, flipping halfway through, until golden brown and cooked through.
Serve with your favorite dipping sauce and enjoy!
Note: Cooking time may vary depending on the size of your scallops and the power of your air fryer, so adjust accordingly.
424. Here's a recipe for air fryer Mediterranean squid rings with couscous:

Ingredients:

1 lb squid rings
1/2 cup all-purpose flour
1/2 tsp garlic powder
1/2 tsp paprika
1/2 tsp dried oregano
Salt and pepper to taste
1 egg, beaten
1/2 cup panko breadcrumbs
Cooking spray
1 cup couscous
1 1/2 cups chicken or vegetable broth
1/4 cup chopped fresh parsley
1/4 cup chopped fresh mint
1/4 cup chopped fresh cilantro
1 lemon, juiced
2 tbsp olive oil

Instructions:

Preheat your air fryer to 400°F.
Rinse the squid rings under cold water and pat them dry with paper towels.
In a shallow dish, mix the flour, garlic powder, paprika, dried oregano, salt, and pepper.
Dip each squid ring into the beaten egg and then coat it in the flour mixture.
Place the panko breadcrumbs in another shallow dish and coat each squid ring in the breadcrumbs.
Lightly spray the squid rings with cooking spray.
Place the squid rings in the air fryer basket in a single layer and cook for 8-10 minutes, flipping halfway through, until they are crispy and golden brown.
While the squid rings are cooking, prepare the couscous according to package instructions, substituting the broth for water.
In a large bowl, mix together the cooked couscous, chopped parsley, chopped mint, chopped cilantro, lemon juice, and olive oil.
Serve the crispy squid rings on top of the couscous mixture. Enjoy!

425. Here's an air fryer recipe for calamari rings with olives:

Ingredients:

1 pound squid rings, thawed if frozen
1/2 cup all-purpose flour
1/2 cup breadcrumbs
1/2 teaspoon paprika
1/2 teaspoon garlic powder
1/2 teaspoon salt
1/4 teaspoon black pepper
1/4 cup pitted Kalamata olives, chopped
1/4 cup chopped fresh parsley
1/4 cup grated Parmesan cheese
2 tablespoons olive oil
Instructions:

Preheat your air fryer to 400°F (200°C).
In a shallow dish, mix together the flour, breadcrumbs, paprika, garlic powder, salt, and black pepper.
Toss the squid rings in the flour mixture until evenly coated.
Place the coated squid rings in the air fryer basket and cook for 8-10 minutes, or until crispy and golden brown. You may need to cook them in batches depending on the size of your air fryer.

While the calamari is cooking, mix together the chopped olives, parsley, Parmesan cheese, and olive oil in a small bowl.
When the calamari is done, transfer it to a serving dish and top with the olive mixture. Serve immediately and enjoy!

426. here is an air fryer recipe for cod fillets with ginger cilantro sauce:

Ingredients:

4 cod fillets
Salt and pepper
1 tablespoon olive oil
1 tablespoon soy sauce
1 tablespoon honey
1 tablespoon fresh grated ginger
2 cloves garlic, minced
Juice of 1 lime
1/4 cup chopped fresh cilantro

Directions:

Preheat the air fryer to 400°F.
Season the cod fillets with salt and pepper.
In a small bowl, whisk together the olive oil, soy sauce, honey, ginger, garlic, lime juice, and cilantro to make the sauce.
Place the cod fillets in the air fryer basket and brush the tops with the sauce.
Cook the cod fillets in the air fryer for 10-12 minutes, or until the fish flakes easily with a fork.
Serve the cod fillets with the remaining sauce on the side.
Enjoy your delicious air fryer cod fillets with ginger cilantro sauce!

427. here's a recipe for American panko fish nuggets in the air fryer:

Ingredients:

1 lb cod fillets, cut into small pieces
1 cup panko breadcrumbs
1/2 cup all-purpose flour
2 eggs, beaten
1 tsp garlic powder
1 tsp paprika
Salt and pepper, to taste
Cooking spray

Instructions:

Preheat the air fryer to 400°F (200°C).
In a shallow dish, mix together the panko breadcrumbs, garlic powder, paprika, salt, and pepper.
In another shallow dish, add the flour.
In a third shallow dish, beat the eggs.
Dip each piece of cod into the flour, then the beaten egg, and finally the panko mixture, pressing the breadcrumbs onto the fish to adhere.
Place the breaded cod nuggets in the air fryer basket in a single layer, and spray with cooking spray.
Air fry for 10-12 minutes, flipping halfway through cooking, until the fish is crispy and cooked through.
Serve hot with your favorite dipping sauce.
Enjoy your crispy and delicious American panko fish nuggets!

428. here's an air fryer recipe for buttered crab legs:

Ingredients:

1 lb crab legs, thawed if frozen
4 tbsp unsalted butter, melted
2 cloves garlic, minced
1 tbsp lemon juice
1 tsp Old Bay seasoning
Salt and pepper, to taste
Fresh parsley, chopped (optional)

Instructions:

Preheat your air fryer to 400°F (200°C).
In a small bowl, mix together melted butter, minced garlic, lemon juice, Old Bay seasoning, salt, and pepper.
Place the crab legs in the air fryer basket, making sure they are not overlapping.
Brush the crab legs generously with the butter mixture.
Air fry the crab legs for 8-10 minutes, until they are heated through and the butter is bubbling.
Serve the crab legs hot, with the remaining butter mixture drizzled over the top and sprinkled with fresh parsley, if desired. Enjoy!

429. Here's a recipe for air fried seafood mix:

Ingredients:

1 lb. seafood mix (shrimp, scallops, calamari, mussels, etc.)
2 tbsp. olive oil
1 tsp. garlic powder
1 tsp. paprika
1 tsp. dried oregano
Salt and pepper to taste
Lemon wedges for serving

Instructions:

Preheat your air fryer to 400°F (200°C).
In a mixing bowl, combine the olive oil, garlic powder, paprika, oregano, salt, and pepper.
Add the seafood mix to the bowl and toss until the seafood is evenly coated in the seasoning.
Place the seafood mix in the air fryer basket and cook for 10-12 minutes, shaking the basket halfway through, until the seafood is crispy and cooked through.
Serve with lemon wedges on the side.
Enjoy your air fried seafood mix!

430. here's an air fryer recipe for golden cod fish fillets:

Ingredients:

4 cod fish fillets
1/2 cup all-purpose flour
1/2 teaspoon garlic powder
1/2 teaspoon onion powder
1/2 teaspoon paprika
1/2 teaspoon salt
1/4 teaspoon black pepper
1/2 cup panko breadcrumbs
1/4 cup grated Parmesan cheese

2 tablespoons olive oil
Lemon wedges, for serving

Instructions:

Preheat the air fryer to 400°F (200°C).
In a shallow bowl, whisk together the flour, garlic powder, onion powder, paprika, salt, and black pepper.
In another shallow bowl, combine the panko breadcrumbs and Parmesan cheese.
Dip each cod fillet into the flour mixture, shaking off any excess, then dip into the breadcrumb mixture, pressing the crumbs to adhere.
Place the breaded fillets into the air fryer basket.
Drizzle the olive oil over the fillets.
Cook the fillets in the air fryer for 10-12 minutes, or until the fish is cooked through and the coating is golden brown and crispy.
Serve the fish fillets with lemon wedges.
Enjoy your crispy and delicious golden cod fish fillets!

431. Here's an air fryer recipe for a cod finger pesto sandwich:

Ingredients:

4 cod fillet fingers
1/2 cup of breadcrumbs
1/2 cup of flour
1 egg, beaten
1/2 cup of pesto sauce
4 sandwich rolls
1/2 cup of arugula
Salt and pepper
Olive oil spray

Instructions:

Preheat your air fryer to 400°F (200°C).
Mix the breadcrumbs, flour, salt, and pepper in a bowl.
Dip the cod fingers into the beaten egg and then into the breadcrumb mixture, making sure they are well coated.
Spray the cod fingers with olive oil spray.
Place the cod fingers in the air fryer basket and cook for 8-10 minutes or until golden brown and crispy.
While the cod fingers are cooking, cut the sandwich rolls in half and spread pesto on one side of each roll.
Once the cod fingers are done, assemble the sandwiches with arugula and the cooked cod fingers.
Serve hot and enjoy!

432. Here's a recipe for air fryer cod cornflake nuggets with avocado dip:

Ingredients:

1 lb cod fillets, cut into bite-sized pieces
2 cups cornflakes, crushed
1 tsp paprika
1/2 tsp garlic powder
1/2 tsp onion powder
1/2 tsp salt
1/4 tsp black pepper
2 eggs
1 avocado

1/4 cup Greek yogurt
1 tbsp lime juice
Salt and pepper, to taste

Instructions:

Preheat the air fryer to 400°F (200°C).
In a bowl, mix together crushed cornflakes, paprika, garlic powder, onion powder, salt, and black pepper.
Beat the eggs in a separate bowl.
Dip each piece of cod into the beaten eggs, then coat with the cornflake mixture.
Place the coated cod pieces in the air fryer basket, making sure they are not touching.
Cook for 8-10 minutes, or until the cod is cooked through and the cornflake coating is golden and crispy.
While the cod is cooking, prepare the avocado dip. Mash the avocado in a bowl, then add Greek yogurt, lime juice, salt, and pepper. Mix well.
Serve the cod nuggets hot with the avocado dip on the side.
Enjoy your delicious and healthy air fryer cod cornflake nuggets with avocado dip!

433. Here's an air fryer recipe for soy sauce glazed cod:

Ingredients:

2 cod fillets
2 tablespoons soy sauce
1 tablespoon honey
1 tablespoon rice vinegar
1 tablespoon sesame oil
1 teaspoon grated ginger
1 clove garlic, minced
1 tablespoon chopped green onions (optional, for garnish)
Sesame seeds (optional, for garnish)

Instructions:

Preheat the air fryer to 400°F (200°C).
In a small bowl, whisk together the soy sauce, honey, rice vinegar, sesame oil, grated ginger, and minced garlic.
Place the cod fillets in a shallow dish or ziplock bag, and pour the soy sauce mixture over the fish. Allow it to marinate for 15-20 minutes.
Remove the cod fillets from the marinade, reserving the marinade.
Place the cod fillets in the air fryer basket in a single layer.
Cook the cod fillets in the air fryer for about 10-12 minutes, or until cooked through and flaky. Flip the fillets halfway through cooking.
While the cod is cooking, pour the reserved marinade into a small saucepan and bring it to a simmer over medium heat. Cook for a few minutes until the sauce thickens slightly.
Once the cod is cooked, remove it from the air fryer and brush the glaze over the fillets.
Garnish with chopped green onions and sesame seeds, if desired.
Serve the soy sauce glazed cod hot with steamed rice and your favorite vegetables.
Enjoy the flavorful and delicious soy sauce glazed cod from your air fryer!

434. Here's an air fryer recipe for gourmet black cod with fennel and pecans:

Ingredients:

2 black cod fillets
1 fennel bulb, thinly sliced

1/4 cup chopped pecans
2 tablespoons olive oil
1 tablespoon lemon juice
1 teaspoon lemon zest
1 teaspoon dried thyme
Salt and pepper, to taste

Instructions:

Preheat the air fryer to 400°F (200°C).
In a bowl, combine the fennel slices, chopped pecans, olive oil, lemon juice, lemon zest, dried thyme, salt, and pepper. Toss well to coat.
Pat the black cod fillets dry with a paper towel and season them with salt and pepper.
Place the seasoned black cod fillets in the air fryer basket.
Spread the fennel and pecan mixture evenly over the top of the black cod fillets.
Cook the black cod in the air fryer for about 10-12 minutes, or until the fish is cooked through and flakes easily with a fork.
Once cooked, remove the black cod fillets from the air fryer and transfer them to serving plates.
Serve the gourmet black cod with fennel and pecans hot, garnished with additional lemon zest and fresh thyme if desired.
Enjoy the flavorful combination of black cod, fennel, and pecans in this gourmet air fryer recipe!

435. Here's an air fryer recipe for pistachio-crusted salmon fillets:

Ingredients:

2 salmon fillets
1/2 cup shelled pistachios, finely chopped
2 tablespoons Dijon mustard
1 tablespoon honey
1 tablespoon lemon juice
1 teaspoon lemon zest
Salt and pepper, to taste
Cooking spray

Instructions:

Preheat the air fryer to 400°F (200°C).
In a bowl, mix together the Dijon mustard, honey, lemon juice, lemon zest, salt, and pepper.
Brush the mustard mixture evenly over the salmon fillets.
Sprinkle the finely chopped pistachios over the top of the salmon, pressing gently to adhere.
Lightly coat the air fryer basket with cooking spray to prevent sticking.
Place the pistachio-crusted salmon fillets in the air fryer basket.
Cook the salmon in the air fryer for about 10-12 minutes, or until the salmon is cooked through and flakes easily with a fork.
Once cooked, remove the salmon fillets from the air fryer and let them rest for a few minutes.
Serve the pistachio-crusted salmon fillets hot, garnished with additional lemon zest if desired.
Enjoy the delicious combination of pistachio crust and tender salmon in this air fryer recipe!

436. Here's an air fryer recipe for Korean kimchi-spiced salmon:

Ingredients:

2 salmon fillets
1/4 cup kimchi, finely chopped
1 tablespoon gochujang (Korean red pepper paste)
1 tablespoon soy sauce

1 tablespoon sesame oil
1 teaspoon honey
1 teaspoon minced garlic
1/2 teaspoon grated ginger
Sesame seeds, for garnish
Sliced green onions, for garnish

Instructions:

Preheat the air fryer to 400°F (200°C).
In a bowl, mix together the kimchi, gochujang, soy sauce, sesame oil, honey, minced garlic, and grated ginger to make the marinade.
Place the salmon fillets in a shallow dish and pour the marinade over them. Make sure the salmon is well coated with the marinade.
Let the salmon marinate for about 15 minutes to allow the flavors to infuse.
Lightly coat the air fryer basket with cooking spray to prevent sticking.
Place the marinated salmon fillets in the air fryer basket.
Cook the salmon in the air fryer for about 10-12 minutes, or until the salmon is cooked through and flakes easily with a fork.
Once cooked, remove the salmon fillets from the air fryer and let them rest for a few minutes.
Garnish the salmon with sesame seeds and sliced green onions before serving.
Serve the Korean kimchi-spiced salmon hot with a side of steamed rice or your favorite veggies for a delicious and flavorful meal. Enjoy!
437. Here's an air fryer recipe for tandoori-style crispy salmon:

Ingredients:

2 salmon fillets
1/4 cup plain yogurt
2 tablespoons tandoori masala spice mix
1 tablespoon lemon juice
1 teaspoon minced garlic
1 teaspoon grated ginger
Salt, to taste
Fresh cilantro leaves, for garnish
Lemon wedges, for serving

Instructions:

Preheat the air fryer to 400°F (200°C).
In a bowl, combine the yogurt, tandoori masala spice mix, lemon juice, minced garlic, grated ginger, and salt. Mix well to make the marinade.
Place the salmon fillets in a shallow dish and pour the marinade over them. Ensure the salmon is well coated with the marinade.
Let the salmon marinate for about 15-20 minutes to allow the flavors to meld.
Lightly coat the air fryer basket with cooking spray to prevent sticking.
Place the marinated salmon fillets in the air fryer basket.
Cook the salmon in the air fryer for about 10-12 minutes, or until the salmon is cooked through and crispy on the outside.
Once cooked, remove the salmon fillets from the air fryer and let them rest for a few minutes.
Garnish the salmon with fresh cilantro leaves and serve with lemon wedges on the side.
Serve the tandoori-style crispy salmon with naan bread, rice, or a fresh salad for a complete meal. Enjoy the delicious flavors!

438. Here's an air fryer recipe for easy salmon with Greek sauce:

Ingredients:

2 salmon fillets
1/4 cup Greek yogurt
2 tablespoons lemon juice
1 tablespoon chopped fresh dill
1 tablespoon chopped fresh parsley
1 teaspoon minced garlic
Salt and pepper, to taste
Lemon wedges, for serving

For the Greek Sauce:

1/2 cup Greek yogurt
2 tablespoons lemon juice
1 tablespoon extra-virgin olive oil
1 tablespoon chopped fresh dill
1 tablespoon chopped fresh parsley
1 teaspoon minced garlic
Salt and pepper, to taste

Instructions:

Preheat the air fryer to 400°F (200°C).
In a bowl, mix together the Greek yogurt, lemon juice, chopped dill, chopped parsley, minced garlic, salt, and pepper to make the marinade.
Place the salmon fillets in a shallow dish and pour the marinade over them. Ensure the salmon is well coated with the marinade.
Let the salmon marinate for about 15-20 minutes to allow the flavors to meld.
Lightly coat the air fryer basket with cooking spray to prevent sticking.
Place the marinated salmon fillets in the air fryer basket.
Cook the salmon in the air fryer for about 10-12 minutes, or until the salmon is cooked through and flakes easily with a fork.
While the salmon is cooking, prepare the Greek sauce by mixing together the Greek yogurt, lemon juice, olive oil, chopped dill, chopped parsley, minced garlic, salt, and pepper in a bowl.
Once the salmon is cooked, remove it from the air fryer and let it rest for a few minutes.
Serve the salmon with a dollop of the Greek sauce on top and garnish with fresh dill and parsley. Serve with lemon wedges on the side.
This easy salmon with Greek sauce is a flavorful and healthy dish that pairs well with a side of roasted vegetables or a Greek salad. Enjoy!

439. Here's an air fryer recipe for salmon cakes:

Ingredients:

2 cans (14.75 ounces each) salmon, drained and flaked
1/2 cup breadcrumbs
1/4 cup mayonnaise
1/4 cup diced red bell pepper
1/4 cup diced red onion
2 tablespoons chopped fresh parsley
1 tablespoon Dijon mustard
1 tablespoon lemon juice
1 teaspoon Old Bay seasoning
1/2 teaspoon salt
1/4 teaspoon black pepper
Cooking spray
For the Lemon Dill Sauce:

1/2 cup mayonnaise
2 tablespoons chopped fresh dill
1 tablespoon lemon juice
Salt and pepper, to taste

Instructions:

In a large bowl, combine the flaked salmon, breadcrumbs, mayonnaise, diced red bell pepper, diced red onion, chopped parsley, Dijon mustard, lemon juice, Old Bay seasoning, salt, and black pepper. Mix well until all ingredients are evenly combined.
Shape the mixture into 4-6 salmon cakes, depending on the desired size.
Preheat the air fryer to 400°F (200°C).
Lightly coat the air fryer basket with cooking spray.
Place the salmon cakes in the air fryer basket, leaving some space between them.
Spray the tops of the salmon cakes with cooking spray to help them brown and crisp.
Cook the salmon cakes in the air fryer for about 10-12 minutes, flipping them halfway through, or until they are golden brown and cooked through.
While the salmon cakes are cooking, prepare the lemon dill sauce by mixing together the mayonnaise, chopped dill, lemon juice, salt, and pepper in a small bowl. Adjust the seasonings to taste.
Once the salmon cakes are done, remove them from the air fryer and let them cool slightly.
Serve the salmon cakes with the lemon dill sauce on the side for dipping.
These air-fried salmon cakes are crispy on the outside, moist on the inside, and packed with delicious flavors. They make a fantastic appetizer or main dish. Enjoy!

440. Here's an air fryer recipe for salmon and spring onion balls:

Ingredients:

1 pound fresh salmon fillets, skinless
1/2 cup breadcrumbs
1/4 cup chopped spring onions (scallions)
2 tablespoons chopped fresh dill
1 tablespoon lemon zest
1 tablespoon lemon juice
1 teaspoon Dijon mustard
1/2 teaspoon salt
1/4 teaspoon black pepper
Cooking spray

For the Dipping Sauce:

1/4 cup mayonnaise
1 tablespoon chopped spring onions (scallions)
1 tablespoon lemon juice
1 teaspoon honey
Salt and pepper, to taste

Instructions:

In a food processor, pulse the salmon fillets until finely chopped. Be careful not to over-process.
In a large bowl, combine the chopped salmon, breadcrumbs, chopped spring onions, fresh dill, lemon zest, lemon juice, Dijon mustard, salt, and black pepper. Mix well until all ingredients are evenly combined.
Shape the mixture into small balls, about 1-2 inches in diameter. You should get around 12-16 balls, depending on the size.
Preheat the air fryer to 400°F (200°C).
Lightly coat the air fryer basket with cooking spray.

Place the salmon and spring onion balls in the air fryer basket, leaving some space between them.
Spray the tops of the balls with cooking spray to help them brown and crisp.
Cook the salmon and spring onion balls in the air fryer for about 10-12 minutes, flipping them halfway through, or until they are golden brown and cooked through.
While the balls are cooking, prepare the dipping sauce by mixing together the mayonnaise, chopped spring onions, lemon juice, honey, salt, and pepper in a small bowl. Adjust the seasonings to taste.
Once the salmon and spring onion balls are done, remove them from the air fryer and let them cool slightly.
Serve the balls with the dipping sauce on the side.
These salmon and spring onion balls are flavorful, crispy on the outside, and tender on the inside. They make a delicious appetizer or can be served as part of a meal. Enjoy!

441. Here's an air fryer recipe for salmon fillets with broccoli:

Ingredients:

2 salmon fillets
2 cups broccoli florets
2 tablespoons olive oil
2 cloves garlic, minced
1 teaspoon lemon zest
1/2 teaspoon salt
1/4 teaspoon black pepper
Lemon wedges, for serving

Instructions:

Preheat the air fryer to 400°F (200°C).
In a small bowl, combine the olive oil, minced garlic, lemon zest, salt, and black pepper.
Place the salmon fillets on a plate or cutting board and brush the olive oil mixture over both sides of the fillets.
Place the salmon fillets in the air fryer basket, skin-side down.
Toss the broccoli florets with the remaining olive oil mixture.
Add the seasoned broccoli florets to the air fryer basket around the salmon fillets.
Cook the salmon and broccoli in the air fryer for about 10-12 minutes, or until the salmon is cooked through and flakes easily with a fork and the broccoli is tender.
Remove the salmon and broccoli from the air fryer and serve immediately with lemon wedges.
This recipe provides a quick and healthy meal with perfectly cooked salmon fillets and tender broccoli. Enjoy!

442. Here's an air fryer recipe for wild salmon with creamy parsley sauce:

Ingredients:

2 wild salmon fillets
1 tablespoon olive oil
Salt and pepper, to taste
1/2 cup plain Greek yogurt
2 tablespoons chopped fresh parsley
1 clove garlic, minced
1 tablespoon lemon juice
1/2 teaspoon Dijon mustard

Instructions:

Preheat the air fryer to 400°F (200°C).
Brush both sides of the salmon fillets with olive oil and season with salt and pepper.

Place the salmon fillets in the air fryer basket, skin-side down.
Cook the salmon in the air fryer for about 10-12 minutes, or until the salmon is cooked through and flakes easily with a fork.
While the salmon is cooking, prepare the creamy parsley sauce. In a small bowl, mix together the Greek yogurt, chopped parsley, minced garlic, lemon juice, and Dijon mustard. Season with salt and pepper to taste.
Once the salmon is done, remove it from the air fryer and let it rest for a few minutes.
Serve the salmon fillets with a dollop of the creamy parsley sauce on top.
Garnish with additional chopped parsley, if desired.
Enjoy your air-fried wild salmon with creamy parsley sauce!
This recipe offers a delicious and healthy way to enjoy wild salmon with a flavorful creamy parsley sauce. Enjoy!

443. Here's an air fryer recipe for sweet Caribbean salmon fillets:

Ingredients:

2 salmon fillets
2 tablespoons brown sugar
1 tablespoon ground allspice
1 tablespoon paprika
1 teaspoon ground cinnamon
1 teaspoon ground nutmeg
1 teaspoon garlic powder
1 teaspoon onion powder
1/2 teaspoon salt
1/4 teaspoon black pepper
1 tablespoon olive oil
Lime wedges, for serving
Fresh cilantro, for garnish

Instructions:

Preheat the air fryer to 400°F (200°C).
In a small bowl, mix together the brown sugar, allspice, paprika, cinnamon, nutmeg, garlic powder, onion powder, salt, and black pepper to create a spice rub.
Rub the spice mixture evenly over both sides of the salmon fillets.
Drizzle the olive oil over the salmon fillets to lightly coat them.
Place the salmon fillets in the air fryer basket.
Cook the salmon in the air fryer for about 10-12 minutes, or until the salmon is cooked through and flakes easily with a fork.
Once the salmon is done, remove it from the air fryer and let it rest for a few minutes.
Serve the sweet Caribbean salmon fillets with lime wedges and garnish with fresh cilantro.
Enjoy your flavorful and sweet air-fried Caribbean salmon!
This recipe combines a delicious blend of spices with a touch of sweetness, creating a flavorful Caribbean-inspired dish. Serve it with lime wedges for a refreshing tang. Enjoy!

444. Here's an air fryer recipe for classic Mediterranean salmon:

Ingredients:

2 salmon fillets
2 tablespoons olive oil
2 cloves garlic, minced
1 teaspoon dried oregano
1 teaspoon dried thyme
1 teaspoon dried basil

1/2 teaspoon salt
1/4 teaspoon black pepper
Juice of 1 lemon
Lemon wedges, for serving
Fresh parsley, for garnish

Instructions:

Preheat the air fryer to 400°F (200°C).
In a small bowl, combine the olive oil, minced garlic, dried oregano, dried thyme, dried basil, salt, and black pepper to create a marinade.
Place the salmon fillets in a shallow dish and pour the marinade over them. Use your hands to gently coat the salmon with the marinade.
Let the salmon marinate for about 15 minutes to allow the flavors to infuse.
Place the marinated salmon fillets in the air fryer basket.
Cook the salmon in the air fryer for about 10-12 minutes, or until the salmon is cooked through and flakes easily with a fork.
Squeeze the juice of 1 lemon over the cooked salmon fillets.
Serve the classic Mediterranean salmon with lemon wedges and garnish with fresh parsley.
Enjoy your delicious and flavorful air-fried Mediterranean salmon!
This recipe features classic Mediterranean flavors like garlic, herbs, and lemon that pair perfectly with salmon. The air fryer ensures a tender and moist salmon fillet with a lovely crisp on the outside. Serve it with lemon wedges and fresh parsley for a beautiful presentation. Enjoy!

445. Here's an air fryer recipe for French trout meunière:

Ingredients:

4 trout fillets
1/4 cup all-purpose flour
Salt and pepper to taste
4 tablespoons unsalted butter
2 tablespoons fresh lemon juice
2 tablespoons chopped fresh parsley
Lemon wedges for serving

Instructions:

Preheat the air fryer to 375°F.
In a shallow dish, combine the flour, salt, and pepper.
Dredge the trout fillets in the flour mixture, shaking off any excess.
Melt the butter in a small saucepan over medium heat. Cook until the butter turns a light brown color and has a nutty aroma, about 5-7 minutes.
Place the trout fillets in the air fryer basket and cook for 8-10 minutes or until the fish is cooked through and flakes easily with a fork.
Drizzle the browned butter over the cooked trout fillets and sprinkle with lemon juice and fresh parsley.
Serve with lemon wedges.
Enjoy your French trout meunière!

446. Here's an air fryer recipe for easy Creole trout:

Ingredients:

4 trout fillets
2 teaspoons Creole seasoning
2 tablespoons olive oil
2 tablespoons lemon juice

1 tablespoon chopped fresh parsley
Lemon wedges for serving

Instructions:

Preheat the air fryer to 375°F.
Pat the trout fillets dry with paper towels.
Rub both sides of the trout fillets with Creole seasoning.
Drizzle the olive oil over the trout fillets and gently massage it to coat.
Place the trout fillets in the air fryer basket and cook for 8-10 minutes or until the fish is cooked through and flakes easily with a fork.
Remove the trout fillets from the air fryer and drizzle with lemon juice.
Sprinkle with chopped parsley.
Serve with lemon wedges.
Enjoy your easy Creole trout!

447. Here's an air fryer recipe for smoked trout frittata:

Ingredients:

4 large eggs
1/4 cup milk
1/2 teaspoon salt
1/4 teaspoon black pepper
1/2 teaspoon smoked paprika
1/2 cup shredded cheddar cheese
2 green onions, sliced
4 ounces smoked trout, flaked
Cooking spray

Instructions:

Preheat the air fryer to 350°F.
In a mixing bowl, whisk together the eggs, milk, salt, black pepper, and smoked paprika.
Stir in the shredded cheddar cheese, green onions, and smoked trout.
Spray a round baking dish or oven-safe dish with cooking spray.
Pour the egg mixture into the prepared dish.
Place the dish in the air fryer basket and cook for 12-15 minutes or until the frittata is set in the center.
Remove the frittata from the air fryer and let it cool slightly before slicing and serving.
Enjoy your delicious smoked trout frittata!

448. Here's an air fryer recipe for baked trout en papillote with herbs:

Ingredients:

2 trout fillets
Salt and pepper to taste
2 tablespoons olive oil
1 tablespoon lemon juice
2 garlic cloves, minced
1 tablespoon fresh dill, chopped
1 tablespoon fresh parsley, chopped
1 tablespoon fresh thyme leaves
Sliced lemon, for garnish

Instructions:

Preheat the air fryer to 375°F.
Season the trout fillets with salt and pepper on both sides.
In a small bowl, mix the olive oil, lemon juice, minced garlic, fresh dill, parsley, and thyme.
Place each trout fillet on a sheet of parchment paper.
Spoon half of the herb mixture over each fillet, spreading it evenly.
Fold the parchment paper over the trout fillets to create a sealed packet.
Place the packets in the air fryer basket and cook for 10-12 minutes or until the trout is cooked through and flakes easily with a fork.
Carefully open the packets and transfer the trout fillets to serving plates.
Garnish with sliced lemon and additional herbs if desired.
Serve hot and enjoy the flavorful baked trout en papillote!
Note: Make sure to adjust the cooking time based on the thickness of your trout fillets. Thicker fillets may require a few extra minutes of cooking.

449. Here's an air fryer recipe for blackened catfish:

Ingredients:

2 catfish fillets
2 tablespoons paprika
1 teaspoon dried thyme
1 teaspoon dried oregano
1 teaspoon garlic powder
1 teaspoon onion powder
1/2 teaspoon cayenne pepper (adjust to your desired level of spiciness)
1/2 teaspoon salt
1/4 teaspoon black pepper
2 tablespoons melted butter or olive oil

Instructions:

Preheat the air fryer to 400°F.
In a small bowl, mix together the paprika, dried thyme, dried oregano, garlic powder, onion powder, cayenne pepper, salt, and black pepper to make the blackening seasoning.
Pat the catfish fillets dry with paper towels.
Brush both sides of the catfish fillets with melted butter or olive oil.
Sprinkle the blackening seasoning mixture evenly over both sides of the catfish fillets, pressing it gently to adhere.
Place the catfish fillets in the air fryer basket, making sure they are not overlapping.
Air fry the catfish fillets for 8-10 minutes, flipping them halfway through cooking, or until the fish is cooked through and flakes easily with a fork.
Remove the catfish fillets from the air fryer and let them rest for a few minutes.
Serve hot with your favorite side dishes, such as coleslaw, roasted vegetables, or rice.
Enjoy the lovely blackened catfish with its flavorful and slightly spicy seasoning!
Note: Cooking time may vary slightly depending on the thickness of the catfish fillets. Adjust the cooking time accordingly to ensure the fish is cooked through.

450. Here's an air fryer recipe for rosemary catfish:

Ingredients:

2 catfish fillets
2 tablespoons olive oil
1 tablespoon chopped fresh rosemary
1 teaspoon minced garlic
1/2 teaspoon salt
1/4 teaspoon black pepper

Lemon wedges, for serving

Instructions:

Preheat the air fryer to 400°F.
In a small bowl, mix together the olive oil, chopped fresh rosemary, minced garlic, salt, and black pepper.
Brush both sides of the catfish fillets with the rosemary mixture.
Place the catfish fillets in the air fryer basket, making sure they are not overlapping.
Air fry the catfish fillets for 8-10 minutes, flipping them halfway through cooking, or until the fish is cooked through and flakes easily with a fork.
Remove the catfish fillets from the air fryer and let them rest for a few minutes.
Serve hot with lemon wedges on the side for squeezing over the fish.
Enjoy the flavorful and aromatic rosemary catfish as a delicious main dish!
Note: Cooking time may vary slightly depending on the thickness of the catfish fillets. Adjust the cooking time accordingly to ensure the fish is cooked through.

451. Here's an air fryer recipe for golden batter fried catfish fillets:

Ingredients:

2 catfish fillets
1 cup all-purpose flour
1 teaspoon salt
1/2 teaspoon paprika
1/4 teaspoon black pepper
1/4 teaspoon garlic powder
1/4 teaspoon onion powder
1/4 teaspoon dried thyme
1/4 teaspoon dried oregano
1/4 teaspoon cayenne pepper (optional, for added heat)
1/2 cup buttermilk
Cooking spray or olive oil, for greasing

Instructions:

Preheat the air fryer to 400°F.
In a shallow bowl, mix together the all-purpose flour, salt, paprika, black pepper, garlic powder, onion powder, dried thyme, dried oregano, and cayenne pepper (if using).
Dip each catfish fillet into the buttermilk, allowing any excess to drip off.
Coat the catfish fillets in the seasoned flour mixture, pressing gently to adhere the flour to the fish.
Place the coated catfish fillets in the air fryer basket, making sure they are not overlapping.
Lightly spray the catfish fillets with cooking spray or brush them with a little olive oil to help achieve a golden and crispy crust.
Air fry the catfish fillets for 10-12 minutes, flipping them halfway through cooking, or until they are golden brown and crispy.
Remove the catfish fillets from the air fryer and let them rest for a few minutes before serving.
Serve the golden batter fried catfish fillets with your favorite dipping sauce or alongside some tartar sauce and lemon wedges.
Enjoy the crispy and flavorful catfish fillets as a tasty seafood dish!
Note: Cooking time may vary slightly depending on the thickness of the catfish fillets. Adjust the cooking time accordingly to ensure the fish is cooked through and the batter is crispy.

452. Here's an air fryer recipe for Jamaican-style fish fillets:

Ingredients:

2 fish fillets (such as red snapper, tilapia, or mahi-mahi)
2 tablespoons Jamaican jerk seasoning
1 tablespoon olive oil
1 lime, juiced
Salt, to taste
Fresh cilantro, chopped (for garnish)

Instructions:

Preheat the air fryer to 400°F.
Pat dry the fish fillets with a paper towel and place them on a plate.
In a small bowl, mix the Jamaican jerk seasoning, olive oil, lime juice, and a pinch of salt.
Brush both sides of the fish fillets with the jerk seasoning mixture, ensuring they are evenly coated.
Place the seasoned fish fillets in the air fryer basket, making sure they are not overlapping.
Air fry the fish fillets for 8-10 minutes, or until they are cooked through and flake easily with a fork.
Once cooked, remove the fish fillets from the air fryer and let them rest for a minute.
Garnish with fresh cilantro and serve the Jamaican-style fish fillets with rice, steamed vegetables, or a side salad.
Enjoy the flavorful and spicy Jamaican fish fillets!
Note: Cooking time may vary depending on the thickness of the fish fillets. Adjust the cooking time accordingly to ensure the fish is cooked through. Additionally, you can adjust the amount of Jamaican jerk seasoning according to your spice preference.

453. Here's an air fryer recipe for ale-battered fish with tartar sauce:

Ingredients:

For the fish:

2 fish fillets (such as cod, haddock, or tilapia)
1 cup all-purpose flour
1 teaspoon baking powder
1/2 teaspoon salt
1/2 teaspoon paprika
1/4 teaspoon black pepper
1/2 cup ale or beer
Cooking spray

For the tartar sauce:

1/2 cup mayonnaise
2 tablespoons chopped dill pickles
1 tablespoon lemon juice
1 tablespoon chopped fresh parsley
1 teaspoon Dijon mustard
Salt and pepper to taste

Instructions:
Preheat the air fryer to 400°F.
In a shallow bowl, whisk together the flour, baking powder, salt, paprika, and black pepper.
Slowly pour in the ale or beer while whisking until the batter is smooth and thick enough to coat the back of a spoon. Adjust the amount of liquid if needed.
Dip each fish fillet into the batter, allowing any excess batter to drip off.
Spray the air fryer basket with cooking spray. Place the battered fish fillets in the basket, making sure they are not overlapping.
Air fry the fish for 8-10 minutes, flipping halfway through, until golden brown and crispy.

While the fish is cooking, prepare the tartar sauce by combining the mayonnaise, chopped dill pickles, lemon juice, chopped parsley, Dijon mustard, salt, and pepper in a small bowl. Stir well to combine.
Once the fish is cooked, remove it from the air fryer and let it cool for a minute.
Serve the ale-battered fish with the tartar sauce on the side for dipping.
Enjoy the crispy and flavorful ale-battered fish with tangy tartar sauce!
Note: Cooking time may vary depending on the thickness of the fish fillets. Adjust the cooking time accordingly to ensure the fish is cooked through and crispy.

454. Here's an air fryer recipe for Parmesan tilapia fillets:

Ingredients:

4 tilapia fillets
1/2 cup grated Parmesan cheese
1/4 cup bread crumbs
1 teaspoon dried oregano
1/2 teaspoon garlic powder
1/2 teaspoon paprika
Salt and pepper to taste
Cooking spray

Instructions:

Preheat the air fryer to 400°F.
In a shallow bowl, combine the grated Parmesan cheese, bread crumbs, dried oregano, garlic powder, paprika, salt, and pepper.
Pat dry the tilapia fillets with a paper towel to remove any excess moisture.
Dip each tilapia fillet into the Parmesan mixture, pressing gently to adhere the coating on both sides.
Spray the air fryer basket with cooking spray. Place the coated tilapia fillets in the basket, making sure they are not overlapping.
Air fry the tilapia for 8-10 minutes, flipping halfway through, until the fish is cooked through and the coating is crispy and golden brown.
Once the tilapia fillets are cooked, remove them from the air fryer and let them cool for a minute.
Serve the Parmesan tilapia fillets with your favorite sides or on a bed of salad.
Enjoy the flavorful and crispy Parmesan-coated tilapia fillets!
Note: Cooking time may vary depending on the thickness of the tilapia fillets. Adjust the cooking time accordingly to ensure the fish is cooked through and the coating is crispy.

455. Here's an air fryer recipe for broiled tilapia:

Ingredients:

4 tilapia fillets
2 tablespoons olive oil
1 tablespoon lemon juice
1 teaspoon paprika
1/2 teaspoon garlic powder
1/2 teaspoon dried thyme
Salt and pepper to taste
Lemon wedges, for serving
Fresh parsley, for garnish

Instructions:

Preheat the air fryer to 400°F.
In a small bowl, mix together the olive oil, lemon juice, paprika, garlic powder, dried thyme, salt, and pepper to create a marinade.

Pat dry the tilapia fillets with a paper towel to remove any excess moisture.
Place the tilapia fillets in a shallow dish and pour the marinade over them. Make sure the fillets are well coated on both sides.
Place the marinated tilapia fillets in the air fryer basket, making sure they are not overlapping.
Air fry the tilapia for 8-10 minutes, or until the fish is cooked through and flakes easily with a fork.
Once the tilapia fillets are cooked, remove them from the air fryer and let them cool for a minute.
Serve the broiled tilapia with lemon wedges and garnish with fresh parsley.
Enjoy the flavorful and tender broiled tilapia!
Note: Cooking time may vary depending on the thickness of the tilapia fillets. Adjust the cooking time accordingly to ensure the fish is cooked through.

456. Here's an air fryer recipe for crispy tilapia bites:

Ingredients:

1 lb tilapia fillets, cut into bite-sized pieces
1/2 cup all-purpose flour
2 eggs, beaten
1 cup breadcrumbs (preferably seasoned)
1/2 teaspoon paprika
1/2 teaspoon garlic powder
1/2 teaspoon salt
1/4 teaspoon black pepper
Cooking spray

Instructions:

Preheat the air fryer to 400°F.
In a shallow dish, mix together the breadcrumbs, paprika, garlic powder, salt, and black pepper.
Set up a dredging station with the flour, beaten eggs, and breadcrumb mixture.
Dip each tilapia bite into the flour, shaking off any excess. Then dip it into the beaten eggs, allowing any excess to drip off. Finally, coat it in the breadcrumb mixture, pressing lightly to ensure it sticks.
Place the breaded tilapia bites in a single layer in the air fryer basket, leaving space between them.
Lightly spray the tops of the tilapia bites with cooking spray.
Air fry the tilapia bites for 8-10 minutes, flipping them halfway through the cooking time, until they are golden brown and crispy.
Once cooked, remove the tilapia bites from the air fryer and let them cool for a minute.
Serve the crispy tilapia bites with your favorite dipping sauce, such as tartar sauce or lemon aioli.
Enjoy the delicious and crunchy air fried tilapia bites!
Note: Cooking time may vary depending on the size and thickness of the tilapia bites. Adjust the cooking time accordingly to ensure they are cooked through and crispy.

457. Here's an air fryer recipe for peppery and lemony haddock:

Ingredients:

2 haddock fillets
1 tablespoon olive oil
1 teaspoon lemon zest
1 teaspoon freshly ground black pepper
1/2 teaspoon salt
1/2 teaspoon garlic powder
1/2 teaspoon paprika
Lemon wedges, for serving

Instructions:

Preheat the air fryer to 400°F.
In a small bowl, mix together the olive oil, lemon zest, black pepper, salt, garlic powder, and paprika to make a marinade.
Pat the haddock fillets dry with a paper towel and place them in a shallow dish or zip-top bag.
Pour the marinade over the haddock fillets, making sure they are evenly coated. Let them marinate for about 10 minutes.
Place the marinated haddock fillets in the air fryer basket in a single layer.
Air fry the haddock for 10-12 minutes, or until it is cooked through and flakes easily with a fork. The cooking time may vary depending on the thickness of the fillets.
Once cooked, remove the haddock from the air fryer and serve hot with lemon wedges.
Enjoy the peppery and lemony haddock as a main dish with your favorite sides, such as roasted vegetables or steamed rice.
Note: Adjust the seasoning according to your taste preferences. You can also add additional herbs or spices to customize the flavor of the haddock.

458. Here's an air fryer recipe for crumbly haddock patties:

Ingredients:

2 haddock fillets
1/4 cup breadcrumbs
1/4 cup grated Parmesan cheese
1/4 cup chopped fresh parsley
1/4 cup chopped green onions
1/4 cup mayonnaise
1 teaspoon Dijon mustard
1/2 teaspoon garlic powder
1/2 teaspoon paprika
Salt and pepper to taste
Lemon wedges, for serving

Instructions:

Preheat the air fryer to 375°F.
In a bowl, flake the haddock fillets into small pieces using a fork.
In a separate bowl, combine the breadcrumbs, Parmesan cheese, parsley, green onions, mayonnaise, Dijon mustard, garlic powder, paprika, salt, and pepper. Mix well.
Add the flaked haddock to the breadcrumb mixture and stir until well combined.
Form the mixture into patties, about 2-3 inches in diameter, and place them on a greased air fryer basket or tray.
Lightly spray or brush the patties with oil to promote browning.
Air fry the haddock patties for 10-12 minutes, flipping them halfway through, until they are golden brown and cooked through.
Remove the patties from the air fryer and let them cool for a few minutes before serving.
Serve the crumbly haddock patties with lemon wedges on the side for squeezing over the patties.
Enjoy the delicious crumbly haddock patties as a main dish or as a sandwich filling with your preferred condiments and toppings.

459. Here's an air fryer recipe for barramundi fillets in the lemon sauce:

Ingredients:

2 barramundi fillets
2 tablespoons olive oil
1 teaspoon lemon zest

2 tablespoons lemon juice
2 cloves garlic, minced
1 tablespoon chopped fresh parsley
Salt and pepper to taste
Lemon slices, for serving

For the lemon sauce:

1/4 cup butter
1/4 cup lemon juice
1 teaspoon lemon zest
1 clove garlic, minced
Salt and pepper to taste
Instructions:

Preheat the air fryer to 400°F.
In a small bowl, combine the olive oil, lemon zest, lemon juice, minced garlic, chopped parsley, salt, and pepper. Mix well.
Place the barramundi fillets in a shallow dish and pour the lemon marinade over them. Ensure the fillets are well coated with the marinade. Let them marinate for 10-15 minutes.
Meanwhile, prepare the lemon sauce by melting the butter in a saucepan over low heat. Add the lemon juice, lemon zest, minced garlic, salt, and pepper. Stir until well combined and heated through. Remove from heat and set aside.
Place the marinated barramundi fillets in the air fryer basket or on the air fryer tray, making sure they are not overcrowded.
Air fry the barramundi fillets for 8-10 minutes, or until they are cooked through and flake easily with a fork.
Remove the fillets from the air fryer and transfer them to serving plates.
Drizzle the prepared lemon sauce over the barramundi fillets and garnish with lemon slices.
Serve the barramundi fillets with lemon sauce alongside your favorite side dishes or salad.
Enjoy the flavorful barramundi fillets in lemon sauce while they're still warm.

460. Here's an air fryer recipe for hot sardine cakes:

Ingredients:

2 cans of sardines, drained and mashed
1/2 cup bread crumbs
1/4 cup grated Parmesan cheese
2 tablespoons chopped fresh parsley
1 tablespoon lemon juice
1 teaspoon lemon zest
1/2 teaspoon paprika
1/4 teaspoon garlic powder
1/4 teaspoon salt
1/4 teaspoon black pepper
1/4 cup all-purpose flour
1 egg, beaten
Cooking spray

Instructions:

Preheat the air fryer to 400°F.
In a mixing bowl, combine the mashed sardines, bread crumbs, Parmesan cheese, chopped parsley, lemon juice, lemon zest, paprika, garlic powder, salt, and black pepper. Mix well until all the ingredients are evenly incorporated.
Shape the mixture into small cakes or patties, about 2-3 inches in diameter.

Place the flour, beaten egg, and additional bread crumbs in separate shallow dishes.
Dip each sardine cake into the flour, then the beaten egg, and finally coat it with bread crumbs, pressing gently to adhere.
Lightly grease the air fryer basket or tray with cooking spray to prevent sticking.
Arrange the coated sardine cakes in a single layer in the air fryer basket or on the air fryer tray. You may need to cook them in batches depending on the size of your air fryer.
Air fry the sardine cakes for 8-10 minutes, flipping them halfway through the cooking time, until they are golden brown and crispy.
Once cooked, transfer the sardine cakes to a serving plate and let them cool slightly before serving.
Serve the hot sardine cakes as an appetizer or main dish, accompanied by your favorite dipping sauce or a side of mixed greens.
Enjoy the flavorful and crispy hot sardine cakes while they're still warm.

461. Here's an air fryer recipe for effortless tuna fritters:

Ingredients:

2 cans of tuna, drained
1/2 cup bread crumbs
1/4 cup finely chopped onion
2 tablespoons chopped fresh parsley
1 tablespoon lemon juice
1 teaspoon Dijon mustard
1/2 teaspoon garlic powder
1/4 teaspoon salt
1/4 teaspoon black pepper
1/4 cup all-purpose flour
1 egg, beaten
Cooking spray

Instructions:

Preheat the air fryer to 400°F.
In a mixing bowl, combine the drained tuna, bread crumbs, chopped onion, chopped parsley, lemon juice, Dijon mustard, garlic powder, salt, and black pepper. Mix well until all the ingredients are evenly incorporated.
Shape the mixture into small fritters or patties, about 2-3 inches in diameter.
Place the flour, beaten egg, and additional bread crumbs in separate shallow dishes.
Dip each tuna fritter into the flour, then the beaten egg, and finally coat it with bread crumbs, pressing gently to adhere.
Lightly grease the air fryer basket or tray with cooking spray to prevent sticking.
Arrange the coated tuna fritters in a single layer in the air fryer basket or on the air fryer tray. You may need to cook them in batches depending on the size of your air fryer.
Air fry the tuna fritters for 8-10 minutes, flipping them halfway through the cooking time, until they are golden brown and crispy.
Once cooked, transfer the tuna fritters to a serving plate and let them cool slightly before serving.
Serve the effortless tuna fritters as an appetizer or main dish, accompanied by your favorite dipping sauce or a side of salad.
Enjoy the tasty and easy-to-make tuna fritters while they're still warm.

462. Here's an air fryer recipe for an air-fried tuna sandwich:

Ingredients:

2 cans of tuna, drained
1/4 cup mayonnaise
2 tablespoons diced red onion

2 tablespoons diced celery
1 tablespoon chopped fresh parsley
1 tablespoon lemon juice
Salt and pepper to taste
4 slices of bread
Lettuce leaves
Sliced tomatoes
Sliced cheese (optional)

Instructions:

In a mixing bowl, combine the drained tuna, mayonnaise, diced red onion, diced celery, chopped parsley, lemon juice, salt, and pepper. Mix well until all the ingredients are thoroughly combined.
Preheat the air fryer to 375°F.
Lightly toast the bread slices if desired.
Divide the tuna mixture evenly among two slices of bread and spread it out in an even layer.
Add lettuce leaves, sliced tomatoes, and sliced cheese (if desired) on top of the tuna mixture.
Place the remaining slices of bread on top to form sandwiches.
Lightly spray the air fryer basket or tray with cooking spray to prevent sticking.
Place the sandwiches in the air fryer basket or on the air fryer tray. You may need to cook them in batches depending on the size of your air fryer.
Air fry the sandwiches for 5-7 minutes, flipping them halfway through the cooking time, until the bread is crispy and the cheese (if added) is melted.
Once cooked, remove the sandwiches from the air fryer and let them cool slightly before serving.
Cut the sandwiches in half, if desired, and serve them warm.
Enjoy the delicious and crispy air-fried tuna sandwiches as a quick and tasty meal.

463. Here's an air fryer recipe for smoked fish quiche:

Ingredients:

1 ready-made pie crust
4 large eggs
1 cup milk
1/2 cup heavy cream
1 cup smoked fish, flaked (such as smoked salmon or trout)
1/2 cup shredded cheese (such as cheddar or Gruyere)
1/4 cup diced red onion
2 tablespoons chopped fresh dill
Salt and pepper to taste

Instructions:

Preheat the air fryer to 350°F.
Place the ready-made pie crust in a pie dish or an air fryer-safe baking dish. Trim any excess crust hanging over the edges.
In a mixing bowl, whisk together the eggs, milk, and heavy cream until well combined.
Add the smoked fish, shredded cheese, diced red onion, chopped dill, salt, and pepper to the egg mixture. Stir until all the ingredients are evenly distributed.
Pour the mixture into the prepared pie crust, spreading it out evenly.
Place the pie dish in the air fryer basket or on the air fryer tray.
Air fry the quiche for 20-25 minutes, or until the center is set and the top is golden brown.
Once cooked, remove the quiche from the air fryer and let it cool slightly before slicing and serving.
Serve the smoked fish quiche warm as a delicious breakfast, brunch, or lunch option.
Enjoy the flavorful and smoky goodness of the air-fried smoked fish quiche!

464. Here's an air fryer recipe for a delicious seafood casserole:

Ingredients:

1 pound mixed seafood (such as shrimp, scallops, and white fish)
1 cup diced bell peppers (any color)
1 cup diced onions
1 cup diced celery
2 cloves garlic, minced
1 can (14 ounces) diced tomatoes, drained
1/2 cup chicken or seafood broth
1/2 cup heavy cream
1 teaspoon dried thyme
1/2 teaspoon paprika
1/2 teaspoon salt
1/4 teaspoon black pepper
1 cup shredded cheese (such as cheddar or Gruyere)
Fresh parsley, chopped (for garnish)

Instructions:

Preheat the air fryer to 375°F.
In a bowl, combine the diced bell peppers, onions, celery, and minced garlic. Toss to mix well.
In the air fryer basket or tray, layer the mixed seafood and the diced vegetable mixture.
In a separate bowl, whisk together the diced tomatoes, chicken or seafood broth, heavy cream, dried thyme, paprika, salt, and black pepper. Pour this mixture over the seafood and vegetables in the air fryer.
Sprinkle the shredded cheese evenly over the top of the casserole.
Place the air fryer basket or tray in the preheated air fryer.
Air fry the seafood casserole for 18-20 minutes, or until the seafood is cooked through and the cheese is melted and golden brown.
Remove the casserole from the air fryer and let it cool for a few minutes.
Garnish with freshly chopped parsley before serving.
Serve the delicious seafood casserole as a main dish with crusty bread or over cooked rice or pasta.
Enjoy the flavorful and comforting seafood casserole straight from the air fryer!

465. Here's an air fryer recipe for sesame halibut fillets:

Ingredients:

2 halibut fillets (6-8 ounces each)
2 tablespoons soy sauce
1 tablespoon sesame oil
1 tablespoon honey
1 tablespoon rice vinegar
1 teaspoon grated fresh ginger
1 teaspoon minced garlic
1 tablespoon sesame seeds
Salt and pepper, to taste
Fresh cilantro, chopped (for garnish)
Lime wedges (for serving)

Instructions:

Preheat the air fryer to 400°F (200°C).
In a small bowl, whisk together the soy sauce, sesame oil, honey, rice vinegar, grated ginger, minced garlic, sesame seeds, salt, and pepper to make the marinade.

Place the halibut fillets in a shallow dish and pour the marinade over them. Let the fillets marinate for 15-20 minutes.
Remove the halibut fillets from the marinade, reserving the marinade for later use.
Place the halibut fillets in the air fryer basket or tray in a single layer.
Air fry the halibut fillets for about 8-10 minutes, or until they are cooked through and easily flake with a fork. Cooking time may vary depending on the thickness of the fillets.
While the halibut is cooking, pour the reserved marinade into a small saucepan and bring it to a simmer over medium heat. Let it simmer for a few minutes until slightly thickened.
Once the halibut fillets are cooked, remove them from the air fryer and drizzle them with the thickened marinade.
Garnish the sesame halibut fillets with fresh cilantro and serve with lime wedges on the side.
Enjoy the flavorful and tender sesame halibut fillets from the air fryer!
Note: Make sure to adjust the cooking time based on the thickness of the fillets to ensure they are cooked through.

466. Here's an air fryer recipe for Oaty fishcakes:

Ingredients:

2 cups cooked white fish (such as cod or haddock), flaked
1 cup mashed potatoes
1/2 cup rolled oats
1/4 cup finely chopped onion
1/4 cup finely chopped celery
1/4 cup chopped fresh parsley
1 egg, beaten
1 tablespoon lemon juice
1 teaspoon Dijon mustard
1/2 teaspoon garlic powder
Salt and pepper, to taste
Olive oil (for brushing)

Instructions:

In a large mixing bowl, combine the flaked fish, mashed potatoes, rolled oats, chopped onion, chopped celery, chopped parsley, beaten egg, lemon juice, Dijon mustard, garlic powder, salt, and pepper. Mix well until all the ingredients are evenly incorporated.
Shape the mixture into small patties, about 2-3 inches in diameter and 1/2-inch thick. Place the patties on a parchment-lined tray.
Preheat the air fryer to 375°F (190°C).
Lightly brush the fishcakes with olive oil on both sides.
Place the fishcakes in the air fryer basket or tray in a single layer, without overcrowding.
Air fry the fishcakes for about 10-12 minutes, flipping them halfway through the cooking time, until they are golden brown and crispy.
Once cooked, remove the fishcakes from the air fryer and let them cool slightly before serving.
Serve the oaty fishcakes with your favorite dipping sauce, such as tartar sauce or a squeeze of lemon.
Enjoy the crispy and flavorful oaty fishcakes from the air fryer!
Note: Cooking time may vary slightly depending on the size and thickness of the fishcakes. Adjust the cooking time as needed to ensure they are cooked through and golden brown.

467. Here's an air fryer recipe for Ponzu Marinated Tuna:

Ingredients:

2 tuna steaks (about 6 ounces each)
1/4 cup Ponzu sauce
1 tablespoon sesame oil

1 tablespoon honey
1 tablespoon grated ginger
1 clove garlic, minced
1 green onion, thinly sliced (for garnish)
Sesame seeds (for garnish)

Instructions:

In a bowl, whisk together the Ponzu sauce, sesame oil, honey, grated ginger, and minced garlic to make the marinade.
Place the tuna steaks in a shallow dish or zip-top bag and pour the marinade over them. Make sure the tuna is well-coated in the marinade. Let it marinate in the refrigerator for at least 30 minutes, or up to 2 hours for more flavor.
Preheat the air fryer to 400°F (200°C) for 5 minutes.
Remove the tuna steaks from the marinade, allowing any excess marinade to drip off.
Place the tuna steaks in the air fryer basket or on the air fryer tray in a single layer.
Air fry the tuna steaks for 4-6 minutes, depending on the desired level of doneness. For medium-rare, cook for about 4 minutes, and for medium, cook for about 6 minutes. Adjust the cooking time slightly for thicker or thinner tuna steaks.
Once cooked to your liking, remove the tuna steaks from the air fryer and let them rest for a few minutes.
Garnish with thinly sliced green onions and sprinkle with sesame seeds.
Serve the Ponzu Marinated Tuna steaks with steamed rice, stir-fried vegetables, or a fresh salad.
Enjoy the flavorful and tender Ponzu Marinated Tuna from the air fryer!
Note: Cooking time may vary depending on the thickness of the tuna steaks and your desired level of doneness. Adjust the cooking time accordingly.

468. Here's an air fryer recipe for Peach Salsa & Beer Halibut Tacos:

Ingredients:

For the Peach Salsa:

2 ripe peaches, peeled and diced
1/2 red onion, finely chopped
1 jalapeño pepper, seeded and finely chopped
1/4 cup fresh cilantro, chopped
Juice of 1 lime
Salt and pepper to taste

For the Beer Halibut:

2 halibut fillets (about 6 ounces each)
1/2 cup all-purpose flour
1 teaspoon paprika
1/2 teaspoon garlic powder
Salt and pepper to taste
1/2 cup beer (your choice of light or amber)
Cooking spray or oil for greasing

For the Tacos:

Soft taco tortillas
Shredded lettuce
Sliced avocado
Lime wedges (for serving)

Instructions:

In a bowl, combine the diced peaches, red onion, jalapeño pepper, cilantro, lime juice, salt, and pepper to make the peach salsa. Set aside to allow the flavors to meld.
Preheat the air fryer to 400°F (200°C) for 5 minutes.
In a shallow dish, mix together the all-purpose flour, paprika, garlic powder, salt, and pepper.
Dip each halibut fillet into the flour mixture, coating it evenly on all sides.
Pour the beer into a separate shallow dish.
Dip the flour-coated halibut fillets into the beer, allowing any excess to drip off.
Place the halibut fillets in the air fryer basket or on the air fryer tray, ensuring they are not overlapping.
Lightly spray the halibut fillets with cooking spray or brush them with a small amount of oil to promote browning.
Air fry the halibut fillets for 8-10 minutes, flipping halfway through, until they are golden brown and cooked through. The internal temperature should reach 145°F (63°C).
Remove the halibut fillets from the air fryer and let them rest for a few minutes.
Warm the soft taco tortillas in a dry skillet or microwave.
To assemble the tacos, place a halibut fillet on each tortilla. Top with shredded lettuce, sliced avocado, and a generous spoonful of the peach salsa.
Squeeze fresh lime juice over the tacos for added brightness.
Serve the Peach Salsa & Beer Halibut Tacos with additional lime wedges on the side.
Enjoy the delicious and flavorful tacos!
Note: You can adjust the spice level of the peach salsa by adding or reducing the amount of jalapeño pepper. Feel free to customize the toppings and garnishes based on your preference.

469. Here's an air fryer recipe for Italian-style white fish:

Ingredients:

2 white fish fillets (such as cod, haddock, or tilapia)
1/4 cup breadcrumbs
2 tablespoons grated Parmesan cheese
1 teaspoon dried Italian herbs (such as basil, oregano, and thyme)
1/2 teaspoon garlic powder
Salt and pepper to taste
1 tablespoon olive oil
Lemon wedges (for serving)

Instructions:

Preheat the air fryer to 400°F (200°C) for 5 minutes.
In a shallow dish, combine the breadcrumbs, grated Parmesan cheese, dried Italian herbs, garlic powder, salt, and pepper.
Brush the white fish fillets with olive oil on both sides.
Dip each fillet into the breadcrumb mixture, pressing lightly to adhere the crumbs to the fish.
Place the breaded fish fillets in the air fryer basket or on the air fryer tray, ensuring they are not overlapping.
Lightly spray the breaded fillets with cooking spray or brush them with a small amount of oil to promote browning.
Air fry the fish fillets for 8-10 minutes, flipping halfway through, until they are golden brown and cooked through. The internal temperature should reach 145°F (63°C).
Remove the white fish fillets from the air fryer and let them rest for a few minutes.
Serve the Italian-style white fish with lemon wedges for squeezing over the fish.
Pair it with your favorite side dishes like roasted vegetables, steamed rice, or a fresh salad.
Enjoy the flavorful and crispy Italian-style white fish!
Note: You can customize the seasoning by adding other herbs and spices that you prefer. Adjust the cooking time based on the thickness of the fish fillets to ensure they are cooked through.

470. Here's an air fryer recipe for mushroom balls with tomato sauce:

Ingredients:

For the mushroom balls:
1 pound (450g) mushrooms, finely chopped
1 small onion, finely chopped
2 cloves garlic, minced
1/2 cup breadcrumbs
1/4 cup grated Parmesan cheese
2 tablespoons chopped fresh parsley
1 teaspoon dried Italian herbs (such as basil, oregano, and thyme)
Salt and pepper to taste
1 egg, beaten
Cooking spray

For the tomato sauce:

1 can (14 ounces/400g) crushed tomatoes
1 tablespoon tomato paste
1 clove garlic, minced
1 teaspoon dried Italian herbs
Salt and pepper to taste

Instructions:

Preheat the air fryer to 380°F (193°C) for 5 minutes.
In a large bowl, combine the chopped mushrooms, onion, minced garlic, breadcrumbs, grated Parmesan cheese, chopped parsley, dried Italian herbs, salt, and pepper. Mix well.
Add the beaten egg to the mushroom mixture and stir until everything is well combined and the mixture holds together.
Shape the mixture into small balls, about 1 inch (2.5 cm) in diameter, and place them on a plate.
Lightly coat the air fryer basket or tray with cooking spray.
Place the mushroom balls in the air fryer basket or on the tray, making sure they are not touching each other.
Spray the mushroom balls with cooking spray to help them crisp up.
Air fry the mushroom balls at 380°F (193°C) for about 12-15 minutes, shaking the basket or flipping the balls halfway through, until they are golden brown and cooked through.
While the mushroom balls are cooking, prepare the tomato sauce. In a small saucepan, combine the crushed tomatoes, tomato paste, minced garlic, dried Italian herbs, salt, and pepper. Heat over medium heat until the sauce is heated through.
Once the mushroom balls are cooked, remove them from the air fryer and serve them with the tomato sauce for dipping.
Enjoy the flavorful and crispy mushroom balls with tangy tomato sauce!
Note: You can customize the seasoning and herbs used in the mushroom balls according to your preference. Feel free to add spices or adjust the amount of garlic and herbs to suit your taste.

471. Here's an air fryer recipe for fried green tomato bites with remoulade sauce:

Ingredients:

For the fried green tomato bites:

2 green tomatoes, sliced into 1/4-inch thick rounds
1 cup all-purpose flour
1 teaspoon paprika
1/2 teaspoon garlic powder

1/2 teaspoon salt
1/4 teaspoon black pepper
2 eggs, beaten
1 cup panko breadcrumbs
Cooking spray

For the remoulade sauce:

1/2 cup mayonnaise
1 tablespoon Dijon mustard
1 tablespoon fresh lemon juice
1 tablespoon chopped fresh parsley
1 tablespoon chopped green onions
1 clove garlic, minced
1/2 teaspoon paprika
1/4 teaspoon cayenne pepper (optional)
Salt and pepper to taste

Instructions:

Preheat the air fryer to 375°F (190°C) for 5 minutes.
In a shallow bowl, combine the flour, paprika, garlic powder, salt, and black pepper. Mix well.
Dip each tomato slice into the flour mixture, coating both sides.
Dip the flour-coated tomato slice into the beaten eggs, allowing any excess to drip off.
Coat the tomato slice with panko breadcrumbs, pressing gently to adhere the breadcrumbs to the tomato.
Place the breaded tomato bites on a plate or wire rack.
Lightly coat the air fryer basket or tray with cooking spray.
Arrange the breaded tomato bites in a single layer in the air fryer basket or on the tray, making sure they are not touching each other.
Spray the tomato bites with cooking spray to help them crisp up.
Air fry the tomato bites at 375°F (190°C) for 8-10 minutes, flipping them halfway through, until they are golden brown and crispy.
While the tomato bites are cooking, prepare the remoulade sauce. In a small bowl, whisk together the mayonnaise, Dijon mustard, lemon juice, chopped parsley, chopped green onions, minced garlic, paprika, cayenne pepper (if using), salt, and pepper.
Once the tomato bites are cooked, remove them from the air fryer and serve them with the remoulade sauce for dipping.
Enjoy the crispy and tangy fried green tomato bites with creamy remoulade sauce!
Note: You can adjust the seasoning and spice level in the remoulade sauce according to your preference. Feel free to add more cayenne pepper for extra heat or adjust the amount of garlic and herbs to suit your taste.

472. Here's an air fryer recipe for roasted tomatoes with a delicious cheese topping:

Ingredients:

4 large tomatoes
2 tablespoons olive oil
1/2 teaspoon dried oregano
1/2 teaspoon dried basil
1/2 teaspoon garlic powder
Salt and pepper to taste
1/2 cup shredded mozzarella cheese
2 tablespoons grated Parmesan cheese
Fresh basil leaves, for garnish (optional)

Instructions:

Preheat the air fryer to 400°F (200°C) for 5 minutes.
Cut the tomatoes in half horizontally and scoop out the seeds and pulp with a spoon.
In a bowl, combine the olive oil, dried oregano, dried basil, garlic powder, salt, and pepper. Mix well.
Brush the cut sides of the tomatoes with the seasoned olive oil mixture.
Place the tomatoes in the air fryer basket or on the tray, cut side up.
Air fry the tomatoes at 400°F (200°C) for 8-10 minutes, or until they start to soften.
In a small bowl, combine the shredded mozzarella cheese and grated Parmesan cheese.
Remove the tomatoes from the air fryer and sprinkle the cheese mixture evenly over the cut side of each tomato.
Return the tomatoes to the air fryer and continue to air fry at 400°F (200°C) for an additional 3-4 minutes, or until the cheese is melted and golden brown.
Carefully remove the roasted tomatoes from the air fryer and let them cool slightly.
Garnish with fresh basil leaves, if desired, and serve as a side dish or as a topping for salads, pasta, or grilled meats.
Enjoy the deliciously roasted tomatoes with a cheesy topping!

473. Here's an air fryer recipe for roasted Brussels sprouts:

Ingredients:

1 pound Brussels sprouts
2 tablespoons olive oil
1 teaspoon garlic powder
1/2 teaspoon salt
1/4 teaspoon black pepper
Instructions:

Preheat your air fryer to 400°F (200°C) for 5 minutes.
Trim the ends of the Brussels sprouts and remove any outer leaves that are wilted or damaged.
Cut the Brussels sprouts in half lengthwise.
In a large bowl, combine the halved Brussels sprouts, olive oil, garlic powder, salt, and black pepper. Toss well to coat the Brussels sprouts evenly.
Place the seasoned Brussels sprouts in the air fryer basket or on the tray in a single layer. If needed, you can cook them in batches.
Air fry the Brussels sprouts at 400°F (200°C) for 12-15 minutes, shaking the basket or flipping the sprouts halfway through cooking.
Check for desired doneness. The Brussels sprouts should be tender and browned on the outside.
Once done, remove the roasted Brussels sprouts from the air fryer and transfer them to a serving dish.
Serve hot as a side dish or as a delicious addition to salads, grain bowls, or roasted vegetable platters.
Enjoy the crispy and flavorful roasted Brussels sprouts straight from the air fryer!

474. Here's an air fryer recipe for honey-glazed baby carrots:

Ingredients:

1 pound baby carrots
2 tablespoons honey
1 tablespoon olive oil
1/2 teaspoon salt
1/4 teaspoon black pepper
Fresh parsley for garnish (optional)

Instructions:

Preheat your air fryer to 400°F (200°C) for 5 minutes.

In a bowl, combine the honey, olive oil, salt, and black pepper. Stir well to make a glaze.
Add the baby carrots to the glaze and toss until they are evenly coated.
Place the glazed baby carrots in the air fryer basket or on the tray in a single layer.
Air fry the carrots at 400°F (200°C) for 10-12 minutes, shaking the basket or flipping the carrots halfway through cooking.
Check for desired tenderness. The carrots should be tender and slightly caramelized.
Once done, remove the honey-glazed baby carrots from the air fryer and transfer them to a serving dish.
Optional: Garnish with fresh parsley for added freshness and color.
Serve hot as a side dish or as a sweet and nutritious snack.
Enjoy the deliciously glazed and tender honey baby carrots made in the air fryer!

475. Here's an air fryer recipe for authentic Spanish Patatas Bravas:

Ingredients:

4 medium potatoes, peeled and cut into 1-inch cubes
2 tablespoons olive oil
1 teaspoon paprika
1/2 teaspoon garlic powder
1/2 teaspoon salt
1/4 teaspoon black pepper

For the Bravas Sauce:

1/4 cup mayonnaise
2 tablespoons ketchup
1 tablespoon hot sauce (adjust according to your preference)
1/2 teaspoon smoked paprika
1/4 teaspoon garlic powder
Salt and pepper to taste

Instructions:

Preheat your air fryer to 400°F (200°C) for 5 minutes.
In a large bowl, combine the olive oil, paprika, garlic powder, salt, and black pepper. Mix well.
Add the potato cubes to the bowl and toss them in the oil and spice mixture until evenly coated.
Place the seasoned potato cubes in the air fryer basket or on the tray in a single layer.
Air fry the potatoes at 400°F (200°C) for 15-20 minutes, shaking the basket or flipping the potatoes halfway through cooking, until they are crispy and golden brown.
While the potatoes are cooking, prepare the Bravas Sauce. In a small bowl, whisk together the mayonnaise, ketchup, hot sauce, smoked paprika, garlic powder, salt, and pepper until well combined.
Adjust the seasoning and hot sauce according to your taste.
Once the potatoes are done, transfer them to a serving dish and drizzle the Bravas Sauce over the top.
Serve the Patatas Bravas hot as a delicious appetizer or side dish.
Enjoy the crispy and flavorful Spanish Patatas Bravas made in the air fryer, accompanied by the spicy Bravas Sauce!

476. Here's an air fryer recipe for delicious potato patties:

Ingredients:

4 large potatoes, boiled and mashed
1/2 cup bread crumbs
1/4 cup grated Parmesan cheese
1/4 cup finely chopped onion
1/4 cup finely chopped parsley
1 teaspoon garlic powder

1/2 teaspoon salt
1/4 teaspoon black pepper
2 eggs, beaten
Cooking spray

Instructions:

In a large bowl, combine the mashed potatoes, bread crumbs, Parmesan cheese, chopped onion, parsley, garlic powder, salt, and black pepper. Mix well until all ingredients are evenly incorporated.
Take a portion of the potato mixture and shape it into a patty. Repeat with the remaining mixture to make additional patties.
Dip each potato patty into the beaten eggs, coating it on both sides.
Preheat your air fryer to 375°F (190°C) for 5 minutes.
Lightly spray the air fryer basket or tray with cooking spray to prevent sticking.
Place the potato patties in a single layer in the air fryer basket or on the tray.
Air fry the potato patties at 375°F (190°C) for 12-15 minutes, flipping them halfway through cooking, until they are golden brown and crispy.
Once the potato patties are cooked, transfer them to a serving plate and serve them hot.
These delicious potato patties can be served as a side dish, snack, or even in burgers. Enjoy the crispy exterior and fluffy interior of these air-fried potato patties!

477. Here's an air fryer recipe for sweet and spicy French fries:

Ingredients:

4 large russet potatoes, cut into thin fries
2 tablespoons olive oil
1 tablespoon brown sugar
1 teaspoon paprika
1/2 teaspoon chili powder
1/2 teaspoon garlic powder
1/2 teaspoon salt
1/4 teaspoon cayenne pepper (adjust to taste)

Instructions:

Preheat your air fryer to 400°F (200°C) for 5 minutes.
In a large bowl, combine the olive oil, brown sugar, paprika, chili powder, garlic powder, salt, and cayenne pepper. Mix well to create the sweet and spicy seasoning.
Place the cut potatoes in the bowl with the seasoning and toss until all the fries are evenly coated.
Lightly spray the air fryer basket or tray with cooking spray to prevent sticking.
Arrange the seasoned fries in a single layer in the air fryer basket or on the tray.
Air fry the fries at 400°F (200°C) for 15-20 minutes, shaking or flipping them halfway through cooking, until they are crispy and golden brown.
Once the fries are cooked, transfer them to a serving dish and serve them hot.
These sweet and spicy French fries are a delicious twist on the classic fries, with a perfect balance of sweetness and heat. Enjoy them as a tasty side dish or snack!

478. Here's an air fryer recipe for curly fries with gochujang ketchup:

Ingredients:

4 medium-sized potatoes
2 tablespoons vegetable oil
1 tablespoon cornstarch
1 teaspoon paprika
1/2 teaspoon garlic powder

1/2 teaspoon salt
1/4 teaspoon black pepper
Cooking spray

For the Gochujang Ketchup:

1/4 cup ketchup
1 tablespoon gochujang paste
1 teaspoon soy sauce
1 teaspoon honey (optional, for sweetness)
1/2 teaspoon garlic powder

Instructions:

Wash and peel the potatoes. Use a Spiralizer or a curly fry cutter to create the curly shape.
In a large bowl, combine the vegetable oil, cornstarch, paprika, garlic powder, salt, and black pepper. Mix well to create a seasoning mixture.
Add the curly potato strands to the bowl and toss until all the strands are evenly coated with the seasoning mixture.
Preheat your air fryer to 400°F (200°C) for 5 minutes.
Lightly spray the air fryer basket with cooking spray to prevent sticking.
Place the seasoned curly potato strands in the air fryer basket, making sure not to overcrowd them. You may need to cook them in batches.
Air fry the curly fries at 400°F (200°C) for 12-15 minutes, shaking or flipping them halfway through cooking, until they are crispy and golden brown.
While the fries are cooking, prepare the gochujang ketchup by mixing together the ketchup, gochujang paste, soy sauce, honey (if using), and garlic powder in a small bowl. Adjust the sweetness and spiciness to your taste.
Once the curly fries are cooked, remove them from the air fryer and serve them hot with the gochujang ketchup.
These curly fries with gochujang ketchup are a delicious and spicy twist on traditional fries. Enjoy them as a tasty appetizer or side dish!

479. Here's an air fryer recipe for traditional jacket potatoes:

Ingredients:

4 medium-sized potatoes
1 tablespoon olive oil
Salt, to taste
Toppings of your choice (e.g., butter, sour cream, cheese, chives, bacon bits)

Instructions:

Preheat your air fryer to 400°F (200°C) for 5 minutes.
Wash the potatoes thoroughly and pat them dry with a paper towel.
Use a fork to prick several holes in each potato to allow steam to escape while cooking.
Rub each potato with olive oil and sprinkle with salt to season the skins.
Place the potatoes in the air fryer basket, making sure they are not overcrowded. You may need to cook them in batches depending on the size of your air fryer.
Air fry the potatoes at 400°F (200°C) for 40-50 minutes, or until the skins are crispy and the insides are soft and tender. Flip the potatoes halfway through cooking to ensure even browning.
Once the potatoes are cooked, carefully remove them from the air fryer using tongs or oven mitts, as they will be hot.
Slice each potato open lengthwise and fluff the insides with a fork.
Serve the jacket potatoes hot with your favorite toppings such as butter, sour cream, cheese, chives, or bacon bits.

These air fryer jacket potatoes are a quick and convenient way to enjoy this classic dish. Customize them with your preferred toppings for a delicious and satisfying meal.

480. Here's an air fryer recipe for cheesy potatoes and asparagus:

Ingredients:

1 pound baby potatoes, halved
1 bunch asparagus, trimmed
2 tablespoons olive oil
1 teaspoon garlic powder
1/2 teaspoon paprika
Salt and pepper, to taste
1 cup shredded cheddar cheese

Instructions:

Preheat your air fryer to 400°F (200°C) for 5 minutes.
In a bowl, combine the halved baby potatoes, trimmed asparagus, olive oil, garlic powder, paprika, salt, and pepper. Toss until the vegetables are coated evenly.
Place the seasoned potatoes and asparagus in the air fryer basket, spreading them out in a single layer. If your air fryer is small, you may need to cook them in batches.
Air fry the potatoes and asparagus at 400°F (200°C) for 15-20 minutes, or until the potatoes are tender and golden brown, and the asparagus is crisp-tender.
Sprinkle the shredded cheddar cheese over the potatoes and asparagus, and continue to air fry for an additional 2-3 minutes, or until the cheese is melted and bubbly.
Carefully remove the cheesy potatoes and asparagus from the air fryer using tongs or a spatula.
Serve hot as a side dish or a light meal.
The combination of cheesy potatoes and asparagus in the air fryer creates a flavorful and satisfying dish. Enjoy the crispy potatoes, tender asparagus, and melted cheese for a delicious meal.

481. Here's an air fryer recipe for balsamic bell pepper bites:

Ingredients:

2 bell peppers (any color), cut into bite-sized pieces
2 tablespoons balsamic vinegar
1 tablespoon olive oil
1 teaspoon dried Italian herbs (such as basil, oregano, or thyme)
Salt and pepper, to taste

Instructions:

Preheat your air fryer to 400°F (200°C) for 5 minutes.
In a bowl, combine the balsamic vinegar, olive oil, dried Italian herbs, salt, and pepper. Whisk well to combine.
Add the bell pepper pieces to the bowl and toss them in the balsamic mixture until they are evenly coated.
Place the coated bell pepper pieces in the air fryer basket, spreading them out in a single layer.
Air fry the bell pepper bites at 400°F (200°C) for 8-10 minutes, or until they are slightly charred and tender, stirring once halfway through the cooking time.
Once done, remove the balsamic bell pepper bites from the air fryer and transfer them to a serving dish.
Serve them as a tasty appetizer or side dish.

The air frying process will enhance the natural flavors of the bell peppers while the balsamic vinegar adds a tangy and slightly sweet taste. Enjoy these balsamic bell pepper bites as a healthy and flavorful snack or accompaniment to your favorite meal.

482. Here's an air fryer recipe for quick beetroot chips:

Ingredients:

2 medium-sized beetroots
1 tablespoon olive oil
Salt and pepper, to taste
Optional seasonings: garlic powder, paprika, dried herbs, etc.

Instructions:

Preheat your air fryer to 375°F (190°C) for 5 minutes.
Peel the beetroots and thinly slice them into chips using a Mandoline slicer or a sharp knife.
In a bowl, toss the beetroot slices with olive oil, salt, pepper, and any desired seasonings, ensuring all slices are coated evenly.
Place the seasoned beetroot slices in a single layer in the air fryer basket, making sure they are not overlapping.
Air fry the beetroot chips at 375°F (190°C) for 10-12 minutes, or until they are crispy and slightly browned, flipping them halfway through the cooking time.
Once done, remove the beetroot chips from the air fryer and let them cool for a few minutes.
Serve them as a healthy and colorful snack.
These air-fried beetroot chips are a great alternative to traditional potato chips. They are crispy, flavorful, and packed with nutrients. Enjoy them on their own or serve them with your favorite dip.

483. Here's an air fryer recipe for Brussels sprouts with garlic aioli:

Ingredients:

1 pound Brussels sprouts
2 tablespoons olive oil
Salt and pepper, to taste
1/4 cup mayonnaise
1 clove garlic, minced
1 tablespoon lemon juice
1/2 teaspoon Dijon mustard

Instructions:

Preheat your air fryer to 400°F (200°C) for 5 minutes.
Trim the ends of the Brussels sprouts and remove any outer leaves that are damaged.
In a bowl, toss the Brussels sprouts with olive oil, salt, and pepper until they are well coated.
Place the Brussels sprouts in a single layer in the air fryer basket, making sure they are not overcrowded.
Air fry the Brussels sprouts at 400°F (200°C) for 12-15 minutes, shaking the basket halfway through, until they are crispy and browned.
While the Brussels sprouts are cooking, prepare the garlic aioli by mixing together the mayonnaise, minced garlic, lemon juice, and Dijon mustard in a small bowl.
Once the Brussels sprouts are done, transfer them to a serving dish and serve them with the garlic aioli on the side.
The Brussels sprouts will be crispy on the outside and tender on the inside, and the garlic aioli adds a delicious creamy and tangy flavor. It's a perfect side dish or appetizer. Enjoy!

484. Here's an easy air fryer recipe for cabbage steaks:

Ingredients:

1 head of cabbage
2 tablespoons olive oil
Salt and pepper, to taste
Optional toppings: grated Parmesan cheese, minced garlic, dried herbs, etc.

Instructions:

Preheat your air fryer to 400°F (200°C) for 5 minutes.
Remove any outer leaves from the cabbage and cut it into thick slices, about 1-inch thick, to create cabbage steaks.
Brush both sides of the cabbage steaks with olive oil and season with salt and pepper. You can also add any additional toppings or seasonings of your choice.
Place the cabbage steaks in a single layer in the air fryer basket. Depending on the size of your air fryer, you may need to cook them in batches.
Air fry the cabbage steaks at 400°F (200°C) for about 10-12 minutes, flipping them halfway through, until they are tender and slightly browned on the edges.
Once cooked, remove the cabbage steaks from the air fryer and serve them hot.
Cabbage steaks cooked in the air fryer have a wonderful texture and flavor. They can be served as a side dish, topped with grated Parmesan cheese or other desired toppings. Enjoy!

485. Here's an air fryer recipe for green cabbage with blue cheese sauce:

Ingredients:

1 head of green cabbage
2 tablespoons olive oil
Salt and pepper, to taste
1/2 cup crumbled blue cheese
1/4 cup sour cream
2 tablespoons mayonnaise
1 tablespoon lemon juice
1 clove garlic, minced
Fresh parsley, chopped (for garnish)

Instructions:

Preheat your air fryer to 400°F (200°C) for 5 minutes.
Remove any outer leaves from the cabbage and cut it into wedges, leaving the core intact to hold the wedges together.
Brush both sides of the cabbage wedges with olive oil and season with salt and pepper.
Place the cabbage wedges in a single layer in the air fryer basket. Depending on the size of your air fryer, you may need to cook them in batches.
Air fry the cabbage wedges at 400°F (200°C) for about 10-12 minutes, flipping them halfway through, until they are tender and slightly charred on the edges.
While the cabbage is cooking, prepare the blue cheese sauce. In a small bowl, combine the crumbled blue cheese, sour cream, mayonnaise, lemon juice, and minced garlic. Stir until well combined.
Once the cabbage wedges are cooked, transfer them to a serving plate. Drizzle the blue cheese sauce over the cabbage wedges and garnish with fresh chopped parsley.
Serve the air-fried cabbage with the blue cheese sauce as a delicious and flavorful side dish.
The combination of the crispy and slightly charred cabbage with the creamy and tangy blue cheese sauce creates a delightful flavor contrast. Enjoy!

486. Here's an air fryer recipe for crispy bell peppers with tartare sauce:

Ingredients:

2 bell peppers (any color), sliced into strips
1/2 cup all-purpose flour
2 large eggs, beaten
1 cup bread crumbs
1/2 teaspoon paprika
1/2 teaspoon garlic powder
Salt and pepper, to taste
Cooking spray
Tartare sauce (store-bought or homemade) for dipping

Instructions:

Preheat your air fryer to 400°F (200°C) for 5 minutes.
In three separate shallow bowls, place the flour, beaten eggs, and bread crumbs.
Add the paprika, garlic powder, salt, and pepper to the bread crumbs. Mix well to combine.
Dip each bell pepper strip first in the flour, shaking off any excess. Then dip it into the beaten eggs, allowing any excess to drip off. Finally, coat the strip with the seasoned bread crumbs, pressing gently to adhere.
Place the coated bell pepper strips in a single layer in the air fryer basket. Depending on the size of your air fryer, you may need to cook them in batches.
Lightly spray the coated bell pepper strips with cooking spray. This will help them become extra crispy.
Air fry the bell pepper strips at 400°F (200°C) for about 8-10 minutes, or until they are golden brown and crispy. Flip them halfway through the cooking time to ensure even browning.
Once cooked, remove the crispy bell pepper strips from the air fryer and let them cool slightly.
Serve the crispy bell pepper strips with tartare sauce for dipping. Enjoy them as a tasty appetizer or snack!
The air fryer helps to achieve a crispy texture on the bell pepper strips without the need for deep frying. The tartare sauce adds a tangy and creamy element that pairs well with the crunchy peppers. Enjoy!

487. Here's an air fryer recipe for Indian fried okra, also known as Bhindi Fry:

Ingredients:

1 pound fresh okra, washed and dried
2 tablespoons cornmeal
2 tablespoons chickpea flour (Besan)
1 teaspoon ground coriander
1/2 teaspoon ground cumin
1/2 teaspoon turmeric powder
1/4 teaspoon red chili powder (adjust to taste)
Salt, to taste
Cooking spray or oil spray
Instructions:

Preheat your air fryer to 400°F (200°C) for 5 minutes.
Trim the ends of the okra and cut them into 1/2-inch thick slices.
In a mixing bowl, combine the cornmeal, chickpea flour, ground coriander, ground cumin, turmeric powder, red chili powder, and salt.
Add the sliced okra to the bowl and toss well to coat the okra evenly with the spice mixture.
Lightly spray the air fryer basket with cooking spray or oil.
Place the coated okra slices in a single layer in the air fryer basket, making sure they are not overlapping.
Air fry the okra at 400°F (200°C) for about 12-15 minutes, shaking the basket or stirring the okra halfway through cooking to ensure even crisping.
Once the okra is golden brown and crispy, remove it from the air fryer.

Serve the Indian fried okra as a side dish or as part of a meal. It pairs well with rice, roti (Indian bread), or as a crunchy snack.
The air fryer helps to achieve a crispy texture on the okra without the need for excessive oil. The combination of spices gives the fried okra a delicious Indian flavor. Enjoy!

488. Here's an air fryer recipe for zucchini fries with Tabasco dip:

Ingredients:

2 medium zucchini
1/2 cup bread crumbs
1/4 cup grated Parmesan cheese
1/2 teaspoon garlic powder
1/2 teaspoon paprika
1/4 teaspoon salt
1/4 teaspoon black pepper
2 eggs, beaten
Cooking spray

Tabasco dip:

1/2 cup mayonnaise
1 tablespoon Tabasco sauce
1 teaspoon lemon juice
Salt and pepper, to taste

Instructions:

Preheat your air fryer to 400°F (200°C) for 5 minutes.
Cut the zucchini into thin fry-like strips.
In a shallow bowl, mix together the bread crumbs, grated Parmesan cheese, garlic powder, paprika, salt, and black pepper.
Dip each zucchini strip into the beaten eggs, allowing any excess to drip off, then coat it in the breadcrumb mixture, pressing lightly to adhere.
Place the coated zucchini strips in a single layer in the air fryer basket, making sure they are not overlapping.
Lightly spray the zucchini fries with cooking spray to help them crisp up.
Air fry the zucchini fries at 400°F (200°C) for about 10-12 minutes, flipping them halfway through, until they are golden brown and crispy.
While the zucchini fries are cooking, prepare the Tabasco dip by combining mayonnaise, Tabasco sauce, lemon juice, salt, and pepper in a small bowl. Stir until well combined.
Once the zucchini fries are done, remove them from the air fryer.
Serve the zucchini fries hot with the Tabasco dip on the side.
The zucchini fries will have a crispy exterior and a tender interior, and the Tabasco dip adds a spicy and tangy kick. Enjoy this delicious and healthier alternative to traditional fries!

489. Here's an air fryer recipe for Parmesan zucchini boats:

Ingredients:

2 large zucchini
1/2 cup grated Parmesan cheese
1/4 cup bread crumbs
1/2 teaspoon garlic powder
1/2 teaspoon dried oregano
1/4 teaspoon salt
1/4 teaspoon black pepper

2 tablespoons olive oil
Fresh parsley, chopped (for garnish)

Instructions:

Preheat your air fryer to 375°F (190°C) for 5 minutes.
Cut each zucchini in half lengthwise. Use a spoon to scoop out the center flesh of the zucchini halves, leaving about a 1/4-inch border around the edges to create "boats".
In a bowl, combine the grated Parmesan cheese, bread crumbs, garlic powder, dried oregano, salt, and black pepper. Mix well.
Brush each zucchini boat with olive oil, inside and out.
Fill each zucchini boat with the Parmesan breadcrumb mixture, pressing it gently into the hollowed-out portion of the zucchini.
Place the zucchini boats in a single layer in the air fryer basket. You may need to cook them in batches depending on the size of your air fryer.
Air fry the zucchini boats at 375°F (190°C) for about 12-15 minutes, or until the zucchini is tender and the topping is golden and crispy.
Once done, remove the zucchini boats from the air fryer and let them cool slightly.
Garnish with fresh parsley and serve hot as a side dish or a light main course.
These Parmesan zucchini boats are flavorful and satisfying, with a crispy topping and tender zucchini.
Enjoy the delicious combination of Parmesan cheese and breadcrumbs in this healthy and tasty recipe!

490. Here's an air fryer recipe for Bulgarian Burek Pepper with Yogurt Sauce:

Ingredients:

4 large bell peppers (red, yellow, or green)
1 cup crumbled feta cheese
1/4 cup chopped fresh parsley
1/4 cup chopped fresh dill
1/4 cup chopped fresh mint
1/4 teaspoon salt
1/4 teaspoon black pepper
1/4 cup olive oil
1 cup plain Greek yogurt
1 garlic clove, minced
1 tablespoon lemon juice
1 tablespoon chopped fresh dill (for the sauce)
Salt and pepper to taste (for the sauce)

Instructions:

Preheat your air fryer to 375°F (190°C) for 5 minutes.
Slice off the top of each bell pepper and remove the seeds and membranes. Set aside.
In a bowl, mix together the crumbled feta cheese, chopped parsley, chopped dill, chopped mint, salt, and black pepper.
Stuff each bell pepper with the feta cheese mixture, filling it to the top.
Brush each stuffed bell pepper with olive oil, making sure to coat the entire surface.
Place the stuffed bell peppers in the air fryer basket in a single layer. You may need to cook them in batches depending on the size of your air fryer.
Air fry the stuffed bell peppers at 375°F (190°C) for about 15-20 minutes, or until the peppers are tender and the cheese is melted and slightly golden.
While the peppers are cooking, prepare the yogurt sauce. In a small bowl, combine the Greek yogurt, minced garlic, lemon juice, chopped dill, salt, and pepper. Mix well.
Once the stuffed bell peppers are done, remove them from the air fryer and let them cool slightly.
Serve the stuffed bell peppers warm, drizzled with the yogurt sauce on top.

These Bulgarian Burek Peppers with Yogurt Sauce are a delicious and flavorful appetizer or side dish. The combination of the creamy feta cheese stuffing and the refreshing yogurt sauce creates a delightful contrast of flavors. Enjoy this traditional Bulgarian recipe made in the air fryer!

491. Here's an air fryer recipe for Green Pea Arancini with Tomato Sauce:

Ingredients:

For the Arancini:

2 cups cooked Arborio rice
1/2 cup cooked green peas, mashed
1/4 cup grated Parmesan cheese
1/4 cup finely chopped onion
2 cloves garlic, minced
1/4 teaspoon dried thyme
1/4 teaspoon dried oregano
Salt and pepper to taste
1/2 cup breadcrumbs
2 large eggs, beaten
Cooking spray

For the Tomato Sauce:

1 can (14 oz) crushed tomatoes
1 tablespoon tomato paste
1 clove garlic, minced
1/2 teaspoon dried basil
1/2 teaspoon dried oregano
Salt and pepper to taste

Instructions:

In a large bowl, combine the cooked Arborio rice, mashed green peas, grated Parmesan cheese, chopped onion, minced garlic, dried thyme, dried oregano, salt, and pepper. Mix well to combine.
Take about 2 tablespoons of the rice mixture and shape it into a small ball. Repeat with the remaining mixture.
Place the breadcrumbs in a shallow dish and dip each rice ball into the beaten eggs, then roll it in the breadcrumbs until coated. Place the coated rice balls on a plate.
Preheat your air fryer to 400°F (200°C) for 5 minutes.
Lightly spray the air fryer basket with cooking spray. Place the coated rice balls in the air fryer basket in a single layer, leaving space between each one.
Air fry the rice balls at 400°F (200°C) for about 12-15 minutes, or until they are crispy and golden brown.
While the rice balls are cooking, prepare the tomato sauce. In a saucepan, combine the crushed tomatoes, tomato paste, minced garlic, dried basil, dried oregano, salt, and pepper. Cook over medium heat for about 10 minutes, stirring occasionally.
Once the rice balls are done, remove them from the air fryer and let them cool slightly.
Serve the Green Pea Arancini warm with the tomato sauce for dipping.
These Green Pea Arancini with Tomato Sauce are a delicious and savory appetizer or snack. The air fryer helps achieve a crispy exterior while keeping the inside moist and flavorful. Enjoy the combination of the creamy rice and green pea filling with the tangy tomato sauce.

492. Here's an air fryer recipe for Aunt's Roasted Carrots with Cilantro Sauce:

Ingredients:

For the Roasted Carrots:

1 pound baby carrots
2 tablespoons olive oil
1 teaspoon ground cumin
1/2 teaspoon paprika
1/2 teaspoon salt
1/4 teaspoon black pepper

For the Cilantro Sauce:

1/2 cup fresh cilantro leaves
2 tablespoons lime juice
2 tablespoons olive oil
1 clove garlic, minced
Salt and pepper to taste

Instructions:

Preheat your air fryer to 400°F (200°C) for 5 minutes.
In a bowl, toss the baby carrots with olive oil, ground cumin, paprika, salt, and black pepper until well coated.
Place the seasoned carrots in the air fryer basket in a single layer, leaving space between each carrot for even cooking.
Air fry the carrots at 400°F (200°C) for about 15-18 minutes, shaking the basket halfway through, until the carrots are tender and slightly caramelized.
While the carrots are cooking, prepare the cilantro sauce. In a blender or food processor, combine the fresh cilantro leaves, lime juice, olive oil, minced garlic, salt, and pepper. Blend until smooth and well combined.
Once the carrots are done, remove them from the air fryer and let them cool slightly.
Serve the Roasted Carrots warm with the Cilantro Sauce drizzled over the top.
These Roasted Carrots with Cilantro Sauce are a flavorful and vibrant side dish. The air fryer helps to achieve a tender and slightly caramelized texture, while the cilantro sauce adds a refreshing and herbaceous touch. Enjoy this delicious and easy-to-make recipe!

493. Here's an air fryer recipe for Mediterranean Eggplant Burgers:

Ingredients:

1 large eggplant
1/2 cup breadcrumbs
1/4 cup grated Parmesan cheese
2 cloves garlic, minced
1/4 cup chopped fresh parsley
1/4 cup chopped fresh basil
1/2 teaspoon dried oregano
1/2 teaspoon salt
1/4 teaspoon black pepper
1/4 cup all-purpose flour (for coating)
2 tablespoons olive oil

For serving:

Burger buns
Lettuce leaves
Sliced tomatoes
Sliced red onions
Tzatziki sauce or your favorite burger toppings

Instructions:

Preheat your air fryer to 400°F (200°C) for 5 minutes.
Slice the eggplant into 1/2-inch thick rounds. Brush both sides of the eggplant slices with olive oil.
In a shallow bowl, combine the breadcrumbs, grated Parmesan cheese, minced garlic, chopped parsley, chopped basil, dried oregano, salt, and black pepper.
Dip each eggplant slice into the breadcrumb mixture, pressing gently to coat both sides evenly.
Place the coated eggplant slices in a single layer in the air fryer basket. You may need to cook them in batches depending on the size of your air fryer.
Air fry the eggplant slices at 400°F (200°C) for about 12-15 minutes, flipping them halfway through, until they are golden brown and crispy.
While the eggplant slices are cooking, prepare your burger buns and desired toppings.
Once the eggplant slices are done, assemble the burgers by placing a slice of eggplant on the bottom bun, followed by lettuce leaves, sliced tomatoes, sliced red onions, and any other toppings of your choice. Add a dollop of tzatziki sauce or your favorite burger sauce.
Serve the Mediterranean Eggplant Burgers immediately and enjoy!
These Mediterranean Eggplant Burgers are packed with flavor and make a delicious vegetarian option. The air fryer helps to achieve a crispy and golden brown exterior while keeping the inside tender and moist. Enjoy these flavorful burgers with your favorite toppings and sauces!

494. Here's an air fryer recipe for Sesame Balsamic Asparagus:

Ingredients:

1 bunch of asparagus
2 tablespoons balsamic vinegar
1 tablespoon soy sauce
1 tablespoon sesame oil
1 tablespoon honey
1 tablespoon sesame seeds
Salt and pepper to taste

Instructions:

Preheat your air fryer to 400°F (200°C) for 5 minutes.
Trim the tough ends of the asparagus spears and place them in a mixing bowl.
In a separate small bowl, whisk together the balsamic vinegar, soy sauce, sesame oil, honey, salt, and pepper to create the marinade.
Pour the marinade over the asparagus spears and toss them well to coat.
Place the marinated asparagus spears in a single layer in the air fryer basket. You may need to cook them in batches depending on the size of your air fryer.
Air fry the asparagus at 400°F (200°C) for about 6-8 minutes, shaking the basket halfway through, until the asparagus is tender and lightly charred.
While the asparagus is cooking, toast the sesame seeds in a dry pan over medium heat until they are lightly golden brown. Set aside.
Once the asparagus is done, transfer them to a serving plate and sprinkle with the toasted sesame seeds.
Serve the Sesame Balsamic Asparagus as a side dish or as a topping for salads or grain bowls.
This air fryer recipe results in tender asparagus with a delicious sesame balsamic flavor. The air fryer quickly cooks the asparagus, giving it a slight char and retaining its natural crunch. The sesame seeds add a nutty and aromatic touch to the dish. Enjoy this flavorful and healthy side dish!

495. Here's an air fryer recipe for Cheesy Eggplant Schnitzels:

Ingredients:

1 large eggplant
1 cup breadcrumbs
1/2 cup grated Parmesan cheese
1 teaspoon dried Italian seasoning
1/2 teaspoon garlic powder
1/2 teaspoon paprika
2 eggs, beaten
Salt and pepper to taste
Cooking spray

Instructions:

Preheat your air fryer to 400°F (200°C) for 5 minutes.
Slice the eggplant into 1/2-inch thick rounds. Sprinkle salt on both sides of the eggplant slices and let them sit for about 10 minutes to draw out excess moisture.
Pat the eggplant slices dry with a paper towel and set aside.
In a shallow bowl, combine the breadcrumbs, grated Parmesan cheese, dried Italian seasoning, garlic powder, paprika, salt, and pepper.
Dip each eggplant slice into the beaten eggs, making sure it is well coated, and then press it into the breadcrumb mixture, ensuring both sides are evenly coated.
Place the coated eggplant slices in a single layer in the air fryer basket. You may need to cook them in batches depending on the size of your air fryer.
Lightly spray the eggplant slices with cooking spray to help them brown and become crispy.
Air fry the eggplant slices at 400°F (200°C) for about 10-12 minutes, flipping them halfway through, until they are golden brown and crispy.
Serve the Cheesy Eggplant Schnitzels hot with your favorite dipping sauce or as a sandwich filling.
These Cheesy Eggplant Schnitzels are a delicious vegetarian alternative to traditional schnitzels. The air fryer method ensures a crispy exterior without the need for deep frying. The combination of breadcrumbs and grated Parmesan cheese adds a cheesy and flavorful coating to the eggplant slices. Enjoy them as a main dish or use them to create tasty sandwiches or wraps.

496. Here's an air fryer recipe for Involtini di Melanzane (Eggplant Rollups):

Ingredients:

2 medium eggplants
1 cup ricotta cheese
1/2 cup grated Parmesan cheese
1/4 cup chopped fresh basil
2 cloves garlic, minced
1 cup marinara sauce
Salt and pepper to taste
Olive oil for brushing
Toothpicks

Instructions:

Preheat your air fryer to 400°F (200°C) for 5 minutes.
Slice the eggplants lengthwise into thin slices, about 1/4 inch thick.
Sprinkle salt on both sides of the eggplant slices and let them sit for about 10 minutes. This helps remove excess moisture from the eggplants.
Pat the eggplant slices dry with a paper towel.
In a bowl, combine the ricotta cheese, grated Parmesan cheese, chopped basil, minced garlic, salt, and pepper. Mix well.
Take an eggplant slice and spread a thin layer of the ricotta mixture onto it. Roll up the slice and secure it with a toothpick. Repeat with the remaining eggplant slices and filling.
Brush the eggplant rollups with olive oil on all sides.

Place the eggplant rollups in a single layer in the air fryer basket. You may need to cook them in batches depending on the size of your air fryer.
Air fry the eggplant rollups at 400°F (200°C) for about 12-15 minutes until they are golden brown and cooked through.
Warm the marinara sauce in a saucepan.
Remove the toothpicks from the eggplant rollups and serve them with the warmed marinara sauce.
These Involtini di Melanzane (Eggplant Rollups) are a delicious and elegant appetizer or side dish. The air fryer method ensures a crispy exterior while keeping the eggplant soft and tender on the inside. The creamy ricotta cheese filling with fresh basil and garlic adds a burst of flavor to the dish. Serve them as is or with a side of warm marinara sauce for dipping. Enjoy!

497. Here's an air fryer recipe for Air Fried Eggplant Bruschetta:

Ingredients:

1 medium eggplant
2 tablespoons olive oil
1 teaspoon Italian seasoning
1/2 teaspoon garlic powder
Salt and pepper to taste
4 slices of baguette or bread of your choice
1 cup diced tomatoes
1/4 cup chopped fresh basil
2 cloves garlic, minced
2 tablespoons balsamic glaze

Instructions:

Preheat your air fryer to 400°F (200°C) for 5 minutes.
Cut the eggplant into 1/2-inch thick slices.
In a bowl, combine olive oil, Italian seasoning, garlic powder, salt, and pepper. Mix well.
Brush both sides of the eggplant slices with the olive oil mixture.
Place the eggplant slices in a single layer in the air fryer basket. You may need to cook them in batches depending on the size of your air fryer.
Air fry the eggplant slices at 400°F (200°C) for about 8-10 minutes, flipping them halfway through, until they are golden brown and crispy.
While the eggplant is air frying, prepare the bruschetta topping. In a separate bowl, combine diced tomatoes, chopped basil, minced garlic, salt, and pepper. Mix well.
Toast the bread slices in a toaster or under a broiler until lightly crispy.
Once the eggplant slices are done, remove them from the air fryer and let them cool slightly.
Assemble the bruschetta by placing a spoonful of the tomato mixture on each bread slice and topping it with an air-fried eggplant slice.
Drizzle the bruschetta with balsamic glaze for added flavor.
Serve the Air Fried Eggplant Bruschetta immediately as an appetizer or light meal.
This recipe combines the crispy texture of air-fried eggplant with the fresh flavors of tomato, basil, and garlic. The balsamic glaze adds a touch of sweetness and tanginess to the dish. Enjoy these delicious and healthier eggplant bruschetta bites!

498. Here's an air fryer recipe for Easy Eggplant & Zucchini Chips:

Ingredients:

1 medium eggplant
1 medium zucchini
1/2 cup breadcrumbs (can use regular or panko breadcrumbs)
1/4 cup grated Parmesan cheese
1/2 teaspoon garlic powder

1/2 teaspoon dried oregano
1/2 teaspoon paprika
Salt and pepper to taste
2 eggs, beaten

Instructions:

Preheat your air fryer to 375°F (190°C) for 5 minutes.
Slice the eggplant and zucchini into thin rounds, about 1/4 inch thick.
In a shallow bowl, combine breadcrumbs, Parmesan cheese, garlic powder, dried oregano, paprika, salt, and pepper. Mix well.
Dip each eggplant and zucchini slice into the beaten eggs, ensuring both sides are coated.
Then, dip the slices into the breadcrumb mixture, pressing gently to adhere the breadcrumbs to the slices.
Place the breaded eggplant and zucchini slices in a single layer in the air fryer basket. You may need to cook them in batches depending on the size of your air fryer.
Air fry the slices at 375°F (190°C) for about 8-10 minutes, flipping them halfway through, until they are golden brown and crispy.
Once done, remove the chips from the air fryer and let them cool slightly before serving.
Serve the Easy Eggplant & Zucchini Chips as a delicious and healthier snack or side dish.
These air-fried eggplant and zucchini chips are crispy, flavorful, and a great way to enjoy these vegetables. You can serve them as a healthier alternative to traditional potato chips or as a tasty side dish with your favorite dipping sauce. Enjoy!

499. Here's an air fryer recipe for Homemade Blooming Onion:

Ingredients:

1 large onion
1 cup all-purpose flour
1 tablespoon paprika
1 tablespoon garlic powder
1 tablespoon onion powder
1/2 teaspoon cayenne pepper (optional, for extra heat)
1 teaspoon salt
1/2 teaspoon black pepper
2 large eggs
1 cup breadcrumbs
Cooking spray

For the dipping sauce:

1/2 cup mayonnaise
2 tablespoons ketchup
1 tablespoon horseradish (optional)
1/2 teaspoon paprika
1/4 teaspoon salt
1/4 teaspoon black pepper

Instructions:

Preheat your air fryer to 375°F (190°C) for 5 minutes.
Cut off the top of the onion and remove the skin. Cut about 1/2 inch from the root end of the onion and peel off the outer layer.
Place the onion on a cutting board, root side up, and make vertical cuts downward towards the root end, about 1/4 inch apart. Be careful not to cut all the way through the onion. Repeat this process all the way around the onion.

In a shallow bowl, combine the flour, paprika, garlic powder, onion powder, cayenne pepper (if using), salt, and black pepper. Mix well.
In another shallow bowl, beat the eggs.
Dip the onion into the flour mixture, making sure to coat it well.
Shake off any excess flour and then dip the onion into the beaten eggs, coating it evenly.
In a separate bowl, place the breadcrumbs. Roll the onion in the breadcrumbs, pressing gently to make sure they adhere to the onion.
Spray the air fryer basket with cooking spray. Place the breaded onion in the basket.
Air fry the onion at 375°F (190°C) for about 20-25 minutes or until it is golden brown and crispy. Rotate the onion halfway through the cooking time for even browning.
While the onion is cooking, prepare the dipping sauce by combining mayonnaise, ketchup, horseradish (if using), paprika, salt, and black pepper in a small bowl. Mix well.
Once the blooming onion is cooked, carefully remove it from the air fryer using tongs and place it on a serving plate.
Serve the Homemade Blooming Onion with the prepared dipping sauce.
Enjoy the crispy and flavorful Homemade Blooming Onion with its delicious dipping sauce. It's a crowd-pleasing appetizer for any occasion!

500. Here's an air fryer recipe for breaded Italian green beans:

Ingredients:

1 lb (450g) fresh green beans
1/2 cup all-purpose flour
2 large eggs, beaten
1 cup breadcrumbs (Italian seasoned or plain)
1/4 cup grated Parmesan cheese
1 teaspoon dried Italian seasoning
1/2 teaspoon garlic powder
1/2 teaspoon salt
1/4 teaspoon black pepper
Cooking spray

For the dipping sauce:

1/2 cup marinara sauce or tomato sauce
1/4 teaspoon dried basil
1/4 teaspoon dried oregano
1/4 teaspoon garlic powder
Pinch of red pepper flakes (optional)
Salt and pepper to taste

Instructions:

Preheat your air fryer to 400°F (200°C) for 5 minutes.
Trim the ends off the green beans and rinse them under cold water. Pat them dry with a paper towel.
In a shallow bowl or plate, combine the breadcrumbs, Parmesan cheese, dried Italian seasoning, garlic powder, salt, and black pepper. Mix well.
Place the flour in a separate shallow bowl or plate, and the beaten eggs in another shallow bowl.
Take a handful of green beans and coat them in flour, shaking off any excess.
Dip the flour-coated green beans into the beaten eggs, allowing any excess to drip off.
Roll the green beans in the breadcrumb mixture, pressing gently to ensure they are evenly coated.
Place the breaded green beans in a single layer in the air fryer basket, making sure they are not touching each other.
Lightly spray the breaded green beans with cooking spray to help them become crispier.

Air fry the green beans at 400°F (200°C) for about 8-10 minutes, or until they are golden brown and crispy. You may need to shake the basket or flip the green beans halfway through the cooking time for even browning.
While the green beans are cooking, prepare the dipping sauce by combining marinara sauce, dried basil, dried oregano, garlic powder, red pepper flakes (if using), salt, and pepper in a small bowl. Mix well.
Once the green beans are cooked, remove them from the air fryer and transfer them to a serving dish.
Serve the breaded Italian green beans hot with the prepared dipping sauce.
Enjoy the crispy and flavorful breaded Italian green beans as a delicious and healthier alternative to traditional fried snacks!

501. Here's an air fryer recipe for Russian-style eggplant caviar:

Ingredients:

2 medium-sized eggplants
2 medium-sized tomatoes, finely chopped
1 small onion, finely chopped
2 cloves of garlic, minced
2 tablespoons olive oil
1 tablespoon white vinegar
Salt and pepper to taste
Fresh herbs (such as parsley or dill) for garnish
Bread or crackers for serving

Instructions:

Preheat your air fryer to 400°F (200°C) for 5 minutes.
Pierce the eggplants several times with a fork to allow steam to escape while cooking.
Place the eggplants in the air fryer basket and cook for 20-25 minutes, or until the skin is charred and the flesh is tender. Flip the eggplants halfway through the cooking time for even roasting.
Remove the eggplants from the air fryer and let them cool for a few minutes.
Once the eggplants are cool enough to handle, cut them in half lengthwise. Scoop out the soft flesh using a spoon and transfer it to a bowl.
Mash the roasted eggplant flesh with a fork until it reaches a smooth consistency. You can also use a blender or food processor for a finer texture.
In a separate pan, heat the olive oil over medium heat. Add the chopped onion and minced garlic, and sauté until they are soft and translucent.
Add the chopped tomatoes to the pan and cook for a few minutes until they start to soften.
Transfer the cooked onion, garlic, and tomatoes to the bowl with the mashed eggplant.
Add the white vinegar, salt, and pepper to the mixture. Stir well to combine all the ingredients.
Allow the Russian-style eggplant caviar to cool to room temperature before serving. This dish can be enjoyed warm or cold.
Garnish with fresh herbs, such as parsley or dill, before serving.
Serve the Russian-style eggplant caviar with bread or crackers as an appetizer or side dish.
Enjoy the rich and flavorful Russian-style eggplant caviar as a delicious addition to your meal!

502. Here's an air fryer recipe for avocado fries with pico de Gallo:

Ingredients:

For the avocado fries:

2 ripe avocados
1 cup breadcrumbs
1/2 teaspoon garlic powder
1/2 teaspoon paprika

1/4 teaspoon salt
1/4 teaspoon black pepper
2 eggs, beaten

For the pico de Gallo:

2 tomatoes, diced
1/2 red onion, finely chopped
1 jalapeño pepper, seeded and finely chopped
1/4 cup chopped fresh cilantro
Juice of 1 lime
Salt and pepper to taste

Instructions:

Preheat your air fryer to 400°F (200°C) for 5 minutes.
Cut the avocados in half lengthwise and remove the pits. Cut each avocado half into thick slices, resembling the shape of fries.
In a shallow bowl, combine the breadcrumbs, garlic powder, paprika, salt, and black pepper. Mix well.
Dip each avocado slice into the beaten eggs, then coat it with the breadcrumb mixture. Make sure to cover all sides evenly.
Place the coated avocado fries in a single layer in the air fryer basket. You may need to cook them in batches depending on the size of your air fryer.
Air fry the avocado fries at 400°F (200°C) for 8-10 minutes, or until they are golden and crispy.
While the avocado fries are cooking, prepare the pico de gallo. In a bowl, combine the diced tomatoes, finely chopped red onion, jalapeño pepper, chopped cilantro, lime juice, salt, and pepper. Mix well to combine.
Once the avocado fries are done, remove them from the air fryer and let them cool slightly.
Serve the avocado fries with the homemade pico de gallo on the side for dipping.
Enjoy the crispy and creamy avocado fries with the fresh and tangy pico de gallo!
Note: It's best to serve the avocado fries immediately after cooking to maintain their crispiness.

503. Here's an air fryer recipe for cheese and cauliflower tater tots:

Ingredients:

2 cups cauliflower florets
1/2 cup shredded cheddar cheese
1/4 cup grated Parmesan cheese
1/4 cup almond flour (or regular all-purpose flour)
1/4 teaspoon garlic powder
1/4 teaspoon onion powder
1/4 teaspoon paprika
1/4 teaspoon salt
1/4 teaspoon black pepper
1 egg, beaten
Cooking spray

Instructions:

Steam the cauliflower florets until they are tender. Drain and let them cool.
Once cooled, place the cauliflower florets in a food processor and pulse until they resemble rice-like grains.
Transfer the cauliflower rice to a clean kitchen towel or cheesecloth and squeeze out as much moisture as possible.

In a mixing bowl, combine the cauliflower rice, shredded cheddar cheese, grated Parmesan cheese, almond flour (or all-purpose flour), garlic powder, onion powder, paprika, salt, and black pepper. Mix well to form a sticky mixture.
Take a tablespoon of the mixture and shape it into a tater tot shape. Repeat with the remaining mixture.
Place the tater tots on a parchment-lined tray or plate and place them in the freezer for about 15-20 minutes to firm up.
Preheat your air fryer to 375°F (190°C) for 5 minutes.
Spray the air fryer basket with cooking spray to prevent sticking.
Place the tater tots in a single layer in the air fryer basket, leaving some space between them.
Air fry the tater tots at 375°F (190°C) for 12-15 minutes, flipping them halfway through, until they are golden brown and crispy.
Remove the tater tots from the air fryer and let them cool for a few minutes before serving.
Serve the cheese and cauliflower tater tots as a delicious snack or as a side dish with your favorite dipping sauce.
Enjoy the crispy, cheesy goodness of these healthier tater tots made with cauliflower!

504. Here's an air fryer recipe for tasty balsamic beets:

Ingredients:

4 medium-sized beets, peeled and sliced into 1/4-inch thick rounds
2 tablespoons balsamic vinegar
1 tablespoon olive oil
1 teaspoon honey (optional)
Salt and pepper to taste
Fresh parsley, chopped (for garnish)

Instructions:

Preheat your air fryer to 375°F (190°C) for 5 minutes.
In a bowl, whisk together the balsamic vinegar, olive oil, honey (if using), salt, and pepper.
Add the beet slices to the bowl and toss them in the balsamic mixture until well coated.
Arrange the beet slices in a single layer in the air fryer basket, making sure they are not overlapping.
Air fry the beets at 375°F (190°C) for 12-15 minutes, flipping them halfway through, until they are tender and slightly caramelized.
Once cooked, remove the beets from the air fryer and let them cool slightly.
Sprinkle the balsamic beets with fresh chopped parsley for added flavor and garnish.
Serve the balsamic beets as a side dish or use them in salads, wraps, or as a flavorful addition to any dish.
Enjoy the sweet and tangy flavor of these air-fried balsamic beets!

505. Here's an air fryer recipe for teriyaki cauliflower:

Ingredients:

1 medium-sized cauliflower, cut into florets
1/4 cup low-sodium soy sauce
2 tablespoons honey or maple syrup
1 tablespoon rice vinegar
1 teaspoon sesame oil
1 teaspoon grated ginger
2 cloves garlic, minced
1 tablespoon cornstarch
Sesame seeds and chopped green onions for garnish

Instructions:

Preheat your air fryer to 375°F (190°C) for 5 minutes.
In a bowl, whisk together the soy sauce, honey (or maple syrup), rice vinegar, sesame oil, grated ginger, minced garlic, and cornstarch to make the teriyaki sauce.
Place the cauliflower florets in a separate bowl and pour the teriyaki sauce over them. Toss until the cauliflower is well coated.
Transfer the coated cauliflower to the air fryer basket, shaking off any excess sauce.
Air fry the cauliflower at 375°F (190°C) for 15-20 minutes, shaking the basket or flipping the cauliflower halfway through, until they are tender and caramelized.
Once cooked, remove the teriyaki cauliflower from the air fryer and let it cool slightly.
Sprinkle with sesame seeds and chopped green onions for garnish.
Serve the teriyaki cauliflower as a delicious side dish or as a vegetarian main course.
Enjoy the savory and sweet flavors of this air-fried teriyaki cauliflower!

506. Here's an air fryer recipe for easy cauliflower popcorn:

Ingredients:

1 medium-sized cauliflower head, cut into small florets
2 tablespoons olive oil
1 teaspoon garlic powder
1/2 teaspoon paprika
1/2 teaspoon salt
1/4 teaspoon black pepper

Instructions:

Preheat your air fryer to 375°F (190°C) for 5 minutes.
In a large bowl, combine the cauliflower florets, olive oil, garlic powder, paprika, salt, and black pepper. Toss until the cauliflower is evenly coated with the seasonings.
Place the coated cauliflower florets in the air fryer basket in a single layer. If needed, you can cook in batches.
Air fry the cauliflower at 375°F (190°C) for 12-15 minutes, shaking the basket or tossing the cauliflower halfway through the cooking time.
Keep a close eye on the cauliflower to ensure it doesn't burn. The cauliflower should be crispy and lightly golden brown.
Once cooked, remove the cauliflower from the air fryer and let it cool slightly before serving.
Serve the cauliflower popcorn as a healthy snack or as a side dish with your favorite dipping sauce.
Enjoy this crispy and flavorful cauliflower popcorn, a nutritious alternative to traditional popcorn!

507. Here's an air fryer recipe for almond-crusted cauliflower florets:

Ingredients:

1 medium-sized cauliflower head, cut into small florets
1 cup almond flour
2 eggs, beaten
1 teaspoon garlic powder
1/2 teaspoon paprika
1/2 teaspoon salt
1/4 teaspoon black pepper
Cooking spray

Instructions:

Preheat your air fryer to 375°F (190°C) for 5 minutes.
In a shallow bowl or plate, combine the almond flour, garlic powder, paprika, salt, and black pepper.

Dip each cauliflower floret into the beaten eggs, allowing any excess to drip off, then roll it in the almond flour mixture, pressing gently to adhere the coating.
Place the coated cauliflower florets in the air fryer basket in a single layer. If needed, you can cook in batches.
Lightly spray the cauliflower florets with cooking spray to help them crisp up.
Air fry the cauliflower at 375°F (190°C) for 12-15 minutes, or until the coating is golden brown and crispy.
Once cooked, remove the cauliflower from the air fryer and let it cool slightly before serving.
Serve the almond-crusted cauliflower florets as a delicious appetizer or as a side dish with your favorite dipping sauce.
Enjoy the crunchy and flavorful almond-crusted cauliflower florets!

508. Here's an air fryer recipe for chili corn on the cob:

Ingredients:

4 ears of corn, husks, and silks removed
2 tablespoons olive oil
1 teaspoon chili powder
1/2 teaspoon paprika
1/2 teaspoon garlic powder
1/2 teaspoon salt
1/4 teaspoon black pepper
Fresh lime wedges, for serving

Instructions:

Preheat your air fryer to 400°F (200°C) for 5 minutes.
In a small bowl, mix together the olive oil, chili powder, paprika, garlic powder, salt, and black pepper.
Brush each ear of corn with the seasoned oil mixture, making sure to coat all sides.
Place the corn in the air fryer basket in a single layer. If needed, you can cook in batches.
Air fry the corn at 400°F (200°C) for 12-15 minutes, or until the kernels are tender and slightly charred.
Carefully remove the corn from the air fryer and let it cool slightly.
Serve the chili corn on the cob with fresh lime wedges for squeezing over the top.
Enjoy the flavorful and spicy chili corn on the cob as a delicious side dish or snack.
Note: Cooking times may vary depending on the size and thickness of the corn. Adjust the cooking time accordingly to ensure the corn is cooked through.
Enjoy the delicious combination of chili seasoning and sweet corn with this air fryer recipe!

509. Here's an air fryer recipe for Cholula seasoned broccoli:

Ingredients:

1 head of broccoli, cut into florets
2 tablespoons olive oil
2 tablespoons Cholula hot sauce (adjust to taste)
1 teaspoon garlic powder
1/2 teaspoon onion powder
1/2 teaspoon paprika
Salt and pepper, to taste

Instructions:

Preheat your air fryer to 400°F (200°C) for 5 minutes.
In a large bowl, combine the olive oil, Cholula hot sauce, garlic powder, onion powder, paprika, salt, and pepper. Mix well.
Add the broccoli florets to the bowl and toss until they are well coated with the seasoning mixture.

Place the seasoned broccoli florets in the air fryer basket in a single layer. If needed, you can cook in batches.
Air fry the broccoli at 400°F (200°C) for 10-12 minutes, or until the florets are tender and slightly crispy on the edges. Shake the basket or toss the broccoli halfway through the cooking time for even browning.
Once cooked, remove the broccoli from the air fryer and serve immediately.
Enjoy the Cholula seasoned broccoli as a delicious side dish or as a topping for salads or bowls.
Feel free to adjust the amount of Cholula hot sauce according to your preference for spiciness. Enjoy the flavorful and spicy Cholula seasoned broccoli prepared in the air fryer!

510. Here's an air fryer recipe for Parmesan broccoli bites:

Ingredients:

1 head of broccoli, cut into florets
1/4 cup grated Parmesan cheese
1/4 cup breadcrumbs
1 teaspoon garlic powder
1/2 teaspoon paprika
Salt and pepper, to taste
1 tablespoon olive oil

Instructions:

Preheat your air fryer to 400°F (200°C) for 5 minutes.
In a large bowl, combine the Parmesan cheese, breadcrumbs, garlic powder, paprika, salt, and pepper. Mix well.
Toss the broccoli florets in the olive oil to coat them evenly.
Add the coated broccoli florets to the bowl with the Parmesan mixture. Gently toss until the florets are well coated.
Place the coated broccoli florets in the air fryer basket in a single layer. If needed, you can cook in batches.
Air fry the broccoli at 400°F (200°C) for 10-12 minutes, or until the florets are tender and the coating is crispy and golden brown. Shake the basket or toss the broccoli halfway through the cooking time for even browning.
Once cooked, remove the broccoli bites from the air fryer and let them cool slightly before serving.
Enjoy the crispy and flavorful Parmesan broccoli bites as a delicious side dish or snack.
Feel free to adjust the seasoning and cheese amounts according to your taste preferences. Enjoy the tasty and crispy Parmesan broccoli bites made in the air fryer!

511. Here's an air fryer recipe for a Catalan-style Escalivada veggie spread:

Ingredients:

1 eggplant
1 red bell pepper
1 yellow bell pepper
1 red onion
2 cloves garlic
2 tablespoons olive oil
1 tablespoon red wine vinegar
Salt and pepper, to taste

Instructions:

Preheat your air fryer to 400°F (200°C) for 5 minutes.

Wash the eggplant, bell peppers, and red onion. Cut the eggplant into thick slices, halve the bell peppers and remove the seeds, and slice the red onion into thick rings.
Place the eggplant slices, bell peppers, red onion rings, and whole garlic cloves in the air fryer basket. Drizzle them with olive oil and season with salt and pepper.
Air fry the vegetables at 400°F (200°C) for 15-20 minutes, or until they are tender and slightly charred, flipping them halfway through the cooking time for even browning.
Once cooked, remove the vegetables from the air fryer and let them cool slightly. Peel the skin off the bell peppers and remove the seeds. Peel the skin off the eggplant slices.
Chop the roasted vegetables into smaller pieces and transfer them to a bowl.
Add red wine vinegar to the bowl and gently toss to combine. Adjust the seasoning with additional salt and pepper, if needed.
Allow the mixture to cool completely before serving. This Catalan-style Escalivada veggie spread can be served as a dip or spread on bread or crackers.
Enjoy the flavorful and smoky Catalan-style Escalivada veggie spread!
Feel free to customize the recipe by adding herbs like parsley or basil, or a drizzle of extra virgin olive oil before serving. Enjoy this delicious and healthy veggie spread made in the air fryer!

512. Here's an air fryer recipe for zucchini and turnip bake:

Ingredients:

2 zucchinis, sliced into rounds
2 turnips, peeled and sliced into rounds
2 tablespoons olive oil
1 teaspoon dried thyme
1 teaspoon dried rosemary
1 teaspoon garlic powder
Salt and pepper, to taste
1/2 cup grated Parmesan cheese

Instructions:

Preheat your air fryer to 400°F (200°C) for 5 minutes.
In a large bowl, combine the zucchini rounds, turnip rounds, olive oil, dried thyme, dried rosemary, garlic powder, salt, and pepper. Toss well to coat the vegetables evenly with the seasoning.
Place the seasoned zucchini and turnip slices in the air fryer basket in a single layer.
Air fry the vegetables at 400°F (200°C) for 12-15 minutes, or until they are tender and lightly browned, flipping them halfway through the cooking time for even browning.
Once cooked, remove the vegetables from the air fryer and transfer them to a baking dish.
Sprinkle the grated Parmesan cheese over the zucchini and turnip slices.
Place the baking dish with the cheese-topped vegetables back into the air fryer and air fry for an additional 2-3 minutes, or until the cheese is melted and golden.
Remove from the air fryer and let it cool for a few minutes before serving.
Serve the zucchini and turnip bake as a side dish or as a vegetarian main course.
Enjoy the delicious and healthy zucchini and turnip bake made in the air fryer!
Feel free to adjust the seasoning and cheese amount according to your taste preferences. Enjoy this flavorful and nutritious vegetable bake!

513. Here's an air fryer recipe for black bean and veggie burgers:

Ingredients:

1 can black beans, drained and rinsed
1 cup cooked quinoa
1/2 cup bread crumbs
1/2 cup finely chopped bell pepper
1/4 cup finely chopped red onion

2 cloves garlic, minced
2 tablespoons chopped fresh parsley
1 teaspoon ground cumin
1/2 teaspoon chili powder
1/2 teaspoon smoked paprika
Salt and pepper, to taste
1 tablespoon olive oil

Instructions:

In a large bowl, mash the black beans with a fork or potato masher until they are mostly mashed but still have some texture.
Add the cooked quinoa, bread crumbs, bell pepper, red onion, garlic, parsley, cumin, chili powder, smoked paprika, salt, and pepper to the bowl. Mix well until all the ingredients are combined.
Form the mixture into burger patties of your desired size and shape.
Preheat your air fryer to 375°F (190°C) for 5 minutes.
Lightly brush or spray the patties with olive oil on both sides.
Place the patties in the air fryer basket in a single layer, leaving some space between each patty.
Air fry the burgers at 375°F (190°C) for 12-15 minutes, flipping them halfway through the cooking time, until they are crisp and golden on the outside.
Once cooked, remove the veggie burgers from the air fryer and let them cool for a few minutes before serving.
Serve the black bean and veggie burgers on buns or lettuce wraps with your favorite toppings and condiments.
Enjoy these delicious and nutritious homemade veggie burgers made in the air fryer!
Feel free to customize the recipe by adding or substituting different vegetables and spices to suit your taste preferences. Enjoy your flavorful and wholesome black bean and veggie burgers!

514. Here's an air fryer recipe for roasted pumpkin with goat cheese:

Ingredients:

1 small pumpkin, peeled, seeded, and cut into cubes
2 tablespoons olive oil
1 teaspoon dried thyme
Salt and pepper, to taste
1/4 cup crumbled goat cheese
Fresh parsley, chopped (for garnish)

Instructions:

Preheat your air fryer to 375°F (190°C) for 5 minutes.
In a bowl, toss the pumpkin cubes with olive oil, dried thyme, salt, and pepper until the pumpkin is well coated.
Place the seasoned pumpkin cubes in the air fryer basket in a single layer. You may need to cook them in batches depending on the size of your air fryer.
Air fry the pumpkin cubes at 375°F (190°C) for 15-20 minutes, shaking the basket or stirring the pumpkin halfway through the cooking time to ensure even browning.
Once the pumpkin cubes are tender and lightly browned, remove them from the air fryer and let them cool slightly.
Transfer the roasted pumpkin to a serving dish and sprinkle the crumbled goat cheese on top.
Garnish with fresh chopped parsley.
Serve the roasted pumpkin with goat cheese as a delicious side dish or appetizer.
The combination of roasted pumpkin and tangy goat cheese creates a delightful flavor contrast. Enjoy the creamy, savory, and slightly sweet taste of this dish!

515. Here's an air fryer recipe for sweet butternut squash with walnuts:

Ingredients:

1 small butternut squash, peeled, seeded, and cut into cubes
2 tablespoons maple syrup
2 tablespoons melted butter
1/2 teaspoon ground cinnamon
1/4 teaspoon ground nutmeg
1/4 cup chopped walnuts
Salt, to taste

Instructions:

Preheat your air fryer to 400°F (200°C) for 5 minutes.
In a bowl, combine the maple syrup, melted butter, ground cinnamon, ground nutmeg, and a pinch of salt.
Add the butternut squash cubes to the bowl and toss them in the maple syrup mixture until well coated.
Place the coated butternut squash cubes in the air fryer basket in a single layer. You may need to cook them in batches depending on the size of your air fryer.
Air fry the butternut squash at 400°F (200°C) for 12-15 minutes, shaking the basket or stirring the squash halfway through the cooking time to ensure even browning.
Sprinkle the chopped walnuts over the cooked butternut squash and give it a gentle toss.
Return the butternut squash to the air fryer and cook for an additional 2-3 minutes until the walnuts are toasted.
Remove the sweet butternut squash with walnuts from the air fryer and transfer it to a serving dish.
Serve warm as a side dish or enjoy it as a sweet and satisfying snack.
The combination of sweet maple syrup, warm spices, and crunchy walnuts adds a delightful twist to the natural sweetness of butternut squash. Enjoy the flavorful and nutty goodness of this dish!

516. Here's an air fryer recipe for spicy vegetable skewers:

Ingredients:

Assorted vegetables of your choice (such as bell peppers, onions, zucchini, cherry tomatoes, and mushrooms)
2 tablespoons olive oil
1 teaspoon paprika
1/2 teaspoon chili powder
1/2 teaspoon garlic powder
1/4 teaspoon cayenne pepper (adjust to your spice preference)
Salt and pepper, to taste
Wooden skewers, soaked in water for 30 minutes to prevent burning

Instructions:

Preheat your air fryer to 400°F (200°C) for 5 minutes.
Cut the vegetables into bite-sized pieces.
In a bowl, whisk together the olive oil, paprika, chili powder, garlic powder, cayenne pepper, salt, and pepper.
Add the vegetables to the bowl and toss them in the spice mixture until well coated.
Thread the seasoned vegetables onto the soaked wooden skewers, alternating different vegetables to create colorful skewers.
Place the vegetable skewers in the air fryer basket in a single layer. You may need to cook them in batches depending on the size of your air fryer.
Air fry the vegetable skewers at 400°F (200°C) for 10-12 minutes, or until the vegetables are tender and slightly charred, turning them halfway through the cooking time.

Remove the spicy vegetable skewers from the air fryer and let them cool for a few minutes before serving.
Serve the vegetable skewers as a delicious and spicy appetizer or side dish. You can also serve them with a side of dipping sauce, such as a yogurt-based dip or spicy salsa.
Enjoy the vibrant flavors and heat of these spicy vegetable skewers, packed with nutritious goodness!

517. Here's an air fryer recipe for tempura veggies with sesame soy sauce:

Ingredients:

For the tempura batter:
1/2 cup all-purpose flour
1/4 cup cornstarch
1/2 teaspoon baking powder
1/2 teaspoon salt
1/2 cup ice-cold water
Assorted vegetables of your choice (such as broccoli florets, bell peppers, sweet potatoes, zucchini, or mushrooms)
Cooking spray
For the sesame soy sauce:
2 tablespoons soy sauce
1 tablespoon rice vinegar
1 teaspoon sesame oil
1 teaspoon honey or maple syrup
1/2 teaspoon grated ginger (optional)
1/2 teaspoon sesame seeds (optional)

Instructions:

Preheat your air fryer to 400°F (200°C) for 5 minutes.
In a mixing bowl, whisk together the all-purpose flour, cornstarch, baking powder, and salt.
Slowly pour in the ice-cold water while continuously whisking until the batter is smooth and lump-free.
Dip the assorted vegetables into the tempura batter, ensuring they are evenly coated.
Lightly coat the air fryer basket with cooking spray to prevent sticking.
Place the battered vegetables in a single layer in the air fryer basket. You may need to cook them in batches depending on the size of your air fryer.
Air fry the tempura veggies at 400°F (200°C) for 8-10 minutes or until they turn golden brown and crispy, flipping them halfway through the cooking time.
While the tempura veggies are cooking, prepare the sesame soy sauce by combining soy sauce, rice vinegar, sesame oil, honey or maple syrup, grated ginger (optional), and sesame seeds (optional) in a small bowl. Stir well to combine.
Once the tempura veggies are done, remove them from the air fryer and let them cool slightly.
Serve the tempura veggies with the sesame soy sauce on the side for dipping.
Enjoy the crispy and flavorful tempura veggies with the delicious sesame soy sauce. It's a perfect appetizer or side dish with a delightful combination of textures and flavors!

518. Here's an air fryer recipe for crispy fried tofu:

Ingredients:

1 block of firm or extra firm tofu
2 tablespoons cornstarch
1 tablespoon soy sauce
1 tablespoon sesame oil
1 teaspoon garlic powder
1/2 teaspoon paprika
1/2 teaspoon salt (adjust to taste)

Cooking spray

Instructions:

Start by pressing the tofu to remove excess moisture. Place the tofu block between two paper towels or clean kitchen towels. Place a heavy object on top, like a cutting board or a few heavy books, and let it sit for about 15-20 minutes. This will help remove the moisture from the tofu and make it crispier when cooked.
After pressing the tofu, cut it into small cubes or rectangular pieces, whichever shape you prefer.
In a bowl, combine cornstarch, soy sauce, sesame oil, garlic powder, paprika, and salt. Mix well to create a thick, smooth batter.
Dip each tofu piece into the batter, making sure it is evenly coated on all sides.
Preheat your air fryer to 400°F (200°C) for 5 minutes.
Lightly coat the air fryer basket with cooking spray to prevent sticking.
Place the coated tofu pieces in a single layer in the air fryer basket, leaving some space between each piece for even cooking.
Air fry the tofu at 400°F (200°C) for 12-15 minutes, flipping the tofu halfway through the cooking time. Adjust the cooking time as needed, depending on your desired level of crispiness.
Once the tofu is golden brown and crispy, remove it from the air fryer and let it cool slightly before serving.
Serve the crispy fried tofu as an appetizer, in stir-fries, or as a protein component in your favorite dishes. Enjoy the crispy texture and flavorful taste of the air-fried tofu. It's a versatile and delicious plant-based option that can be enjoyed in various dishes!

519. Here's an air fryer recipe for classic French Ratatouille:

Ingredients:

1 eggplant, diced
1 zucchini, diced
1 yellow squash, diced
1 red bell pepper, diced
1 yellow bell pepper, diced
1 onion, diced
3 garlic cloves, minced
2 tablespoons olive oil
1 can (14 oz) diced tomatoes
1 teaspoon dried thyme
1 teaspoon dried oregano
1/2 teaspoon dried basil
Salt and pepper to taste
Fresh basil leaves, for garnish (optional)

Instructions:

Preheat your air fryer to 400°F (200°C) for 5 minutes.
In a large bowl, combine the diced eggplant, zucchini, yellow squash, red bell pepper, yellow bell pepper, onion, and minced garlic.
Drizzle the olive oil over the vegetables and toss to coat them evenly.
Transfer the vegetable mixture to the air fryer basket, making sure they are in a single layer.
Air fry the vegetables at 400°F (200°C) for 15-20 minutes, stirring once halfway through the cooking time. Cook until the vegetables are tender and slightly charred.
In the meantime, in a separate bowl, combine the diced tomatoes, dried thyme, dried oregano, dried basil, salt, and pepper.
Once the vegetables are cooked, pour the tomato mixture over them in the air fryer basket. Gently stir to combine.
Air fry the ratatouille for an additional 5-10 minutes at 400°F (200°C) to let the flavors meld together.

Remove the ratatouille from the air fryer and let it cool slightly before serving.
Garnish with fresh basil leaves, if desired, and serve as a side dish or main course. It pairs well with crusty bread, rice, or pasta.
Enjoy the flavorful and vibrant classic French Ratatouille made in your air fryer!

520. Here's an air fryer recipe for Indian Aloo Tikki:

Ingredients:

3 large potatoes, boiled and mashed
1/2 cup bread crumbs
1/4 cup finely chopped onion
2 tablespoons chopped fresh coriander (cilantro)
1 teaspoon grated ginger
1 teaspoon grated garlic
1/2 teaspoon cumin powder
1/2 teaspoon coriander powder
1/4 teaspoon red chili powder (adjust to taste)
1/2 teaspoon garam masala
Salt to taste
2 tablespoons vegetable oil (for brushing)

Instructions:

In a large bowl, combine the mashed potatoes, bread crumbs, chopped onion, chopped coriander, grated ginger, grated garlic, cumin powder, coriander powder, red chili powder, garam masala, and salt. Mix well to form a smooth mixture.
Divide the mixture into equal portions and shape them into round patties or Tikkis.
Preheat your air fryer to 380°F (193°C) for 5 minutes.
Place the aloo tikkis in the air fryer basket, making sure to leave some space between them for even cooking.
Air fry the tikkis at 380°F (193°C) for 10 minutes. Flip them halfway through the cooking time to ensure they cook evenly.
After 10 minutes, brush the tikkis with a little vegetable oil for a crispy texture.
Continue air frying for another 5 minutes or until the tikkis are golden brown and crispy.
Remove the aloo tikkis from the air fryer and let them cool slightly before serving.
Serve the aloo tikkis hot with mint chutney, tamarind chutney, or tomato ketchup.
Enjoy the delicious and crispy Indian Aloo Tikki made in your air fryer!

521. Here's an air fryer recipe for roasted balsamic veggies:

Ingredients:

2 cups mixed vegetables (such as bell peppers, zucchini, mushrooms, cherry tomatoes, and red onion), cut into bite-sized pieces
2 tablespoons balsamic vinegar
2 tablespoons olive oil
1 teaspoon dried herbs (such as thyme, rosemary, or Italian seasoning)
Salt and pepper to taste

Instructions:

Preheat your air fryer to 400°F (200°C) for 5 minutes.
In a bowl, combine the balsamic vinegar, olive oil, dried herbs, salt, and pepper. Mix well.
Add the mixed vegetables to the bowl and toss them in the balsamic mixture until they are evenly coated.
Place the coated vegetables in the air fryer basket, spreading them out in a single layer.

Air fry the veggies at 400°F (200°C) for about 12-15 minutes, shaking the basket or stirring the veggies halfway through the cooking time to ensure even browning.
Check the vegetables for desired doneness. If you prefer them softer, you can cook them for a few minutes longer.
Once the veggies are cooked to your liking, remove them from the air fryer and transfer them to a serving dish.
Serve the roasted balsamic veggies as a side dish or as a topping for salads, wraps, or grain bowls.
Enjoy the flavorful and roasted balsamic veggies made in your air fryer!

522. Here's an air fryer recipe for crispy nachos:

Ingredients:

1 bag of tortilla chips
1 cup shredded cheese (such as cheddar or Mexican blend)
1/2 cup diced tomatoes
1/2 cup diced red onion
1/2 cup sliced black olives
1/4 cup sliced jalapeños (optional)
1/4 cup chopped fresh cilantro
Sour cream, guacamole, and salsa for serving

Instructions:

Preheat your air fryer to 375°F (190°C) for 5 minutes.
Arrange a layer of tortilla chips on the bottom of the air fryer basket, making sure they are spread out in a single layer.
Sprinkle a layer of shredded cheese evenly over the chips.
Add a layer of diced tomatoes, red onion, black olives, and jalapeños (if using).
Repeat the layers of tortilla chips, cheese, and toppings until you have used up all the ingredients, making sure to end with a layer of cheese on top.
Place the basket in the air fryer and cook at 375°F (190°C) for about 5-7 minutes, or until the cheese is melted and bubbly.
Carefully remove the basket from the air fryer and sprinkle the chopped cilantro over the nachos.
Serve the crispy nachos immediately with sour cream, guacamole, and salsa on the side.
Enjoy the delicious and crispy nachos made in your air fryer! It's a perfect party snack or appetizer.

523. Here's an air fryer recipe for charred broccolini with lemon caper sauce:

Ingredients:

1 bunch of broccolini, trimmed
2 tablespoons olive oil
Salt and pepper to taste
2 tablespoons capers, drained
2 tablespoons lemon juice
1 clove garlic, minced
1/4 teaspoon red pepper flakes (optional)
Lemon wedges for serving

Instructions:

Preheat your air fryer to 400°F (200°C) for 5 minutes.
In a bowl, toss the broccolini with olive oil, salt, and pepper until well coated.
Place the broccolini in a single layer in the air fryer basket. If necessary, cook them in batches to avoid overcrowding.

Air fry the broccolini at 400°F (200°C) for 8-10 minutes, or until they are charred and tender-crisp. Shake the basket once or twice during cooking for even browning.
While the broccolini is cooking, prepare the lemon-caper sauce. In a small bowl, combine the capers, lemon juice, minced garlic, and red pepper flakes (if using). Mix well.
Once the broccolini is done, remove it from the air fryer and transfer to a serving plate.
Drizzle the lemon-caper sauce over the broccolini.
Serve the charred broccolini with lemon-caper sauce hot, and garnish with lemon wedges.
Enjoy the delicious charred broccolini with zesty lemon-caper sauce made in your air fryer! It's a flavorful and healthy side dish.

524. Here's an air fryer recipe for a delicious winter vegetable traybake:

Ingredients:

2 large carrots, peeled and cut into chunks
2 parsnips, peeled and cut into chunks
1 large sweet potato, peeled and cut into chunks
1 small butternut squash, peeled, seeds removed, and cut into chunks
1 red onion, peeled and cut into wedges
2 tablespoons olive oil
1 teaspoon dried rosemary
1 teaspoon dried thyme
Salt and pepper to taste

Instructions:

Preheat your air fryer to 400°F (200°C) for 5 minutes.
In a large bowl, toss the carrots, parsnips, sweet potato, butternut squash, and red onion with olive oil, dried rosemary, dried thyme, salt, and pepper until well coated.
Place the seasoned vegetables in a single layer in the air fryer basket. If necessary, cook them in batches to avoid overcrowding.
Air fry the vegetables at 400°F (200°C) for 15-20 minutes, or until they are tender and lightly browned, stirring once or twice during cooking for even browning.
Once the vegetables are done, remove them from the air fryer and transfer to a serving platter.
Serve the winter vegetable traybake as a side dish with your favorite main course.
Enjoy the delicious and flavorful winter vegetable traybake made in your air fryer! It's a hearty and nutritious dish perfect for the colder months.

525. Here's an air fryer recipe for a delicious winter root vegetable medley:

Ingredients:

2 large carrots, peeled and cut into chunks
2 parsnips, peeled and cut into chunks
2 beets, peeled and cut into chunks
2 turnips, peeled and cut into chunks
2 tablespoons olive oil
1 teaspoon dried thyme
1 teaspoon dried rosemary
Salt and pepper to taste

Instructions:

Preheat your air fryer to 400°F (200°C) for 5 minutes.
In a large bowl, combine the carrots, parsnips, beets, turnips, olive oil, dried thyme, dried rosemary, salt, and pepper. Toss until the vegetables are evenly coated with the seasoning.

Place the seasoned vegetables in a single layer in the air fryer basket. If necessary, cook them in batches to avoid overcrowding.
Air fry the vegetables at 400°F (200°C) for 15-20 minutes, or until they are tender and lightly browned, stirring once or twice during cooking for even browning.
Once the vegetables are done, remove them from the air fryer and transfer to a serving platter.
Serve the winter root vegetable medley as a side dish with your favorite main course.
Enjoy the flavorful and nutritious medley of winter root vegetables made in your air fryer! It's a perfect dish to enjoy during the colder months.

526. Here's an air fryer recipe for turmeric-crispy chickpeas:

Ingredients:

1 can (15 ounces) chickpeas, drained and rinsed
1 tablespoon olive oil
1 teaspoon ground turmeric
1/2 teaspoon ground cumin
1/2 teaspoon paprika
1/4 teaspoon garlic powder
1/4 teaspoon salt (adjust to taste)
Freshly ground black pepper to taste

Instructions:

Preheat your air fryer to 390°F (200°C) for 5 minutes.
Pat dry the chickpeas using a clean kitchen towel or paper towels.
In a bowl, combine the olive oil, ground turmeric, ground cumin, paprika, garlic powder, salt, and black pepper. Mix well.
Add the dried chickpeas to the bowl and toss to coat them evenly with the spice mixture.
Place the seasoned chickpeas in the air fryer basket in a single layer. If necessary, cook them in batches to avoid overcrowding.
Air fry the chickpeas at 390°F (200°C) for 15-20 minutes, shaking the basket halfway through to ensure even cooking.
Once the chickpeas are crispy and golden brown, remove them from the air fryer and let them cool slightly before serving.
Enjoy the turmeric crispy chickpeas as a healthy and flavorful snack or as a topping for salads or bowls.
These turmeric crispy chickpeas make a delicious and nutritious snack or topping. They are packed with flavor and have a delightful crunch from the air frying process. Enjoy!

527. Here's an air fryer recipe for Middle Eastern Veggie Kofta:

Ingredients:

1 cup cooked chickpeas, drained and rinsed
1 cup grated zucchini, squeezed to remove excess moisture
1 small onion, finely chopped
2 cloves garlic, minced
1/4 cup chopped fresh parsley
1/4 cup chopped fresh cilantro
1/4 cup bread crumbs
2 tablespoons olive oil
1 teaspoon ground cumin
1 teaspoon ground coriander
1/2 teaspoon ground turmeric
1/2 teaspoon paprika
1/4 teaspoon cayenne pepper (optional, for spice)
Salt and pepper to taste

Instructions:

Preheat your air fryer to 400°F (200°C) for 5 minutes.
In a food processor, combine the cooked chickpeas, grated zucchini, chopped onion, minced garlic, fresh parsley, fresh cilantro, bread crumbs, olive oil, ground cumin, ground coriander, ground turmeric, paprika, cayenne pepper (if using), salt, and pepper. Pulse until well combined and the mixture comes together.
Shape the mixture into small kofta shapes or cylinders using your hands.
Place the shaped kofta in the air fryer basket in a single layer, leaving some space between them. If necessary, cook them in batches.
Air fry the veggie kofta at 400°F (200°C) for 12-15 minutes, flipping them halfway through, until they are golden brown and crispy.
Once cooked, remove the veggie kofta from the air fryer and let them cool slightly before serving.
Serve the Middle Eastern Veggie Kofta with pita bread, hummus, tahini sauce, or a side salad.
These Middle Eastern Veggie Kofta are flavorful and packed with healthy ingredients. Enjoy them as a vegetarian main course or as part of a Mezze platter.

528. Here's an air fryer recipe for Air-Fried Cheesy Ravioli:

Ingredients:

1 package of refrigerated cheese ravioli
1 cup breadcrumbs
1/2 cup grated Parmesan cheese
2 eggs, beaten
1/2 teaspoon Italian seasoning
1/4 teaspoon garlic powder
Marinara sauce, for serving

Instructions:

Preheat your air fryer to 400°F (200°C) for 5 minutes.
In a shallow bowl, mix together the breadcrumbs, grated Parmesan cheese, Italian seasoning, and garlic powder.
Dip each ravioli into the beaten eggs, allowing any excess to drip off, and then coat it in the breadcrumb mixture. Press gently to adhere the breadcrumbs to the ravioli.
Place the coated ravioli in a single layer in the air fryer basket, leaving some space between them. If necessary, cook them in batches.
Air fry the ravioli at 400°F (200°C) for 6-8 minutes, flipping them halfway through, until they are golden brown and crispy.
Once cooked, remove the ravioli from the air fryer and let them cool slightly before serving.
Serve the Air-Fried Cheesy Ravioli with marinara sauce for dipping.
These crispy and cheesy ravioli make a delicious appetizer or snack. They are quick and easy to prepare in the air fryer, and the result is a delightful, crispy texture with a gooey cheese filling. Enjoy!

529. Here's an air fryer recipe for Cashew & Chickpea Balls:

Ingredients:

1 can chickpeas, drained and rinsed
1/2 cup cashews
1/4 cup breadcrumbs
2 tablespoons nutritional yeast
2 tablespoons fresh parsley, chopped
1 teaspoon ground cumin
1/2 teaspoon paprika

1/2 teaspoon garlic powder
Salt and pepper, to taste
Olive oil spray

Instructions:

In a food processor, combine the chickpeas, cashews, breadcrumbs, nutritional yeast, parsley, cumin, paprika, garlic powder, salt, and pepper. Pulse until well combined and the mixture starts to come together.
Shape the mixture into small balls, about 1 inch in diameter, and place them on a plate.
Preheat your air fryer to 375°F (190°C) for 5 minutes.
Lightly spray the chickpea balls with olive oil to help them crisp up.
Place the chickpea balls in the air fryer basket in a single layer, leaving some space between them. If necessary, cook them in batches.
Air fry the balls at 375°F (190°C) for 12-15 minutes, flipping them halfway through, until they are golden brown and crispy.
Once cooked, remove the chickpea balls from the air fryer and let them cool slightly before serving.
Serve the Cashew & Chickpea Balls as a tasty appetizer or snack. They are great on their own or served with a dipping sauce of your choice.
These cashew and chickpea balls are packed with flavor and have a nice crunchy texture when air fried. They make a delicious and protein-rich vegetarian option for any occasion. Enjoy!

530. Here's an air fryer recipe for Chili Falafel with Cheesy Sauce:

Ingredients:

For the falafel:

1 can chickpeas, drained and rinsed
1/2 cup fresh cilantro, chopped
1/2 cup fresh parsley, chopped
1 small onion, chopped
3 cloves garlic, minced
1 tablespoon olive oil
1 teaspoon ground cumin
1 teaspoon ground coriander
1 teaspoon chili powder
1/2 teaspoon salt
1/4 teaspoon black pepper
1/4 teaspoon cayenne pepper (optional)
1/2 cup breadcrumbs

For the cheesy sauce:

1/2 cup shredded cheddar cheese
1/4 cup milk
1 tablespoon butter
1 tablespoon all-purpose flour
Salt and pepper, to taste

Instructions:

In a food processor, combine the chickpeas, cilantro, parsley, onion, garlic, olive oil, cumin, coriander, chili powder, salt, black pepper, and cayenne pepper. Pulse until the mixture is well combined but still slightly chunky.
Transfer the mixture to a mixing bowl and stir in the breadcrumbs. Mix well until the mixture holds together when squeezed.

Preheat your air fryer to 375°F (190°C) for 5 minutes.
Shape the falafel mixture into small balls or patties, about 1 inch in diameter.
Lightly spray the air fryer basket with cooking spray. Place the falafel in a single layer in the basket, leaving some space between them. If necessary, cook them in batches.
Air fry the falafel at 375°F (190°C) for 12-15 minutes, flipping them halfway through until they are crispy and golden brown.
While the falafel is cooking, prepare the cheesy sauce. In a small saucepan, melt the butter over medium heat. Add the flour and cook for 1-2 minutes, stirring constantly.
Gradually whisk in the milk until smooth. Continue cooking and stirring until the sauce thickens.
Remove the saucepan from the heat and stir in the shredded cheddar cheese until melted and smooth.
Season with salt and pepper to taste.
Once the falafel is cooked, serve them with the cheesy sauce on the side for dipping.
This chili falafel with cheesy sauce makes a flavorful and satisfying vegetarian dish. Enjoy them as an appetizer, snack, or even as a main course.

531. Here's an air fryer recipe for Quinoa and Veggie Stuffed Peppers:

Ingredients:

4 bell peppers (any color), tops removed and seeds removed
1 cup cooked quinoa
1 cup mixed vegetables (such as diced zucchini, corn, carrots, and peas)
1/2 cup diced onion
2 cloves garlic, minced
1 tablespoon olive oil
1 teaspoon dried herbs (such as oregano, basil, or thyme)
1/2 teaspoon cumin
1/2 teaspoon paprika
Salt and pepper, to taste
1/2 cup shredded cheese (such as cheddar, mozzarella, or pepper jack)
Fresh parsley or cilantro, for garnish

Instructions:

Preheat your air fryer to 375°F (190°C) for 5 minutes.
In a skillet, heat the olive oil over medium heat. Add the onion and garlic and cook until softened and translucent.
Add the mixed vegetables to the skillet and cook until tender. Season with dried herbs, cumin, paprika, salt, and pepper. Stir in the cooked quinoa and mix well.
Stuff the mixture into the hollowed-out bell peppers, pressing down gently to fill them evenly.
Place the stuffed peppers in the air fryer basket, standing upright. If necessary, cook them in batches.
Air fry the stuffed peppers at 375°F (190°C) for 15-20 minutes, or until the peppers are tender and the filling is heated through.
Sprinkle the shredded cheese over the top of each stuffed pepper and air fry for an additional 2-3 minutes, or until the cheese is melted and bubbly.
Carefully remove the stuffed peppers from the air fryer and let them cool slightly before serving.
Garnish with fresh parsley or cilantro, if desired, and serve warm.
These quinoa and veggie stuffed peppers are nutritious, flavorful, and easy to prepare in the air fryer. They make a delicious vegetarian main course or side dish. Enjoy!

532. Here's an air fryer recipe for Fava Bean Falafel with Tzatziki:

Ingredients for Fava Bean Falafel:

1 cup dried fava beans
1 small onion, finely chopped
3 cloves garlic, minced

1/4 cup fresh parsley, chopped
1/4 cup fresh cilantro, chopped
1 teaspoon ground cumin
1 teaspoon ground coriander
1/2 teaspoon baking soda
Salt and pepper, to taste
Olive oil, for brushing

Ingredients for Tzatziki:

1 cup Greek yogurt
1/2 cucumber, grated and squeezed to remove excess moisture
1 clove garlic, minced
1 tablespoon fresh lemon juice
1 tablespoon fresh dill, chopped
Salt and pepper, to taste

Instructions:

Soak the dried fava beans in water overnight. Drain and rinse the beans thoroughly.
In a food processor, combine the soaked fava beans, onion, garlic, parsley, cilantro, cumin, coriander, baking soda, salt, and pepper. Pulse until the mixture is well combined and forms a coarse paste.
Shape the falafel mixture into small patties or balls and place them on a parchment-lined tray.
Preheat your air fryer to 375°F (190°C) for 5 minutes.
Lightly brush the falafel patties or balls with olive oil on both sides.
Place the falafel in the air fryer basket, making sure to leave some space between them. If necessary, cook them in batches.
Air fry the falafel at 375°F (190°C) for 12-15 minutes, flipping them halfway through cooking, until they are golden brown and crispy.
While the falafel are cooking, prepare the tzatziki sauce by combining the Greek yogurt, grated cucumber, minced garlic, lemon juice, chopped dill, salt, and pepper in a bowl. Mix well.
Serve the air-fried fava bean falafel with tzatziki sauce on the side for dipping.
Enjoy the crispy and flavorful fava bean falafel with refreshing tzatziki sauce!
This recipe is a delightful twist on traditional falafel, using fava beans instead of chickpeas for a unique flavor. The air fryer ensures a crispy exterior while keeping the inside tender. Enjoy the falafel as a snack, appetizer, or as part of a delicious Mediterranean-inspired meal.

533. Here's an air fryer recipe for Greek Halloumi Cheese with Veggies:

Ingredients:

8 ounces of Halloumi cheese, cut into thick slices
1 red bell pepper, sliced
1 yellow bell pepper, sliced
1 zucchini, sliced
1 red onion, sliced
2 tablespoons olive oil
1 teaspoon dried oregano
Salt and pepper, to taste
Lemon wedges, for serving

Instructions:

Preheat your air fryer to 400°F (200°C) for 5 minutes.
In a bowl, combine the sliced bell peppers, zucchini, and red onion. Drizzle with olive oil and sprinkle with dried oregano, salt, and pepper. Toss to coat the veggies evenly.

Place the seasoned veggies in the air fryer basket and cook for 10-12 minutes, shaking or flipping the veggies halfway through, until they are tender and slightly charred.
Remove the air fryer basket and carefully place the Halloumi cheese slices on top of the cooked veggies.
Return the air fryer basket to the air fryer and cook for an additional 3-5 minutes until the cheese is golden brown and slightly melted.
Carefully remove the air fryer basket from the air fryer and let the Halloumi and veggies cool slightly.
Serve the Greek Halloumi cheese and veggies with lemon wedges on the side for squeezing over the cheese.
Enjoy the delicious combination of crispy, salty Halloumi cheese with the roasted flavors of the veggies.
This recipe is a fantastic way to enjoy the unique taste and texture of Halloumi cheese, along with flavorful roasted vegetables. The air fryer helps achieve a crispy exterior on the cheese while keeping it soft and gooey inside. Serve this dish as an appetizer, side dish, or even as a light lunch or dinner option.

534. Here's an air fryer recipe for Green Vegetable Rotini Pasta Bake:

Ingredients:

8 ounces of rotini pasta
2 cups broccoli florets
1 cup peas (fresh or frozen)
1 cup spinach leaves
1/2 cup diced zucchini
1/2 cup diced bell pepper (any color)
1/2 cup diced onion
2 cloves garlic, minced
2 tablespoons olive oil
1 cup shredded mozzarella cheese
1/4 cup grated Parmesan cheese
1/2 teaspoon dried basil
1/2 teaspoon dried oregano
Salt and pepper, to taste

Instructions:

Cook the rotini pasta according to the package instructions until al dente. Drain and set aside.
In a large bowl, combine the cooked pasta, broccoli florets, peas, spinach, zucchini, bell pepper, onion, and garlic.
Drizzle olive oil over the vegetables and pasta. Season with dried basil, dried oregano, salt, and pepper. Toss to coat everything evenly.
Preheat your air fryer to 375°F (190°C) for 5 minutes.
Transfer the vegetable and pasta mixture into a baking dish or an air fryer-safe pan.
Sprinkle the shredded mozzarella cheese and grated Parmesan cheese evenly over the top.
Place the baking dish or pan in the air fryer basket and cook for 15-20 minutes, or until the cheese is melted and golden brown.
Carefully remove the baking dish or pan from the air fryer using oven mitts.
Allow the pasta bake to cool slightly before serving.
Serve the Green Vegetable Rotini Pasta Bake as a delicious and nutritious main dish or side dish.
This recipe combines the goodness of green vegetables with flavorful pasta and melted cheese. The air fryer helps create a crispy and cheesy topping while ensuring the vegetables remain tender and cooked to perfection. Enjoy this wholesome and satisfying dish as a comforting meal for the whole family.

535. Here's an air fryer recipe for Easy Vegetable Croquettes:

Ingredients:

2 cups mashed potatoes
1 cup finely chopped mixed vegetables (carrots, peas, corn, bell peppers, etc.)
1/4 cup grated cheddar cheese
1/4 cup breadcrumbs
1/4 cup finely chopped fresh parsley
2 tablespoons finely chopped onion
1 teaspoon garlic powder
1/2 teaspoon paprika
Salt and pepper, to taste
1/4 cup all-purpose flour
1 egg, beaten
Cooking spray

Instructions:

In a large bowl, combine mashed potatoes, mixed vegetables, cheddar cheese, breadcrumbs, parsley, onion, garlic powder, paprika, salt, and pepper. Mix well until all the ingredients are evenly combined.
Take a small portion of the mixture and shape it into a croquette patty. Repeat with the remaining mixture.
Place the croquettes on a baking sheet lined with parchment paper.
In three separate shallow bowls, place the all-purpose flour, beaten egg, and breadcrumbs.
Dip each croquette into the flour, ensuring it's coated evenly. Then dip it into the beaten egg, allowing any excess to drip off. Finally, coat the croquette in breadcrumbs, pressing lightly to adhere.
Preheat your air fryer to 400°F (200°C) for 5 minutes.
Lightly spray the air fryer basket with cooking spray to prevent sticking.
Place the coated croquettes in the air fryer basket, making sure they are not touching each other.
Cook the croquettes in the air fryer for 12-15 minutes, flipping them halfway through, until they are golden brown and crispy.
Remove the croquettes from the air fryer and let them cool for a few minutes before serving.
Serve the Easy Vegetable Croquettes as a tasty appetizer, side dish, or even as a vegetarian burger patty.
These vegetable croquettes are a delightful way to enjoy a medley of veggies in a crispy and flavorful form. The air fryer helps achieve a golden exterior while keeping the inside soft and tender. Feel free to serve them with your favorite dipping sauce or enjoy them as is. They are sure to be a hit!

536. Here's an air fryer recipe for Asian-style Spring Rolls:

Ingredients:

8 spring roll wrappers
1 cup shredded cabbage
1 cup shredded carrots
1 cup bean sprouts
1/2 cup sliced bell peppers
1/2 cup sliced cucumber
1/4 cup chopped fresh cilantro
2 tablespoons soy sauce
1 tablespoon rice vinegar
1 tablespoon sesame oil
1 teaspoon grated ginger
1 teaspoon minced garlic
1/2 teaspoon sugar
Cooking spray

Instructions:

In a large bowl, combine shredded cabbage, carrots, bean sprouts, bell peppers, cucumber, and cilantro.
In a separate small bowl, whisk together soy sauce, rice vinegar, sesame oil, grated ginger, minced garlic, and sugar.
Pour the sauce over the vegetable mixture and toss well to coat all the ingredients.
Take one spring roll wrapper and place it on a clean surface. Spoon about 2 tablespoons of the vegetable filling onto the center of the wrapper.
Fold the sides of the wrapper over the filling, then roll it tightly from the bottom up, similar to rolling a burrito. Seal the top edge with a bit of water to help it stick.
Repeat the process with the remaining wrappers and filling.
Preheat your air fryer to 375°F (190°C) for 5 minutes.
Lightly spray the air fryer basket with cooking spray to prevent sticking.
Place the spring rolls in the air fryer basket, making sure they are not touching each other.
Cook the spring rolls in the air fryer for 8-10 minutes, flipping them halfway through, until they are golden brown and crispy.
Remove the spring rolls from the air fryer and let them cool for a few minutes before serving.
Serve the Asian-style Spring Rolls with your favorite dipping sauce, such as sweet chili sauce or peanut sauce.
These air-fried spring rolls are a healthier alternative to the traditional deep-fried version, as they require less oil. The air fryer helps achieve a crispy texture while keeping the filling inside soft and flavorful. Enjoy these delicious Asian-style spring rolls as an appetizer, snack, or even as a light meal.

537. Here's an air fryer recipe for Egg & Cauliflower Rice Casserole:

Ingredients:

2 cups cauliflower rice
4 large eggs
1/4 cup diced onions
1/4 cup diced bell peppers
1/4 cup diced tomatoes
1/4 cup grated Parmesan cheese
1/4 cup shredded cheddar cheese
2 tablespoons chopped fresh parsley
1 tablespoon olive oil
1/2 teaspoon garlic powder
1/2 teaspoon dried oregano
Salt and pepper to taste

Instructions:

Preheat your air fryer to 375°F (190°C) for 5 minutes.
In a skillet, heat olive oil over medium heat. Add diced onions, bell peppers, and tomatoes. Sauté for 2-3 minutes until the vegetables are slightly softened.
Add cauliflower rice to the skillet and continue cooking for another 2-3 minutes until the cauliflower rice is tender.
Season the cauliflower rice mixture with garlic powder, dried oregano, salt, and pepper. Stir well to combine the flavors.
In a separate bowl, beat the eggs and add grated Parmesan cheese. Mix until well combined.
Pour the egg and cheese mixture over the cauliflower rice mixture in the skillet. Stir everything together until the eggs are evenly distributed.
Transfer the mixture into a greased baking dish or a small oven-safe dish that fits inside the air fryer basket.
Sprinkle shredded cheddar cheese on top of the mixture.
Place the baking dish in the preheated air fryer and cook for 15-20 minutes until the eggs are set and the cheese is melted and slightly golden brown.
Carefully remove the casserole from the air fryer and let it cool for a few minutes.

Garnish with chopped fresh parsley before serving.
This Egg & Cauliflower Rice Casserole is a healthy and low-carb alternative to traditional rice-based casseroles. The air fryer helps cook the casserole evenly and gives it a nice texture. You can customize this recipe by adding your favorite vegetables or spices to suit your taste. Enjoy this flavorful and satisfying casserole as a light meal or as a side dish.
538. Here's an air fryer recipe for Greek-style stuffed bell peppers:

Ingredients:

4 large bell peppers (any color)
1 cup cooked quinoa
1/2 cup diced tomatoes
1/2 cup diced cucumber
1/4 cup chopped Kalamata olives
1/4 cup crumbled feta cheese
2 tablespoons chopped fresh parsley
2 tablespoons chopped fresh dill
2 tablespoons lemon juice
1 tablespoon olive oil
1 teaspoon dried oregano
Salt and pepper to taste

Instructions:

Preheat your air fryer to 375°F (190°C) for 5 minutes.
Cut off the tops of the bell peppers and remove the seeds and membranes from the inside.
In a mixing bowl, combine cooked quinoa, diced tomatoes, diced cucumber, chopped Kalamata olives, crumbled feta cheese, chopped fresh parsley, chopped fresh dill, lemon juice, olive oil, dried oregano, salt, and pepper. Mix well until all ingredients are evenly combined.
Stuff each bell pepper with the quinoa mixture, pressing it down gently to fill the cavity.
Place the stuffed bell peppers in the preheated air fryer basket. Depending on the size of your air fryer, you may need to cook them in batches.
Cook the stuffed bell peppers in the air fryer for 15-20 minutes until the peppers are tender and slightly charred on the edges.
Carefully remove the stuffed bell peppers from the air fryer and let them cool for a few minutes before serving.
Garnish with additional fresh herbs, if desired, and serve hot.
These Greek-style stuffed bell peppers are filled with a flavorful combination of quinoa, fresh vegetables, feta cheese, and herbs. The air fryer cooks the peppers to perfection, giving them a delicious roasted flavor. They can be served as a light lunch or dinner, and they make a great side dish as well. Enjoy these Greek-inspired stuffed bell peppers as a healthy and tasty meal option!

539. Here's an air fryer recipe for Poblano & Tomato Stuffed Squash:

Ingredients:

2 medium-sized yellow squash
2 poblano peppers
1 cup diced tomatoes
1/2 cup cooked quinoa
1/4 cup chopped onion
2 cloves garlic, minced
1/4 cup shredded cheddar cheese
2 tablespoons chopped fresh cilantro
1 tablespoon olive oil
1 teaspoon ground cumin
Salt and pepper to taste

Instructions:

Preheat your air fryer to 375°F (190°C) for 5 minutes.
Cut the yellow squash in half lengthwise and scoop out the seeds to create a hollow cavity.
Place the squash halves in the air fryer basket, cut side up.
Rub the inside of the poblano peppers with olive oil and place them in the air fryer basket alongside the squash.
Air fry the squash and poblano peppers for about 10 minutes until they are slightly tender and have a roasted appearance.
Remove the squash and poblano peppers from the air fryer and let them cool for a few minutes.
Once cooled, dice the roasted poblano peppers and set aside.
In a mixing bowl, combine the diced tomatoes, cooked quinoa, chopped onion, minced garlic, shredded cheddar cheese, chopped cilantro, ground cumin, salt, and pepper. Mix well to combine all the ingredients.
Gently fold in the diced roasted poblano peppers into the tomato-quinoa mixture.
Spoon the tomato-quinoa mixture into the hollowed cavities of the roasted squash halves.
Place the stuffed squash halves back into the air fryer basket.
Air fry the stuffed squash for another 5-7 minutes until the filling is heated through and the cheese is melted and bubbly.
Carefully remove the stuffed squash from the air fryer and let them cool slightly before serving.
Garnish with additional chopped cilantro, if desired, and serve hot.
These Poblano & Tomato Stuffed Squash make a delicious and nutritious meal. The combination of roasted poblano peppers, diced tomatoes, quinoa, and cheese creates a flavorful filling for the tender yellow squash. The air fryer gives them a slightly charred and roasted flavor, making them even more delicious. Enjoy these stuffed squash as a main course or as a side dish for a complete and satisfying meal!

540. Here's an air fryer recipe for Cheesy English Muffins:

Ingredients:

2 English muffins, split
4 slices of cheese (cheddar, Swiss, or your favorite cheese)
2 tablespoons butter, softened
1 teaspoon garlic powder
1 teaspoon dried parsley flakes

Instructions:

Preheat your air fryer to 350°F (175°C) for 5 minutes.
Spread the softened butter on the cut sides of the English muffins.
Sprinkle garlic powder and dried parsley flakes evenly over the buttered surfaces.
Place a slice of cheese on the bottom half of each English muffin.
Place the English muffins in the air fryer basket, cheese side up.
Air fry the English muffins for about 5 minutes, or until the cheese is melted and bubbly, and the muffins are toasted to your desired crispness.
Carefully remove the English muffins from the air fryer and let them cool for a minute.
Press the top halves of the English muffins onto the melted cheese to create a sandwich.
Serve the cheesy English muffins warm.
These Cheesy English Muffins are quick and easy to make in the air fryer. The combination of melted cheese, garlic butter, and toasted English muffins creates a delicious snack or breakfast option. Feel free to customize the recipe by adding your favorite toppings such as sliced tomatoes, cooked bacon, or fresh herbs. Enjoy the warm and gooey goodness of these cheesy treats!

541. Here's an air fryer recipe for Cheesy Vegetable Quesadillas:

Ingredients:

4 small tortillas (corn or flour)
1 cup shredded cheese (cheddar, Monterey Jack, or a blend)
1/2 cup diced bell peppers (any color)
1/2 cup diced red onion
1/2 cup sliced mushrooms
1/2 cup chopped spinach
1 teaspoon olive oil
1/2 teaspoon cumin
1/2 teaspoon chili powder
Salt and pepper to taste
Salsa, guacamole, or sour cream for serving (optional)

Instructions:

Preheat your air fryer to 375°F (190°C) for 5 minutes.
In a skillet, heat the olive oil over medium heat. Add the diced bell peppers, red onion, and mushrooms. Sauté for 3-4 minutes until the vegetables are slightly softened.
Add the chopped spinach to the skillet and cook for an additional 1-2 minutes until wilted. Season with cumin, chili powder, salt, and pepper. Mix well.
Place two tortillas on a clean surface. Sprinkle half of the shredded cheese evenly over each tortilla.
Divide the sautéed vegetable mixture equally between the two tortillas, spreading it over the cheese.
Top each tortilla with the remaining shredded cheese.
Place the quesadillas in the air fryer basket and cook for 5-6 minutes until the tortillas are crispy and the cheese is melted.
Carefully remove the quesadillas from the air fryer and let them cool for a minute.
Cut each quesadilla into wedges and serve warm with salsa, guacamole, or sour cream, if desired.
These Cheesy Vegetable Quesadillas are packed with flavorful sautéed vegetables and gooey melted cheese. You can customize the recipe by adding other vegetables or spices according to your preference. Enjoy these delicious and crispy quesadillas as a snack, appetizer, or light meal!

542. Here's an air fryer recipe for Italian-style stuffed mushrooms:

Ingredients:

12 large mushrooms (portobello or cremini)
1/2 cup bread crumbs
1/4 cup grated Parmesan cheese
1/4 cup chopped fresh parsley
2 cloves garlic, minced
2 tablespoons olive oil
1/2 teaspoon dried oregano
1/2 teaspoon dried basil
Salt and pepper to taste
Instructions:

Preheat your air fryer to 375°F (190°C) for 5 minutes.
Clean the mushrooms by wiping them with a damp paper towel to remove any dirt. Remove the stems and set them aside.
In a mixing bowl, combine the bread crumbs, Parmesan cheese, chopped parsley, minced garlic, olive oil, dried oregano, dried basil, salt, and pepper. Mix well until the ingredients are evenly incorporated.
Take a spoonful of the breadcrumb mixture and stuff it into the cavity of each mushroom cap. Press the mixture gently to ensure it sticks to the mushroom.
Place the stuffed mushroom caps in the air fryer basket. You may need to work in batches depending on the size of your air fryer.

Air fry the stuffed mushrooms for 10-12 minutes, or until the mushrooms are tender and the breadcrumb topping is golden brown and crispy.
Remove the stuffed mushrooms from the air fryer and let them cool for a few minutes before serving.
Garnish with additional chopped parsley, if desired, and serve hot as an appetizer or side dish.
These Italian-style stuffed mushrooms are a flavorful and satisfying appetizer that is perfect for entertaining or enjoying as a snack. The air fryer helps to achieve a crispy breadcrumb topping while keeping the mushrooms moist and tender. Enjoy!

543. Here's an air fryer recipe for chili roasted pumpkin with orzo:

Ingredients:

1 small pumpkin, peeled, seeds removed, and cut into bite-sized cubes
2 tablespoons olive oil
1 teaspoon chili powder
1/2 teaspoon smoked paprika
1/2 teaspoon garlic powder
Salt and pepper to taste
1 cup cooked orzo pasta
1/4 cup crumbled feta cheese
Fresh parsley, chopped (for garnish)

Instructions:

Preheat your air fryer to 400°F (200°C) for 5 minutes.
In a bowl, toss the pumpkin cubes with olive oil, chili powder, smoked paprika, garlic powder, salt, and pepper. Ensure the pumpkin is evenly coated with the seasoning.
Place the seasoned pumpkin cubes in the air fryer basket. You may need to work in batches depending on the size of your air fryer.
Air fry the pumpkin cubes for 12-15 minutes, or until they are tender and slightly caramelized, flipping them halfway through the cooking time.
While the pumpkin is cooking, cook the orzo pasta according to the package instructions. Drain and set aside.
Once the pumpkin is cooked, transfer it to a serving bowl. Add the cooked orzo pasta and gently toss to combine.
Sprinkle the crumbled feta cheese over the pumpkin and orzo mixture.
Garnish with fresh chopped parsley.
Serve the chili roasted pumpkin with orzo as a delicious and satisfying side dish or as a vegetarian main course.

544. Here's an air fryer recipe for Portuguese-style veggies with cheese:

Ingredients:

2 cups mixed vegetables (such as bell peppers, zucchini, eggplant, and cherry tomatoes), sliced
2 tablespoons olive oil
1 teaspoon smoked paprika
1/2 teaspoon garlic powder
Salt and pepper to taste
1/2 cup shredded cheese (such as cheddar, mozzarella, or a blend)
Fresh parsley, chopped (for garnish)

Instructions:

Preheat your air fryer to 400°F (200°C) for 5 minutes.
In a bowl, toss the mixed vegetables with olive oil, smoked paprika, garlic powder, salt, and pepper. Ensure the vegetables are evenly coated with the seasoning.

Place the seasoned vegetables in the air fryer basket. You may need to work in batches depending on the size of your air fryer.
Air fry the vegetables for 8-10 minutes, or until they are tender and slightly charred, tossing them halfway through the cooking time.
Once the vegetables are cooked, transfer them to an oven-safe dish.
Sprinkle the shredded cheese over the vegetables.
Place the dish with the vegetables and cheese back into the air fryer and air fry for an additional 2-3 minutes, or until the cheese is melted and bubbly.
Remove from the air fryer and garnish with fresh chopped parsley.
Serve the Portuguese-style veggies with cheese as a delicious and flavorful side dish.
This recipe combines the vibrant flavors of Portuguese cuisine with the convenience of air frying. The combination of the seasoned and charred vegetables with the melted cheese creates a delightful dish that can be enjoyed as a side or even a light main course. Enjoy the taste of Portugal in this simple and tasty recipe!

This recipe combines the earthy sweetness of roasted pumpkin with the bold flavors of chili powder and smoked paprika. The orzo pasta adds a nice texture and the crumbled feta cheese adds a tangy and creamy element. Enjoy this comforting and flavorful dish!

545. Here's an air fryer recipe for Southern-style corn cakes:

Ingredients:

1 cup yellow cornmeal
1/2 cup all-purpose flour
1 tablespoon granulated sugar
1 teaspoon baking powder
1/2 teaspoon baking soda
1/2 teaspoon salt
1/4 teaspoon cayenne pepper (optional, for some heat)
1 cup buttermilk
1 large egg
2 tablespoons unsalted butter, melted
1 cup canned corn kernels, drained
Cooking spray

Instructions:

In a large bowl, whisk together the cornmeal, flour, sugar, baking powder, baking soda, salt, and cayenne pepper (if using).
In a separate bowl, whisk together the buttermilk, egg, and melted butter.
Pour the wet ingredients into the dry ingredients and stir until just combined. Do not over mix.
Gently fold in the corn kernels.
Preheat your air fryer to 400°F (200°C) for 5 minutes.
Lightly grease the air fryer basket with cooking spray.
Using a 1/4 cup measuring cup, scoop the batter and drop it onto the greased basket, spacing them apart.
Flatten each mound slightly with the back of a spoon to form a round shape.
Air fry the corn cakes in batches for 8-10 minutes, flipping them halfway through, until they are golden brown and cooked through.
Remove the corn cakes from the air fryer and let them cool slightly before serving.
Serve the Southern-style corn cakes warm as a side dish or as a base for other toppings or sauces.
These air-fried Southern-style corn cakes are crispy on the outside and tender on the inside. They make a delightful side dish for any Southern-inspired meal or can be enjoyed on their own as a snack. The sweet corn kernels add bursts of flavor, and the touch of cayenne pepper adds a subtle heat if desired.
Enjoy these delicious corn cakes with your favorite toppings or dips!

546. Here's an air fryer recipe for eggplant gratin with a mozzarella crust:

Ingredients:

1 large eggplant, sliced into 1/4-inch thick rounds
Salt
1 cup marinara sauce
1 cup shredded mozzarella cheese
1/4 cup grated Parmesan cheese
1/4 teaspoon dried oregano
1/4 teaspoon dried basil
Fresh basil leaves, for garnish (optional)

Instructions:

Place the eggplant slices on a paper towel-lined baking sheet and sprinkle them with salt. Let them sit for 15-20 minutes to draw out excess moisture.
After 20 minutes, pat the eggplant slices dry with paper towels to remove the moisture.
Preheat your air fryer to 375°F (190°C) for 5 minutes.
Lightly grease the air fryer basket with cooking spray.
Place the eggplant slices in a single layer in the air fryer basket. You may need to do this in batches, depending on the size of your air fryer.
Air fry the eggplant slices for 8-10 minutes, flipping them halfway through, until they are tender and lightly browned. Remove them from the air fryer and set aside.
Preheat your oven to 400°F (200°C).
In a baking dish, spread a thin layer of marinara sauce on the bottom.
Arrange half of the air-fried eggplant slices in a single layer over the sauce.
Sprinkle half of the shredded mozzarella cheese and grated Parmesan cheese over the eggplant slices.
Sprinkle half of the dried oregano and dried basil over the cheese.
Repeat the layers with the remaining eggplant slices, cheese, and herbs.
Place the baking dish in the oven and bake for 15-20 minutes, or until the cheese is melted and golden brown.
Remove the gratin from the oven and let it cool for a few minutes.
Garnish with fresh basil leaves, if desired, and serve warm.
This eggplant gratin with a mozzarella crust is a delicious and satisfying dish. The air-fried eggplant slices add a crispy texture, while the marinara sauce, melted mozzarella, and Parmesan cheese create a flavorful and cheesy topping. The dried oregano and basil add a hint of Italian seasoning. Serve this gratin as a side dish or a vegetarian main course, and enjoy the wonderful combination of flavors and textures.

547. Here's an air fryer recipe for vegetable and goat cheese tian:

Ingredients:

2 medium zucchini, sliced into thin rounds
2 medium yellow squash, sliced into thin rounds
2 large tomatoes, sliced into thin rounds
1 red onion, thinly sliced
2 cloves garlic, minced
1 tablespoon olive oil
Salt and pepper, to taste
4 ounces goat cheese, crumbled
Fresh basil leaves, chopped, for garnish (optional)

Instructions:

Preheat your air fryer to 375°F (190°C) for 5 minutes.

In a large bowl, combine the zucchini, yellow squash, tomatoes, red onion, minced garlic, olive oil, salt, and pepper. Toss well to coat the vegetables with the oil and seasonings.
Lightly grease the air fryer basket with cooking spray.
Arrange the vegetable slices in the air fryer basket in an alternating pattern, stacking them vertically to create a tian.
Air fry the vegetable tian at 375°F (190°C) for 15-18 minutes, or until the vegetables are tender and slightly caramelized.
Remove the vegetable tian from the air fryer and sprinkle the crumbled goat cheese evenly over the top.
Return the vegetable tian to the air fryer and air fry for an additional 2-3 minutes, or until the goat cheese is slightly melted and golden.
Remove the vegetable and goat cheese tian from the air fryer and let it cool for a few minutes.
Garnish with fresh basil leaves, if desired, and serve warm.
This vegetable and goat cheese tian is a delightful and flavorful dish. The air fryer helps to roast the vegetables to perfection, giving them a slightly caramelized exterior while keeping them tender inside. The crumbled goat cheese adds a creamy and tangy element to the dish. Serve this tian as a side dish or a vegetarian main course, and enjoy the wonderful combination of flavors and textures.

548. Here's an air fryer recipe for chickpea and spinach casserole:

Ingredients:

2 cans (15 ounces each) of chickpeas, drained and rinsed
4 cups fresh spinach leaves
1 small onion, finely chopped
2 cloves garlic, minced
1 teaspoon ground cumin
1 teaspoon paprika
1/2 teaspoon turmeric
1/2 teaspoon salt
1/4 teaspoon black pepper
1/4 teaspoon cayenne pepper (optional, for added heat)
1 cup tomato sauce
1/4 cup vegetable broth
1/4 cup chopped fresh cilantro (optional, for garnish)

Instructions:

Preheat your air fryer to 375°F (190°C) for 5 minutes.
In a bowl, combine the chickpeas, spinach, onion, garlic, cumin, paprika, turmeric, salt, black pepper, and cayenne pepper (if using). Mix well to coat the chickpeas and spinach with the spices.
Lightly grease an oven-safe dish that fits in your air fryer basket.
Transfer the chickpea and spinach mixture to the greased dish and spread it out evenly.
In a separate bowl, whisk together the tomato sauce and vegetable broth. Pour the mixture over the chickpea and spinach mixture in the dish.
Place the dish in the air fryer basket and air fry at 375°F (190°C) for 20-25 minutes, or until the casserole is heated through and the flavors have melded together.
Remove the casserole from the air fryer and let it cool for a few minutes.
Garnish with chopped fresh cilantro, if desired, and serve warm.
This chickpea and spinach casserole is a nutritious and flavorful dish. The air fryer helps to heat the casserole evenly and infuse the flavors of the spices into the chickpeas and spinach. The combination of spices gives the dish a delightful taste, and the tomato sauce adds a tangy element. Serve this casserole as a main course or a hearty side dish, and enjoy the protein and fiber-rich goodness of chickpeas and the nutritional benefits of spinach.

549. Here's an air fryer recipe for Dilled zucchini egg cakes:

Ingredients:

2 medium zucchini, grated
1 small onion, finely chopped
2 cloves garlic, minced
3 large eggs
1/4 cup all-purpose flour
2 tablespoons fresh dill, chopped
1/2 teaspoon baking powder
Salt and pepper to taste
Cooking spray

Instructions:

Start by squeezing excess moisture from the grated zucchini using a clean kitchen towel or paper towels. This step will prevent the cakes from being too watery.
In a mixing bowl, combine the grated zucchini, chopped onion, minced garlic, eggs, flour, dill, baking powder, salt, and pepper. Mix well until all ingredients are combined.
Preheat your air fryer to 375°F (190°C) for 5 minutes.
Lightly coat the air fryer basket or tray with cooking spray.
Scoop about 1/4 cup of the zucchini mixture and drop it onto the greased air fryer basket or tray. Use the back of a spoon to flatten and shape the mixture into a cake.
Repeat the process with the remaining zucchini mixture, leaving some space between the cakes in the air fryer basket or tray.
Place the basket or tray in the preheated air fryer and cook the zucchini egg cakes at 375°F (190°C) for 10-12 minutes, or until they turn golden brown and crispy.
Once cooked, carefully remove the zucchini egg cakes from the air fryer and let them cool for a few minutes before serving.
Serve the dilled zucchini egg cakes as a light and flavorful appetizer or as a side dish. They can be enjoyed on their own or with a dipping sauce of your choice.
These dilled zucchini egg cakes are a delicious and healthy way to enjoy zucchini. The air fryer helps to achieve a crispy texture on the outside while keeping the inside moist and tender. The addition of fresh dill adds a refreshing flavor to the cakes, and the combination of zucchini, onion, and garlic provides a savory taste. These cakes can be enjoyed as a light meal, snack, or even as a side dish to accompany your favorite main course.

550. Here's an air fryer recipe for roasted veggies with penne pasta:

Ingredients:

2 cups mixed vegetables (such as bell peppers, zucchini, eggplant, and cherry tomatoes)
2 tablespoons olive oil
1 teaspoon Italian seasoning
1/2 teaspoon garlic powder
Salt and pepper to taste
8 ounces penne pasta (or any pasta of your choice)
Fresh basil leaves, chopped (for garnish)
Grated Parmesan cheese (optional, for serving)

Instructions:

Preheat your air fryer to 400°F (200°C) for 5 minutes.
In a large mixing bowl, combine the mixed vegetables, olive oil, Italian seasoning, garlic powder, salt, and pepper. Toss well to coat the vegetables evenly with the seasoning.
Place the seasoned vegetables in a single layer in the air fryer basket or tray. Cook at 400°F (200°C) for about 12-15 minutes, or until the vegetables are roasted and tender. Shake or flip the vegetables halfway through the cooking time to ensure even browning.

While the vegetables are cooking, cook the penne pasta according to the package instructions until al dente. Drain the cooked pasta and set aside.
Once the vegetables are done, remove them from the air fryer and set aside.
In a large serving bowl, combine the roasted vegetables and cooked penne pasta. Toss gently to mix well.
Garnish the roasted veggies and pasta with fresh chopped basil leaves.
Serve the roasted veggies with penne pasta as a delicious and healthy meal. You can optionally sprinkle grated Parmesan cheese on top for added flavor, if desired.
This recipe combines the goodness of roasted vegetables with penne pasta for a flavorful and satisfying dish. The air fryer helps to roast the vegetables to perfection, bringing out their natural sweetness and adding a delicious charred flavor. The combination of different vegetables adds variety and color to the dish, while the Italian seasoning and garlic powder provide a savory and aromatic taste. The penne pasta adds a comforting and hearty element to the dish. You can customize the vegetables and seasoning according to your preference and even add a drizzle of olive oil or your favorite sauce for extra flavor. Enjoy!

551. Here's an air fryer recipe for tomato sandwiches with feta and pesto:

Ingredients:

4 slices of bread (your choice of bread, such as whole wheat or sourdough)
2 large tomatoes, sliced
1/2 cup crumbled feta cheese
2 tablespoons pesto sauce
Fresh basil leaves, for garnish (optional)

Instructions:

Preheat your air fryer to 350°F (175°C) for 5 minutes.
Spread pesto sauce on one side of each bread slice.
Place the tomato slices on two bread slices, dividing them evenly.
Sprinkle crumbled feta cheese over the tomato slices.
Top the tomato and feta with the remaining two bread slices, pesto side down, to form sandwiches.
Place the sandwiches in the air fryer basket or tray.
Air fry at 350°F (175°C) for about 4-5 minutes, or until the bread is toasted and crispy.
Carefully remove the sandwiches from the air fryer and let them cool for a minute.
Slice the sandwiches in half if desired and garnish with fresh basil leaves.
Serve the tomato sandwiches with feta and pesto as a delicious and refreshing meal.
The air fryer provides a quick and convenient way to toast the bread slices, giving them a nice crunch while keeping the inside soft. The combination of juicy tomato slices, creamy feta cheese, and flavorful pesto creates a delightful burst of flavors. Feel free to add extra ingredients such as lettuce or cucumber slices for added freshness and texture. Enjoy these delicious tomato sandwiches as a light lunch or a satisfying snack!

552. Here's an air fryer recipe for cheesy green beans and egg cups:

Ingredients:

1 cup fresh green beans, trimmed and cut into bite-sized pieces
4 large eggs
1/4 cup shredded cheddar cheese
2 tablespoons grated Parmesan cheese
Salt and pepper to taste
Cooking spray

Instructions:

Preheat your air fryer to 350°F (175°C) for 5 minutes.
In a mixing bowl, whisk together the eggs, cheddar cheese, Parmesan cheese, salt, and pepper.
Spray the cups of a muffin tin with cooking spray to prevent sticking.
Divide the green beans evenly among the muffin cups.
Pour the egg mixture over the green beans, filling each cup about 3/4 full.
Place the muffin tin in the air fryer basket or tray.
Air fry at 350°F (175°C) for about 10-12 minutes, or until the egg cups are set and slightly golden on top.
Carefully remove the muffin tin from the air fryer and let it cool for a few minutes.
Use a knife or silicone spatula to gently loosen the egg cups from the muffin tin.
Serve the cheesy green beans and egg cups warm as a nutritious and flavorful breakfast or brunch option.
The air fryer provides a quick and efficient way to cook the green beans and eggs together, resulting in a delicious combination. The addition of cheddar and Parmesan cheese adds a savory and cheesy flavor to the dish. Feel free to customize the recipe by adding other vegetables or herbs according to your preference. These cheesy green beans and egg cups are not only tasty but also packed with protein and nutrients. Enjoy!

553. Here's an air fryer recipe for jalapeño and bean tacos:

Ingredients:

4 large flour tortillas
1 cup cooked black beans, drained and rinsed
1 jalapeno pepper, thinly sliced
1/2 red onion, thinly sliced
1 bell pepper, thinly sliced
1 tablespoon olive oil
1 teaspoon chili powder
1/2 teaspoon cumin
Salt and pepper to taste
Optional toppings: shredded lettuce, diced tomatoes, avocado slices, cilantro, lime wedges, sour cream, salsa

Instructions:

Preheat your air fryer to 350°F (175°C) for 5 minutes.
In a mixing bowl, combine the black beans, jalapeño pepper, red onion, bell pepper, olive oil, chili powder, cumin, salt, and pepper. Toss until the vegetables are coated in the spices and oil.
Place the seasoned vegetables in the air fryer basket or tray and spread them out in a single layer.
Air fry at 350°F (175°C) for about 10-12 minutes, or until the vegetables are tender and slightly charred, stirring halfway through the cooking time.
Warm the flour tortillas in the air fryer for a few seconds to make them pliable.
Fill each tortilla with the roasted jalapeño and bean mixture.
Top with your preferred optional toppings such as shredded lettuce, diced tomatoes, avocado slices, cilantro, lime wedges, sour cream, or salsa.
Serve the jalapeño and bean tacos immediately while warm.
The air fryer provides a convenient way to roast the jalapeños and beans, giving them a delicious smoky flavor. The combination of the spicy jalapeños, savory beans, and crunchy vegetables makes these tacos flavorful and satisfying. Feel free to adjust the spice level by adding more or fewer jalapeño slices according to your preference. Enjoy these jalapeño and bean tacos as a tasty and vegetarian-friendly meal option!

554. Here's an air fryer recipe for air-fried veggie sushi:

Ingredients:

4 nori seaweed sheets

2 cups sushi rice, cooked and seasoned with rice vinegar
Assorted vegetables (e.g., cucumber, carrot, avocado, bell pepper), thinly sliced
Soy sauce, for dipping
Pickled ginger, for serving
Wasabi, for serving

Instructions:

Preheat your air fryer to 350°F (175°C) for 5 minutes.
Place a nori seaweed sheet on a clean surface or sushi mat.
Spread a thin layer of sushi rice evenly over the nori sheet, leaving about an inch of space at the top.
Arrange your choice of thinly sliced vegetables in a row across the center of the rice.
Starting from the bottom, roll the nori sheet tightly around the vegetables, using a sushi mat or your hands to help shape it.
Repeat the process with the remaining nori sheets and fillings.
Lightly brush or spray the rolled sushi with a little oil to help with browning.
Place the sushi rolls in the air fryer basket or tray, making sure they are not touching each other.
Air fry at 350°F (175°C) for about 5-7 minutes, or until the sushi rolls are crispy and lightly golden.
Remove the sushi rolls from the air fryer and let them cool for a few minutes.
Use a sharp knife to slice each roll into bite-sized pieces.
Serve the air-fried veggie sushi with soy sauce, pickled ginger, and wasabi on the side.
The air fryer provides a quick and easy way to achieve a crispy texture on the outside of the sushi rolls while keeping the vegetables inside fresh and flavorful. You can get creative with the vegetable fillings, using your favorite combinations or adding additional ingredients like tofu, sprouts, or herbs. Enjoy this air-fried veggie sushi as a tasty and healthier alternative to traditional deep-fried sushi.

555. Here's an air fryer recipe for potato-filled bread rolls:

Ingredients:

2 cups all-purpose flour
1 teaspoon instant yeast
1 teaspoon sugar
1/2 teaspoon salt
1/4 cup warm milk
2 tablespoons melted butter
1 cup mashed potatoes (cooled)
1/2 teaspoon garlic powder
1/2 teaspoon dried herbs (such as thyme or parsley)
Salt and pepper to taste
Optional: grated cheese or chopped herbs for topping

Instructions:

In a large mixing bowl, combine the flour, instant yeast, sugar, and salt.
Add the warm milk and melted butter to the dry ingredients. Mix well until a dough forms.
Transfer the dough to a floured surface and knead for about 5 minutes until smooth and elastic.
Place the dough in a greased bowl, cover with a clean kitchen towel, and let it rise in a warm place for about 1 hour or until doubled in size.
In a separate bowl, mix the mashed potatoes, garlic powder, dried herbs, salt, and pepper to taste. Set aside.
Once the dough has risen, punch it down to release the air.
Divide the dough into small portions and shape each portion into a ball.
Flatten each dough ball with your palm and place a spoonful of the potato filling in the center.
Gently fold the edges of the dough over the filling and pinch them together to seal.
Place the filled rolls on a greased air fryer basket or tray, leaving space between them.
Optional: Sprinkle grated cheese or chopped herbs on top of the rolls for added flavor.

Preheat the air fryer to 350°F (175°C) for 5 minutes.
Air fry the potato-filled bread rolls at 350°F (175°C) for 12-15 minutes or until golden brown and cooked through.
Remove the rolls from the air fryer and let them cool slightly before serving.
These potato-filled bread rolls make a delicious snack or appetizer. The air fryer helps achieve a crispy and golden exterior while keeping the inside soft and flavorful. Serve them warm on their own or with your favorite dipping sauce. Enjoy!

556. Here's an air fryer recipe for Mexican Chile Relleno:

Ingredients:

4 large poblano peppers
1 cup shredded Monterey Jack or Oaxaca cheese
1/2 cup all-purpose flour
3 large eggs
1/2 teaspoon salt
1/4 teaspoon black pepper
1/4 teaspoon paprika
Cooking spray

Optional toppings:

Red or green salsa
Sour cream
Chopped cilantro
Diced tomatoes
Sliced avocado

Instructions:

Preheat your air fryer to 375°F (190°C).
Place the poblano peppers on a baking sheet and broil them in the oven on high for 5-7 minutes, turning them occasionally until the skin is blistered and charred. Alternatively, you can roast them directly in the air fryer for about 10 minutes, turning them halfway through.
Remove the peppers from the oven or air fryer and transfer them to a bowl. Cover the bowl with plastic wrap and let them steam for about 10 minutes. This will help loosen the skin.
After steaming, carefully peel off the skin from each pepper. Make a lengthwise slit on one side of each pepper and remove the seeds and membranes.
Stuff each pepper with the shredded cheese, making sure to close the slit as much as possible.
In a shallow dish, combine the flour, salt, black pepper, and paprika. In a separate bowl, beat the eggs.
Dip each stuffed pepper into the flour mixture, shaking off any excess. Then dip it into the beaten eggs, ensuring it is well coated.
Place the coated peppers in the air fryer basket or tray, making sure they are not touching each other.
Lightly spray them with cooking spray.
Air fry the chile rellenos at 375°F (190°C) for about 10-12 minutes until the coating is crispy and golden brown, and the cheese is melted and bubbly.
Carefully remove the chile rellenos from the air fryer and let them cool for a few minutes.
Serve the chile rellenos with your choice of toppings, such as salsa, sour cream, chopped cilantro, diced tomatoes, or sliced avocado.
Enjoy these delicious air-fried Mexican chile rellenos as a main dish or appetizer. The air fryer helps achieve a crispy coating while maintaining the flavor and texture of the peppers. It's a tasty and healthier alternative to deep-fried versions.

557. Here's an air fryer recipe for crispy mozzarella sliders:

Ingredients:

1 pound ground beef
1/2 teaspoon salt
1/4 teaspoon black pepper
1/4 teaspoon garlic powder
1/4 teaspoon onion powder
1/4 teaspoon paprika
1/4 teaspoon dried oregano
8 small slider buns
8 small mozzarella cheese slices
1 cup panko breadcrumbs
Cooking spray
Marinara sauce for dipping

Instructions:

Preheat your air fryer to 375°F (190°C).
In a mixing bowl, combine the ground beef, salt, black pepper, garlic powder, onion powder, paprika, and dried oregano. Mix well until all the ingredients are evenly incorporated.
Divide the beef mixture into 8 equal portions and shape them into small patties that will fit the slider buns.
Place a slice of mozzarella cheese on top of 4 of the beef patties. Top each cheese-topped patty with another plain patty, sealing the edges to enclose the cheese.
Place the panko breadcrumbs in a shallow dish. Coat each stuffed beef patty with the breadcrumbs, pressing gently to adhere.
Spray the air fryer basket or tray with cooking spray to prevent sticking. Place the coated sliders in the air fryer, ensuring they are not touching each other.
Lightly spray the tops of the sliders with cooking spray to promote browning and crispiness.
Air fry the sliders at 375°F (190°C) for about 10-12 minutes until the patties are cooked through and the breadcrumbs are golden brown and crispy.
Carefully remove the sliders from the air fryer and let them cool for a few minutes.
Assemble the sliders by placing each patty on a slider bun. Serve with marinara sauce for dipping.
These crispy mozzarella sliders are perfect for a quick and flavorful meal. The air fryer helps achieve a crispy exterior while keeping the interior juicy and cheesy. Enjoy them as a delicious appetizer or as a satisfying main dish.

558. Here's an air fryer recipe for vegetable tortilla pizza:

Ingredients:

4 small tortillas
1/2 cup pizza sauce
1 cup shredded mozzarella cheese
1/2 cup sliced bell peppers
1/2 cup sliced mushrooms
1/4 cup sliced red onions
1/4 cup sliced black olives
1 tablespoon olive oil
1/2 teaspoon dried oregano
Salt and pepper to taste
Fresh basil leaves for garnish (optional)

Instructions:

Preheat your air fryer to 400°F (200°C).
Brush the tortillas lightly with olive oil on both sides. This will help them crisp up in the air fryer.
Place the tortillas in the air fryer basket or tray, making sure they are not overlapping.

Air fry the tortillas for about 2 minutes to crisp them up slightly.
Remove the tortillas from the air fryer and spread an even layer of pizza sauce on each tortilla.
Sprinkle shredded mozzarella cheese evenly over the sauce on each tortilla.
Arrange the sliced bell peppers, mushrooms, red onions, and black olives on top of the cheese.
Sprinkle dried oregano, salt, and pepper over the vegetables.
Return the topped tortillas to the air fryer and air fry for an additional 5-7 minutes until the cheese is melted and bubbly.
Carefully remove the vegetable tortilla pizzas from the air fryer and let them cool for a few minutes.
Garnish with fresh basil leaves, if desired, and serve hot.
These vegetable tortilla pizzas are a quick and easy way to enjoy a tasty and healthier pizza option. The air fryer helps crisp up the tortilla crust while keeping the toppings flavorful and gooey. Customize the toppings to your liking and enjoy a delicious homemade pizza in no time!

559. Here's an air fryer recipe for Spanish-style Huevos Rotos (Broken Eggs):

Ingredients:

2 large potatoes
2 tablespoons olive oil
Salt and pepper to taste
4 eggs
Chopped fresh parsley for garnish
Optional toppings: Serrano ham or bacon, grated cheese, sautéed vegetables

Instructions:

Peel the potatoes and cut them into thin, matchstick-like strips.
In a bowl, toss the potato strips with olive oil, salt, and pepper until evenly coated.
Preheat your air fryer to 400°F (200°C).
Place the seasoned potato strips in the air fryer basket or tray, making sure they are spread out in a single layer.
Air fry the potatoes for about 12-15 minutes, shaking or flipping them halfway through, until they are golden and crispy.
While the potatoes are cooking, heat a non-stick skillet over medium heat on the stovetop and fry the eggs to your desired doneness (e.g., sunny-side up or over-easy).
Once the potatoes are done, transfer them to a serving plate or individual plates.
Carefully place the fried eggs on top of the potatoes.
If desired, you can add optional toppings such as crumbled Serrano ham or bacon, grated cheese, or sautéed vegetables.
Sprinkle chopped fresh parsley over the eggs and potatoes for garnish.
Serve the Huevos Rotos immediately while the eggs are still warm and the potatoes are crispy.
Huevos Rotos is a popular Spanish dish that combines crispy potatoes with broken eggs, creating a delicious and satisfying meal. Feel free to customize the toppings and seasonings to your liking, and enjoy this tasty Spanish-style dish made in the air fryer!

560. Here's an air fryer recipe for a homemade pie with root vegetables:

Ingredients:

For the crust:

1 ¼ cups all-purpose flour
½ teaspoon salt
½ cup cold unsalted butter, cut into small cubes
3-4 tablespoons ice water

For the filling:

2 cups mixed root vegetables (such as carrots, parsnips, sweet potatoes, and turnips), peeled and diced
1 small onion, diced
2 cloves garlic, minced
1 tablespoon olive oil
1 teaspoon dried thyme
Salt and pepper to taste
1 cup vegetable broth
2 tablespoons all-purpose flour
½ cup milk (or non-dairy milk)
½ cup shredded cheese of your choice (such as cheddar or Gruyere)
Fresh parsley for garnish (optional)

Instructions:

Preheat your air fryer to 375°F (190°C).
In a large bowl, combine the flour and salt for the crust. Add the cold butter cubes and use a pastry cutter or your hands to mix until the mixture resembles coarse crumbs.
Gradually add the ice water, one tablespoon at a time, and mix until the dough comes together. Form the dough into a ball, cover with plastic wrap, and refrigerate for about 30 minutes.
In the meantime, prepare the filling. In a skillet, heat the olive oil over medium heat. Add the diced onion and minced garlic and sauté until softened and fragrant.
Add the diced root vegetables to the skillet and sprinkle with dried thyme, salt, and pepper. Cook for about 5 minutes until the vegetables start to soften.
In a small bowl, whisk together the vegetable broth and flour until well combined. Pour the mixture into the skillet with the vegetables and stir well.
Add the milk to the skillet and continue cooking, stirring occasionally, until the mixture thickens. Remove from heat and let it cool slightly.
On a lightly floured surface, roll out the chilled dough into a circle large enough to fit your pie dish.
Transfer the rolled-out dough to your pie dish and gently press it down to fit. Trim any excess dough hanging over the edges.
Pour the cooled vegetable filling into the pie crust and spread it evenly.
Sprinkle the shredded cheese on top of the filling.
Place the pie dish in the air fryer basket or tray and air fry for about 20-25 minutes, or until the crust is golden and the filling is bubbly.
Remove the pie from the air fryer and let it cool for a few minutes.
Garnish with fresh parsley, if desired, and serve the homemade root vegetable pie warm.
Enjoy your delicious homemade pie with a medley of flavorful root vegetables! The air fryer provides a convenient and efficient way to achieve a golden and crispy crust while cooking the filling to perfection.

561. Here's an air fryer recipe for plantain fritters:

Ingredients:

2 ripe plantains
1/4 cup all-purpose flour
1/4 cup cornmeal
1/4 teaspoon baking powder
1/4 teaspoon salt
1/4 teaspoon ground cinnamon (optional)
Vegetable oil (for spraying)

Instructions:

Preheat your air fryer to 375°F (190°C).
Peel the plantains and cut them into small chunks. Place the plantain chunks in a bowl.

In a separate bowl, whisk together the flour, cornmeal, baking powder, salt, and ground cinnamon (if using).
Add the dry mixture to the bowl of plantain chunks and gently mix until the plantain chunks are coated with the mixture.
Using your hands or a spoon, shape the plantain mixture into small fritter patties.
Lightly spray the air fryer basket or tray with vegetable oil to prevent sticking.
Place the plantain fritters in the air fryer basket or tray in a single layer, leaving some space between each fritter.
Air fry the fritters at 375°F (190°C) for about 10-12 minutes, flipping them halfway through the cooking time, until they are golden brown and crispy.
Once cooked, transfer the plantain fritters to a plate lined with paper towels to absorb any excess oil.
Serve the plantain fritters warm as a snack or side dish. They can be enjoyed on their own or paired with your favorite dipping sauce or salsa.
These air-fried plantain fritters make a delicious and healthier alternative to traditional fried fritters. The air fryer helps achieve a crispy texture while minimizing the use of oil. Enjoy the tasty combination of sweet plantains with a crispy exterior!

562. Here's an air fryer recipe for baked Mediterranean Shakshuka: (While Shakshuka is traditionally cooked on the stovetop, you can create a delicious baked version using an air fryer)

Ingredients:

1 tablespoon olive oil
1 small onion, diced
1 red bell pepper, diced
2 cloves garlic, minced
1 can (14 ounces) diced tomatoes
1 teaspoon ground cumin
1 teaspoon ground paprika
1/2 teaspoon ground cayenne pepper (adjust to taste)
Salt and pepper to taste
4-6 large eggs
Fresh parsley, chopped (for garnish)

Instructions:

Preheat your air fryer to 375°F (190°C).
Heat the olive oil in a skillet or pan over medium heat.
Add the diced onion and red bell pepper to the skillet and sauté for 5-7 minutes, until softened.
Add the minced garlic and cook for an additional minute.
Stir in the diced tomatoes, ground cumin, ground paprika, and ground cayenne pepper. Season with salt and pepper to taste.
Cook the tomato mixture for about 10 minutes, allowing the flavors to meld together and the sauce to thicken slightly.
Transfer the tomato mixture to a baking dish that fits inside your air fryer basket or tray.
Create wells in the tomato mixture and crack the eggs into the wells.
Place the baking dish in the air fryer basket or tray and air fry at 375°F (190°C) for about 8-10 minutes, or until the eggs are cooked to your desired level of doneness.
Once cooked, carefully remove the baking dish from the air fryer.
Garnish with fresh chopped parsley.
Serve the baked Mediterranean shakshuka hot, with crusty bread or pita on the side for dipping.
Enjoy the flavorful combination of the tomato and pepper sauce with perfectly baked eggs. This air fryer recipe offers a unique twist on the classic stovetop shakshuka dish.

563. Here's an air fryer recipe for Brussels sprouts with raisins and pine nuts:

Ingredients:

1 pound Brussels sprouts, trimmed and halved
2 tablespoons olive oil
2 tablespoons balsamic vinegar
1/4 cup raisins
1/4 cup pine nuts
Salt and pepper to taste

Instructions:

Preheat your air fryer to 400°F (200°C).
In a mixing bowl, combine the Brussels sprouts, olive oil, balsamic vinegar, raisins, pine nuts, salt, and pepper. Toss until the Brussels sprouts are evenly coated.
Place the Brussels sprouts mixture in the air fryer basket or tray, spreading them out in a single layer.
Air fry at 400°F (200°C) for 12-15 minutes, shaking the basket or flipping the sprouts halfway through cooking, until they are crispy and browned.
Carefully remove the Brussels sprouts from the air fryer and transfer to a serving dish.
Serve the air-fried Brussels sprouts with raisins and pine nuts as a delicious side dish or as part of a main meal.
The combination of caramelized Brussels sprouts, sweet raisins, and crunchy pine nuts makes for a tasty and nutritious dish. Enjoy!

SWEETS & DESSERTS

564. Here's an air fryer recipe for Spanish churros con chocolate:

Ingredients:

For the churros:

1 cup all-purpose flour
1 cup water
2 tablespoons unsalted butter
1 tablespoon granulated sugar
1/2 teaspoon salt
1/2 teaspoon vanilla extract

For the chocolate sauce:

1 cup dark chocolate, chopped
1/2 cup heavy cream
1/4 cup milk
1 tablespoon granulated sugar
1/2 teaspoon vanilla extract
For coating:
1/2 cup granulated sugar
1 teaspoon ground cinnamon

Instructions:

In a saucepan, combine the water, butter, sugar, salt, and vanilla extract. Bring the mixture to a boil over medium heat.
Remove the saucepan from heat and add the flour all at once. Stir quickly until the mixture forms a smooth dough.
Transfer the dough to a piping bag fitted with a star tip.
Preheat your air fryer to 375°F (190°C).

Pipe the dough into long strips directly into the preheated air fryer basket, cutting the dough with scissors as needed. Leave enough space between the churros for them to expand.
Air fry the churros at 375°F (190°C) for 8-10 minutes or until they turn golden brown and crispy.
Meanwhile, prepare the chocolate sauce. In a microwave-safe bowl, combine the chopped dark chocolate, heavy cream, milk, granulated sugar, and vanilla extract. Microwave in 30-second intervals, stirring in between, until the chocolate is melted and the mixture is smooth.
In a shallow bowl, mix together the granulated sugar and ground cinnamon.
Once the churros are cooked, remove them from the air fryer and immediately roll them in the cinnamon-sugar mixture to coat.
Serve the warm churros with the homemade chocolate sauce for dipping.
Enjoy your homemade Spanish churros con chocolate!

565. Here's an air fryer recipe for chocolate and peanut butter fondants:

Ingredients:

4 ounces dark chocolate
1/4 cup unsalted butter
1/4 cup granulated sugar
2 large eggs
2 tablespoons all-purpose flour
2 tablespoons cocoa powder
1/4 cup creamy peanut butter
Powdered sugar, for dusting
Vanilla ice cream or whipped cream (optional)

Instructions:

Preheat your air fryer to 360°F (180°C).
In a microwave-safe bowl, melt the dark chocolate and butter together in the microwave, stirring occasionally until smooth.
In a separate bowl, whisk together the granulated sugar and eggs until well combined.
Add the melted chocolate and butter mixture to the egg and sugar mixture. Stir until fully incorporated.
Sift in the all-purpose flour and cocoa powder. Mix until smooth and well combined.
Grease small ramekins or silicone muffin cups with cooking spray or butter.
Fill each ramekin or cup halfway with the chocolate batter.
Place a small dollop of peanut butter in the center of each ramekin or cup.
Top with more chocolate batter to cover the peanut butter completely.
Place the filled ramekins or cups in the preheated air fryer basket. Cook at 360°F (180°C) for 10-12 minutes or until the edges are set and the centers are slightly gooey.
Remove the fondants from the air fryer and let them cool for a few minutes.
Carefully remove the fondants from the ramekins or cups and dust with powdered sugar.
Serve the chocolate and peanut butter fondants warm, optionally with a scoop of vanilla ice cream or a dollop of whipped cream.
Enjoy your delicious chocolate and peanut butter fondants made in the air fryer!

566. Here's an air fryer recipe for a delicious mock blueberry pie:

Ingredients:

2 cups fresh or frozen blueberries
1/4 cup granulated sugar
1 tablespoon lemon juice
1 tablespoon cornstarch
1/2 teaspoon ground cinnamon
1 refrigerated pie crust
1 tablespoon milk or beaten egg (for egg wash)

Powdered sugar (for dusting, optional)
Whipped cream or vanilla ice cream (for serving, optional)

Instructions:

Preheat your air fryer to 375°F (190°C).
In a bowl, combine the blueberries, granulated sugar, lemon juice, cornstarch, and cinnamon. Stir until the blueberries are coated with the mixture.
Roll out the pie crust and cut it into desired shapes, such as circles or strips, to create a lattice pattern or a solid top crust.
Place the blueberry mixture into a small oven-safe dish or ramekin, leaving some space for the crust.
Carefully arrange the pie crust pieces over the blueberry filling, creating a lattice pattern or covering the entire top.
Brush the crust with milk or beaten egg for a golden finish.
Place the pie dish in the air fryer basket and cook at 375°F (190°C) for about 20-25 minutes or until the crust is golden brown and the filling is bubbly.
Once cooked, remove the mock blueberry pie from the air fryer and let it cool for a few minutes.
Dust with powdered sugar if desired.
Serve the mock blueberry pie warm, optionally with a dollop of whipped cream or a scoop of vanilla ice cream.
Enjoy your delicious mock blueberry pie made in the air fryer!

567. Here's an air fryer recipe for French sour cherry clafoutis:

Ingredients:

1 cup sour cherries, pitted
3/4 cup all-purpose flour
1/2 cup granulated sugar
3 large eggs
1 cup milk
1 teaspoon vanilla extract
Pinch of salt
Powdered sugar (for dusting)

Instructions:

Preheat your air fryer to 320°F (160°C).
In a mixing bowl, whisk together the flour, sugar, and salt.
In a separate bowl, beat the eggs, then add the milk and vanilla extract. Mix well.
Gradually add the dry ingredients to the wet ingredients, whisking until the batter is smooth and well combined.
Grease a round baking dish that fits into your air fryer basket.
Arrange the pitted sour cherries in a single layer at the bottom of the baking dish.
Pour the batter over the cherries, making sure they are evenly covered.
Place the baking dish in the air fryer basket and cook at 320°F (160°C) for about 25-30 minutes or until the clafoutis is set and lightly golden on top.
Remove the clafoutis from the air fryer and let it cool for a few minutes.
Dust the clafoutis with powdered sugar before serving.
Serve warm or at room temperature.
Enjoy your delicious French sour cherry clafoutis made in the air fryer!

568. Here's an air fryer recipe for chocolate fudge squares:

Ingredients:

1 cup semisweet chocolate chips

1/2 cup unsalted butter
1 cup granulated sugar
2 large eggs
1 teaspoon vanilla extract
3/4 cup all-purpose flour
1/4 cup cocoa powder
1/4 teaspoon salt
Optional toppings: chopped nuts, chocolate chips, or powdered sugar

Instructions:

Preheat your air fryer to 320°F (160°C).
In a microwave-safe bowl, combine the chocolate chips and butter. Heat in the microwave in 30-second intervals, stirring in between, until the chocolate and butter are melted and smooth.
In a separate bowl, whisk together the sugar, eggs, and vanilla extract until well combined.
Gradually add the melted chocolate mixture to the sugar-egg mixture, whisking continuously.
In another bowl, sift together the flour, cocoa powder, and salt. Gradually add the dry ingredients to the chocolate mixture, stirring until just combined. Be careful not to over mix.
Grease a square baking dish that fits into your air fryer basket. Pour the fudge batter into the greased dish, spreading it evenly.
Place the baking dish in the air fryer basket and cook at 320°F (160°C) for about 20-25 minutes or until a toothpick inserted into the center comes out with moist crumbs.
Remove the baking dish from the air fryer and let the fudge cool completely in the dish.
Once cooled, cut the fudge into squares. You can sprinkle chopped nuts, chocolate chips, or powdered sugar on top for added decoration.
Serve and enjoy the delicious chocolate fudge squares!
Note: Cooking times may vary depending on the air fryer model, so keep an eye on the fudge as it cooks to avoid overcooking.

569. Here's a recipe for classic Crème Brûlée:

Ingredients:

1/2 cup milk
2 egg yolks
2/3 cup light cream
2 2/3 tbsp sugar granulated
1 dash of vanilla extract

Add the milk, light cream, egg yolks, and a few drops of vanilla extract to a bowl and whip uniformly.
Heat to simmer in a pan on low and stir in 1⅔ tbsp of sugar to dissolve.
Once the sugar has dissolved, pour it into ramekins. Preheat the air fryer to 375°F.
Cook for 25-30 mins. Using an oven mitt, test that it is set by gently shaking it.
Bring to air temperature.
Sprinkling the remainder of the sugar evenly across the top.
Caramelize the layer of sugar using a small culinary torch.
Enjoy!

570. Here's an air fryer recipe for vanilla and chocolate brownies:

Ingredients:

1 cup all-purpose flour
1/2 cup unsweetened cocoa powder
1/2 teaspoon baking powder
1/4 teaspoon salt
1/2 cup unsalted butter, melted

1 cup granulated sugar
2 large eggs
1 teaspoon vanilla extract
1/2 cup chocolate chips (optional)

Instructions:

Preheat your air fryer to 325°F (160°C). If your air fryer doesn't have a temperature setting, preheat it to the equivalent.
In a mixing bowl, whisk together the flour, cocoa powder, baking powder, and salt until well combined.
In a separate bowl, mix the melted butter and granulated sugar until smooth.
Add the eggs and vanilla extract to the butter-sugar mixture and whisk until well combined.
Gradually add the dry ingredients to the wet ingredients, stirring until just combined. Be careful not to over mix.
If desired, fold in the chocolate chips.
Grease a square baking pan or line it with parchment paper. Pour the brownie batter into the prepared pan and spread it evenly.
Place the baking pan in the air fryer basket and cook for 18-20 minutes, or until a toothpick inserted into the center comes out with a few moist crumbs. The cooking time may vary slightly depending on your air fryer model, so keep an eye on the brownies towards the end.
Once cooked, remove the brownies from the air fryer and let them cool in the pan for a few minutes.
Carefully transfer the brownies to a wire rack to cool completely before cutting into squares.
Serve the vanilla and chocolate brownies as is or with a scoop of ice cream for an extra indulgent treat.
Enjoy your delicious vanilla and chocolate brownies made in the air fryer!

571. Here's an air fryer recipe for easy lemony cheesecake:

Ingredients:

For the crust:

1 cup graham cracker crumbs
3 tablespoons unsalted butter, melted
1 tablespoon granulated sugar

For the filling:

16 ounces cream cheese, softened
1/2 cup granulated sugar
2 large eggs
1/4 cup fresh lemon juice
1 tablespoon lemon zest
1 teaspoon vanilla extract

For the topping:

1/2 cup sour cream
2 tablespoons powdered sugar
1 tablespoon fresh lemon juice
Lemon slices, for garnish (optional)

Instructions:

Preheat your air fryer to 325°F (160°C). If your air fryer doesn't have a temperature setting, preheat it to the equivalent.

In a bowl, mix the graham cracker crumbs, melted butter, and granulated sugar until well combined.
Press the mixture into the bottom of a greased or parchment-lined round cake pan that fits in your air fryer.
In another bowl, beat the cream cheese and granulated sugar until smooth and creamy. Add the eggs, one at a time, beating well after each addition. Stir in the lemon juice, lemon zest, and vanilla extract until everything is well combined.
Pour the cream cheese mixture over the crust in the cake pan, spreading it evenly.
Place the cake pan in the air fryer basket and cook for about 30-35 minutes, or until the edges are set but the center is slightly jiggly.
While the cheesecake is cooking, prepare the topping by mixing the sour cream, powdered sugar, and lemon juice in a small bowl until well combined.
Once the cheesecake is done, remove it from the air fryer and let it cool in the pan for about 10 minutes.
Spread the sour cream topping evenly over the surface of the cheesecake.
Place the cheesecake back in the air fryer for another 5 minutes to set the topping.
Remove the cheesecake from the air fryer and let it cool completely at room temperature.
Once cooled, refrigerate the cheesecake for at least 4 hours, or preferably overnight, to set.
When ready to serve, garnish with lemon slices if desired.
Slice and enjoy your easy lemony cheesecake made in the air fryer!

572. Here's an air fryer recipe for apple caramel relish:

Ingredients:

2 apples, peeled, cored, and finely chopped
1/4 cup brown sugar
2 tablespoons unsalted butter
1/4 teaspoon ground cinnamon
1/4 teaspoon vanilla extract
Pinch of salt

Instructions:

Preheat your air fryer to 375°F (190°C). If your air fryer doesn't have a temperature setting, preheat it to the equivalent.
In a small saucepan, melt the butter over medium heat. Add the brown sugar and stir until dissolved.
Add the chopped apples, ground cinnamon, vanilla extract, and a pinch of salt to the saucepan. Stir well to combine all the ingredients.
Cook the mixture for about 5-7 minutes, stirring occasionally, until the apples are tender and the caramel has thickened slightly.
Transfer the apple caramel relish to a heatproof bowl or dish that fits in your air fryer.
Place the bowl or dish in the air fryer basket and cook for an additional 5-7 minutes, or until the relish is bubbly and the edges start to caramelize.
Carefully remove the relish from the air fryer and let it cool slightly before serving.
Serve the apple caramel relish as a topping for pancakes, waffles, ice cream, or as a dip for apple slices.
Enjoy the sweet and delicious apple caramel relish made in your air fryer!

573. Here's an air fryer recipe for oat and walnut granola:

Ingredients:

2 cups old-fashioned oats
1 cup walnuts, chopped
1/4 cup honey or maple syrup
2 tablespoons coconut oil, melted
1 teaspoon vanilla extract
1/2 teaspoon ground cinnamon
Pinch of salt

Optional: dried fruits, such as raisins or cranberries

Instructions:

Preheat your air fryer to 300°F (150°C). If your air fryer doesn't have a temperature setting, preheat it to the equivalent.
In a large bowl, combine the oats, walnuts, honey or maple syrup, melted coconut oil, vanilla extract, ground cinnamon, and a pinch of salt. Stir well to ensure all the dry ingredients are coated with the honey or maple syrup and coconut oil.
Transfer the mixture to the air fryer basket, spreading it out evenly.
Place the basket in the air fryer and cook for 15 minutes, stirring the granola halfway through to ensure even browning.
After 15 minutes, check the granola for desired crispness. If it needs more time, cook for an additional 5 minutes, keeping a close eye on it to prevent burning.
Once the granola is golden brown and crispy, remove the basket from the air fryer and let the granola cool completely.
If desired, mix in dried fruits, such as raisins or cranberries, for added sweetness and flavor.
Store the cooled granola in an airtight container.
Enjoy your homemade oat and walnut granola! Serve it with milk or yogurt, sprinkle it over smoothie bowls, or enjoy it as a crunchy snack.

574. Here's an air fryer recipe for white chocolate pudding:

Ingredients:

2 cups whole milk
1/4 cup granulated sugar
3 tablespoons cornstarch
1/8 teaspoon salt
4 ounces white chocolate, chopped
1 teaspoon vanilla extract
Optional toppings: whipped cream, grated white chocolate, berries

Instructions:

In a medium saucepan, whisk together the milk, sugar, cornstarch, and salt until well combined.
Place the saucepan over medium heat and cook, stirring constantly, until the mixture thickens and comes to a gentle boil.
Remove the saucepan from the heat and add the chopped white chocolate. Stir until the chocolate is completely melted and the mixture is smooth.
Stir in the vanilla extract.
Pour the pudding mixture into individual serving bowls or ramekins.
Preheat your air fryer to 325°F (165°C). If your air fryer doesn't have a temperature setting, preheat it to the equivalent.
Place the bowls or ramekins in the air fryer basket, making sure they are evenly spaced.
Air fry the pudding for about 10 minutes, or until it is set and has a slightly golden top.
Carefully remove the pudding from the air fryer and let it cool to room temperature.
Once cooled, cover the pudding with plastic wrap and refrigerate for at least 2 hours, or until chilled and set.
Serve the white chocolate pudding chilled, and if desired, garnish with whipped cream, grated white chocolate, or fresh berries.
Enjoy your creamy and indulgent white chocolate pudding!

575. Here's an air fryer recipe for soft buttermilk biscuits:

Ingredients:

2 cups all-purpose flour
2 teaspoons baking powder
1/2 teaspoon baking soda
1/2 teaspoon salt
1/4 cup unsalted butter, cold and cubed
3/4 cup buttermilk
Optional: melted butter for brushing on top

Instructions:

In a mixing bowl, whisk together the flour, baking powder, baking soda, and salt.
Add the cold, cubed butter to the dry ingredients. Use a pastry cutter or your fingers to cut the butter into the flour mixture until it resembles coarse crumbs.
Make a well in the center of the mixture and pour in the buttermilk. Stir until just combined, being careful not to over mix. The dough should be slightly sticky.
Turn the dough out onto a floured surface and gently knead it a few times to bring it together.
Roll the dough out to a thickness of about 1/2 inch. Use a biscuit cutter to cut out biscuits from the dough. Place the biscuits on a parchment-lined tray.
Preheat your air fryer to 375°F (190°C). If your air fryer doesn't have a temperature setting, preheat it to the equivalent.
Place the biscuits in the air fryer basket, leaving some space between them.
Air fry the biscuits for about 8-10 minutes, or until they are golden brown and cooked through.
Remove the biscuits from the air fryer and let them cool slightly before serving.
Optional: Brush the tops of the biscuits with melted butter for added flavor and shine.
Serve the soft buttermilk biscuits warm as a delicious side dish or for breakfast. Enjoy their fluffy and tender texture!

576. Here's an air fryer recipe for orange sponge cake:

Ingredients:

4 large eggs
3/4 cup granulated sugar
1 teaspoon vanilla extract
1/2 cup vegetable oil
1/4 cup fresh orange juice
1 tablespoon orange zest
1 cup all-purpose flour
1 teaspoon baking powder
Pinch of salt

Instructions:

In a mixing bowl, beat the eggs and sugar together until pale and fluffy.
Add the vanilla extract, vegetable oil, orange juice, and orange zest to the egg mixture. Mix well to combine.
In a separate bowl, whisk together the flour, baking powder, and salt.
Gradually add the dry ingredients to the wet ingredients, folding gently until just combined. Be careful not to over mix.
Preheat your air fryer to 325°F (163°C). If your air fryer doesn't have a temperature setting, preheat it to the equivalent.
Grease a round cake pan that fits inside the air fryer basket.
Pour the batter into the greased cake pan and smooth the top with a spatula.
Place the cake pan in the air fryer basket and cook for about 25-30 minutes, or until a toothpick inserted into the center of the cake comes out clean.
Once the cake is cooked, carefully remove the cake pan from the air fryer and let it cool in the pan for a few minutes.

Transfer the cake to a wire rack and allow it to cool completely before serving.
You can serve the orange sponge cake as is or dust it with powdered sugar for an extra touch. Enjoy the light and citrusy flavor of this delicious cake!

577. Here's an air fryer recipe for almond and berry crumble:

Ingredients:

2 cups mixed berries (such as strawberries, blueberries, or raspberries)
1 tablespoon lemon juice
1/4 cup granulated sugar
1/2 cup all-purpose flour
1/4 cup rolled oats
1/4 cup sliced almonds
1/4 cup brown sugar
1/4 teaspoon ground cinnamon
3 tablespoons unsalted butter, melted

Instructions:

In a bowl, combine the mixed berries, lemon juice, and granulated sugar. Toss gently to coat the berries with the sugar and lemon juice mixture.
In a separate bowl, mix together the flour, rolled oats, sliced almonds, brown sugar, and ground cinnamon. Stir until well combined.
Drizzle the melted butter over the dry ingredients and mix until the mixture resembles coarse crumbs.
Preheat your air fryer to 350°F (175°C). If your air fryer doesn't have a temperature setting, preheat it to the equivalent.
Transfer the berry mixture into a baking dish that fits inside the air fryer basket.
Sprinkle the almond crumble mixture evenly over the top of the berries.
Place the baking dish in the air fryer basket and cook for about 15-20 minutes, or until the berries are bubbling and the crumble topping is golden brown.
Once cooked, carefully remove the baking dish from the air fryer and let it cool slightly.
Serve the almond and berry crumble warm, and optionally, with a scoop of vanilla ice cream or whipped cream.
Enjoy the delicious combination of sweet berries and crunchy almond crumble in this delightful dessert made in the air fryer!

578. Here's an air fryer recipe for Madrid-style almond meringues:

Ingredients:

3 large egg whites
1/2 cup granulated sugar
1/4 teaspoon almond extract
1/4 teaspoon lemon juice
1 cup ground almonds
Powdered sugar, for dusting

Instructions:

In a clean mixing bowl, beat the egg whites on medium speed until frothy.
Gradually add the granulated sugar, almond extract, and lemon juice to the egg whites while continuing to beat. Increase the speed to high and beat until stiff peaks form.
Gently fold in the ground almonds until well combined.
Preheat your air fryer to 320°F (160°C). If your air fryer doesn't have a temperature setting, preheat it to the equivalent.
Line the air fryer basket with parchment paper or silicone baking mat.

Using a spoon or a piping bag, drop dollops of the meringue mixture onto the prepared parchment paper, forming small mounds.
Place the meringues in the air fryer basket, leaving some space between each meringue to allow for even cooking.
Air fry the meringues at 320°F (160°C) for about 15-20 minutes, or until they are lightly golden and crispy on the outside.
Once cooked, carefully remove the meringues from the air fryer and let them cool completely on a wire rack.
Dust the cooled meringues with powdered sugar before serving.
Enjoy these delightful Madrid-style almond meringues with their crispy exterior and chewy interior!

579. Here's an air fryer recipe for white chocolate cookies:

Ingredients:

1/2 cup unsalted butter, softened
1/2 cup granulated sugar
1/2 cup packed light brown sugar
1 large egg
1 teaspoon vanilla extract
1 1/2 cups all-purpose flour
1/2 teaspoon baking soda
1/4 teaspoon salt
1 cup white chocolate chips

Instructions:

In a mixing bowl, cream together the softened butter, granulated sugar, and brown sugar until light and fluffy.
Add the egg and vanilla extract to the butter mixture and mix until well combined.
In a separate bowl, whisk together the all-purpose flour, baking soda, and salt.
Gradually add the dry ingredients to the wet ingredients, mixing until just combined. Be careful not to over mix.
Fold in the white chocolate chips until evenly distributed throughout the dough.
Shape the dough into tablespoon-sized balls and place them on a parchment-lined air fryer basket. Leave some space between the cookies for spreading.
Preheat your air fryer to 325°F (163°C). If your air fryer doesn't have a temperature setting, preheat it to the equivalent.
Place the cookie-filled air fryer basket into the preheated air fryer and cook for 8-10 minutes, or until the cookies are golden brown on the edges.
Once the cookies are cooked, carefully remove them from the air fryer and let them cool on a wire rack.
Enjoy your delicious white chocolate cookies!
Note: Cooking times may vary depending on the model and size of your air fryer, so keep an eye on the cookies as they cook to prevent them from burning.

580. Here's an air fryer recipe for chocolate and raspberry cake:

Ingredients:

1 1/2 cups all-purpose flour
1/2 cup unsweetened cocoa powder
1 1/4 teaspoons baking powder
1/2 teaspoon baking soda
1/4 teaspoon salt
1/2 cup unsalted butter, softened
1 cup granulated sugar
2 large eggs

1 teaspoon vanilla extract
1 cup buttermilk
1 cup fresh raspberries

For the chocolate ganache:

1/2 cup heavy cream
1 cup semisweet chocolate chips

Instructions:

In a mixing bowl, whisk together the flour, cocoa powder, baking powder, baking soda, and salt. Set aside.
In a separate large mixing bowl, cream together the softened butter and granulated sugar until light and fluffy.
Add the eggs one at a time, beating well after each addition. Stir in the vanilla extract.
Gradually add the dry ingredients to the wet ingredients, alternating with the buttermilk, beginning and ending with the dry ingredients. Mix until just combined.
Gently fold in the fresh raspberries into the cake batter.
Preheat your air fryer to 325°F (163°C). If your air fryer doesn't have a temperature setting, preheat it to the equivalent.
Grease a round cake pan that fits into your air fryer with butter or cooking spray. Pour the cake batter into the prepared pan.
Place the cake pan into the preheated air fryer basket. Cook for 25-30 minutes, or until a toothpick inserted into the center of the cake comes out clean.
Once the cake is cooked, remove it from the air fryer and let it cool in the pan for a few minutes. Then transfer it to a wire rack to cool completely.
To make the chocolate ganache, heat the heavy cream in a saucepan over medium heat until it begins to simmer. Remove from heat and stir in the chocolate chips until smooth and melted.
Once the ganache has cooled slightly and thickened, pour it over the cooled cake.
Garnish the cake with additional fresh raspberries, if desired.
Slice and serve your delicious chocolate and raspberry cake!
Note: Cooking times may vary depending on the model and size of your air fryer, so keep an eye on the cake as it bakes to ensure it doesn't overcook.

581. Here's an air fryer recipe for effortless pecan pie:

Ingredients:

1 refrigerated pie crust
1 cup light corn syrup
1 cup granulated sugar
3 large eggs
1 teaspoon vanilla extract
2 tablespoons melted butter
1 1/2 cups pecan halves

Instructions:

Preheat your air fryer to 325°F (163°C). If your air fryer doesn't have a temperature setting, preheat it to the equivalent.
Unroll the refrigerated pie crust and place it in a pie dish, pressing it into the bottom and up the sides.
In a mixing bowl, combine the light corn syrup, granulated sugar, eggs, vanilla extract, and melted butter. Whisk until well combined.
Stir in the pecan halves, making sure they are evenly coated with the mixture.
Pour the pecan mixture into the prepared pie crust.

Place the pie dish into the preheated air fryer basket. Cook for 30-35 minutes, or until the filling is set and the crust is golden brown.
Remove the pie from the air fryer and let it cool completely before serving.
Slice and enjoy your effortless pecan pie!
Note: Cooking times may vary depending on the model and size of your air fryer, so keep an eye on the pie as it bakes to ensure it doesn't overcook.

582. Here's an air fryer recipe for pineapple cake:

Ingredients:

1 1/2 cups all-purpose flour
1 teaspoon baking powder
1/2 teaspoon baking soda
1/4 teaspoon salt
1/2 cup unsalted butter, softened
1 cup granulated sugar
2 large eggs
1 teaspoon vanilla extract
1 cup crushed pineapple, drained
1/4 cup pineapple juice
Optional: powdered sugar for dusting

Instructions:

Preheat your air fryer to 325°F (163°C). If your air fryer doesn't have a temperature setting, preheat it to the equivalent.
In a mixing bowl, whisk together the all-purpose flour, baking powder, baking soda, and salt. Set aside.
In another bowl, cream together the softened butter and granulated sugar until light and fluffy.
Beat in the eggs one at a time, followed by the vanilla extract.
Add the crushed pineapple and pineapple juice to the wet ingredients and mix until well combined.
Gradually add the dry ingredients to the wet ingredients, mixing until just combined. Be careful not to over mix.
Grease a round cake pan that fits inside your air fryer basket and pour the batter into it.
Place the cake pan into the preheated air fryer basket. Cook for 25-30 minutes, or until a toothpick inserted into the center comes out clean.
Remove the cake from the air fryer and let it cool in the pan for a few minutes, then transfer it to a wire rack to cool completely.
Once cooled, you can dust the cake with powdered sugar if desired.
Slice and serve your delicious pineapple cake!
Note: Cooking times may vary depending on the model and size of your air fryer, so keep an eye on the cake as it bakes to ensure it doesn't overcook.

583. Here's an air fryer recipe for lemon-glazed cupcakes:

Ingredients for cupcakes:

1 1/2 cups all-purpose flour
1 teaspoon baking powder
1/4 teaspoon baking soda
1/4 teaspoon salt
1/2 cup unsalted butter, softened
3/4 cup granulated sugar
2 large eggs
1 teaspoon vanilla extract
1 tablespoon lemon zest
1/4 cup fresh lemon juice

1/4 cup milk
Ingredients for lemon glaze:
1 cup powdered sugar
2 tablespoons fresh lemon juice
1 teaspoon lemon zest

Instructions:

Preheat your air fryer to 325°F (163°C). If your air fryer doesn't have a temperature setting, preheat it to the equivalent.
In a mixing bowl, whisk together the all-purpose flour, baking powder, baking soda, and salt. Set aside.
In a separate bowl, cream together the softened butter and granulated sugar until light and fluffy.
Beat in the eggs one at a time, followed by the vanilla extract.
Add the lemon zest, lemon juice, and milk to the wet ingredients and mix until well combined.
Gradually add the dry ingredients to the wet ingredients, mixing until just combined. Be careful not to over mix.
Line a cupcake pan with cupcake liners and spoon the batter evenly into the liners, filling each about 2/3 full.
Place the cupcake pan into the preheated air fryer basket. Cook for 12-15 minutes, or until a toothpick inserted into the center of a cupcake comes out clean.
While the cupcakes are cooking, prepare the lemon glaze. In a small bowl, whisk together the powdered sugar, lemon juice, and lemon zest until smooth.
Once the cupcakes are done, remove them from the air fryer and let them cool for a few minutes.
Transfer the cupcakes to a wire rack to cool completely.
Once the cupcakes are completely cooled, drizzle the lemon glaze over the top of each cupcake.
Allow the glaze to set before serving.
Enjoy your delicious lemon-glazed cupcakes!

584. Here's an air fryer recipe for cinnamon-grilled pineapples:

Ingredients:

1 pineapple, peeled, cored, and sliced into rings
2 tablespoons melted butter
2 tablespoons brown sugar
1 teaspoon ground cinnamon
Pinch of salt
Optional: Vanilla ice cream or whipped cream for serving

Instructions:

Preheat your air fryer to 400°F (200°C). If your air fryer doesn't have a temperature setting, preheat it to the equivalent.
In a small bowl, combine the melted butter, brown sugar, ground cinnamon, and salt. Mix until well combined.
Brush both sides of the pineapple rings with the cinnamon mixture.
Place the pineapple rings in a single layer in the air fryer basket. If needed, cook them in batches to avoid overcrowding.
Cook the pineapple rings in the air fryer for 6-8 minutes, flipping them halfway through the cooking time, until they are caramelized and slightly charred.
Remove the grilled pineapple rings from the air fryer and let them cool for a few minutes.
Serve the cinnamon-grilled pineapples as a delicious dessert on their own, or pair them with vanilla ice cream or whipped cream for an extra treat.
Enjoy the sweet and flavorful cinnamon-grilled pineapples!

585. Here's a simple recipe for coffee cake that you can make in an air fryer:

Ingredients:

1 ½ cups all-purpose flour
¾ cup granulated sugar
½ cup unsalted butter softened
½ cup sour cream
2 eggs
1 teaspoon baking powder
½ teaspoon baking soda
½ teaspoon vanilla extract
¼ teaspoon salt

For the Streusel Topping:

¼ cup all-purpose flour
¼ cup granulated sugar
2 tablespoons unsalted butter, cold
1 teaspoon ground cinnamon

Instructions:

In a mixing bowl, combine the softened butter and granulated sugar. Cream them together until light and fluffy.
Add the eggs one at a time, mixing well after each addition. Then add the sour cream and vanilla extract, and mix until well combined.
In a separate bowl, whisk together the flour, baking powder, baking soda, and salt. Gradually add the dry ingredients to the wet ingredients, mixing until just combined. Be careful not to over mix.
Preheat your air fryer to 320°F (160°C) for a few minutes.
Grease a round cake pan or a baking dish that fits in your air fryer.
Pour the cake batter into the greased pan, spreading it evenly.
In a small bowl, combine the streusel topping ingredients: flour, sugar, butter, and cinnamon. Use a fork or your fingers to mix the ingredients until crumbly.
Sprinkle the streusel topping over the cake batter, covering it evenly.
Place the cake pan in the preheated air fryer and cook for about 25-30 minutes, or until a toothpick inserted into the center comes out clean.
Once the coffee cake is done, carefully remove it from the air fryer and let it cool in the pan for a few minutes.
Cut into slices and serve warm. Enjoy your delicious air-fried coffee cake!
Note: Cooking times may vary depending on the model and size of your air fryer, so keep an eye on the cake as it bakes to prevent overcooking.

586. Here's a recipe for peach almond flour cake that you can make in an air fryer:

Ingredients:

2 cups almond flour
1/2 cup granulated sugar
1/4 cup unsalted butter, melted
3 large eggs
1/4 cup milk (dairy or non-dairy)
1 teaspoon vanilla extract
1/2 teaspoon almond extract
1 teaspoon baking powder
1/4 teaspoon salt
2 medium peaches, pitted and sliced

Instructions:

In a large mixing bowl, combine the almond flour, granulated sugar, melted butter, eggs, milk, vanilla extract, almond extract, baking powder, and salt. Stir until well combined and smooth.
Grease a round cake pan or baking dish that fits in your air fryer.
Pour the cake batter into the greased pan, spreading it evenly.
Arrange the sliced peaches on top of the batter, pressing them gently into the batter.
Preheat your air fryer to 320°F (160°C) for a few minutes.
Place the cake pan in the preheated air fryer and cook for about 30-35 minutes, or until a toothpick inserted into the center comes out clean.
Once the cake is done, carefully remove it from the air fryer and let it cool in the pan for a few minutes.
Slice and serve the peach almond flour cake warm or at room temperature.
Enjoy your delicious air-fried peach almond flour cake!

587. Here's a recipe for dark rum pear pie that you can make in an air fryer:

Ingredients:

For the Pie Crust:

2 ½ cups all-purpose flour
1 tablespoon granulated sugar
1 teaspoon salt
1 cup unsalted butter, cold and cut into small pieces
6-8 tablespoons ice water

For the Filling:

4 large pears, peeled, cored, and sliced
¼ cup dark rum
¼ cup granulated sugar
2 tablespoons all-purpose flour
1 teaspoon ground cinnamon
½ teaspoon ground nutmeg
¼ teaspoon salt
1 tablespoon lemon juice

For the Topping:

¼ cup all-purpose flour
¼ cup granulated sugar
2 tablespoons unsalted butter, cold and cut into small pieces

Instructions:

In a large mixing bowl, combine the flour, sugar, and salt for the pie crust. Add the cold butter pieces and use a pastry cutter or your fingers to cut the butter into the flour mixture until it resembles coarse crumbs.
Gradually add the ice water, one tablespoon at a time, mixing with a fork until the dough comes together. Be careful not to over mix. Form the dough into a disk, wrap it in plastic wrap, and refrigerate for at least 30 minutes.
In a separate bowl, combine the sliced pears, dark rum, sugar, flour, cinnamon, nutmeg, salt, and lemon juice. Toss gently until the pears are coated evenly. Let the mixture sit for 10-15 minutes to allow the flavors to meld.
Preheat your air fryer to 375°F (190°C) for a few minutes.
On a lightly floured surface, roll out the chilled pie crust into a circle large enough to fit your pie pan.
Place the crust in the pan and press it gently against the bottom and sides.
Pour the pear filling into the pie crust, spreading it evenly.

In a small bowl, combine the flour and sugar for the topping. Add the cold butter pieces and use a pastry cutter or your fingers to cut the butter into the flour mixture until it resembles coarse crumbs.
Sprinkle the topping mixture over the pear filling, covering it evenly.
Place the pie pan in the preheated air fryer and cook for about 30-35 minutes, or until the crust is golden brown and the filling is bubbly.
Once the pie is done, carefully remove it from the air fryer and let it cool in the pan for a few minutes.
Slice and serve the dark rum pear pie warm or at room temperature.
Enjoy your delicious air-fried dark rum pear pie!

588. Here's a recipe for yummy moon pies that you can make in an air fryer:

Ingredients:

For the Cookies:

1 ½ cups all-purpose flour
½ cup unsweetened cocoa powder
1 teaspoon baking powder
¼ teaspoon salt
½ cup unsalted butter softened
1 cup granulated sugar
1 large egg
1 teaspoon vanilla extract
¼ cup milk
For the Marshmallow Filling:
1 cup marshmallow creme or marshmallow fluff
¼ cup unsalted butter, softened
1 cup powdered sugar
½ teaspoon vanilla extract

For the Chocolate Coating:

8 ounces dark or semi-sweet chocolate, chopped
2 tablespoons coconut oil

Instructions:
In a mixing bowl, whisk together the flour, cocoa powder, baking powder, and salt.
In a separate bowl, cream together the softened butter and granulated sugar until light and fluffy. Add the egg and vanilla extract, and mix until well combined.
Gradually add the dry ingredients to the wet ingredients, alternating with the milk. Mix until just combined to form a dough. Do not over mix.
Preheat your air fryer to 350°F (175°C) for a few minutes.
Roll out the dough on a lightly floured surface to about ¼-inch thickness. Use a round cookie cutter to cut out circles of dough.
Place the dough circles on a parchment-lined baking sheet and transfer them to the preheated air fryer.
Cook for about 8-10 minutes, or until the cookies are firm to the touch. You may need to cook them in batches depending on the size of your air fryer.
While the cookies are cooling, prepare the marshmallow filling. In a mixing bowl, beat together the marshmallow creme, softened butter, powdered sugar, and vanilla extract until smooth and creamy.
Once the cookies are completely cooled, spread a dollop of the marshmallow filling onto the bottom side of one cookie. Place another cookie on top to form a sandwich. Repeat this process with the remaining cookies and filling.
Place the assembled moon pies on a parchment-lined baking sheet and transfer them to the refrigerator to chill for about 20-30 minutes.
In a microwave-safe bowl, melt the chopped chocolate and coconut oil together in short intervals, stirring in between, until smooth and melted. Be careful not to overheat.

Dip each chilled moon pie into the melted chocolate, coating it completely. Place the coated moon pies back on the parchment-lined baking sheet.
Once all the moon pies are coated, transfer the baking sheet to the refrigerator to allow the chocolate coating to set and harden.
Once the chocolate has hardened, your yummy air-fried moon pies are ready to enjoy!
Note: The cooking times in the air fryer may vary, so keep an eye on the cookies to ensure they don't overcook or burn.

589. Here's a recipe for air-fried donuts that you can make in an air fryer:

Ingredients:

For the Donuts:

2 cups all-purpose flour
¼ cup granulated sugar
2 teaspoons baking powder
½ teaspoon salt
½ teaspoon ground cinnamon (optional)
¾ cup milk (dairy or non-dairy)
2 tablespoons unsalted butter, melted
1 large egg
1 teaspoon vanilla extract

For the Glaze:

1 cup powdered sugar
2-3 tablespoons milk (dairy or non-dairy)
1 teaspoon vanilla extract

For the Toppings (optional):

Sprinkles, chopped nuts, shredded coconut, etc.

Instructions:

In a mixing bowl, whisk together the flour, sugar, baking powder, salt, and ground cinnamon (if using).
In a separate bowl, whisk together the milk, melted butter, egg, and vanilla extract until well combined.
Gradually add the wet ingredients to the dry ingredients, stirring until just combined. Be careful not to over mix; a few lumps are okay.
Cover the bowl with plastic wrap and let the dough rest for 10-15 minutes.
Preheat your air fryer to 350°F (175°C) for a few minutes.
Lightly grease the air fryer basket with cooking spray or brush with oil.
Scoop the donut batter into a piping bag or a large zip-top bag with a corner snipped off.
Pipe the batter into the prepared air fryer basket, forming donut shapes. You can make traditional ring-shaped donuts or smaller donut holes.
Cook the donuts in the air fryer for about 5-7 minutes, or until they are golden brown and cooked through. You may need to cook them in batches depending on the size of your air fryer.
While the donuts are cooling, prepare the glaze. In a shallow bowl, whisk together the powdered sugar, milk, and vanilla extract until smooth and well combined. Adjust the consistency by adding more milk or powdered sugar as needed.
Once the donuts are cool enough to handle, dip each one into the glaze, coating it completely. Place the glazed donuts on a wire rack to allow the excess glaze to drip off.
If desired, sprinkle your chosen toppings onto the freshly glazed donuts before the glaze sets.
Allow the glaze to set for a few minutes before serving the air-fried donuts.
Enjoy your delicious homemade air-fried donuts!

590. Here's a recipe for tropical pineapple fritters that you can make in an air fryer:

Ingredients:

1 cup all-purpose flour
2 tablespoons granulated sugar
1 teaspoon baking powder
¼ teaspoon salt
½ teaspoon ground cinnamon
1 large egg
½ cup milk (dairy or non-dairy)
1 teaspoon vanilla extract
1 ½ cups fresh pineapple chunks
Vegetable oil, for greasing
Powdered sugar, for dusting (optional)

For the Dipping Sauce:

½ cup powdered sugar
1 tablespoon lime juice
2 tablespoons pineapple juice

Instructions:

In a mixing bowl, whisk together the flour, sugar, baking powder, salt, and ground cinnamon.
In a separate bowl, whisk together the egg, milk, and vanilla extract until well combined.
Gradually add the wet ingredients to the dry ingredients, stirring until just combined. Do not over mix.
Gently fold in the fresh pineapple chunks into the batter.
Preheat your air fryer to 350°F (175°C) for a few minutes.
Lightly grease the air fryer basket with vegetable oil.
Drop spoonfuls of the pineapple batter into the greased basket, forming fritters. Space them out to ensure even cooking.
Cook the fritters in the air fryer for about 8-10 minutes, flipping them halfway through, or until they are golden brown and cooked through. You may need to cook them in batches depending on the size of your air fryer.
While the fritters are cooking, prepare the dipping sauce. In a small bowl, whisk together the powdered sugar, lime juice, and pineapple juice until smooth and well combined.
Once the fritters are done, transfer them to a wire rack to cool for a few minutes.
Dust the warm fritters with powdered sugar, if desired.
Serve the tropical pineapple fritters warm with the prepared dipping sauce.
Enjoy the delightful tropical flavors of these air-fried pineapple fritters!

591. Here's a recipe for honey and plum homemade rice that you can make in an air fryer:

Ingredients:

1 cup jasmine rice (or any type of rice you prefer)
2 cups water
2 plums, pitted and sliced
2 tablespoons honey
1 tablespoon unsalted butter
1/2 teaspoon cinnamon
1/4 teaspoon salt
Chopped fresh mint or basil for garnish (optional)

Instructions:

Rinse the jasmine rice under cold water until the water runs clear. Drain the rice well.
In a saucepan, combine the rinsed rice and water. Bring to a boil over medium-high heat. Once boiling, reduce the heat to low, cover, and simmer for about 15-20 minutes, or until the rice is tender and the water is absorbed.
Preheat your air fryer to 350°F (175°C) for a few minutes.
In a bowl, combine the sliced plums, honey, butter, cinnamon, and salt. Toss well to coat the plums.
Transfer the honey and plum mixture to an air fryer-safe baking dish or tray.
Place the dish or tray with the plum mixture into the preheated air fryer. Cook for about 10-12 minutes, stirring halfway through, or until the plums are soft and caramelized.
Once the rice is cooked, fluff it with a fork and transfer it to a serving dish.
Remove the honey and plum mixture from the air fryer and spoon it over the cooked rice. Gently mix to incorporate the flavors.
Garnish with chopped fresh mint or basil, if desired.
Serve the honey and plum homemade rice warm as a side dish or a light dessert.
Enjoy the sweet and fragrant flavors of this air-fried honey and plum rice!

592. Here's a recipe for chocolate soufflé that you can make in an air fryer:

Ingredients:

4 ounces semisweet chocolate, chopped
3 tablespoons unsalted butter
3 large eggs, separated
1/4 cup granulated sugar, divided
1 teaspoon vanilla extract
Pinch of salt
Powdered sugar, for dusting (optional)
Whipped cream or vanilla ice cream, for serving (optional)

Instructions:

Preheat your air fryer to 375°F (190°C) for a few minutes.
In a microwave-safe bowl, melt the chopped chocolate and butter together in short intervals, stirring in between, until smooth and melted. Set aside to cool slightly.
In a separate mixing bowl, beat the egg yolks and half of the granulated sugar (2 tablespoons) until pale and creamy. Stir in the vanilla extract and the melted chocolate mixture until well combined.
In another clean mixing bowl, beat the egg whites and salt using an electric mixer until soft peaks form. Gradually add the remaining granulated sugar (2 tablespoons) and continue beating until stiff peaks form.
Gently fold about one-third of the beaten egg whites into the chocolate mixture to lighten it. Then, carefully fold in the remaining egg whites until no streaks remain.
Grease individual ramekins with butter and lightly dust them with granulated sugar. Fill each ramekin with the chocolate soufflé mixture, leaving about 1/4-inch space from the top.
Place the filled ramekins in the preheated air fryer basket. Cook for about 10-12 minutes, or until the soufflés have risen and are set in the center.
Carefully remove the ramekins from the air fryer using oven mitts or tongs, as they will be hot.
Dust the soufflés with powdered sugar, if desired, and serve immediately.
For an extra touch, serve the chocolate soufflés with whipped cream or vanilla ice cream.
Enjoy your decadent and fluffy air-fried chocolate soufflés!

593. Here's a recipe for no-flour lime cupcakes that you can make in an air fryer:

Ingredients:

4 large eggs, separated
1/2 cup granulated sugar
Zest of 2 limes

Juice of 1 lime
1/4 cup melted unsalted butter
1/2 cup ground almonds
1/2 teaspoon baking powder
Pinch of salt
Powdered sugar, for dusting (optional)
Lime slices or zest, for garnish (optional)

Instructions:

In a mixing bowl, beat the egg yolks and granulated sugar together until pale and creamy. Add the lime zest, lime juice, and melted butter. Mix well.
In a separate bowl, combine the ground almonds, baking powder, and salt. Stir to mix.
Gradually add the almond mixture to the egg yolk mixture, stirring until well combined.
In another clean mixing bowl, beat the egg whites using an electric mixer until stiff peaks form.
Gently fold the beaten egg whites into the almond mixture until no streaks remain.
Preheat your air fryer to 325°F (165°C) for a few minutes.
Line a cupcake tin with cupcake liners or silicone molds. Fill each mold with the batter, about 3/4 full.
Place the cupcake tin in the preheated air fryer. Cook for about 12-15 minutes, or until the cupcakes are set and a toothpick inserted into the center comes out clean.
Carefully remove the cupcakes from the air fryer and let them cool in the tin for a few minutes before transferring them to a wire rack to cool completely.
Once cooled, dust the cupcakes with powdered sugar, if desired.
For garnish, you can top each cupcake with a slice of lime or sprinkle some lime zest over the powdered sugar.
Enjoy the zesty and gluten-free goodness of these lime cupcakes made in your air fryer!

594. Here's a recipe for a cheat apple pie that you can make in an air fryer:

Ingredients:

2 cups diced apples (about 2 medium-sized apples)
2 tablespoons granulated sugar
1 teaspoon ground cinnamon
1 tablespoon lemon juice
1 tablespoon cornstarch
1 tablespoon unsalted butter, melted
1 package refrigerated pie crusts (2 crusts)
1 egg, beaten (for egg wash)
1 tablespoon turbinado sugar (optional, for sprinkling)

Instructions:

In a mixing bowl, combine the diced apples, granulated sugar, ground cinnamon, lemon juice, and cornstarch. Toss until the apples are coated in the mixture.
Preheat your air fryer to 375°F (190°C) for a few minutes.
Roll out one pie crust and use it to line a greased or parchment-lined air fryer basket or tray.
Spoon the apple mixture onto the pie crust, leaving a border around the edges.
Drizzle the melted butter over the apple mixture.
Roll out the second pie crust and place it over the apple filling. Press the edges of the crusts together to seal.
Use a sharp knife to cut a few slits in the top crust to allow steam to escape.
Brush the top crust with a beaten egg to give it a shiny finish. Sprinkle with turbinado sugar, if desired, for a bit of extra sweetness and crunch.
Place the pie in the preheated air fryer and cook for about 20-25 minutes, or until the crust is golden brown and the apples are tender. You may need to adjust the cooking time based on the size and power of your air fryer.

Once the pie is cooked, carefully remove it from the air fryer and let it cool slightly before serving.
Serve your cheat apple pie warm, either on its own or with a scoop of vanilla ice cream for a delicious treat!
Note: Air fryers can vary in temperature and cooking times, so keep an eye on the pie as it cooks to prevent over-browning.

595. Here's a recipe for apricot and lemon flapjacks that you can make in an air fryer:

Ingredients:

1 1/2 cups rolled oats
1/2 cup dried apricots, chopped
Zest of 1 lemon
1/4 cup honey or maple syrup
1/4 cup unsalted butter, melted
1 tablespoon lemon juice
1/4 teaspoon vanilla extract
Pinch of salt

Instructions:

Preheat your air fryer to 325°F (165°C) for a few minutes.
In a mixing bowl, combine the rolled oats, chopped dried apricots, and lemon zest.
In a separate microwave-safe bowl, heat the honey or maple syrup, melted butter, lemon juice, vanilla extract, and salt together until the mixture is warm and well combined.
Pour the warm honey or maple syrup mixture over the oat mixture. Stir well to coat all the ingredients evenly.
Line the air fryer basket or tray with parchment paper or a silicone mat.
Spread the flapjack mixture evenly in the lined air fryer basket or tray, pressing it down gently to compact it.
Place the filled basket or tray in the preheated air fryer. Cook for about 15-18 minutes, or until the edges are golden brown and the flapjacks are set.
Carefully remove the flapjacks from the air fryer and let them cool in the basket or tray for a few minutes.
Once cooled, cut the flapjacks into squares or rectangles.
Serve the apricot and lemon flapjacks as a delightful snack or a quick breakfast on the go.
Enjoy the delicious combination of apricot and lemon flavors in these air-fried flapjacks!

596. Here's a simple recipe for fruit skewers that you can make in an air fryer:

Ingredients:

Assorted fruits of your choice (such as strawberries, pineapple chunks, grapes, melon, and kiwi)
Wooden skewers
Instructions:

Preheat your air fryer to 375°F (190°C) for a few minutes.
While the air fryer is preheating, prepare your fruits by washing and cutting them into bite-sized pieces. Make sure the pieces are large enough to be skewered.
Thread the fruit pieces onto the wooden skewers, alternating between different fruits to create a colorful arrangement.
Once the skewers are assembled, lightly spray or brush them with a little oil to prevent sticking.
Place the fruit skewers in the preheated air fryer basket or on a tray. If using a tray, you may need to flip the skewers halfway through cooking.
Cook the fruit skewers in the air fryer for about 4-6 minutes, or until the fruits are slightly caramelized and tender. The exact cooking time may vary depending on the size and type of fruits used.
Carefully remove the fruit skewers from the air fryer using tongs or oven mitts, as they will be hot.
Let the skewers cool for a few minutes before serving.

Enjoy your delicious and colorful fruit skewers as a refreshing snack or a healthy dessert option!
Note: Keep an eye on the skewers as they cook in the air fryer to prevent overcooking or burning. Adjust the cooking time as needed based on the desired doneness of the fruits.

597. Here's a recipe for mom's lemon curd that you can make in an air fryer:

Ingredients:

Zest of 2 lemons
1/2 cup freshly squeezed lemon juice (about 4 lemons)
1/2 cup granulated sugar
4 large eggs
1/4 cup unsalted butter, melted

Instructions:

Preheat your air fryer to 325°F (165°C) for a few minutes.
In a heatproof bowl, combine the lemon zest, lemon juice, granulated sugar, and eggs. Whisk together until well combined.
Place the bowl in the air fryer basket or on a tray. Cook for about 10-12 minutes, stirring every 2-3 minutes, or until the mixture thickens and coats the back of a spoon.
Once the lemon curd has thickened, remove the bowl from the air fryer and let it cool for a few minutes.
Gradually whisk in the melted butter until smooth and well incorporated.
Pour the lemon curd into clean, sterilized jars or containers.
Let the lemon curd cool completely at room temperature, then cover and refrigerate for at least 1-2 hours to allow it to set and thicken further.
Mom's lemon curd is now ready to be enjoyed! Use it as a spread on toast, pancakes, or scones, or incorporate it into various desserts and baked goods.
Note: The cooking time may vary slightly depending on the size and power of your air fryer. Keep an eye on the lemon curd as it cooks to prevent overcooking or curdling. Stirring frequently helps ensure a smooth and creamy texture.

598. Here's a recipe for molten lava mini cakes that you can make in an air fryer:

Ingredients:

1/2 cup semisweet chocolate chips
1/4 cup unsalted butter
1/4 cup granulated sugar
2 large eggs
1/4 teaspoon vanilla extract
2 tablespoons all-purpose flour
Pinch of salt
Optional toppings: powdered sugar, fresh berries, whipped cream, or vanilla ice cream

Instructions:

Preheat your air fryer to 375°F (190°C) for a few minutes.
In a microwave-safe bowl, melt the chocolate chips and butter together in short intervals, stirring in between, until smooth and melted. Set aside to cool slightly.
In a separate mixing bowl, whisk together the granulated sugar, eggs, and vanilla extract until well combined.
Gradually pour the melted chocolate mixture into the egg mixture, stirring constantly, until smooth.
Sift in the all-purpose flour and add a pinch of salt. Gently fold the dry ingredients into the chocolate mixture until just combined. Be careful not to over mix.
Grease small ramekins or silicone molds that will fit in your air fryer basket.
Divide the batter equally among the prepared ramekins or molds, filling them about 3/4 full.

.he filled ramekins or molds in the preheated air fryer basket. Cook for about 6-8 minutes, or until ɹges are set and the center is still slightly jiggly.
/ully remove the ramekins or molds from the air fryer using oven mitts or tongs, as they will be hot.
.he mini cakes cool in the ramekins or molds for a few minutes. Then, gently invert them onto ving plates.
,rve the molten lava mini cakes immediately, while they are still warm and gooey in the center.
ptionally, you can dust the cakes with powdered sugar and serve them with fresh berries, whipped ;ream, or vanilla ice cream for a delightful presentation and added flavor.
Enjoy the rich and decadent molten lava mini cakes made in your air fryer!

599. Here's a recipe for snickerdoodle poppers that you can make in an air fryer:

Ingredients:

1 can refrigerated biscuit dough (8 biscuits)
3 tablespoons unsalted butter, melted
1/4 cup granulated sugar
2 teaspoons ground cinnamon

For the cinnamon sugar coating:

1/4 cup granulated sugar
1 teaspoon ground cinnamon

For the glaze (optional):

1/2 cup powdered sugar
1-2 tablespoons milk
1/2 teaspoon vanilla extract

Instructions:

Preheat your air fryer to 350°F (175°C) for a few minutes.
In a small bowl, combine the granulated sugar and ground cinnamon for the cinnamon sugar coating. Set aside.
Open the can of refrigerated biscuit dough and separate the biscuits.
Cut each biscuit into quarters to create bite-sized pieces.
Dip each biscuit quarter into the melted butter, ensuring it is well coated.
Roll the butter-coated biscuit piece in the cinnamon sugar-coating mixture, pressing gently to adhere the sugar.
Place the coated biscuit pieces in a single layer in the air fryer basket or on a tray lined with parchment paper or a silicone mat.
Cook the snickerdoodle poppers in the air fryer for about 6-8 minutes, or until golden brown and cooked through. You may need to adjust the cooking time based on the size and power of your air fryer.
Meanwhile, if desired, prepare the glaze by whisking together the powdered sugar, milk, and vanilla extract in a small bowl until smooth. Adjust the consistency with more milk if needed.
Once the snickerdoodle poppers are cooked, remove them from the air fryer and let them cool for a few minutes.
If using the glaze, drizzle it over the poppers while they are still warm.
Serve the snickerdoodle poppers as a delicious sweet treat, either warm or at room temperature.
Enjoy the delightful snickerdoodle poppers made in your air fryer! They are perfect for sharing and enjoying a cup of coffee or tea.

600. Here's a recipe for blueberry muffins that you can make in an air fryer:

Ingredients:

1 3/4 cups all-purpose flour
1/2 cup granulated sugar
2 teaspoons baking powder
1/4 teaspoon baking soda
1/4 teaspoon salt
1/2 cup milk
1/4 cup unsalted butter, melted
1/4 cup plain yogurt
1 large egg
1 teaspoon vanilla extract
1 cup fresh blueberries

Instructions:

Preheat your air fryer to 325°F (165°C) for a few minutes.
In a mixing bowl, whisk together the all-purpose flour, granulated sugar, baking powder, baking soda, and salt.
In a separate bowl, whisk together the milk, melted butter, plain yogurt, egg, and vanilla extract until well combined.
Pour the wet ingredients into the dry ingredients. Stir until just combined. Do not over mix.
Gently fold in the fresh blueberries, being careful not to break them.
Line the muffin tin with paper liners or silicone muffin cups.
Divide the batter evenly among the muffin cups, filling each one about 2/3 full.
Place the muffin tin in the preheated air fryer. Cook for about 12-15 minutes, or until a toothpick inserted into the center of a muffin comes out clean.
Carefully remove the muffin tin from the air fryer and let the muffins cool in the tin for a few minutes before transferring them to a wire rack to cool completely.
Once cooled, the blueberry muffins are ready to be enjoyed!
These blueberry muffins are perfect for breakfast or as a snack throughout the day. They're moist, fluffy, and bursting with juicy blueberries.

Made in the USA
Monee, IL
01 August 2023

40314242R00175